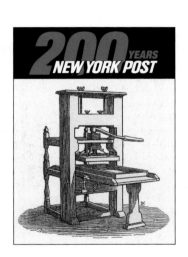

THE POST'S NEW YORK

Celebrating 200 Years of New York City through the Pages and Pictures of the *New York Post*

Compiled by Antonia Felix and The Editors of the *New York Post*

HarperResource

An Imprint of HarperCollins Publishers

FIRST EDITION

Designed by: Timothy Shaner and Christopher Measom

Library of Congress Cataloging-in-Publication has been applied for.

ISBN 0-06-621135-2

01 02 03 04 05 RRD 10 0 9 7 6 5 4 3 2 1

Contents

NEW YORK POST

LATE CITY FINAL

MONDAY, MAY 18, 1998 / Early sun, mid 80s / Weather: Page 67 ★★   http://www.nypost.com/   • • • • 35¢

PERFECT!

Wells becomes only 2nd Yankee to accomplish baseball's most amazing feat

Teammates hoist pitcher David Wells after his historic 4-0 perfect-game victory over Minnesota yesterday at Yankee Stadium.

Full coverage begins on Pages 2-3.

New York Post: Francis Specker

Foreword

There's no city like New York, and there's no newspaper like the *New York Post*.

For 200 years, a succession of distinguished *Post* journalists have chronicled the triumphs and tragedies of this city as it grew from its humble origin on the southern tip of Manhattan, became the glittering capital of the world, then endured the nightmarish terrorist attack on the World Trade Center.

It's a fascinating story told for the first time through the pages of the only newspaper in America that has been published continuously for two centuries.

It's the story of the remarkable people who shaped this city, their determination and their dynamism, their sacrifices and their sorrows, and about the heroes and villains that made the headlines.

Just as New York grew and changed to meet its new challenges, so has the *Post*—evolving from Alexander Hamilton's first four-page sheet in 1801 to today's crisp, colorful editions published from our new state-of-the-art presses inaugurated during this, our bicentennial year.

Everyone at the *Post* is proud of the paper's long and fascinating history. At the start of the 21st century, the *Post*'s commitment to New York is stronger than ever. This book is a tribute to everyone affiliated with the *Post* for the past 200 years and to the city that is its home.

Ken Chandler
Publisher

OPPOSITE: *Front page of May 18, 1998, celebrates Yankee pitcher David Wells' perfect game over the Minnesota Twins.*

Introduction

New York's Tell-It-Like-It-Is Paper

By STEVE DUNLEAVY, *New York Post* **Columnist**

Our founder, Alexander Hamilton, breathed his last on the Lower East Side, a week and a day after Independence Day in 1804. He was brought back to Manhattan following his infamous duel with Aaron Burr, across the Hudson, in Weehawken, N.J. Hamilton felt his old rival needed a stern lesson in manners—but instead he came out on the wrong end of a piece of lead.

The founder of what was to become the great New York tabloid departed this earth as tabloid fodder.

One hundred and eighty years later, T-shirts and coffee cups could be found on that same Lower East Side emblazoned "Headless Body in Topless Bar"—the *Post* Page One classic that sent the purists of the Columbia School of Journalism into apoplexy.

From losing your life to losing your head, somehow we are always scalded by the elitists for sticking to our guns.

But praise be, this city is peopled by people, not elitists . . . and, we the people love it?

Sights, sounds, smells, the whole nine yards. Los Angeles, Chicago, Washington, we are not. Get it? Got it? Good.

Professor Terrence Moran, of the Department of Culture and Communications of New York University said:

"What has been consistent about the *New York Post* since it was founded in 1801 as a media outlet for the Federalist Party to its role as a liberal force opposing

LEFT: *A* Post *reporter working a story, 1930s. (* Post *photo)*

McCarthyism in the 1950s, to its current role of in-your-face irreverent pro-American, pro-capitalist, tell-it-like-it-is journalism, is the fact that the *Post* and its readers have been as one, sharing the same values and world views and advocacy journalism.

"The *Post* knows its readers and its readers know the *Post*.

"In academic media jargon, it's called a participatory audience. Makes pretty good sense to me."

And it makes pretty good sense to the people at the *Post*.

We would rather touch the city's heart than be touched by a Pulitzer Prize. Being politically correct for eggheads might be okay for some newspapers but we are about people.

Are we tooting our own horn? Well, if you read our sports pages and don't feel you have been behind home plate, then you don't like baseball. We take you out to the ball game.

You read our City Hall coverage and you know you are in town.

If you care about money, and we hope you do, our business pages will take you straight to the concrete canyons of Wall Street with a blueprint to the world of the bulls and bears.

People call some columns gossip columns. No, "gossip" means something that is swapped among people without their knowing the facts. But our people report.

Those columns take you by the hand into the hallways, living rooms and yes, sometimes, reluctantly, into the bedrooms of the rich and famous. If the rich and famous want to be rich and famous, well, there always is a downside to life.

Far afield, the massive empire of News Corp. sweeps from the desert sands of the Middle East to the gilded corridors of the parliaments of Europe, to the steamy intrigues of Asia.

We are not ashamed of being active supporters of our police and fire departments at a time when other media treat them as journalistic dartboards.

Our Washington Bureau throws bricks and bouquets to the politicians who serve and the politicians who succeed in serving.

Okay, you could say self-praise is no recommendation.

But let's face it; we live at record speed in a big, lusty, laughing, crying and noisy town.

And the *Post* is all that . . . an echo, a mirror, a replica of the Big Apple that we so love to polish.

Like New York, we are serious, sophisticated, sensational, sensual, serene and surprising, with no excuses for who we are.

It's just a doggone pleasure to get off the elevator on the 10th floor of our building and go to work on a real hometown newspaper.

ABOVE: *Two members of Broadway's* A Chorus Line *reading the* Post's *tribute to the show, 1983. (* Post *photo by Lenore Davis)* OPPOSITE: *New York Mayor Rudy Giuliani—the world's biggest Yankees fan—holds up the* Post *after the 2000 Subway Series. (* Post *photo by Francis Specker)*

Top-Selling Post Editions

Date	Headline	Copies Sold
10/6/81	SADAT SLAIN	1,048,800
6/6/68	NOW RKF	1,020,697
8/1/77	SON OF SAM	1,013,059

NEW-YORK E

TUESDAY, NOVE

NEW-YORK E

TUESDAY, NOVE

NEW-YORK E

TUESDAY, NOVE

NEW-YORK E

TUESDAY, NOVE

ENING POST.

DER 17, 1801.

N

ENING POST.

DER 17, 1801.

N

ENING POST.

DER 17, 1801.

N

ENING POS

Part I

1801–1850

DER 17, 1801.

N

NEW YORK POST

Decade One

1801–1810

On November 16, 1801, the postal service delivered the first issue of the *New York Evening Post* to its subscribers. As one of six daily newspapers in the city, the *Post* was a broadsheet journal of four pages, approximately three of which were taken up with advertisements.

Newspapers played a vital role in the rough and tough political climate of the young republic as rival political factions fought for power. Alexander Hamilton and a group of Federalists wanted a new journal in which to express their views, and at a gathering in the home of Archibald Gracie, one of the city's wealthiest merchants, the *Post* was born. The building, now known as Gracie Mansion, is the official home of the Mayor of New York. Tragically, Hamilton died only three years later—killed in 1804 at the age of 47 in a duel with his political nemesis, Aaron Burr.

The Quintessential New Yorker

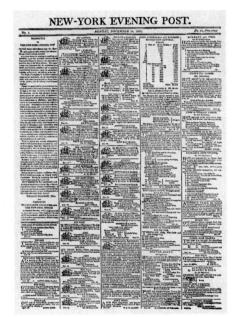

NEW-YORK EVENING POST.

Revolutionary soldier, eminent lawyer and economist, first Secretary of the Treasury and vital proponent of the Constitution, Alexander Hamilton had distinguished himself in American politics by the time he co-founded the *New York Evening Post* at the age of 44.

Hamilton's youth did not foretell his remarkable career. An illegitimate child born on Nevis in the British West Indies, he dreamed of adventure and a life beyond the Caribbean islands. His father, James Hamilton, was a Scot who claimed an aristocratic ancestry and failed at several business ventures. He never married Alexander's mother, Rachel Fawcett Lavien, but abandoned her and their two sons shortly after they moved to another Caribbean island, St. Croix. There, 11-year-old Alexander began working as a clerk in a trading post—his initiation into the world of finance and commerce. At age 17, Alexander's intelligence and strong character won him the respect of St. Croix's Presbyterian minister, who took up a collection for the boy's formal education. He was sent to New York and, after some preparatory schooling, studied law at King's College (now Columbia University).

With the start of the American Revolution, Hamilton joined the militia and became captain of the New York Artillery Company. After two years of battle, General Washington invited the young officer to join his staff, and Hamilton spent the next four years as a lieutenant colonel, fitting in very comfortably with the gentlemanly, aristocratic circle of officers surrounding Washington.

With the end of the war, the well-respected soldier became a prominent lawyer with his own practice on Wall Street. An eloquent speaker, he was a powerful advocate of Federalist ideas such as a strong central government. Hamilton joined up with James Madison and John Jay to write a series of 85 newspaper articles, known as the Federalist Papers, which served as a handbook for supporters of the Constitution. Self-confident, articulate and persuasive, Hamilton was the driving force behind New York's ratifying the Constitution. Representing New York, he signed the Constitution with George Washington and 37 others in Philadelphia on September 17, 1787. The Federalists believed that the Constitution contained the best formula for America's strength and prosperity. Those who opposed it, such as Patrick Henry and Thomas Paine, didn't think that a republican form of government could work on a national scale. They also feared that the new Constitution didn't adequately protect the rights of the individual. These anti-Federalists considered themselves true heirs of the spirit of the Revolution. The Federalists were successful, however, in getting all 13 states to ratify the Constitution, and when George Washington took office as the first

OPPOSITE: *The portrait of Alexander Hamilton that appears on the United States' ten-dollar bill.* ABOVE: *Front page of the first edition of the* New-York Evening Post, *November 16, 1801.*

"A Style Far Superior to That of Any Other Newspaper"

The *Post*'s first printer, Michael Burnham, outdid himself with high-quality production design for the new paper. The original *Post* was printed on one large sheet that was folded once to create four pages. Each page measured 19.5 inches tall by 14 inches wide, and the type was set from four completely new, beautifully cut fonts. Papers traditionally used only two fonts, and the *Post*'s enhanced look and superior quality of paper used caught the eye of those in the trade. One paper in Philadelphia described the new *Post* as a paper published "in a style by far superior to that of any other newspaper in the United States."

Out of 20 columns, 14 or 15 were filled with ads from merchants. This heavy ad revenue supported the *Post*'s high-quality production costs.

For FREIGHT or CHARTER,
The Ship VENUS, Lemuel
Bunce, master, burthen 199 tons.—

TWENTY-SIX Hhds. West-India and
New-England Rum,

JOHN & Wm. TABELE,
260, *Pearl-street,*

TROY, LANSINGBURGH AND WATERFORD
NAVIGATION LOTTERY.

When George Washington took office as the first President of the United States, he appointed Alexander Hamilton the first Secretary of the Treasury.

ALEXANDER HAMILTON'S LIFE

1757
January 11. Born on the Island of Nevis in the British West Indies

1771
Settles in New York City and studies at King's College

1775
Organizes and becomes captain of a New York City artillery company at the start of the Revolutionary War

1777
Begins service as aide-de-camp to General George Washington with the rank of lieutenant colonel (until 1781)

1780
Marries Elizabeth Schuyler

1782–1783
Delegate to the Continental Congress (age 25)

1783
Opens law office in New York City

1787
Delegate to Constitutional Convention

1787–1788
Co-authors the pro-Constitution Federalist Papers

1789
Appointed first Secretary of the Treasury of the U.S., a post he holds until 1795

1795
Returns to New York to resume his law practice

1801
Co-founds the *New York Evening Post*

1804
Fatally wounded July 11 in a duel with longtime political enemy Aaron Burr

LEFT *A portrait of 19-year-old Alexander Hamilton as captain of the New York Artillery Company, 1776.* RIGHT: *Illustration of 19th-century New York.*

President of the United States, he appointed Alexander Hamilton the first Secretary of the Treasury.

The Treasury was one of only four federal departments, and in this powerful post Hamilton made his greatest contributions to the nation. His complex strategy to put the country on firm economic footing, the "Hamiltonian system," formed solutions for tackling the nation's most critical problem: the $50 million war debt. Hamilton argued that the debt should be on the shoulders of the federal government, and his plan also included establishing a national bank to standardize and control the currency and encouraging wealthy Americans to invest in manufacturing and business.

Hamilton's small government salary made it difficult for him to provide for his large family of eight children, so in 1795 he resigned from the Treasury and returned to New York to resume his law practice. His income quickly rose from $3,500—his pay as head of the Treasury—to $12,000 a year as one of New York's leading lawyers. Titles to land ownership were in great flux after the Revolutionary War, and the city's 50 lawyers—including Alexander Hamilton and Aaron Burr—thrived by taking on such cases.

With the creation of the *New-York Evening Post* in 1801, Hamilton had a vehicle for voicing his Federalist political views. Although his name was never published as a byline in the paper, his views were closely narrated by—if not directly dictated to—*Post* editor William Coleman. Three years after the launch of the paper, Hamilton was mortally wounded in a duel with Aaron Burr. He died the day after the duel, July 12, 1804, at the age of 47.

NEW-YORK EVENING POST.

No. 1. | *MONDAY, NOVEMBER* 16, 1801. | *No.* 40, *Pine-street*

PROSPECTUS OF THE NEW-YORK EVENING POST

THE Editor will endeavor that this Paper shall appear in a dress worthy of the liberal patronage which is already promised.

As it must derive its principal support from the Merchants of our City, particular attention will be bestowed on whatever relates to that large and respectable class of our fellow-citizens. The earliest Commercial Information will be industriously collected, and faithfully presented; and we hope that the advertising department may, for convenience, [illegible], and accuracy, vie with any in the city.

The design of this paper, is to diffuse among the people correct information on all interesting subjects; to inculcate just principles in religion, morals and politics; and to cultivate a taste for sound literature.

Though we openly profess our attachment to that system of politics denominated FEDERAL, because we think it the most conducive to the welfare of the community, and the best calculated to ensure permanency to our present form of government, yet we disapprove of that spirit of dogmatism which lays exclusive claim to infallibility; and willingly believe that honest and virtuous men are to be found in each party. Persuaded that the great body of the people of this country only want correct information, to enable them to judge of what is really best; and believing that nothing will so directly conduce to this desirable end, as candid and liberal discussion; this paper shall be equally free to all parties. All Communications, therefore, shall be inserted with equal impartiality, and equal secrecy as it respects the name of the author; reserving, however, the right of subjoining a reply whenever we shall consider it necessary or proper. But it would be inconsistent with the rules which we have prescribed to ourselves, not to declare explicitly that we never will give currency to any thing scurrilous, indecent, immoral, or profane, or which may contravene the essential principles of social order.

While we shall be duly studious of originality, we shall avail ourselves of the contents of the various News-papers, Pamphlets, Magazines and Reviews printed in our own country, or elsewhere; since it cannot be of any moment, as it respects the public, whether an interesting piece of information, or a well written essay, which they have probably never seen, has appeared in any other paper or not.

In a word, as our great design is to disseminate sound just principles, which [illegible] and indeed [illegible] of good Government, [illegible] steady eye upon this one primary object, [illegible] neglect no means by which [illegible] will be best promoted.

Having thus given a general outline of our Plan, we think it needless to make an [illegible] display of professions. We rely for support on what shall [illegible] the intrinsic merit of the paper itself.

As it is necessary that the Editor should exercise his own judgement on determining on the propriety of inserting any Original Communication, it will relieve him from an unpleasant embarrassment in this part of his duty, to have them transmitted to him without the names of the Authors.

WILLIAM COLEMAN, Editor.

POSTSCRIPT.

There will be attached to the above [illegible] THE NEW-YORK HERALD [illegible] published *Wednesdays* and *Saturdays* [illegible] a COUNTRY PAPER. The terms are *Three* [illegible] *Dollars* per annum, payable at the end of every six months to agents appointed, of which timely notice will be given.

FOR SALE BY HOFFMAN & SETON

TWELVE hhds assorted Glass Ware,
2 boxes Lustrings,
1 trunk white Kid Gloves,
600 boxes Soap and Candles,
60 bales Cinnamon, entitled to drawback.
Nov. 16.

SUGARS.

TWENTY Hhds. will be landed this day from the schooner John, from St. Croix, and will be sold low on the wharf, by application to JOHN PATRICK, No. 4 William-street.

WHO HAS IN STORE,
St. Croix Sugars in hhds. and bbls. some of prime quality, and which he will sell reasonable.
Nov. 16

NEW-YORK BREAD COMPANY.

AT a meeting of the Directors, held this day, it was resolved that a *Superintendant*, who

---

FOR LONDON,

The staunch regular trading ship JULIANA, R. Roath, master, will be dispatched in 10 or 12 days, having all her cargo on board. For freight or passage, having superior accommodations, apply on board at Old-slip, or to
COIT & WOOLSEY,
93 Murray's wharf.

Who have received per the Mercury from Liverpool,
A consignment of DRY GOODS, which will be sold at a moderate advance, consisting of 2 bales Coatings, 4 do. Rose Blankets, 10 cases Hats, 4 do. Hosiery, and 20 trunks Calicoes, Chintzes, Q[illegible], Muslins, Velverets, Corduroys, Thicksets, &c. &c. Nov 16

FOR CALCUTTA,

The well known ship CITIZEN, C. Blakeman, master, burthen [illegible] tons, was built in Philadelphia of live oak and red cedar, and coppered in Liverpool about 11 months since, and in every respect is well fitted for the voyage, and is intended to be dispatched with all convenient speed. She will take on board merchandize or specie on [illegible] and will return direct to this port with goods, the manufacture of that country, to which effect she will be provided with a Supercargo, competent to the business of the voyage; and it is probable she may touch on her outward passage at Teneriffe, 150 or 200 pipes of wine will there be received on freight, if a contract for the same is made before sailing from here, terms of which, or freight or passage direct Calcutta, apply to HOYT & TOM

WHO HAVE FOR SALE,
600 boxes Havannah Sugars assorted
150,000 Spanish Segars, 30 crates Earthenware
2 hhds. and 3 bbls. St. Croix Sugars.
Nov. 16

FOR HULL,

The British brig MINERVA, captain M'Bride. Said brig lays at Bowne's wharf, and will sail about the first of December. For freight of 600 barrels, apply to the captain on board or to
JOHN KNOX,
Nov. 15. No. 27 Water street.

FOR GREENOCK,

The good and substantial British Brig RECOVERY, D. Campbell, master; will sail with all convenient dispatch, having a considerable part of her freight now engaged. For the remainder, or Passage, apply to the master on board, at the wharf adjoining the new Bath, north river, or to
SMITH and WYCKOFF,
Nov 16. No. 211 Pearl-street.

FOR AMSTERDAM,

The ship MAGNET, [illegible] Marsh, master, a substantial good vessel, burthen about 300 tons and will be ready to take on board in a few days. If immediate application be made, the freight will be taken on very moderate terms; for which, or passage, having good accommodations, apply to
SMITH & WYCKOFF,
Nov. 16. No. 211 Pearl-street.

FOR BORDEAUX

The brig [illegible] lying at White's wharf, North-river, is now ready to take in, and can be dispatched in ten days. For freight or passage apply to
Nov. 16 W. M. SETON.

FOR MARTINIQUE,

Five Hundred Barrels will be taken on freight in a good vessel for Martinique, if immediate application is made to
SUYDAM & WYCKOFF,
Nov. 16. No. 31 [illegible]-street.

For Norfolk and Richmond,

The remarkable fine new Schooner [illegible]RION, William [illegible], Master, a regular trader, will sail in the course of seven days. For freight or passage, having elegant accommodations, apply on board, at Jones' wharf, Coffee house-slip, or to
BETHUNE & SMITH,
Nov. 16. Murray's Wharf.

FOR SALE,

The ship [illegible], just arrived from Waterford, lying at the Fly-market, burthen 260 tons, or thereabouts, stows well, sails fast, and is extremely well found. For terms apply to
Nov. 16 GOUVERNEUR & KEMBLE.

FOR SALE.

RUSSIA GOODS.—The cargo of the ship Oliver Ellsworth, Joseph Skinner, master, from St. Petersburgh, consisting of Hemp, Iron, Duck, Sheetings, &c.

ALSO,

The said ship, burthen 400 tons, is a remarkable fast sailing and staunch vessel; has made but one voyage, and is in complete order for sea. Apply to
COIT & WOOLSEY,
Nov. 16. No. 93 Murray's wharf.

FOR SALE

ST. CROIX RUM.—Thirty puncheons, received per Schooner Dispatch, Paine, master, from St. Croix.

ALSO,

The said Schooner, burthen 110 tons; well calculated to carry Stock or Lumber on deck; is a staunch vessel and well found. Apply to

---

FOR SALE or CHARTER,

The schooner NEW-YORK, burthen 135 tons, built of live-oak and cedar, and in every respect a staunch good vessel. For terms of sale apply to
JOHN OZVILL, 9 Beekman-street, or
RICHD. I. TUCKER, 103 Water-street.
14 boxes Havanna brown sugar, and
9 tierces arrow root, are offered for sale on liberal terms, by RICHARD I. TUCKER, Nov. 16. 2w

For Sale, Freight or Charter,

The remarkable fast sailing ship SALLY, burthen about 265 tons—stows well, and in every respect a complete vessel. For terms apply to
ROBERT I. THURSTON,
Nov 16. [illegible] No. 297 Water-street.

For FREIGHT or CHARTER,

The ship HIRAM, Captain Jocelin, burthen 142 tons; a fine vessel, sails fast, and is well found; will be ready to receive a cargo in 12 days. For terms apply to
JAMES & SAMUEL WATSON,
No. 111 Front, or 44 Broad-street

Who will land from said ship in a day or two,

[illegible] hhds. Jamaica Rum of high proof,	18 bales Natchez Cotton,
650 Cherry and Walnut Plank & Scantling,	2 bbls. Beaver Fur,
	31 hhds. good Sugar for retailing.

THEY HAVE ALSO FOR SALE,

150 boxes Brown Soap	250 firkins Butter, of the best quality, for shipping,
60 do. Mould Candles	
59 bbls. Boston Beef,	
1100 sides Soal Leather	Nov. 16

For FREIGHT or CHARTER,

The Ship VENUS, Lemuel Bunce, master, burthen 199 tons.—Apply to
Nov. 16. WILLIAM NEILSON & Co.

For FREIGHT or CHARTER
for the West-Indies,

The brig GENIUS, burthen 90 tons, Daniel Cornwall, master—a remarkable fast sailer. Apply to the captain on board at Old slip, or to
JOHN MURRAY & SON,
Nov. 17 No. 269 Pearl street.

FOR FREIGHT or CHARTER,

The new and substantial British ship CHARLES, James Moyes, master, burthen per register 250 tons (will carry 450 tons.) She is on her first voyage. Please apply to
JOHN MAC GREGOR,
Nov. 16. 84 Broad-way.

For FREIGHT or CHARTER,

The ship NEPTUNE, burthen about 200 tons, stows well and is in complete order for sea. For terms, Apply to MINTURN & BARKER.
Nov 16.

FREIGHT
For Copenhagen or Hamburgh,

The bark [illegible], Captain Gabriel [illegible], is ready to receive [illegible] either of the above places, if application is made to the Captain on board, at Gouverneur's wharf,
Nov. 16 GOUVERNEUR & KEMBLE.

WANTED TO CHARTER,

Three or four vessels, drawing under 10 feet water, to load with lumber at Newbern, N. Carolina for Jamaica, By
Nov. 16. DICKSON & STOCKHOLM.

For FREIGHT or CHARTER
to a port in Europe or the West-Indies,

The ship NANCY, burthen about 220 tons. For terms apply to
JOHN MURRAY & SON,
Nov. 16. No. 269 Pearl-street.

FOR CHARTER,
To any of the West-India Islands,

The brig FRANCIS NIXON, burthen 150 tons, [illegible]. Apply to HOFFMAN & SETON,
Nov. 16 No. 67 Wall-street.

For Sale, Freight or Charter,

The good ship JASON, captain [illegible], 240 tons burthen, laying at Beaver-lane wharf, north-river.—She is ready to take in, and may sail to sea at a very trifling expence.
ARMSTRONG & SMITH,
No. 221 Water-street.

THEY HAVE ALSO FOR SALE,
Just received from Madeira,

10 pipes London particular		
[illegible] ditto market	Madeira Wine.	
[illegible] hogshead ditto		
[illegible] quarter cask ditto.		

N. B. Subject to foreign drawback. Nov. 16.

THE SHIP MERCHANT'S FAVOURITE,

Is compleated and will be delivered in New-York or Philadelphia. Her dimensions are as follow, viz.—Whole length of keel 81 feet 8 inches—breadth about 28 feet—lower hold 11 feet 7 inches—between decks 6 feet 1 inch—transom 20 feet 3 inches. Her plank hand-sawed, long and thick, with navel timbers bolted on the keel, both decks running flush. Her measurement is from 340 to 350 carpenter's tonnage. She may be seen in 12 or 14 hour's sail from New-York. The Proprietor was [illegible] in the construction of the above ship

---

TROY, LANSINGBURGH AND WATERFORD
NAVIGATION LOTTERY.

SCHEME.

1	Prize of	20,000 Dollars is	20,000
1		10,000	10,000
1		5,000	5,000
1		2,000	2,000
3		1,000	3,000
20		500	10,000
60		200	12,000
150		100	15,000
340		50	17,000
600		20	12,000
9,600		10	96,000
1	First drawn number		1,000
1	do. on the 5th day		1,000
1	do.	10th day	1,000
1	do.	15th	2,000
1	do.	20th	2,000
1	do.	25th	2,000
1	do.	30th	2,000
1	do.	35th	3,000
1	do.	40th	3,000
1	do.	45th	5,000
1	do.	50th	1,000
10,788	Prizes	Dollars	225,000
26,712	Blanks.		
37,500	Tickets at 6 Dolls. is	Dls.	225,000

Subject to a Deduction of 15 per cent.

☞ Less than two and a half Blanks to a Prize.

The Managers will certainly commence drawing in the City of New-York, *on the first Tuesday in May next*, and will continue to draw 750 Tickets each day until completed, as they have disposed of the LOTTERY to a Company of Gentlemen in this city, who are to sell the Tickets at the original price of *Six Dollars*, until the first of December.

This Lottery is for the purpose of raising *Thirty Thousand Dollars*, to improve the Navigation of Hudson's River, between the City of Albany and the Villages of Troy, Lansingburgh, and Waterford—Agreeably to Three several Acts of the Legislature of this State

DAVID GELSTON,
[illegible] TEN EYCK,
JOHN BORDMAN, } *Managers.*

The Tickets in the above Lottery are for sale at GAINE & TEN EYCK's Book-store, No. 148 Pearl-street.—Prize Tickets in the New-York State Road Lottery taken in payment. Nov 16 tf

THE COUNCIL of APPOINTMENT having thought proper to displace the subscribers from their former business as Auctioneers, they have (from the recommendation of many of their friends) commenced the Wholesale and Retail Grocery Business, at their old *Auction Store*, No. 143, Pearl-Street, where they will be happy to receive the orders of their friends and public in general. They have selected a choice assortment of the following articles, which they will dispose of on the lowest terms—

[illegible] hhds. 3d and 4th proof St. Croix Rum,
3 do. Country Rum,
5 pipes Gin, 100 cases old Claret,
31 pipes
17 hhds. and } superior [illegible]
64 qr. casks
[illegible] qr. casks old Sherry [illegible]
18 pipes old Lisbon do.
4 do. London [illegible]
[illegible] Hibbert's first [illegible]
20 boxes superior quality [illegible]
100 boxes & 30 jars fresh [illegible]
100 boxes Havannah Suga[illegible]
4 pipes Old Cogniac B[illegible]
30 boxes playing Cards [illegible] Manufactory.
30 chests Hyson
60 do. Hyson Skin }
30 do. Souchong
together with a general assor[illegible]
Nov. 16 H. G. [illegible]

BETHUNE & SMITH [illegible]
HAVE FOR [illegible]

EIGHTY-FIVE hogsh[illegible] Petersburg Tobacco,
13 kegs Richmond manufa[illegible]
850 bbls kiln dried India[illegible] quality—500 bushels southern [illegible]
5 casks bottled Scotch Ale,
One pipe London particula[illegible]
One hundred boxes Tin Pl[illegible]
17 cases mens and boys co[illegible] Brittannias—subject to drawb[illegible]
19 trunks and cases jacon[illegible] net Muslins,
1 case Nuns Thread, No. 1 [illegible]
3 bales blue Duffel Plaiding[illegible]
6 trunks saleable and select[illegible]
550 crates Earthen-ware, [illegible] Spanish market, and subject [illegible]
15 casks assorted Glass-War[illegible]

JOHN KNOX—97 W[illegible]
HAS FOR S[illegible]

TWENTY-SIX Hhd[illegible] New-England Rum,
23 hhds. Sugar,
20 hhds. plain and cut Glass,
30 hhds. Lamp Black,
50 crates and 20 hhds. assorte[illegible]
12 tons American Cordage, of first qua[illegible]
100 bbls. Indian Meal, 10 hhds. Virgi[illegible]
100 barrels Virginia superfine Flour.
Nov. 16.

HECTOR SCOTT,
125 *Pearl-street,*

HAS just received per the Maryland from London, and Connecticut from Liverpool, a general assortment of SEASONABLE GOODS, to be sold low by the package.

M'CREADY AND REID,
No. 91 William-Street,

HAVE received, by the late arrivals from Europe, a general assortment of DRY GOODS, which will be sold on reasonable terms, wholesale and retail—Among which are the following articles, viz.—
9 bales superfine Rose Blankets,
1 do. red, white and yellow Flannels,
5 cases Cambric Muslins, from 1/6 to 5s sterling pr yard,
3 do. Nuns Thread, from No. 8 to 64,
3 do. purple Shawls,
1 do. fancy do.
1 do. three threaded Cotton Yarn,
1 do. Women's Hose, from 3 to 18s pr pair,
2 do. Scotch damask Table Cloths, elegant patterns, from 5-4ths to 8 by 10.
Nov. 16. 1m.

JOHN & Wm. TABELE,
260, *Pearl-street,*

HAVE received by the late arrivals from London, a large and general assortment of 7-8 and 9-8 fancy calicoes & chintzes, do. furniture do. 9-8, 3-4 and 6-4 camel hair shawls in cases assorted, Book and jaconet muslin, 9-8 and 6-4 cambric, do. Dimities, Irish linens, womens white, black and coloured silk gloves and mitts, mens and womens cotton and worsted stockings, mens black and coloured silk stockings, broadcloths, cassimeres, coatings and duffels, thicksetts, callimancoes, durants, and tabborets, black India sattins, sewing silks, twist, &c.

And by the Hebe, from Amsterdam,
White and brown platillas, britannias, superfine blue and black cloths, bed-ticks, white linen hdkfs, bordered, tapes and bobbins, hair ribbon, velvet ribbon, black lace, &c.
Also on hand, about 15 ton pig lead, Nov. 16.

JOHN & WILLIAM TABELE,
No. 260 *Pearl-Street,*

HAVE imported in the snow Anna, capt. Koper, from Bremen, the following articles, viz.—
White and brown Platillas, Britannias, Sheetings, Brown and white Hessians, Brown Rolls, Ticklenburghs and Osnaburgs, Best Raven Duck. Nov. 16.

THE SUBSCRIBER has for sale, remaining from the cargo of the ship Santeim, from Calcutta, an assortment of WHITE PIECE GOODS;—

ALSO,	50 hhds. Jamaica Rum
50 tierces Rice,	10,000 Pieces White Nankeens,
15 bales Sea-Island Cotton,	A quantity of Large Bottles in cases,
29 tierces and 34 bls Jamaica Coffee,	And as usual, OLD MADEIRA WINE, fit for immediate use.

Nov. 16 ROBERT LENOX.

RICHARD & JOHN THORNE,
No. 141 *Pearl-street,*

HAVE just imported by the Factor from [illegible] from Liverpool [illegible] GOODS [illegible]

[illegible] borders, and net fringe,
Do. do. net fringe,
Do. do. plain.—Just received and will be sold low by the case or dozen, by
JOHN & Wm. TABELE,
Nov. 16. No. 260, Pearl-street.

FOR SALE,

ONE hundred chests Hyson Tea, of the Severn's cargo—70 hhds. prime St. Croix Sugar—83,000 lbs. Demarara coffee. Apply to I. [illegible]

The Post's Mission

In the first issue, the *Post*'s prospectus declared that the paper would:

- support Federalism
- provide space for communication from Democrats
- give special attention to matters concerning New York merchants
- provide timely commercial information such as ship arrivals and departures
- provide interesting and noteworthy clips from newspapers, pamphlets, magazines and reviews
- publish letters from the community

Founding the Post

Who, Where and Why

Eighteen hundred one was a dark year for the Federalists, who had lost all the major elections. Democratic Republican Thomas Jefferson was president, Democratic Republicans ruled both houses of Congress, and in New York, they swept the state elections from the governor to the legislature.

Federalists like Alexander Hamilton feared that the new government would be the downfall of the struggling new nation. One of the major issues that separated the Federalists from the Democratic Republicans concerned the power of the national government and that of the states. Hamilton felt that the strength of the United States lay in a strong, self-sufficient federal government and that the states, if left primarily to themselves, would aggressively threaten the unity of the country. As the head of the Treasury Department during George Washington's presidency, Hamilton had created financial policies built upon his ideas of a strong central government.

Before the elections, Hamilton had written a bitter piece against his fellow Federalist, President John Adams, and the rift between the two widened. The Federalist Party had broken into two main factions—those loyal to Hamilton and those loyal to Adams. With his party virtually disintegrating everywhere except in New York City, Hamilton decided to put his complete focus on his law practice. He would maintain the voice of his Federalist Party in a new daily newspaper, the *New-York Evening Post*.

This journal would allow Hamilton and the New York Federalists to defend themselves against the John Adams Federalist faction, restore Federalist prestige in the nation and express opinions against the Republicans.

In May and June of 1801, Hamilton and a few of his associates met to draft their plan of the *Post*. The group consisted of three of Hamilton's lawyer friends, Robert Troup, John Wells and William Coleman; former Mayor Richard Varick; Commissioner of Bankruptcy Caleb S. Riggs; and merchant William Woolsey. Coleman, a bright, frank, energetic young man with a remarkable flair for the written word, was chosen as editor.

The group circulated a founders list among trusty Federalists, asking each to contribute a minimum of $100. About $10,000 in capital was needed to launch the paper, and Hamilton himself contributed $1,000.

Hamilton had the support of almost all of commercial New York. Topping the *Post*'s first subscriber list of 600 people were some of the most wealthy and powerful names in the city including John Jacob Astor, fur business-owner and entrepreneur, who would become a New York real-estate mogul and the richest man in the country; Daniel D. Tompkins, future Vice President of the United States and a four-term Governor of New York; and

Archibald Gracie, one of New York's richest merchants.

Although the *Post* was often referred to as "Hamilton's Journal" or "Hamilton's Gazette," Alexander Hamilton did not openly declare himself the author of any articles or advertise his affiliation with the paper. Jeremiah Mason, a contemporary of Coleman, asked him about Hamilton's role:

"Does [Hamilton] write in your paper?"

"Never a word."

"How, then, does he assist?"

"As soon as I see him, he begins in a deliberate manner to dictate and I to note down in shorthand; when he stops, my article is completed."

The *Evening Post* took its place in the struggling young nation as the leading Federalist paper. But this was only the first voice of a journal that would outlast its founders, its party affiliation, its format, its first decade and much more.

To spread its message beyond New York, the *Post* also published a special, once-a-week edition called the *Herald* for out-of-town subscribers. This paper gave the New York City Federalists a national voice, reaching readers in cities from Boston to Savannah. Its name was changed in 1817 to the *New York Evening Post for the Country*, and it was published until 1919.

ABOVE: *John Jay, who co-wrote the Federalist Papers with Alexander Hamilton and was Governor of New York when the* Post *was founded, was a leading supporter of the paper.* CENTER: *John Astor, one of the first subscribers to the new paper. (Post 100th Anniversary supplement)*

The First New York Knick

Knickerbocker, the character who came to symbolize New York City's Dutch origins, originated in the pages of the *Post* in 1809, thanks to an elaborate literary hoax perpetrated by author Washington Irving and *Post* editor William Coleman.

Irving placed an advertisement in the paper, asking for information on a missing elderly person by the name of Diedrich Knickerbocker, who, the ad said, had vanished suddenly from his home and "is not entirely in his right mind." A few days later, a second ad asked for more information, this time saying that Knickerbocker had left behind a "curious manuscript."

Soon after, a third *Post* ad declared that Knickerbocker's creditors would publish the manuscript in order to satisfy his debts. Knickerbocker, of course, didn't really exist—the book, *A History of New York from the Beginning of the World to the End of the Dutch Dynasty*, was written by Irving, although it was published in Knickerbocker's name.

Now widely known as *Knickerbocker's History of New York*, the book was 26-year-old Irving's first commercial success. In it, he delivered a comical satirical history of the Dutch settlers and their influence on New York. The book also introduced a new word to the language: A New Yorker who could trace his ancestry to the Dutch came to be known as a Knickerbocker. The word was also applied to the first American group of writers, which included Irving.

RIGHT: *Washington Irving, standing, delivering his comical Knickerbocker advertisement to the* Post *in 1809.* BELOW: *Wall and William Streets, New York City, 1801. (Illustrations from Post 100th Anniversary supplement)*

DECADE OF DUELS

Death of the Founder's Son

Alexander Hamilton's untimely death in a duel was tragically foreshadowed by the death of his eldest son, Philip.

Just days after the founding of the *Post*, 20-year-old Philip was killed in a duel brought on by a slight a man made about his father. *Post* editor William Coleman described the facts in an article that appeared on November 24, 1801. His last paragraph is an outcry against this "horrid custom" and a call for laws to prohibit it once and for all.

DIED.

This morning, in the 20th year of his age, Philip Hamilton, eldest son of General Hamilton—murdered in a duel.

As the public will be anxious to know the leading particulars of this deplorable event, we have collected the following, which may be relied upon as correct.

On Friday evening last, young Hamilton and young Price, sitting in the same box with Mr. George I. Eacker, began in levity a conversation respecting an oration delivered by the latter in July, and made use of some expressions respecting it, which were overheard by Eacker, who asked Hamilton to step into the lobby; Price followed—here the expression, damned rascal, was used by Eacker to one of them, and a little scuffle ensued; but they soon adjourned to a public house:—an explanation was then demanded, which of them the offensive expression was meant for; after a little hesitation, it was declared to be intended for each: Eacker then said, as they parted, I expect to hear from you; they replied, you shall; and challenges followed. A meeting took place, between Eacker and Price, on Sunday morning; which, after exchanging four shots each, was finished by the interference of the seconds.

Yesterday afternoon, the fatal duel was fought between young Hamilton, and Eacker. Hamilton received a shot thro' the body the first discharge, and fell without firing. He was brought across the ferry to his father's house, where he languished of the wound till this morning, when he expired.

"By 1804, dueling had become an American fixture. And for another thirty years or more, its popularity would continue to grow. The chance of dying in a pistol duel was relatively slim. Flintlocks often misfired. And even in the hands of an experienced shooter, accuracy was difficult. Generally, pistols had to be discharged within three seconds; to take aim for a longer time period was considered dishonorable."

—from the PBS documentary *The Duel*

He was a young man of amiable disposition and cultivated mind; much esteemed and affectionately beloved by all who had the pleasure of his acquaintance.

Reflections on this horrid custom must occur to every man of humanity; but the voice of an individual or of the press must be ineffectual without additional, strong and pointed legislative interference. Fashion has placed it upon a footing which nothing short of this can control.

1803—Publishing Becomes Deadly

Two years after Philip Hamilton was killed, the *Post* was again at the center of a famous duel. After a heated exchange in the press between editor William Coleman and a Democratic rival, the two men took their battle to Love Lane (21st Street), armed with pistols. In the dusk of the evening, Coleman took the better shot and killed his opponent. According to one observer, the editor brushed himself off and went on his way "as if nothing had occurred, at least nothing unusual in the life of an editorial publisher."

ABOVE: *Post* editor William Coleman shoots and kills a political enemy *in his famous duel of 1803. (Post 100th Anniversary supplement)*

Stray Cows and Bondage

Advertisements from the 1800s

ONE CENT REWARD.

RANAWAY from the subscriber, an indent
ed apprentice, named HENRY DEGROOT.
This is to forbid any person harboring or trusting
said boy—and whoever will apprehend, or return
him to the subscriber, shall be entitled to the above
reward, but no charges.
Feb. 28 1w   JOHN MARSHALL.

A YOUNG NEGRO WOMAN,
TWENTY-ONE years of age, to be sold
for want of employment. She is capable of
all kinds of work, and is an excellent cook. For
terms enquire of the printer.   March 4

PUBLIC BALL.

MR. LALLIET respectfully informs the
Ladies and Gentlemen of New-York that
his annual BALL, will be on TUESDAY the 25th
inst. at the CITY ASSEMBLY ROOM, Broadway.
Tickets $1 each, to be had of Mr. L. No. 55,
Maiden Lane.   Feb. 1

CONCERT & BALL.

MADEMOISELLE BEZE, respectfully
informs her friends and the public that she
will give a CONCERT & BALL, on TUESDAY,
11th March, at the CITY-HOTEL.
Tickets $1 each to be had at Mr. Paff's Store,
No. 56, Maiden Lane, or at Mrs. Beze, No. 138,
Pearl-street.
Particulars in future advertisements. Feb 18

A STRAY COW.

STRAYED from the owner, a midd'e sized
Red Cow, with a white face and a white streak
on her back. It is supposed she is somewhere in
this city. A liberal reward will be given to any
person who will return her to No. 93 Front-street.
Dec 15

LOST.—Yesterday afternoon in Broadway or
Upper Robinson-street, a Topaz Breast Pin,
set in Gold with a row of Pearl around. Also, a-
bout three weeks since a Topaz Bracelet, set in
the same manner. A suitable reward will be given
for the delivery of one or both at No. 23 Upper
Robinson-street.   Sep. 30

ABOVE: *Dozens of shipping ads appeared in every edition of the* Post *in the 19th century, including those on the front page of the first edition, shown on page 17. Most shipping ads were accompanied by the ship illustration above.*

NEW-YORK EVENING POST.
THURSDAY, NOVEMBER 19, 1801.   No. 40, Pine-street.

NEW YORK, 1801

Population: 60,515

Area: The city extended from the Battery at the tip of the island to one mile north, just south of what is now Houston Street. Beyond lay countryside dotted with farms.

Mayor: Edward Livingston

Governor of New York: George Clinton

Post Newspaper Price: $3.50/year

Staten Island Ferry Fare: 2 shillings

Theater Ticket, Best Seat: $1.00

Columbia College Tuition: $8.00 to each professor

(all dollar figures non-adjusted)

NEW YORK CITY'S DAILY NEWSPAPERS IN 1801

Daily Advertiser 1785–1809

New-York Gazette 1788–1840

Commercial Advertiser 1797–1804

Mercantile Advertiser 1798–1933

American Citizen 1800–1810

New-York Evening Post 1801–present

ABOVE: *Map of Manhattan, 1783. (New York Historical Society)*

FINAL CONFLICT

The Alexander Hamilton– Aaron Burr Duel

Alexander Hamilton and Aaron Burr were fierce political rivals who had more than one public confrontation in the small environs of New York City. They called a truce in 1800 to collaborate as the defense team in the famous Levi Weeks murder trial (in which the court clerk was William Coleman, soon to be Hamilton's choice as founding editor of the *Evening Post*), but four years later their mutual animosity would culminate in a deadly showdown.

For fifteen years Hamilton had thwarted Burr's major political moves including attempts at the presidency and the governorship of New York. In 1804 Aaron Burr was Vice President of the United States, but this position did not shield him from Hamilton's bitter criticism. Hamilton publicly described Burr as "a dangerous man and one who ought not to be trusted with the reins of government," a statement that drove Burr to demand an apology and retraction. After an exchange of angry correspondence, Burr challenged Hamilton to a duel.

Hamilton's oldest son, Philip, had died in a duel three years previously and Hamilton was vehemently opposed to the custom. He felt bound to defend his honor, however, and agreed to meet Burr at a dueling site on a cliff edge just across the Hudson River in New Jersey (dueling was illegal in New York). At this point in his life, Hamilton had settled into a deeper faith that compelled him to refrain from shooting and taking a human life. He planned to participate but not fire. The evening before the duel, Hamilton wrote a personal statement outlining his feelings on the matter and stored it with his last will and testament. His note stated that "the scruples of a Christian have determined me to expose my own life to any extent rather than subject myself to the guilt of taking the life of another." He vowed to "reserve and throw away" his first fire in the hopes that the pause would provide an "opportunity to Col. Burr to pause and to reflect."

At seven a.m. on July 11, 1804, Burr, Hamilton and their seconds met on the rocky ledge below the Weehawken plain. Hamilton, being the one who had been challenged, had the choice of weapons. He chose the same set of pistols that had been used by his son in his fatal duel, a custom-made, ornate pair belonging to his brother-in-law.

In spite of Hamilton's vow, both parties did fire their pistols that early morning. The exact course of events is somewhat blurred by the contrasting accounts of the duel that followed, but historians are certain that two shots were fired—with a few seconds' interval between them—one hitting Hamilton about four inches above his right hip and one possibly hitting a tree a few feet above and to the side of Burr's head. Eyewitness accounts do not solidly identify who shot first, and the mystery remains whether Burr fired first and caused a jolt that forced the trigger in Hamilton's hand or whether Hamilton shot first and purposely missed, forcing Burr to take his shot in accord with the code duello.

Alexander Hamilton and Aaron Burr dueled on a New Jersey cliff ledge below Weehawken, New Jersey. (New York Public Library) OPPOSITE: *The week following Hamilton's death, heavy black borders lined the columns of the paper as an expression of mourning.*

Burr appeared surprised and unhappy with his deadly shot. He tried to move toward the fallen Hamilton, but his second pulled him away and rushed him to his boat. Burr struggled to turn back but was not permitted. When the attending physician, Dr. David Hosack, knelt down to examine Hamilton, the wounded man said, "This is a mortal wound, Doctor." He slipped into unconsciousness, was carried to the boat and taken to the home of his good friend James Bayard in New York. The doctor gave Hamilton laudanum, a mixture of alcohol and opium, for the pain. He died the next afternoon at two o'clock, surrounded by a small group including his wife and seven children and the Episcopal bishop of New York. Hamilton was 47 years old. Two days after his death, an enormous funeral march carried his coffin to the burial grounds of Trinity Church. Mourners in the ceremony included military officers, students and faculty of Columbia College, city politicians and hundreds of citizens.

Burr was condemned in the press as a cold-blooded killer and indicted for both dueling and murder. He fled the city and would make history again when charged with treason, although he was acquitted.

Black Borders

The day of Alexander Hamilton's funeral was the only day the *Post* has ever suspended publication due to a death. For one week, all the news columns were outlined with heavy black borders to give the entire paper a look of mourning. Crushed with grief, editor William Coleman couldn't bring himself to write his promised sketch of "him whom I can never cease to mourn as the best of friends, and the greatest and most virtuous of men."

NEW-YORK EVENING POST.

No. 827 — *MONDAY, JULY 16, 1804.* — *No. 40 Pine-Street*

NOTICE...All persons indebted to the late Copartnership of George Ferguson & Co. are requested to make immediate payment to the subscribers, who have received an assignment of all the estate and effects of the said Copartnership for the benefit of all the creditors of the said George Ferguson & Co. And the creditors are also requested to present their respective demands, duly authenticated to Thomas Eddy, of the city of New-York, that they may receive such dividend as may hereafter be made of the estate and effects so assigned as aforesaid.

Richard Hartshorne,
Henry Shotwell,
James Byrd,
Thomas Eddy.

July 11 3w

BY order of John B. Prevost, Esquire, Recorder of the city of New-York, Notice is hereby given to *Dat & Brocar*, absent debtors, and all others whom it may concern, that on application and due proof to him, the said John B. Prevost, pursuant to the directions of the act of the Legislature of the state of New York, entitled, "An act for relief against absconding and absent debtors," passed 21st of March, 1801, he hath directed all the estate, real and personal, within the city and county of New-York, belonging to the said Dat & Brocar, to be attached and safely kept—And that unless the said Dat & Brocar do discharge their debts within one year after the notice of such seizure, all their estate, real and personal, will be sold for the payment and satisfaction of their creditors.

May 18 3m BOYD & DEY, Att's

BY order of John B. Prevost, Esquire, Recorder of the city of New-York—Notice is hereby given to Benjamin Wayne, of Boston, in the Commonwealth of Massachusetts, ship-master, an absent debtor, and all others whom it may concern, That on application made to the said Recorder, by a creditor of the said Benjamin Wayne, pursuant to an act of the Legislature of the state of New-York entitled "An act for relief against absconding and absent debtors," passed 21st March 1801, the said Recorder has directed all the estate, real and personal, of the said Benjamin Wayne to be seized, and that unless the said Benjamin Wayne shall discharge his debts within one year after the publication of this notice, all his estate, real and personal, will be sold for the payment and satisfaction of his creditors. New-York, 25th May, 1804.

JAMES SCOTT SMITH, Att'y. May 23 3m

At a General Assembly of the state of Connecticut, holden at Hartford in said State, on the second Thursday of May, A. D. 1804.

UPON the Petition of Jesse S. Peck, of Wallingford, in New-Haven County, against his creditors, praying an act of Insolvency in his favor, shewing to this Assembly among other things that many of his creditors dwell out of this State and in places unknown to the petitioner, and praying that said petition may be continued to the next session of the General Assembly, to be holden at New-Haven on the second Thursday in October, 1804, for the purpose of notifying said creditors and all others concerned, of the pendency of said petition, by advertising notice of the same in such newspapers and for such lengths of time as this Assembly may direct, as by petition on file. Dated April 10, 1804.

Resolved by this Assembly, That said petition be continued to the next Session of the General Assembly, to be holden at New-Haven on the second Thursday in October, 1804, and that the petitioner give notice to said creditors and to all others concerned, of the pendency of said petition, and that they appear at said last mentioned Session of Assembly, on the second day of said Session (if they see cause) then and there to shew reasons (if any they have) why the prayer of said petition should not be granted; by causing a copy of this Resolve to be published in the Evening Post, printed in the city of New-York, and in the Connecticut Courant, printed at Hartford in this State, at least three weeks successively.

A true Copy of Record,

EXAMINED,

By SAMUEL WYLLYS, *Sec'ry.*

June 29 3w*

IN CHANCERY.

Hester Gouverneur, and others, Executors, &c. of Nicholas Gouverneur, deceased, vs. Herman G. Rutgers, and others.

IN *pursuance of a decretal order made in the above cause by the Court of Chancery of the State of New-York, will be sold under the superintendance of the subscriber, at Public Auction, at the Tontine Coffee-House, in the City of New-York, on the twenty first day of August, 1804, at one of the clock in the afternoon, a certain lot of ground and dwelling house thereon, described in a mortgage thereof made by Herman G. Rutgers, and Sarah his wife, to Nicholas Gouverneur, as follows, to wit, "all that certain messuage or dwelling house and lot of ground, No. 5 situate in Cedar-street, late little Queen-street, in the City of New-York, butted, bounded and described as follows, to wit, on the north or rear by a lot of ground belonging to the devisees of Joseph Haynes, deceased, on the west by another house and lot of the said devisees; on the east by the house and lot of ground belonging to John Harris Cruger, on the south by the said Cedar-street, containing in breadth in front twenty-five feet and one inch, in the rear twenty-three feet and six inches, in length on the south east side one hundred and thirteen feet six inches, and in length on the north west side one hundred and twelve feet seven inches," together with all and singular, the appurtenances, &c. thereunto belonging. Dated the 15th day of June, 1804.*

THOMAS COOPER,
Master in Chancery.

July 9

TO BE SOLD, a Country Retreat, situated in the pleasant village of Jamaica, on Long-Island, on the corner formed by the post-road, and the road leading to Black Stump, Flushing, &c. containing one acre of ground, or upwards, in a high state of cultivation, inclosed in a substantial fence, and abounding with a great variety of fruit and flowering trees, shrubs and plants. On the premises are a double two story dwelling house, a spacious barn, and other out-houses, a cistern and well of excellent water, with a pump in each. The improvements have been lately made, are replete with every convenience, and in excellent repair.—the house contains four rooms on each floor, besides three garret rooms, a milk room, kitchen, and two cellars, and has six fire places, two of them with marble and other suitable chimney ornaments.—The village contains three places of public worship, several seminaries of education, and affords the convenience of procuring supplies of all kinds.—Stages and market waggons are daily passing to and from New-York.

Possession may be had immediately if required, and terms made known by applying on the premises.

June 14 f. tf

BUILDING LOTS...Three Lots on Broadway, and one acre of ground on Kips Bay, fronting on the Harlem road—For sale by

JOHN HAGGERTY,
July 5 2w 82 William-street.

WANTED a Dry Nurse, none need apply without good recommendations—enquire at this office. July 9

For HAMBURGH,

The ship Lydia, capt. Tredwell, lying at Pier No. 9, has more than one half of her freight engaged, for the remainder or for passage apply to

GEORGE ERICH,
93 Front-street.

The Lydia will proceed to Lubeck, should the blockade of Hamburgh continue.

June 27 1m

TRINIDAD.

Freight for 40 hhds. is wanted on board a good vessel bound to the Island of Trinidad. Apply to

JOHN MURRAY & SONS,
July 12 269 Pearl-street.

FOR ANTIGUA,

And will stop at Barbadoes or Dominique if freight offers, the brig ACTRESS, Edward Tinker, master. She is now graving and will sail in ten days: For freight or passage, (having excellent accommodations) apply to

A. KIRKPATRICK,
July 12 7 Fair-street.

For NEW-ORLEANS,

The brig WILLIAM, P. W. Pailiet, Master, has two thirds of her cargo engaged, and will be dispatched soon as possible—For freight of the residue or passage, apply to

JACOB & THOS. WALDEN,
66 South-street.

Who offer for sale landing from said vessel.

110 Hhds New-Orleans Sugar, strong grained and of superior quality.
34 bales Cotton,

IN STORE,

170 Qr. casks Sherry Wine of the most approved brands.
35 bbls Cider Brandy, strong proof & good flav.
4 pipes old L. P. Madeira Wine,
500 Red oak Hhds Shooks, best quality.

July 10 2w

ST. DOMINGO COFFEE in bags, barrels and Tierces, about 3000 wt. with Certificate—For sale by

MAXWELL HYSLOP,
18 Broadway.

Freight for Jamaica,

A good vessel bound to the port Kingston, may have a few barrels of Provisions and a quantity of Lumber by applying as above.

June 18.

Wanted to Purchase,

Two Schooners of about 100 tons each—Apply to

GRANT FORBES, & Co.

Who have in Store

Louisiana Sugars of the *first* quality for the scale, in parcels suitable to the retailers. Also, 82 hhds and 20 bbls Clayed Sugars. June 23

For Sale, Freight or Charter,

The new brig WILLIAM TELL, burthen 120 tons by Carpenter's measurement, Et Glad, master, just arrived from Poughkeepsie, where she was built; she is a faithful built and burthensome vessel, and will be fitted for sea with dispatch. If she should not be sold when completely fitted, a freight to Cadiz or Lisbon would be preferred. Apply to,

CALDWELL & FOOTE,
June 22 74 South-street.

FOR SALE,

(A GREAT BARGAIN)

The brig HAMILTON, a prize vessel, purchased in the West-Indies, about 150 tons burthen, British built, and is coppered. She may be examined at the foot of James-street—For terms apply to

May 15 ROBERT LENOX.

EBENEZER STEVENS, 222 Front-street, has for sale,

3500 lbs. first quality New-Orleans Indigo
60 pipes Barcelona Brandy,
4 do Cognac
50 do Sicily Madeira Wine
6 bales French Coffee Bags, best quality
3 do French Paper Hangings
2 do Umbrellas
2 cases Fowling pieces, single & double barrll'd
1 do common and embroidered Fans, Snuff Boxes and Pocket Books
2 do Ladies Straw and Crape Bonnets
2 do Fancy Articles, Chambray, Gauze, Plumes, Ornaments for Gowns, Wreaths and Garlands of Flowers, Diadems, &c. and
2 cases Ladies extra long Silk Gloves

ALSO,

The very fast sailing brig ENTERPRIZE, burthen 164 tons, pierced for 16 guns, and is in complete order. July 7

FOR SALE,

The beautiful fast sailing Pilot Boat DASH, as she arrived from Port-au-Prince, burthen 51 tons, Inventory and conditions of sale to be known by application to

GILBERT ROBERTSON & Co.

July 10

For Sale Freight or Charter,

The schooner MARGARET, now lying at the subscribers Lumber Yard, burthen 99 1-2 tons, is a strong vessel and newly sheathed; will be ready to receive a cargo in 2 or 3 days—For terms apply to

BROADIE & DENNISTOWN,
July 10 146 Washington-street.

WANTED TO CHARTER,

(for a port in the Mediterranean)

A good vessel, burthen about 150 or 160 tons, immediate dispatch will be given. Apply to

JOHN MURRAY & SONS,
July 2 No. 269 Pearl-street.

SICILY MADEIRA WINE....50 pipes, of first quality, now landing from the brig Ann, from Marsala—For sale by

EBENEZER STEVENS,
222 Front-street.

Also,

7 hhds. Clayed Sugar,
5 do. Muscovado do.
7 barrels of Coffee.

From the brig Diamond, from Guadaloupe.

June 16

CLARET, NANKEENS, TOBACCO, &c.

JOHN M'VICKAR & Co. No. 3 Barclay-street, have on hand the following consignments, which they will dispose of on accommodating terms.

23 hhds Prime Richmond Tobacco,
840 pieces Blue Nankeens,
100 boxes Claret, each containing 2 dozen, and
A quantity of Lignum Vitæ. July 7

RAISINS, SPERM CANDLES & GUNPOWDER TEA—

50 casks Raisins, 50 boxes Muscatel do
65 boxes Spermaceti Candles
10 chests Gunpowder Tea landing this day

For Sale by

BRUCE & MORISON.

They have also in Store

140 hhds prime Codfish
20 hhds Jamaica Spirits
20 pipes Cognac and Barcelona Brandy
12 do Hollands Gin
40 casks Hibberts Brown Stout
30 Qr casks Sherry Wine
7 pipes Madeira Wine
3 do Old Lisbon

First quality Claret in cases of 1 & 2 doz. each

15 chests Hyson }
25 do Young Hyson } TEAS of latest importations.
30 do Souchong }
25 do Bohea }

Flotant and Spanish Indigo
Bullocks Cheese, 75 bags Race Ginger
Demi Johns and 12 bales soft shell'd Almons
Chocolate and Coffee
200 lb Nutmegs, 200 do Cloves
Cassai, Ginger, Pepper, Rice, Barley
Basket Salt, Citron, Mace, Mustard, &c. with a number of other articles which they will dispose of Wholesale and Retail. June 22

GUN-POWDER & FOWLING PIECES.

Just received, and for sale by the subscribers.

120 qr. casks single seal British Powder, a very approved quality,
20 do. double seal do.
20 do. cannister do.
300 do. tower proof do.
120 do. double do. do.
30 do. glazed do. do.
4 cases well assorted Fowling Pieces, and long deck Guns, and
2 do. twisted stub do in cases, with implements.

ROBERT BACH & Co.
June 1 145 Pearl street.

ONEIDA'S CARGO.

A FEW boxes best chop Hyson Tea of this Cargo yet on hand—Also,

Hyson Chulan in small boxes for families

Imperial Tea,	Fans
Nankeens,	China Ware
Silks,	Rhubarb and

China Root, &c.—For sale by Wm. Leffingwell, No. 50 Wall-street, or at

LEFFINGWELL & DUDLEYS,
May 11 No 116 Front street

DUNSTABLE BONNETS, RUSSIA HEMP, &c....

2 boxes straw and chip Bonnets, of the first quality, with fancy chip Plumes,
11 tons St. Petersburg Hemp,
1 cask Felt Hats,
180 bbls. Mess, Prime and Cargo Beef,
30 do. Cargo Pork,

A few bbls. Prime Pork—For sale by

LEBBEUS LOOMIS,
June 9 43 William-street.

SUGAR & MOLASSES, of the first quality—Will commence Landing this day, from on board the schooner Hampshire, from Trinidad, at Stevens'-wharf,

52 hhds. }
48 barrels, } Muscovado Sugar,
27 hhds. Molasses—For sale by

JOHN MURRAY & SONS,
May 21 269 Pearl-street.

TELESCOPES, MAPS, BUNTING, &c. —Imported in the ship Jupiter, Law, from London, 3 cases and 12 casks, containing an handsome assortment of—

Telescopes, Quadrants,
Maps of the coast of America, West-Indies and Europe,
Buntings white and coloured,
Sail Needles, Paints in kegs and Paint Brushes, with a variety of other articles in the Ship Chandelery line, which are offered for sale on very moderate terms, by

JOHN MURRAY & SONS;
May 23 269 Pearl-street.

TO commence landing on Monday, the 18th June, the cargo of the brig Albatross, captain Woldes, from Leghorn.

6 boxes Marble Slabs,
300 Marble Tiles
116 pipes Corsica }
83 hhds. French } Wine,
350 boxes Soap, 6 boxes Manna,
12 bags Aniseeds, 189 boxes Olives,
17 boxes Straw Hats,
8 do. Silk do. 2 boxes Silks,
12 bags Juniper Berries,
2 boxes Black Crapes,
3 do. Chip Hats,
2 do. Straw Rims,
8 do. Writing Paper, of excellent quality,
2 do. Saffron,
527 do. Oil—For sale by

JOHN MURRAY & SONS,
June 16 269 Pearl-street.

OLIVER WOLCOTT & Co.

OFFER FOR SALE,

FIFTEEN bales Allahabad Cossas,
4 do. Jelapore Sawns,
4 do. blue Handkerchiefs,
10 do. Chintzes,
11 do. Twine,
307 bags Pepper,
120 do Ginger,
288 do Sugar, part of the cargo of the ship Allegany. June 21

JOHN M'VICKAR & Co. have received per the ship Susan, John O'Connor, master, from Dublin, a further supply of—

7-8 and 4-4 Linens,
3-4 and 10-4 Diapers,
5-4 Sheetings,
Long Lawns and Table Cloths.

Also on hand,

100 cases Claret, two dozen each.

June 4

HEMP, IRON, LINEN, INK, WINE, &c....For Sale,

Russia Hemp, Iron, Diapers, and Sail Duck,
Irish Linens, Sheetings, and Ticken, assorted,
Irish Whiskey, 4th proof, and Glassware,
A few kegs Printers Ink,
10 pipes superior quality Port Wine,
Old Madeira Wine, from $3 to 5 per gallon.

Apply to LOW & WALLACE,
April 6 tf 24 Broadway.

BAR LEAD, SHOT, NAILS & CHEESE,

896 kegs Patent Shot,
100 barrels }
50 kegs } BAR LEAD
20 casks Nails assorted
5 Hampers Cheese, received per ship Cotton-Planter, from Liverpool---For sale by

ROBERT GILLESPIE.

June 26

PORTER, COPPERAS, BARK, WINE, CORDAGE & HATS....

150 casks Hibberts best Brown Stout,
30 hhds. Copperas,
60 do Quercitron Oak Bark,
104 coils Cordage.
5 pipes old London Particular Madeira Wine,
2 cases low priced Hats—For sale by

COIT & PHILLIPS,
Corner of Carlisle and Washington streets.

May 12

LE ROY, BAYARD & M'EVERS, have for sale the following articles, which they will dispose of on reasonable terms, for approved notes

Madras Handkerchiefs, in bales,
Mock Madras do. do.
Vantapaulam do. do.
Ginghams, do.
Sussackars, do.
Napkins, do.
Twilled Silk Hdkfs. in boxes }
50 cadies colored Sewing Silk, } from Canton.
50 do. black do. do. }

Also,

A few bales of Hessians. April 24

STERLING PLATE & PLATED WARE.

THOMAS WARREN,
No. 61 MAIDEN-LANE,

HAS just opened and for sale an elegant assortment of the above articles, with a general assortment of—

Cutlery and Japan Ware,
Knife Cases and Tea Caddies,
Andirons, Shovels and Tongs,
Officers Swords, Sashes and Epaulets,
Prussia Binding, Vellum Lace, Cord, &c.

ALSO,

30 cases Pins, well assorted,
4 do. Metal, Plated and Gilt Buttons,

May 4

ROBERT LENOX,

HAS for sale, by the latest arrivals, the following Goods—

By the ship Grace, Peace and Plenty, and Nancy, from Calcutta,

A complete and well selected assortment of PIECE GOODS, Cotton, Lines and Twine, a large proportion of which is calculated for Sugar Bakers.

Ginger, Gunny Bags,
Gum Shillac, Gum Copal, and
Sugar, of a very superior quality.

By the ship Alleghany, from Madras,

A very handsome assortment of Pullicat, Ventapolam and Masulipatam Hdkfs. of the newest and most fashionable patterns.

By the ship Silenus, from Cape of Good Hope,

600 bags Brazil Sugar,
12 boxes Window Glass,
150 pieces Ebony Wood, and
5000 pounds Sapan Wood.

Also, by former arrivals,

A few boxes of Madras superfine Chintz,
100 pipes fine flavored Barcelona Brandy,
270 cases Bordeaux Claret,
A few tons Lignumvitæ,
A quantity of cases of 6 bottles, containing 4 gallons each, and
Old full-bodied MADEIRA WINE, fit for present use. May 15

GUNS, SWORDS, EPAULETTS, &c.....

3 cases first quality double barrel Guns,
1 do Hair trigger and pocket Pistols,
1 do Epauletts, Cords, Fancy Plumes, Wreaths, Fringes, Laces, &c.
1 do Military Feathers,
6 do Plated Ware, Castors, &c.
1 do Gigg Whips,
2 trunks Watch Glasses,
1 do Silk and Cotton Suspenders,
1 cask Cutlery,
1 do Brittania Metal Tea Pots,
1 do Plating Mills 4 to 8 inches,

Received by the Martha, from London; Cotton-Planter, Oliver Ellsworth and Josiah Collins, from Liverpool, and for sale by

LEMUEL WELLS, & Co.

June 30 eod 1m

MADEIRA WINE....3 pipes and 14 hhds. choice picked London Particular Madeira Wine, 4 years old, now landing at Murray's-wharf, for sale by LOW & WALLACE.

Also in store,

Russia Hemp, Sail Duck and Diapers,
Madrass Hdkfs. Ginghams, &c.
30 hhds. assorted Irish Glass,
12 kegs Printers Ink,
80 hhds. Draught Porter,
Old Madeira Wine, from three to five dollars per gallon, and
Superior Port and Claret Wines, in bottle & wood

June 8 tf

EDWARD L. SCHIEFFELIN,

HAVING entered into co-partnership with Mr. JONATHAN SCHIEFFELIN, business will in future be conducted at the Store lately occupied by James Thomson, corner of Maiden lane and Pearl street, under the firm of

J. & E. SCHIEFFELIN,

Who have for sale a general assortment of *Drugs and Medicines*, which they will dispose of on the most reasonable terms, amongst which are, viz.

1000 lb Rhubarb,	50 doz large white skins
800 lb Yellow Bark,	3 cases Aq. Fortis,
1500 lb Sarsaparilla,	2 carboys Oil Vitriol
500 lb Camomile Flowers,	40 lb Oil of Mint.
6 doz superior Castor Oil,	1000 lb Liquorice,
150 lb Nutmegs,	1000 lb Flor. Sulphur
200 lb Cloves,	1000 lb Salts,
200 lb Windsor Soap	7 lb Pulv. Feb. Antim.
1000 doz Wash Balls,	COLOURS.
100 doz Roll Pomatum,	200 lb Mineral Green, No. 1 & 4,
200 lb Camphor,	100 lb Rose Pink,
200 lb Quicksilver,	Litharge, Blue Verditer,
1000 lb Pearl Barley,	Naples Yellow, Patent
200 lb Ol. Lavender,	Yellow, &c.
1000 lb Rad. Gentian,	200 lb Cantharides.

MEDICINE CHESTS

From six dollars to twenty, and upwards, with new improved directions, and a general assortment of Patent Medicines, &c. May 21

RICE, SUGAR, AND RUM.....

180 tierces New Rice,
13 hogsheads Jamaica Rum,
5 hogsheads Sugar,

Now landing, and for sale by

EBENEZER STEVENS,
May 23 222 Front-street

NEWEST FASHION.

CHIMNEY GLASSES....A few very elegant ones are now offered for sale by JOHN DIXEY, at his Looking Glass Store, 118 William-street,

As they are the first articles of this kind finished agreeably to the present prevailing fashion in Europe, it is hoped they will merit the attention of persons of taste.

Also, an extensive assortment of Pier Glasses, Gerandoles, Widow Cornices, &c. in the newest and most approved stile. March 28 eod

NOW Landing at Walton's-wharf, from on board the ship Fame, from Bourdeaux, and for sale by the subscribers,

503 pipes best 4th proof Cognac Brandy,
700 boxes Claret Wine,
100 do. Capers, Olives and Anchovies,
100 baskets best Sweet Oil.

Also in Store,

300 bags Ginger,
200 casks Rice and 10 bags Cloves.

June 18 MINTURN & CHAMPLIN.

BOURS, MAC GREGOR & Co. have received by the Telegraphe and Ontario, from Liverpool, and Brandywine Miller, from Greenock, the following Goods, which they offer for sale by the package or less quantity, on reasonable terms—

2 cases fancy and boss Trimmings, Cotton Edgings, and white Silk Laces,
1 case black and white silk Bands and Tassels, white silk Epaulets, new patterns,
1 do. black Patinet Laces and Lace Cloaks,
1 do. elegant 6 4 laced and soft mull muslins, and fashionable finish'd Shawls.

Also, by the late arrivals from Calcutta,

34 packages, consisting of—

Mow, Jallapore and Johanna } MAMOODIES,
Jugdea, Lekipore and Chattabully } BAFTAS,
Jallapore and Mow } SANNAS,
Beerbhoom Gurrahs,
Cossas and Company do.
Checks and Persians June 4

FOR SALE, 9 casks White Wine Vinegar, just received from Bordeaux.—Apply to

LE ROY, BAYARD & M'EVERS,
June 13 66 Broadway.

INDIA GOODS, imported in the ship Alleghany, G G Coffin, master, from Calcutta, viz

86 bales Piece Goods, assorted,
7 do. Twine,
619 bags }
20 chests } Sugar,
272 bags heavy Pepper,
67 do. Ginger—For sale by

BENJ. WOOLSEY ROGERS & Co.
April 26 225 Pearl-street.

SAMUEL MURGATROYD, No. 14 Stone street, has for sale,

277 cases of Claret,
36 cases sweet White Wine,
14 half casks White Wine,
9 tierces White Wine Vinegar,

Imported in the brig Rolla, from Bordeaux.

May 30 eod tf

BRANDY, OIL, BEANS, &c...

3 hhds and 38 bbls Cyder Brandy
11 bbls Linseed Oil
200 bbls White Beans
10 hhds Yellow Corn Meal.—For sale by

GURDON & DANIEL BUCK,
June 26 84 South-street.

ST. CROIX SUGAR....30 Hhds, & 24 bbls. of the first quality of Muscovado Sugar, just imported in the brig Mountaineer, Rodgers, and 6 Hhds. and 43 bbls. of the first quality Muscovado Sugar, imported in the brig Phoenix, capt Goodrich, both from St. Croix, will be landed tomorrow at the old slip and for sale by

CHARLES D. GOOLD.

July 9 1w

NOTICE.---By order of John B. Prevost, Esq Recorder of the city of New-York—Notice is hereby given to the persons constituting the co-partnership, or house of trade of Dat and Brocar of Cape Francois, merchants, absent debtors, and all others whom it may concern, that on application and due proof made to him the said Recorder, pursuant to the directions of the act of the Legislature of the state of New-York, entitled, "An act for relief against absconding and absent debtors," passed March 21, 1801, he hath directed all the estate of the said persons as constituting the said co-partnership or house of trade of Dat and Brocar, to be seized, and that unless they discharge their debts within one year after this public notice, all their estate will be sold for the payment of their debts. Dated, New-York 20th April, 1805.

April 20 F 3m

ROBERT DUNLAP,

Merchant Taylor, 57 Chatham street,

RETURNS his sincere thanks to his customers and the public in general for their past favors, and hopes by strict attention to his business, to merit a continuance of their patronage.

N. B. Mens wearing apparel of every decription made on the shortest notice—and should any garment made for a gentleman, not fit him, he is at liberty to return it free of expence. June 6 tf

IN CHANCERY.

BUILDING LOTS AT BROOKLYN,

FOR SALE.

The President, Directors and Company of the Bank of New-York, vs. Comfort Sands, Henry Sands, & Isaac Kibbe.

A *DECRETAL order having been made in the above cause, by the court of Chancery of the state of New-York, whereby the mortgaged premises mentioned in the pleadings in the said cause, are directed to be sold at Public Auction, in the city of New-York, by one of the Masters of the said Court—The subscriber gives notice, that the sales of the said mortgaged premises will commence at Public Auction, at the Tontine Coffee House, in the city of New-York, on TUESDAY, the third day of July, 1804, at twelve of the clock, A. M. and will be continued by adjournment from time to time, until the same shall be completed.*

The said mortgaged premises are situate at Brooklyn, in the County of Kings, in this State, and consist of Building Lots of different dimensions, to the number of six hundred and upwards, as numbered on a certain map thereof, which may be seen at the office of the subscriber.

Some of the said Lots will be sold separately, and others of them in such parcels as to the subscriber shall appear likely to be most beneficial to the parties interested therein.

On some of the said lots there are dwelling houses, buildings, and other improvements. Dated June 11, 1804.

THOMAS COOPER,
June 11 Master in Chancery.

P. S. The sales of the above property will be resumed and continued on Tuesday the 31st inst. at 12 of the clock, in the forenoon, at the Tontine Coffee-House in the city of New-York, to which time the said sales have been adjourned by the subscriber. Dated 10th July, 1804.

THOMAS COOPER,
July 11. Master in Chancery.

FOR SALE OR TO LEASE, the HOUSE and Lot adjoining Mr. Abeuus, on the east corner of the common, near the Episcopal Church, Newark. There is on the premises every convenience necessary for a family, a good garden, with a beautiful grass lot in the rear, and a new barn. For terms apply to ELIAS VAN ARSDALE, Newark, or

JOHNSON TUTTLE,
No. 31 Nassau-street, New-York.

April 14

Decade Two

1811-1820

As New York's population grew by about 30,000 in this decade, so did its level of noise, dirty streets, crowded housing districts, crime, public drunkenness and other problems. The *Post* carried many editorials and articles about civic concerns, some of which led to new city policies. Manhattan was a rugged town, with pigs freely roaming the streets, obnoxious cart drivers racing up and down Broadway to the peril of everyone who got in their way, piles of garbage from butcheries and shops littering the streets, and daily alarms of fires in homes and commercial buildings.

The threat of war against Britain turned to reality in the summer of 1812, and the *Post*, which had always spoken out against such a war, declared it "madness" for Congress to declare war on a country with such a powerful navy.

Broadway and City Hall, 1819. (Post 100th Anniversary supplement)

Filthy Streets and Other Calamities

The Post Speaks Out

In its first decades, the *Post* reported on issues that concerned the daily lives of New York's ever-growing population. Letters from the editor and concerned citizens railed against the awful conditions of the streets, the noise and pranks of hooligans, the unfair abuse of lotteries in taking money from the poor (which

helped bring forth a new law against lotteries), the failings of the ill-managed public health agency, and more.

The city's Board of Health was reluctant to report outbreaks of yellow fever and other diseases in fear that it would chase away trade. During outbreaks of yellow fever, thousands of people fled the city—at times nearly half the population—including the editor of the *Post*, who, during one epidemic, moved the offices of the paper to the outskirts of the city (present-day Greenwich Village). The *Post*'s demand for public information about health crises led to reform in the Board of Health and its policies. The following excerpts reveal the scope of health and safety matters that were brought to light in the *Post*'s first decades:

On unsanitary food:

"You can scarcely pass through any one street in the city without running against a greasy table, with plates of sickly oysters displayed, well peppered with dust, and swarms of flies feeding upon them."

On yellow fever and the spread of disease:

"It is notorious that notwithstanding the prevalence

of a malignant disease, and when great exertions are made to check its destroying progress, the streets of this city are in a most noxious state; and will continue to increase in putridity, unless we are favored with some refreshing rains to clear them."

"That the disease exists in this city I believe is universally admitted, but the real extent or limits of it is not known; upon this point our citizens are left to their imagination and to public report. Is this system of conduct, this profound silence, calculated to prevent or lessen alarm? I believe not—I believe it is productive of every evil it is intended to guard against. . . . Every vessel that is even suspected should be removed from our wharves, and if the fever be ascertained to arise from such vessel, every adjoining vessel should also be removed to the stream or the quarantine ground. . . . In whatever part of the town the disease appears let the physician be enjoined to make a report of the case. . . . If practicable, let the sick be immediately removed into the country."

On fire safety:

"This morning, about 5 o'clock, the city was again alarmed by the cry of fire. . . . We sincerely hope the time is not far distant when no wooden buildings will be suffered to remain in the city. Such a measure undoubtedly would bear hard on some individuals; but the general good seems to render it indispensably necessary."

On bad roads and streets:
"Every street in the city is thronged with hogs."

"[Broadway is in] such a state of neglect and ruin that no one could drive through it after dark but at the hazard of limbs and life."

"The collection of filth and manure now lying in heaps, or which has been heaped in Wall, Pearl, Water, and Front Streets, near the Coffee-House, and left there, will astonish those who are fond . . . of a walk there."

"Citizens find the dog returning to his filth, and the hog to its wallowing . . . what was rank is ranker still. Nothing could be worse than the collection of manure, offals, garbage, and rotten vegetables, with which [we are] surrounded . . . the very walks of [our] streets [are] the place of deposit for the very vilest of all filth."

"The ice and snow on our sidewalks have rendered them so slippery as to make the walking not only difficult and painful, but uncommonly dangerous. Serious accidents are taking place every day, and every body who walks the streets should do it with the peril of broken limbs before his eyes. The evening before last a man fell on the sidewalks and broke his leg . . . and this morning a smart girl fell and broke her arm. . . . Our housekeepers could hardly do a greater duty, than to clear the ice from the sidewalk, in front of their dwellings."

On patent medicines:
"[We denounce] the quack medicines and quack advertisements which . . . so much distinguish and disgrace the city."

Ads for potions and elixirs were often seen in the Post, but the paper was strict about weeding out quack products and refused to advertise them.

On noise:
"The measured ditty of the young sweep at daybreak, upon the chimney top; the tremendous nasal yell of 'Ye rusk!'; the sonorous horn that gives dreadful note of 'gingerbread!'; and the echoing sound of 'Hoboy!' at midnight . . . bellowing out their filthy ditties!"

On lotteries:
"Look at the crowd of poor, ragged wretches that beset the office-keeper's doors the morning after the day's drawing is over, waiting with their little slips in their hands, to hear their fate, and the yesterday's earnings ready to be given to the harpies that stand gaping for the pittance."

"We once more desire lottery office-keepers not to send to this office, for publication, any advertisements, offering, directly or indirectly, any tickets in foreign lotteries for sale. They shall not appear. They must look elsewhere for some one to aid them in evading the law."

THE Irish Lottery Office, 222 Broadway, opposite the Park — Virginia Dismal Swamp Lottery, No 4, was drawn in Richmond yesterday. Capitals $20,000, 10,000, 6000, 5000, 4000, 2910, 12 of 1,000, 18 of 500, &c. &c.
ERIN GO BRAGH
Price of Tickets—Whole only $5; half $2 50

A lottery ad from June 1817. Foreign lotteries were illegal, but some of their ads were cleverly worded so as to fool the readers—and the editor— about their origins.

Madness of War

Excerpts from two editorials written during the War of 1812:

June 20, 1812
It is now ascertained that an unconditional Declaration of War against Great Britain has passed both houses of Congress, and has become a law.

We have very little disposition to remark on this unprecedented measure at this time; but we cannot help expressing our regret that such madness (for we can call it nothing better) should have seized a majority of our Representatives at Washington.

For the government of a country, without armies, navies, fortifications, money or credit and in direct contradiction to the voice of the people, to declare war against a power which is able in a few months time to sweep from the ocean millions of property belonging to the people of that country, is an act of imprudence, not to say wickedness, such as, perhaps, was never before known since civil government was established.

August 27, 1814
THE CITY OF WASHINGTON DESTROYED—This day we have the disagreeable task of recording the capture and destruction of the city of Washington, the Capital of the United States!

Six months ago, no one could have thought such an event could have possibly taken place. But this is the age of wonders! . . . This city situated at such a distance from the ocean and only approachable with shipping by long, crooked and narrow rivers, on a spot selected above all others as the most secure from foreign invasion—who could have supposed that it could so easily have been destroyed by an enemy?

What shall we think of such things? Where have our men at the head of affairs been all this time? . . . Was there no means of defending the property of the nation? Can men who manage in this way be fit to govern a great and free people? Let their constituents answer.

Post Editor Takes a Beating—1818

In the 19th century, newspaper editors freely wrote harsh and cutting criticisms of rival editors and others who drew their scorn. William Coleman was no exception. In early 1818, he described the shocking and scandalous behavior of prominent Democrat Henry B. Hagerman, who had molested an innkeeper while traveling in upstate New York.

Coleman's rants in the *Evening Post* outraged Hagerman to the point of cold-blooded violence. On the evening of April 11, he snuck up behind Coleman at the corner of Murray and Church Streets and attacked him with the butt of a rawhide whip. The editor fell to the ground, was repeatedly struck and kicked and left for dead in a bloody heap. He survived, but never fully recovered.

Two years after the attack, a court awarded the editor $4,000 in damages. The money was little comfort, however, because Coleman suffered strokes of paralysis and failing health until his death in 1829.

ABOVE: *William Coleman, first editor of the* Post. LEFT: *New York street scene, 1800s. (Illustrations from Post 100th Anniversary supplement)*

SCUDDER'S AMERICAN MUSEUM.
No 21 CHATHAM-STREET.

THIS interesting place of public resort has lately been enriched with a great variety of new articles ; some of which have never before been exhibited in any collection of the kind in America. Among the articles added, within a few months, are the American Forest, exhibiting a view of the game animals of our country ; a number of beautiful and rare birds from different parts of the Globe, with a variety of shells &c. &c. too many to enumerate in an advertisement. The Beasts and birds are exhibited in their natural shape and colour ; and as it has been the wish of the proprietor to excel in preparing and exhibiting his articles, he wishes his friends and the friends of science to examine his collection, and judge for themselves how far he has succeeded in his attempts.

April 20

ABOVE: *Stuffed animals of many kinds, "too many to enumerate in an advertisement." April 20, 1812.*

Naked Truths and Opera

Advertisements from the 1810s

STEAM BOATS.

FOR Philadelphia, the RARITON & PHŒNIX Steam Boats, being connected with elegant and commodious Stages, have formed a complete line to and from Philadelphia. The Rariton will leave New-York every MONDAY, WEDNESDAY AND FRIDAY at seven, and Brunswick on TUESDAY, THURSDAY and SATURDAYS at six o'clock in the morning, touching at the usual places going and returning. Breakfast, Dinner and Tea on board.—For passage apply to the captain at Steam-Boat-wharf, north side Battery.

April 3. tf

HUDSON RIVER STEAM-BOATS.
FOR THE INFORMATION OF THE PUBLIC

THE PARAGON, capt. Wiswall, will leave New-York every Saturday afternoon, at 5 o'clock.

MUTUAL INSURANCE COMPANY OF THE CITY OF NEW-YORK.
(The oldest Institution for Insurance against fire in this city.)

NAKED TRUTHS.—TO THE CURIOUS.

THE public have now an opportunity of viewing a large and interesting collection of LIVING ANIMALS, at the corner of Duane-street, second door from the corner of Broadway.

A RED LION of the largest species, just arrived from the Coast of Africa, in the brig Francis, Captain Britten, of New-York. This animal was taken by the Arabs in the Interior, and brought down to Senegal.

The form of the LION is the best model of strength joined to agility. Its anger is noble, its courage magnanimous, and its temper susceptible of grateful impressions. It has often been known to despise weak and defenceless animals, thrown to be devoured by it—to live in habits of cordiality with it—to share subsistance, and even give it a preference when its portion of food was scanty.

A living OSTRICH, 5 feet high.
The Greenland BEAR, and a BEAR from Lake Ontario.
A PELICAN of the wilderness—his bill will hold 10 quarts of water.
A WILD MOUNTAIN RAM, with a horn growing out of his forehead 15 inches in length.
A large male ELK.
An American EAGLE, caught in Kentucky.
Two MAN MOZETS, from the East Indies.
The ALLIGATOR, the SEA TIGER, the African APE, and a number of different animals, not mentioned, making 16 different and curious animals, from different parts of the world. Also, a number of painted Views of several battles of the late war.

Admittance 25 cents. Hours of Exhibition from 9 in the morning till 9 in the evening.

Feb 19 tf

ROBERT DAVIES having entered in partnership with STEPHEN WHEATON, in the fancy chair manufacturing, inform their friends and the public, that the business in future will be carried on under the firm of
WHEATON & DAVIES.

WHEATON and DAVIES, fancy chair manufacturers, have removed from No. 15 Bowery to No. 153 Fulton-street, opposite St. Paul's Church, where they offer for sale an elegant assortment of curled maple painted, ornamented, landscape, sewing and rocking chairs, loungees, settees, sofas, music stools, &c. ☞ Old chairs repaired, painted, and ornamented.

may 30

NEW CIRCUS

NEAR THE STONE BRIDGE, BROADWAY.

Last week but two of the Company's Performing On MONDAY, September 1st 1817, and every evening during the week (Saturday excepted.)

Mr. Campbell, the Flying Phenomena, will take a surprising leap over 3 horses, the wonderful Pony standing on the other two Horses backs.

Horsemanship by Mr. Blackmore, who, among a variety of Feats, will stand on his head on the neck of a Quart Bottle! the Horse in full speed.

Mr. Campbell will ascend a Pole eighteen feet high and will place his breast upon it, and in that state will turn round like a Fly of a Jack, with his Hands and Feet expanded in the air. Never attempted by any other person.

Mr. Williams will go through his elegant performance on the Tight Rope, Clown to the Rope Mr. Campbell.

A grand Equestrian Entree, with all those beautiful horses.

Mrs. Williams will display the whole of her astonishing Equilibriums on the Slack Wire.

Still Vaulting by the troop of Flying Phenomena—Clown, Mr. Campbell.

Equestrian Exercises, and the six Divisions of the Broad Sword, by Mrs. Williams.

The wonderful Pony, (only 35 inches high.)

Master Yeaman, the Flying Horseman, will introduce the Peasant's Frolic, or Flying Wardrobe, and Ladies Fashions in Paris.

Mr. Blackmore will exhibit his wonderful performances on the Slack Rope.

The entertainment to conclude with the Hunted Tailor, by Mr. Parker.

Tickets sold and places taken at the Circus every day of Performance, from 11 till 2 o'clock.

Doors to be opened at 6 o'clock; the performance to commence at 7 o'clock; price of admission—boxes $1; children under 12 years of age, 50 cents; Pit 75 cents; children 50 cents; Gallery 50 cents.

Ladies and gentlemen taught the polite art of Riding by Mr. West and W. West, Riding Masters.

N. B. The Circus will be opened but a few weeks, in consequence of Mr. West's engagement at Baltimore. Au 30

FLATBUSH AND BATH STAGE.

JOHN HUNTER informs his old customers and the public in general that he intends running a convenient and commodious Stage, from his old noted stand, Old Ferry; to leave his Hotel at 10 o'clock in the morning, arrive at Bath at 11; leave Bath at 5 o'clock, and arrive at Brooklyn at 6 o'clock.

N. B. Elegant Horses and Gigs to let at any moment for any route on the Island.

may 15 1m*

Messrs. GILLES & ETIENNE'S
Third and last Didactic and Academical
CONCERT.

☞ On WEDNESDAY EVENING, March 12th, 1817, at the City Hotel, to begin at half past 7 o'clock.

PROGRAMME.
PART I.

1. Overture to Lodoiska, . . . Kreutzer
2. French Air, from the Opera of Concert Interrompu, sung by Mrs. L. Bertea.
3. French Air, with variations, from the Opera of Secret, executed on the hautboy by Mr. Gilles, senr. . . Kreutzer
4. Italian Duetto, from the Opera of Romeo and Juliette, sung by Mrs. L. and Mr. T. . . . . . . Zingarelli
5. Scotch Rondo, executed on the piano forte by Mr. Etienne, . . . Cramer
PART II.
1. Extract from the Opera of Helena, Mehul
2. Italian Scene, from the Opera of Tancrede, sung by Mrs. L. . . Rossini
3. Grande Concertante for hautboy, piano and violoncello, executed by Mr. Gilles, senr. Gilles junr. and M. Etienne, ... Widerker.
4. Quatuor, from the Opera of Molinara, sung by Mrs. L. Mr. Gilles, senr. Mr. Etienne, and Mr. M. . . Paisiello
5. Fantaine, composed for violoncello and piano forte, with songs extracted from the Opera of Cendrillon, executed by Mr. Gilles, junr. and Mr. Etienne, ... Gilles, jr
6. Finale. Mch 11 2t

FOR SALE,

A STOUT, young negro wench and child. She is honest and sober, is sold because her services are no longer wanted by the family and may be had very low—Apply at No. 3 Beach-street.

April 9 1m*

Fire, Robbery and Racing

Three public notices from the spring of 1812:

Melancholly!—On Saturday last the new dwelling house of Stephen Wilcox, Esq who lives in the north part of this town, was entirely consumed by FIRE.—In the house was about four hundred and sixty dollars in paper—and such was the rapidity of the flames after the discovery, that the whole was destroyed, together with the wearing apparel, furniture, and provisions.—Thus, in a moment, has an aged man, who is unable to labor, been reduced from a state of affluence, almost to poverty. We think his situation peculiarly calculated to awaken public sympathy in his behalf.

STOP THIEF!
STOLEN, out of a writing desk, in a sleeping room in the Mechanic-hall, on Saturday night, a single cased gold WATCH, maker's name M'Creary, London, with gold chain, two seals and ring; on one of the seals was cut H.V. with a device of a sheaf of wheat. Also, $25 in notes of the city banks, and two Portuguese gold coins of $8 each, 4 of $4 each, and 4 of $2 each. A reward of $120 will be paid on the detection of the thief, so that it may lead to the recovery of the property; or $60 will be paid on the watch and chain being left at John M'Lean's, 35 William-street, and no questions asked.

It is particularly requested, should any of the above articles be offered for sale, the person may be detained, and notice given as above.

Charleston Races.—More expectation has been excited in the sporting world respecting the races at Charleston the present season than for many years. The races it seems commenced on Wednesday, 24th Feb. by four colts starting for 2 miles heats, which was won with ease by Mr. Winn's Timoleon; first heat in 4m. the second in 3m. 49s. On Tuesday the proprietor's cup was run for 3 miles heats, which was won by Mr. Winn's Lady Lightfoot, in 3 heats; 3d heat 3m. 59s. On Wednesday the jockey club purse was run for 4 miles heats, for $1000 (7 horses entered); which was won with ease by Col. Richardson's B.H. Transport; 1st heat in 7m. 54s; the 2d in 7m. 58s. "contrary to the expectation of the knowing ones."

Decade Three

1821- 1830

With the arrival of lawyer-poet William Cullen Bryant in 1826, the *Post* entered a long era under the leadership of one of America's most respected men of letters. Bryant worked at the *Post* for 52 years, and his long career with the paper spanned the Civil War era. He was outspoken against the institution of slavery, which he once described as "a dreadful injustice" that "perverts [and] corrupts every humane and generous sentiment."

The majority of the *Post*'s pages continued to be devoted to advertising in this decade, and a number of ads collected for this chapter include illustrations that were very popular with the merchants who posted them.

Robert Fulton was one of the first to open steamboat service across the rivers of greater New York. (Illustration from Post 100th Anniversary supplement)

Laureate at the Helm

William Cullen Bryant: Lawyer-Poet-Newspaperman

> *❝I do not like politics . . . [but] you know politics and a bellyfull are better than poetry and starvation.❞*
>
> —WILLIAM CULLEN BRYANT

Trained as a lawyer, respected as a newspaper editor and renowned as a poet, William Cullen Bryant is a giant figure in the *Post*'s past.

He joined the paper after leaving his post as co-editor of a literary journal that was failing financially. Just when he thought he'd have to return to the law and leave the literary life behind, he received the offer from the *Post*. Bryant considered himself a poet and man of letters, and the world of journalism in 1826 was a far cry from the lofty intellectual realm to which he was accustomed, but the literary life could not support him and his small family. After accepting the job, he wrote to his wife, Fanny: "The establishment is an extremely lucrative one. It is owned by two individuals, Mr. Coleman and Mr. Burnham. The profits are estimated at about thirty thousand dollars a year, fifteen to each proprietor. This is better than poetry and magazines!"

The reluctant newspaperman began a career that would span 52 years, turning the *Post* into an influential humanitarian paper that took up the causes of free men and free trade in a dark era of the nation's history.

Most of Bryant's long life was taken up with running a daily newspaper, but history remembers him most as a poet. His most famous poems, such as "To a Waterfowl" and "Thanatopsis," reflect the nature-loving man who grew up roaming the Berkshires and discovering deep truth and inspiration in nature.

ABOVE: *William Cullen Bryant. (From Allan Nevins'* The Evening Post: A Century of Journalism*)*

CITY INTELLIGENCE.

Mr. John Warner, a painter by trade, while leaning against a tree in Broadway, looking at the fire in Chamber street, last evening, suddenly dropped down dead.

§ § §

Fire Crackers.—A house in John street, near the Arcade, was discovered to be on fire between 12 and 1 o'clock last night. The fire originated from some crackers, that had been thrown on the house by a parcel of careless boys in the evening.

§ § §

We understand that twenty-nine men, women and children were yesterday taken from one cellar in James street, by Mr. Schureman, Visitor of the Alms House, in a state of extreme wretchedness. The corpse of a child that had been dead since Tuesday last, was also found in the same tenement, and the whole presented a spectacle of filth disgusting beyond expression. Part of the inmates of the dwelling were sent to the Penitentiary and part to the Alms House.

§ § §

The gentlemen dog-holders in the vicinity of No.— State street and the stables in the rear on Pearl street, are hereby notified that the attention of Mr. Watson, the Dog Register, is particularly requested to them, and unless the nuisance is immediately abated, means will be taken by the neighborhood to relieve themselves (by indictment or destruction) from the inconvenience occasioned by the incessant howling and barking through the night of ten or twenty curs, terriers, setters, &c.

§ § §

Caution.—We would caution all persons going out, or coming into the city, in carriages or on horseback, to take the Bowery road, as the upper end of Broadway is made impassable by digging out and regulating to its proper level. On commencing the work, a fence was put up to warn travellers and prevent accidents; but by carelessness of the workmen, or in some other unaccountable way, the fence was left down last evening, and a gentleman on horse back, coming into the city, rode off the perpendicular precipice of seven feet, and was taken into a neighboring house so badly hurt, that he was speechless when our informant left him. The horse broke his hind leg in the fall.

§ § §

Four notorious pickpockets have been seen, for a few days past, hovering about the purlieus of the Post Office in this city, and whenever there is a greater press for letters than usual, mingling with the crowd in order to find an opportunity of exercising their vocation. These gentry, we are informed, have a most forlorn and dismal aspect, on account of the present hard times, from which they suffer as much as those who pursue the more reputable occupations. . . . The moment there is a little crowd formed, one of them comes hastily up and claps his hands on the back of one of the outermost persons, pushing him with all his might, as if his life depended on getting at the Post Office window. Immediately after him comes another, and then a third, all busy in crowding and shoving, while the fourth, with his hands disengaged, hovers around the circle in quest of a well-stored and unguarded pocket.

§ § §

Murder.—A white man by the name of John Roland, was murdered last evening . . . near Rivington street, by James Bowne, a black.—The following circumstances were detailed before the Coroner's Jury this morning: The deceased had retired to bed in the early part of the evening, with Charlotte Cornish, a black woman.— He was intoxicated at the time. About 7 o'clock, Bowne came to the door and requested to come in, saying he wanted a light. He was let in by another black woman, who was in the room, and becoming noisy, was desired by Roland to be peaceable. Bowne then seized a stick about 3 1/2 feet long, and struck Roland on the head with it. Deceased cried murder, and Bowne immediately struck three or four blows more, saying at the time "d——n you, I'll give you something to balloo for." He left the room and after a light was brought, came back again, and was told he had killed Roland. He exclaimed "He's only drunk; he'll come over it soon." The verdict of the jury is "That the deceased came to his death in consequence of blows inflicted on the left side of his head . . . by the blows, which were so heavy that they were distinctly heard in the adjoining house."

§ § §

The house keepers, store keepers and street keepers in Broadway are in a state of almost open insurrection. "Our suffering," say they, "is untolerable. We can neither see, sit, walk nor breathe with any comfort. Which ever way we turn, nothing meets us, but dust—dust—dust.—Dust, we are in very deed. We eat dust, we breathe dust, we feel dust, we absolutely wear dust. From dust we rise in the morning; and, in the evening to dust we return. Is there no remedy for this grievance, no cure in the Marble House, to street inspector there? By all that is sweet and clean and comfortable, we beseech you Mr. B. or Mr. C. or Mr. H., or whoever else may have this matter in charge, send us some relief—send it, we beseech you, send it quickly." CIVIS.

BELOW: *Broadway, 1830. (Post 100th Anniversary supplement)*

The Fat Lady Won't Sing Here

Theater, both dramatic and musical, was wildly popular in New York in the 1800s. Light operetta, such as the *Siege of Belgrade*, which played at the Park Theater in the winter of 1826, was filled with thrilling songs that highlighted the skills of the singers.

The *Post* was smitten with the leading lady of *The Siege of Belgrade*, as expressed in the excerpts of a review from December 16:

> We cannot resist our strong inclination to speak once more of the very interesting and highly gifted female stranger who has lately made her debut on our boards. On Thursday evening, Mrs. Knight made her fifth appearance at the Park Theater, in the opera of the Siege of Belgrade. . . . Her playing was marked, as it always is, with a naivete, life, and graceful action, that left the spectator nothing to wish for.

An evening of pleasant songs in English was much preferred to a night of grand opera, at least for the critics at the *Post*. In an article of August 12, 1826, the *Post* proclaimed that New York—as well as the rest of the nation—was not yet ready for this Old World art form:

New-York Opera.—This dramatic speculation has proved

THEATRE.

THIS Evening, the *Siege of Belgrade*.—Lilla, Mrs. Knight, in which character she will sing several favorite songs. After which the ballet of La Petitte Vendangeuse. To conclude with *Paul Pry*. Tomorrow, for the benefit of Mrs. Barnes, Venice Preserved and Aladdin.

On Saturday, the Stranger, by Mr Barry, his first appearance in America.

a failure as was anticipated. There is no city in the Union yet ripe for this species of entertainment. N. York with the greatest share of wealth is still without that class of persons who in the crowded capitals of Europe frequent places of public entertainment from the mere fashion and expensiveness of the luxury rather than from the wish of refined enjoyment.

Now, New-York has always a large population, either settled or migratory. She is still however, more like Liverpool than London—more like Bordeaux than Paris. The pursuits of her wealthy citizens are in closer connexion with the counting house than the coteries of fashion.

THE NEW-YORK EVENING POST.

MONDAY, JUNE 27, 1825.   NO. 49 WILLIAM-STREET.

NEW YORK, 1825
Population: **202,589**
Mayor: **William Paulding**
Governor of New York: **DeWitt Clinton**
Post Newspaper Price: **$10.00/year**
Staten Island Ferry Fare: **12.5¢**
Theater Ticket, Best Seat: **50¢–$1.00**
Columbia College Tuition: **$80.00/year**
(all dollar figures non-adjusted)

■ **Developed Areas**

An Early Post Style Guide

Bryant insisted on a pure, simple style of writing in the *Post*, refusing to stoop to the level of "barbaric" vocabulary used in other papers. For the benefit of young staffers, he published a list of words to avoid entitled *index expurgatorius*. These condemned words included:

Artiste (for artist)
Bagging (for capturing)
Banquet (for dinner or supper)
Casket (for coffin)
Commence (for begin)
Cortege (for procession)
Devouring element (for fire)
Gents (for gentlemen)

Juvenile (for boy)
Lengthy (for long)
Pants (for pantaloons)
Raid (for attack)
Realized (for obtained)
Repudiate (for reject)
Sensation (for noteworthy event)

Hats, Horses and Highboys

Advertisements from the 1820s

BOOTS! BOOTS! BOOTS!—Z. THAYER & CO. No. 1 Bowery, are daily receiving additions to their former extensive stock of boots and shoes, all of which they are retailing at the lowest cash prices. Reasonable deductions to those who purchase by the quantity. The following are their retailing prices, viz:

500 pair warr'd calf skin boots, city work,				4 50
300 do	do	do	do 2d rate,	3 50
250 do	do	seal skin do	sewed,	3 50
275 do	do	do	do pegged,	2 75
500 do	do	do	do nailed,	2 50
150 do	calf skin & horse skin do, sewed,			2 50
560 do	boys calf skin boots,			2 25 to 3 50
250 do	short cow hide do			3 00
200 do	long	do	do	3 50

Likewise, ladies', misses' and children's boots and shoes; gentlemen's and boys' shoes and laced boots proportionably low.

COFFINS. Shrouds, &c. of all descriptions, may be obtained in the basement story of the New York Spectaculum, 330 Chatham, opposite Roosevelt street, by E. HOUGHTON, who has taken great pains to have the assortment, quality, and prices, such as cannot fail to satisfy every applicant. The public are invited to call & examine the superior workmanship of coffins, and the plan of one so constructed as to prevent a body's being taken for the purpose of dissection. He would also inform the public, that he takes the whole charge of funerals, and furnishes every thing necessary.   o24 tf

CARPETING.—Just rec'd by the latest arrivals an extensive assortment of light English Ingrain and Brussels Carpeting, consisting of new and elegant patterns, selected expressly for this market, together with a general assortment of Floor Cloths, fig'd and plain Floor Baizes, Table and Piano Covers, India Mats and Matting, Hearth Rugs, &c. Also, a general assortment of Venetian and dark Ingrain Carpeting, for sale at 96 Division st.   J. & J. H. SACKETT.

CHARLES POOL, Maker and Importer of Optical, Mathematical, and Philosophical Instruments, No. 9 Wall street, opposite the Church, offers for sale—Spectacles mounted in gold, silver, tortoise shell, and steel, with the finest white or coloured glasses, or Brazil pebbles; Telescopes, simple and compound; Microscopes, Camera Obscuras, Prisms; Magic Lanterns, and other optical instruments. Also, parlour, marine and mountain Barometers, with a large assortment of Thermometers, suitable for all purposes; Hydrometers, Saccharometers, Plate and Cylinder Electrical Machines, Air Pumps, Tape and Chain Measures, Drawing Instruments, Theodolites, Circumferenters, Levels, &c. N. B. Barometers, Thermometers, &c. &c. accurately repaired.   m22 1m*

MRS DODGE respectfully informs her patrons and the ladies in general, that she continues her Writing Academy at No. 49 Canal street, near Broadway.

Mrs. D. teaches the plain running hand, and the various ornamental hands; and engages to enable every pupil, who conforms strictly to her directions, to write a fair and beautiful hand in twenty lessons.

Young ladies who learn of Mrs D acquire a *habit* and *manner* of writing at once easy, graceful and elegant. Ladies of middle life who have heretofore either entirely neglected this important branch of Education, or wanting opportunity to perfect themselves earlier, have delayed until they think they are almost "too old to learn." attain in a few lessons, to that beauty of penmanship which surprises, while it delights themselves, and even the venerable matron is pleased in tracing the first rudiments of the chirographic art, to revive the recollections and associations of the vernal morn of life.

Often in six, and always in ten lessons, pupils who before knew not how to shape a letter, have acquired a fair and legible hand.

Mrs. D. also instructs her pupils, individually, in the art of making a good Pen.

From those ladies who wish to acquire in the shortest possible time, an easy, graceful, and elegant hand writing, Mrs. D. respectfully solicits a call—at the same time she will be happy to exhibit for inspection, specimens of the improvement of her pupils in the art of penmanship, which tend in a high degree to establish the decided superiority of her mode of instruction.

A select class will be taught in the evening.   d13 2w

HAT STORE. No. 53 Chatham, nearly opposite Chambers-st.—The subscriber feeling grateful for the patronage bestowed on him since his commencement in business wishes to inform his former customers, and the public in general, that he still continues to keep on hand, a general assortment of first rate HATS, of the most fashionable kind, of every description, which he offers for sale on the most accommodating terms.

N. B. Gentlemen wishing to purchase by the quantity, would do well to call and examine for themselves.   THOMAS YATES.

Liquid Grecian Rouge

THIS very excellent toilette article is offered to the public, with the utmost confidence of its perfect innocence upon those who use it; and it stands unrivalled for the very beautiful, and, at the same time, perfectly natural color which it imparts. It has for some length of time been before the public, and has always given the greatest satisfaction. For sale by the proprietor's agent,   MISS St. MARTIN,
359 Broadway, and by
MRS. BOWER, 36 Maiden lane.
J. L. SCHIEFFELIN, 334 Broadway.
Every description of Leghorn work executed in a superior manner, by MISS ST. MARTIN, 359 Broadway.   m22

MAHOGANY CHAIRS.—The subscriber keeps constantly on hand, at 174 Chambers street, second door below Washington street, Mahogany Chairs of various patterns, being his own work, and warranted equal to any in the city.

THOMAS L. BROWER.

For Tarrytown, Sing Sing and Peekskill.

The steam boat ARIEL, Captain Requa, will leave the foot of Murray st. every Monday, Wednesday and Friday, at 8 o'clock A. M. for the above places, leaving Peekskill every Tuesday, Thursday and Saturday mornings at 11 o'clock, stopping at the wharves each way. On Sundays will be despatched for Sing Sing and intermediate places at 7 o'clock A. M. and returning the same day— Fare to Sing Sing 50 cents, Peekskill 75.   a1 tf

HORSES FOR SALE

Fourteen first rate Horses, just from the country, viz. three pair of carriage horses, one pair of poney's 5 hands high, six remarkable fine saddle and gig horses—can be seen at Townsend Cock's livery stable, Brooklyn.   17 6t

IMPORTANT TO THE CONSUMPTIVE. A safe and valuable preperation, which has proved successful in practice, and its reputation well established within the last eight months, is now offered to those afflicted, to stop the ravages of that cruel disease, the consumption of the lungs. Its good effects may be learned on trial by those afflicted. Prepared and sold at No. 29 Bowery, corner of Bayard street.
a4 3t   MOSES S. LITTLE.

THE young *gentleman* who last evening at half past ten *purloined* from Downing's Oyster Cellar, in Broad street, a cane in form of a watch club, will be polite enough to send it to the owner, at No. 59 Pearl street.   d5 1t

THIS is to certify that Betsey Gabril my wife has left my house and I forbid all persons harboring or trusting her, for I will not pay any debts of her contracting after this date. December 8. 1826.   FRANCIS GABRIL.
d8 3t†

SELF DEFENCE. WILLIAM FULLER, begs leave to inform his friends and the Gentlemen in general of New York, that he has just returned from England, and has taken the large Room at the Shakspeare Hotel, Nassau street, for the purpose of giving lessons in the above named manly science, whereby Gentlemen after a few lessons are enabled to chastise those who may offer violence, and protect themselves against the attack of the ruffian.

To open on Wednesday the 22d. Terms to be known on application as above.   n 20 6t

TO LET, That convenient two story brick house No. 19 Howard street, being in complete order; a very suitable residence for a genteel family. Enquire on the premises, or of Isaac Lawrence, Esq. at the Branch Bank.   d5

NEW YORK POST

Decade Four
1831-1840

The abolition movement was loud and outspoken in the 1830s, yet heavily opposed in New York. The *Post* was the only paper in the city to speak up for the rights of the abolitionists, fiercely defending their constitutional rights.

Manhattan, which by 1840 reached a population of more than 300,000, was still plagued by fires, crime and other hazards of a growing metropolis. The Great Fire of 1835 was the worst the city had seen, reported the next morning under the headline UNPARALLELED CONFLAGRATION! ENORMOUS DESTRUCTION OF PROPERTY IN THE WARD OF THIS CITY!!!

Another calamity of the decade was the cholera epidemic of 1832, one of the worst in the 19th century.

Wall Street, 1831, in a sepia watercolor by Charles Burton (New York Historical Society)

Dreadful Injustice

Slavery

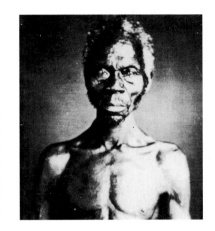

"The *Evening Post* believed slavery a curse," wrote the paper's biographer Allan Nevins in 1922. William Cullen Bryant felt that slavery was the hottest issue of the day when he returned to his job in 1836 after a long visit to Europe. For the next 25 years he ran editorials about the vices of slavery, such as those excerpted here:

> Shall the United States no longer be known as the home of the free and the asylum of the oppressed, but as the hope of the slave and the oppressor of the poor?

> The greatest disgrace inflicted upon labor is inflicted by the institution of slavery. Those who support it—we mean the negro owners or the negro-drivers of the South—openly declare that he who works with his hands is on the level with the slave. They cannot think otherwise, so long as they are educated under the influence of this dreadful injustice. It perverts all the true relations of society, and corrupts every humane and generous sentiment.

> There were 26,533 slaves embarked on board Brazilian vessels, on the African coasts, between the first of July 1825, and the first of July 1826, for the Rio de Janeiro market. Of these poor creatures 1,540 died on the passage; and 24,728 were landed at the Brazilian capital. The traffic in human flesh and blood must be uncommonly active, when nearly 25,000 unfortunate Africans are annually imported to Rio alone.

Poet-editor William Cullen Bryant's anti-slavery view was also evident when he printed his lengthy poem, "The African Chief," in the *Post*. This ballad describes the true story of a man from the Solima nation, a majestic chief who was the brother of the king. The 64-line poem begins with this stanza:

> Chained in the market place he stood,
>   A man of giant frame.
> Amid the gathering multitude
>   That shrunk to hear his name—
> All stern of look and strong of limb,
>   His dark eye on the ground:—
> And silently they gazed on him,
>   As on a lion bound.
> Vainly, but well, that chief had fought,
>   He was a captive now,
> Yet pride, that fortune humbles not,
>   Was written on his brow.
> The scars his dark broad bosom wore,
>   Showed warrior true and brave;
> A prince among his tribe before,
>   He could not be a slave.

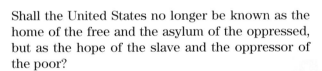

ABOVE: *This photo of Renty of the Congo—a slave in South Carolina—was taken as part of a scientific study in 1850. (Harvard Library)*

EVENING POST.

MONDAY, AUGUST 6.

The appearance which New York presents to one who views it the present time from the midst of the Hudson or from the opposite shore of New Jersey, a spectacle scarce less unusual and solemn than to one who visits what were two months since its crowded and noisy places of business. The number of persons who have left the city is estimated at upwards of one hundred thousand people, including persons of all classes and occupations. So many domestic fires have been put out, and the furnaces of so many manufactories have been extinguished, that the dense cloud of smoke which always lay over the city, inclining in the direction of the wind, is now so thin as often to be scarcely discernible, and the buildings of the great metropolis appear with unusual clearness and distinctness. On a fair afternoon, the corners of the houses, their eaves and roofs appear as sharply defined as if the spectator stood close by their side, and from the walks at Hoboken you may count the dormer windows in any given block of buildings. The various colours of the edifices appear also with an astonishing vividness, while the usual murmur from the streets is scarcely heard.

38

Deserted City

The Cholera Epidemic of 1832

In the summer of 1832, nearly 100,000 residents of New York City—half the population of Manhattan—fled to the country to escape the devastating cholera epidemic that had broken out in June. By the end of the year, 3,513 people died from the disease. This was one of the most severe cholera epidemics to hit the city in the 19th century, second only to the epidemic of 1849 that would cause the death of more than 5,000. The *Post* regularly published the Board of Health's reports on the status of the disease, as shown here (from August 6). The accompanying article describes the strange, desolate look of the abandoned city in which "the usual murmur from the streets is scarcely heard."

In June of 1832, the following message by a writer identified as "Aqua" was inserted into the foreign reports page:

> In the midst of the exciting alarm of the approaching Cholera, a little advice to our young men would perhaps not be without its effect. Every description of medicine has received its due need of praise; but Sir, who has mentioned aquatic sports? Manly and physical as it is, the bracing sea breeze, the early rising incident from the same, are all calculated to preserve that gentle perspiration of body and elasticity of mind so necessary in the midst of a prevailing epidemic. These are in my opinion the true preventives, and which every young man should take advantage of.   AQUA.

Two ads for cholera cures from August 1832. Reports of cures as detailed in these ads were in error: the "uneasiness in the stomach" that could be cured by the remedy was caused by the flu or some other stomach upset, not cholera. Doctors were unable to differentiate between stomach problems and the initial stages of cholera as the symptoms were very similar.

The cause of cholera was not known in 1832, and Pasteur's discoveries would not confirm the germ theory of disease until later in the century. In spite of this lack of scientific knowledge, many felt that the spread of the illness was connected to unsanitary living conditions (another popular theory held that cholera was a punishment from God on the sinful).

The city acted quickly with the outbreak, setting up several hospitals, evacuating the worst slums and housing the residents in other buildings, and cleaning the streets of waste and filth that had built up for decades. Animal carcasses, garbage and other debris was shoveled up and the streets were swept, cleaned and covered in tons of lime.

Doctors were under the false assumption that they could cure the disease if it was caught in its early stages. The *Post* carried ads for a variety of such treatments, but the reports of cures stated in the ads were in error. The pills and salves that "cured" the stomach cramps of the initial stages of the disease had no effect on cholera—the ailment from which these "fortunate" patients suffered was not cholera in its initial stage, but a simple stomach upset. Doctors could not tell the difference between the two.

THIS DAY.
REPORT OF THE BOARD OF HEALTH.
Monday, Aug. 6—10 o'clock, A. M.

1	139 Reed	
1	35 Columbia	
1	Pike, cor Cherry	dead
1	110 Madison	
1	398 Cherry	dead
1	109 Clinton	
1	117 do	
1	100 do	
1	421 Grand *	dead
2	37 Pitt	
1	25 Willet	
1	150½ Broome*	dead
1	24 do	
1	67 Goerick	
1	65 do	
1	49 Lewis	
1	20 Chrystie	
1	129 Delancy	
1	142 Suffolk (rear)	
1	119 Willet	
1	121 do	
1	41 Christopher	dead
1		dead
1	22 Oak	dead
1	240 Cherry	dead
1	36 Essex	

MOB!

The Post Defends Freedom of Speech

On a hot night in July 1834, a group of white New Yorkers launched an all-out attack on the blacks living in the neighborhood known as Five Points. Two churches were demolished, a school was nearly ripped down, twenty houses were wrecked and looted, and many of those blacks who didn't flee northward into the open fields were severely beaten.

The rioters, fed up with the abolitionists, had taken their fury out upon the blacks whose cause was in hot debate. Talk of freeing slaves was hurting commerce in the city, as businesses were losing the patronage of Southern merchants. The *Post* boldly stood up against the mob, proclaiming that freedom of speech was the right of every citizen, including the wildly unpopular abolitionists. After the Five Points riot, the *Post* wrote:

Let [the rioters] be fired upon, if they dare collect

together again to prosecute their infamous designs. Let those who make the first movement toward sedition be shot down like dogs—and thus teach to their infatuated followers a lesson which no milder course seems sufficient. . . . We would recommend that the whole military force of the city be called out . . . and that the troops be directed to fire upon the first disorderly assemblage.

A journal in Boston hailed the *Post*'s courage in making a stand, saying: "The *Evening Post* was the only daily paper in that city which condemned the riots with manly denunciation."

The subject blew up again the following summer when the United States Post Office refused to deliver some abolitionist mail. Postmaster General Amos Kendall upheld the decision of a postmaster in Charleston, South Carolina, to reject abolitionist letters and documents. The Charleston postmaster argued that the material was insurrectionary and dangerous, and the postal boss agreed. In an outraged editorial, the *Post* lashed out against this blatant violation of free speech:

Neither the general postoffice, nor the general government itself, possesses any power to prohibit the

The Five Points section of Manhattan, scene of one of the city's most violent riots in 1834. (New York Historical Society)

"If the government once begins to discriminate as to . . . what is safe and what unsafe in tendency, farewell, a long farewell, to our freedom."

—EDITORIAL, AUGUST 1835

transportation by mail of abolition tracts. On the contrary, it is the bounden duty of the government to protect the abolitionists in their constitutional right of free discussion. . . . If the government once begins to discriminate as to . . . what is safe and what unsafe in tendency, farewell, a long farewell, to our freedom.

The two pieces above and many other passionate editorials of the decade were written by assistant editor William Leggett, a bold and unrestrained writer who has gone down in history as one of the most potent and controversial editors in American journalism. Always ready to defend civil rights, he supported unpopular causes such as the first trade unions. In an editorial printed in 1834, he rages at the wealthy for stomping on the rights of the poor and defends the right of workers to organize:

The tyrant is changed from the steel-clad feudal baron . . . at the head of thousands of ruffian followers, to a mighty civil gentleman. . . . He is the sly, selfish, grasping and insatiable tyrant, the people are now to guard against. A CONCENTRATED MONEY POWER; a usurper in the disguise of a benefactor [who] pretends to be manacled only so that he may the more safely pick our pockets, and lord it over our rights.

Where is the danger of a combination of the labouring classes . . . in defence of their menaced rights? Have they not the right to act in concert, when their opponents act in concert?

The Power of (Not) Advertising

Assistant editor William Leggett took great liberties running the *Post* while Editor in Chief Bryant was on an extended vacation in Europe in the 1830s. In addition to his fierce editorials against the banking industry and the upper class who tried to suppress the unions (causes Bryant also took up with a passion), he alienated many important customers by making a major change in the look of the paper.

Leggett thought that the stock-cut illustrations used in the ads "cluttered up" the page, and stopped printing them in 1834. Shipping companies and advertisers of all kinds were outraged and swiftly took their business elsewhere. This caused a steep drop in revenue, and the illustrations were added once again after Leggett's retirement.

Assistant Editor William Leggett (from Post 100th Anniversary supplement)

Four samples of stock-cut illustrations that were deleted for a time to make the front page look less cluttered.

41

The Great Fire of 1835

On the bitterly cold night of December 16, the temperature a mere three degrees above zero, fire broke out in a store and quickly spread through the entire section of Wall, South and Broad Streets. The fire destroyed 674 buildings, including the offices of three newspapers: the *Daily*, *Gazette* and *American*. Reporting on the fire the next morning, the *Post* gave a dramatic summary of events (this page also prominently displays, at top, the paper's endorsement of Van Buren in the upcoming 1836 election):

THE EVENING POST.

THURSDAY, DECEMBER 17.

For President.
MARTIN VAN BUREN.
For Vice President.
RICHARD M. JOHNSON.

UNPARALLELLED CONFLAGRATION!
ENORMOUS DESTRUCTION OF PROPERTY IN
THE FIRST WARD OF THIS CITY ! ! !

The night of the sixteenth of December, 1835, will long be memorable in the history of this city for the occurrence of one of the most destructive fires that ever desolated a great metropolis. The scene of devastation presented this morning beggars description.

We have taken from the only two papers published this morning, the imperfect accounts they present. How far, how very far, short they fall of the dreadful reality, those, and they are thousands, who have already visited the site of destruction can bear testimony.

The firemen exerted themselves to the utmost. But what could be expected of them on such a merciless night as last night, with the thermometer but three degrees above zero, and the water freezing into a solid mass the instant it fell? We have heard of some persons who were out all that awful night, and had their clothes frozen so stiff upon them, that they were obliged to cut them from their bodies.

The marines from Brooklyn are on duty guarding the masses of property exposed in the streets, with muskets and fixed bayonets.

It is the opinion of many persons that the fire insurance companies are all, or nearly all, inevitably bankrupt.

A gentleman told us that he heard the first alarm and repaired to Exchange street, where he found the flames proceeding from the third story window of the store over Messrs. Bailey, Keeler & Remsen. After a short time, it burst forth from the building in a vast volume, and making a gigantick stride, communicated at once with the stores of Arthur Tappan and others, on the opposite side of Hanover square.

The Post Office is removed, temporarily, to the rear

"The Great Fire of 1835 as Seen from Williamsburgh, Long Island" by Nicollino Calyo. (New York Historical Society)

Voice of Reason: Post Predicts the Crash of 1837

In response to claims in 1835 that the country had no debt, the *Post* ran a biting editorial to shed light on the truth. Contrary to being solvent, the nation was mired in debt and heading toward disaster, warned the *Post*, and the people "are plunging deeper and deeper into the bottomless pit of unredeemed and irredeemable obligations. . . . Who will pay the piper for all this political and speculative dancing?" the paper asked.

As warned, wild speculations in real estate, overextension of loans by banks and other events led to a severe financial collapse two years later. The panic of 1837—an avalanche of failed banks and businesses—affected people in every walk of life. In April alone, 250 businesses shut down in New York, and within two months the city's financial losses reached nearly $100 million.

Exterior and interior of the New York Stock Exchange in the early 1800s. (Illustrations from Post 100th Anniversary supplement)

Post's Defense of Amistad Slave Revolt

The big story in the Eastern cities in the autumn of 1839 concerned the ship *Amistad*, taken over by the black slaves on board. The mutineers were imprisoned when they landed in Connecticut, and the story stirred up the abolitionists in New York. From the outset, the *Post* published articles about the injustice of seizing the men and called for their release.

Editor Bryant called upon his friend Theodore Sedgwick, Jr., to research the legal aspects of the case and printed his findings. One of Sedgwick's articles (September 17, 1839), excerpted here, expressed the *Post*'s support of the slaves' cause:

The Amistad Negroes.—This day is appointed for the trial of these men before the United States Circuit Court at Hartford—Judge Thompson, the presiding Judge.

We await with deepest interest the issue of the judicial proceedings in the case which commences to-day. If it is possible to extend over these men the protection of the shadow of the free American Eagle, let them of course have the benefit of the most liberal construction of every point arising in the case. They have every human sympathy on their side. . . .

Nor can we doubt that, independently of the force of the moral sense of the civilized world, England will see well in the present case to the execution of the treaty, which must result in the restoration of these poor fellows to the homes from which they have been so atrociously stolen.

Two days later, the *Post* reported the fate of one of the captives:

Death of Another African.—Another of the captured Africans named Bulwa (or Woolah) died on Saturday night. This is the third who has died in this city, and the thirteenth since their leaving Havana. One more remains sick in this city . . . several are still affected with the white flux, the disease which has proved fatal to so many of them.

In February 1841 the Supreme Court ruled that the Africans were free men, and later that year they sailed home to Sierra Leone.

ABOVE: *A woodcut illustration of the* Amistad *slave revolt. (New York Historical Society)*

NEW YORK POST

Decade Five
1841-1850

New York's great tide of immigration began to swell in this decade, with Brooklyn alone increasing in population by almost 100,000. The city didn't have a solid infrastructure to provide some of the basic necessities for this population explosion, however, such as street upkeep or a good police force. With the help of *Post* editorials and articles, the citizens had a stronger voice in airing their complaints and demands, and some important changes were made as a result. The idea of providing the police department with uniforms, a practice that had been used with great success in London, was first brought up in the *Post*. Another significant event launched in an editorial was the construction of Central Park, first suggested by Editor in Chief William Cullen Bryant.

The growing city sprawls along both sides of Broadway, 1848. (Illustration from Post 100th Anniversary supplement)

Post Editor Fathers Central Park

"If the public authorities, who expend so much of our money in laying out the city, would do what is in their power, they might give our vast population an extensive pleasure ground of shade and recreation in these sultry afternoons, which we might reach without going out of town." —Editorial, 1844

THE EVENING POST.
WEDNESDAY EVENING, JULY 3, 1844

A NEW PUBLIC PARK

The heats of summer are upon us, and while some are leaving the town for shady retreats in the country, others refresh themselves with short excursions to Hoboken and New Brighton, or other places among the beautiful environs of our city. If the public authorities, who expend so much of our money in laying out the city, would do what is in their power, they might give our vast population an extensive pleasure ground for shade and recreation in these sultry afternoons, which we might reach without going out of town.

In an editorial dated July 3, 1844, William Cullen Bryant proposed "an extensive pleasure ground for shade and recreation" in the city. He suggested cutting paths through the woods that covered the land between 68th and 77th Streets. For the next nine years, businessmen, landowners and politicians discussed the idea, and in 1853 the state legislature authorized the city to purchase more than 700 acres of land for the park.

Building the park became one of the city's greatest public works projects of the 19th century. Approximately 20,000 people were put to work, from stonecutters and engineers to laborers and gardeners. Central Park opened in the winter of 1859, offering its ice rinks, carriage lanes and walking paths to an appreciative city—and fulfilling Bryant's long-awaited dream of a natural oasis in the heart of the city.

Following is Bryant's complete editorial from 1844:

A New Public Park

The heats of summer are upon us, and while some are leaving the town for shady retreats in the country, others refresh themselves with short excursions to Hoboken or New Brighton, or other places among the beautiful environs of our city. If the public authorities, who expend so much of our money in laying out the city, would do what is in their power, they might give our vast population an extensive pleasure ground of shade and recreation in these sultry afternoons, which we might reach without going out of town.

On the road to Harlem, between Sixty-eighth street on the south, and Seventy-seventh street on the north, and extending from the Third Avenue to the East River, is a tract of beautiful woodland, comprising sixty or seventy acres, thickly covered with old trees, intermingled with a variety of shrubs. The surface is varied in a very striking and picturesque manner, with craggy eminences and hollows, and a little stream runs through the midst.

The swift tides of the East River sweep its rocky shores, and the fresh breeze of the bay comes in, on every warm summer afternoon, over the restless waters. The trees are of almost every species that grows in our woods:—the different varieties of oak, the birch, the linden, the mulberry, the tulip tree, and others: the azalea, the Kalmia, and other flowering shrubs are in bloom here at their season, and the ground in spring is gay with flowers.

There never was a finer situation for a public garden of a great city. Nothing is wanted but to cut winding paths through it, leaving the woods as they now are, and introducing here and there a jet from the Croton aqueduct, the streams from which would make their own waterfalls over the rocks, and keep the brook running through the place always fresh and full. In the English Garden at Munich, a pleasure ground of immense extent, laid out by our countryman Count Rumford, into which half the population pours itself on summer evenings, the designer of the grounds was obliged to content himself with artificial rocks, brought from a distance and cemented together, and eminences painfully heaped up from the sand of the plain. In the tract of which we speak, nature has done almost everything to our lands, excepting the construction of paths.

As we are now going on, we are making a belt of muddy docks all round the island. We should be glad to see one small part of the shore without them, one place at least where the tides may be allowed to flow pure, and the ancient brim of rocks which borders the waters left in its original picturesqueness and beauty. Commerce is devouring inch by inch the coast of the island, and if we would rescue any part of it for health and recreation it must be done now.

All large cities have their extensive public grounds and gardens, Madrid and Mexico their Alamedas, London its Regent's Park, Paris its Champs-Élysées, and Vienna its Prater. There are none of them, we believe, which have the same natural advantages of the picturesque and beautiful which belong to this spot. It would be of easy access to the citizens, and the public carriages which now rattle in almost every street in this city, would take them to its gates. The only objection which we can see to the place would be the difficulty of persuading the owners of the soil to part with it.

If any of our brethren of the public press should see fit to support this project, we are ready to resign in their favor any claim to the credit of originally suggesting it.

A sketch of projected plans for Central Park by Roswell Graves, Jr. (New York Historical Society)

CITY INTELLIGENCE.

About 1 o'clock on Saturday the horse attached to a baker's cart, which was left standing untied in front of No. 5 Centre Market place, started off at a rapid speed down Orange street, and running on the side walk knocked down two children, one of which, the child of Mr. Donald, of No. 155 Orange street, being run over, is so seriously injured that its recovery is doubtful.

§ § §

Fatal Accident.—Two Men Drowned.—Last evening, soon after dusk, three men, who were all grossly intoxicated, fell into the East river from off pier No. 10. An alarm was given, and one of them was saved, but the other two were drowned. Their bodies were this morning recovered . . . they are said to have been laborers employed on the wharf assisting to discharge a vessel's cargo, and that the drowning was purely accidental.

§ § §

Drowned.—Two young men on Sunday morning went into the East river in a skiff for the purpose of fishing. When but a little way from the shore the boat upset and both were drowned. Both their bodies were recovered.

§ § §

Yesterday, during the progress of the ceremonies at the Mass Temperance meeting at the foot of Forty-ninth street, the stage erected for the speakers gave way, and a man named William Dobbs was so crushed by the weight of it, that it is thought he is dangerously injured.

§ § §

Quite a crowd of spectators congregated together yesterday afternoon, on the corner of Maiden Lane and Broadway, to see a lady cowhide a gentleman. It appears that a Mrs. Rhode, who occupies the cane and whip store on the corner, had a glass show case standing outside her door, and this gentleman, who keeps the trunk shop in the basement, being annoyed at this case, either on purpose or by accident, broke the glass in the case. This enraged the lady, and she seized a rawhide, and laid it on the shoulders of the trunk maker in right good earnest, to the great merriment of all the bystanders. The trunk maker finding himself in rather a peculiar situation, beat a retreat into his basement to avoid the lash, and the laugh of the spectators.

§ § §

Missing.—Yesterday morning a young girl named Minerva Farren, 20 years old, left the residence of Mrs. Hunt, No. 727 Greenwich street, and has not since been heard of. She is of a dark complexion, and about five feet high; and had on when she left a straw colored silk hat, a light colored worsted shawl, and a striped dress. She is a tailoress by trade, and it is thought that her mind is deranged.

§ § §

At half-past one o'clock this morning, the store of Van Kleek & Storms, No. 172 West street, was found open, with the key in the door. Policeman McLaughlin went inside to see that all was safe, when he found the porter lying behind the door in a state of intoxication.

§ § §

An elderly woman, in a state of intoxication, was nearly run over by an omnibus last evening, near the Carlton House. She was knocked down by the horses, but was rescued from her dangerous situation by a policeman.

§ § §

Fire.—At 2 o'clock this morning, a fire broke out in a stable in the rear of No. 554 Broome street, but was extinguished before much damage was done. It is clear, from the number of stables that have been fired of late, that the city is infested with a gang of incendiaries who seek in this way to plunder the citizens. Every one should be on the look out.

§ § §

An attempt was made on Sunday afternoon to rob the grocery store of David Gould, No. 38 Lewis street, but the burglars becoming frightened, ran away without securing their booty. Mr. Gould is a poor man, but very industrious and it is to be hoped that the rascals will be caught, should they make another attempt.

§ § §

A Deserter.—A man named Peter Lyon, a sailor belonging to the United States Service, ran away from the Navy Yard a few days since, and went to live with his wife Ann, but having too great love for liquor, he got drunk, and gave his wife a severe beating, for which she caused him to be arrested, and desired to have him sent back to the Navy Yard. He was accordingly detained.

§ § §

FIRE.—The alarm in the 5th district, last evening, proceeded from house 78 Reade street, near Church. The fire was in the 3d story, caused by the bursting of a hanging spirit lamp, in use by a German tailor, who rising from his shop board, knocked it down.

§ § §

The Tribune says that a poor woman with two children made her way into the Governor's Room yesterday, and throwing herself on her knees before the Governor, began pouring out so vociferous a prayer for the pardon of her husband from the Penitentiary, that she was taken away by force. She had a couple of letters to the Governor which he took and put in his pocket.

§ § §

Indians.—The attractions at Stewart's new store was partially eclipsed this morning, by the greater novelty at Howard's Hotel, in Broadway, where there are no less than twenty three Indians, including squaws and one little papoose. These Indians arrived here yesterday on their way from Iowa to Washington city, under the direction of General Fletcher, whither they proceed tomorrow morning by direction of the President, that he may have a talk with them in regard to their lands in Iowa. They belong to the Winnebago tribe. Their faces are painted fantastically and many of them look as though they had come in contact with a charcoal dealer, who as a token of love had left the print of his four fingers on either cheek.

AMERICAN MUSEUM AND GARDENS, corner of Broadway and Ann street— Opposite St. Paul's Church— P. T. BARNUM, manager.—
WONDER OF CREATION.
INCREASED EXCITEMENT!
☞ In consequence of the immense crowds of Ladies and Gentlemen which have visited the Museum during the last week, and being aware that thousands of persons have been unable to see the Mermaid, who are desirous of doing so, the Manager has, at an immense expense, made arrangements with the proprietor to exhibit at the Museum, for one week more, the greatest curiosity in the world—the REAL MERMAID!
No extra charge for admittance to the Museum.
In order to accommodate the immense number of visitors which daily attend here, there will, this week, be a splendid
DAY PERFORMANCE EVERY AFTERNOON.
commencing at 4 o'clock—the performance in the day being precisely the same as that in the evening.
Mr HARRINGTON, the celebrated Magician and Ventriloquist from Boston, is engaged. Also the MYSTERIOUS GIPSY GIRL can be consulted privately during the day MISS TAYLOR, the popular vocalist from the Park Theatre—LA PETITE CELESTE, ALBINO LADY, BALLOON ASCENSIONS, FANCY GLASS BLOWING, and 500,000 Curiosities.
Admittance to the whole, Museum, Garden and Entertainments, 25 cents; Children half price.

P.T. Barnum's museum of "500,000 curiosities" on Broadway presents a "REAL MERMAID!" in September 1842.

The first uniforms designed for New York City's police. (New York Police Department Museum: on exhibit)

Demand for a Police Force— with Uniforms

By 1844, New York City's population had swelled to 500,000. Its ragtag community protection force of constables and night watchmen only numbered 1,132 men—far too few to handle the growing problems of violence, drunkenness and chaos of the all-but-lawless metropolis. The *Post* cried out for a better police force and helped raised public awareness about the importance of creating a better police system to bring law and order to the streets.

In 1843, an editorial stated:

We maintain a body of watchmen, but they are of no earthly use, except here and there to put an end to a street brawl, and sometimes to pick up a drunken man and take him to the watch house. In some cases, they have been suspected of being in a league with the robbers. At present, we hear of a new case of housebreaking about as often as every other day.

Of course there will be no end to this evil, until there

A volunteer fire brigade battles a roaring city blaze in the mid-1800s. (Illustration from Post 100th Anniversary supplement)

"Our city swarms with daring and ingenious rogues."

—EDITORIAL, 1843

is a reform of the police regulations—until a police of better organization and more efficiency shall be introduced. Our city swarms with daring and ingenious rogues, many of whom have been driven from the Old World, and who find no difficulty in exercising their vocation here with perfect impunity.

The following year, another editorial complained that "our city, with its great population and vast extent, can hardly be said to have a police." The paper also suggested outfitting the police in uniforms, explaining that a uniformed policeman could be easily identified by those in trouble, exude more authority and be less inclined to loitering on duty. With the help of the *Post*'s relentless call for reform, a "Day and Night Police" force was established in 1845. According to the new handbook, each officer was required to "wear the emblem of office on the left breast." This first step in creating an identifiable look for the force was followed up by uniforms in 1850.

Aqueduct Opens

Ushered in during a sensational Fourth of July celebration, the Croton Aqueduct began providing the city with fresh water in 1842. The system, constructed of iron pipes and brick masonry, spanned 41 miles from the Croton Dam in upstate New York to a distributing reservoir on 42nd Street and Fifth Avenue, where the New York Public Library now stands.

The *Post* reported on the festivities the following day:

The National Jubilee was celebrated yesterday with that hilarity which should ever characterize its observance.

An immense concourse assembled to witness the introduction of the Croton water into the reservoir at Forty-second street, which was successfully admitted at sunrise, and continued to flow in during the day, amid the roar of artillery and the cheers of the multitude.

There were several splendid civic processions, among which several mechanic societies, and the Hibernian Benevolent Association, made a fine display.

In 1847, a park was built adjacent to the aqueduct and renamed Bryant Park in 1884 in honor of *Post* editor William Cullen Bryant.

The lunch room in the A.T. Stewart store, which opened in 1846. (New York Historical Society)

Bargains for Millionaires

Large department stores appeared in the city in the mid-1800s, creating a new institution that would come to be one of the most identifying marks of big American cities. The first big store was A.T. Stewart, opened on September 21, 1846, on Broadway between Reade and Chambers Streets. Later dubbed the "Marble Palace," this lavish store was the first commercial building designed with a marble facade. A crushing throng of thousands arrived on opening day to see the magnificent domed atrium, gleaming mahogany cabinets and ornate fixtures. According to a *Post* article published on the following day, millionaires from uptown couldn't resist making a trip to take advantage of the low, set prices:

Stewart's Store.—This store, according to previous announcement, was opened yesterday, for the sale of goods as well as to allow persons who desired to examine the building. The crowd of people that visited there could hardly be numbered, and yet an attempt was made to do so, which resulted in the conviction that the average number for each hour was about one thousand. It was found necessary to station policemen at the main entrance for the purpose of preventing the crowd from stockading the door, as well as to protect the visitors from the unwelcome contact with pickpockets. It is said that Mssrs. Stewart & Co. sold an immense quantity of goods. It looked quite strange to see the beautiful carriages of the millionaires stopping on the shilling side of Broadway to purchase dry goods.

1851–1900

Decade Six

1851-1860

ABOVE: *Abraham Lincoln made his first East Coast appearance in New York City in 1860. (National Archives and Records Administration)* PREVIOUS PAGE: *Civil War battlefield. (National Archives and Records Administration)*

Between the launching of the *Post* in 1801 and the year 1851, hundreds of daily papers had come and gone in New York. The most revolutionary change in that span of time occurred in the 1830s with the launch of papers that carried human-interest stories geared at a mass audience— at a price of one cent. Among these papers, known as the penny press, the best known were the *Sun* (1833) and the *New York Herald* (1835). Papers throughout the country adopted the mass-appeal tactic to some degree, including the *Post* with its "City Intelligence" pieces about crime, accidents, deaths and other true-life dramas. The style of these pieces, however, never came close to the sensationalism of the penny presses, on orders of the editor in chief.

Editor William Cullen Bryant introduced New York to Republican nominee hopeful Abraham Lincoln in February 1860 when he was chosen to be the emcee at Lincoln's first address at Cooper Union. The two men admired each other, and when Lincoln became president rumors spread that he would appoint Bryant to a government post. The newspaperman had no interest in leaving the *Post*, however, and he denied that any offers had been made.

NY Welcomes Lincoln

❝[Lincoln is] a living bulwark against the advance of slavery.❞

—Editor in Chief William Cullen Bryant

On a snowy February night in 1860, a crowd gathered at the newly opened Cooper Union in New York City to hear an address by one of the candidates for the Republican presidential nomination. Abraham Lincoln made his first address to an East Coast audience that evening in the large, 2,000-seat auditorium. The moderator of the event, *Post* Editor in Chief William Cullen Bryant said he felt privileged to present such "a living bulwark against the advance of slavery" to the audience.

Lincoln's address was a great success, drawing frequent bursts of applause and ending with a rousing standing ovation. The Midwesterner completely won over the crowd, and his speech convinced Bryant to endorse him as the Republican candidate of choice. Lincoln was impressed with Bryant, too; after returning home he wrote, "It is worth a visit from Springfield, Illinois, to New York to make the acquaintance of such a man as William Cullen Bryant."

The *Post* printed Lincoln's speech in full the day after the address, but it would be one of only two New York papers to champion Lincoln and rejoice in his nomination that spring. The paper's anti-slavery position had never been popular with the businesses who provided much of the paper's advertising revenue, and the editor's support of Lincoln did nothing to help the situation. "Our position upon the anti-slavery question was by no means a popular one with the merchants upon whom the New York papers depended largely for their support," recalled Managing Editor Parke Godwin. "Most of our importers were closely connected with the South, and, of course, our position brought us into disfavor with all their Southern customers."

After Lincoln won the election, Bryant wrote to him urging that he appoint Salmon P. Chase as secretary of state. Chase was an anti-slavery activist and lawyer well known for his courtroom defense of runaway slaves and the whites who helped them. Lincoln considered Bryant's suggestion seriously and appointed Chase to his cabinet, but as secretary of the Treasury rather than secretary of state. On his way to Washington to take office, Lincoln stopped in New York and spent a few hours with Bryant to discuss the issues of the day.

With the start of the war, the New York business community gradually returned its patronage to the *Post*, and the paper thrived. Even those critical of Lincoln kept their politics to themselves and chose the *Post* for their ads and notices. "It was only when the tide turned," wrote Godwin, "that we rose, almost at a bound, into financial favor. After the first year of the war, all the bankers and speculators who had bonds to sell took our columns at any price we chose to ask." They put their ads in the *Post* because the paper used a high-quality layout with expensive type that advertisers loved. "The *Evening Post* became," wrote Godwin, "the organ for the most exclusive and expensive advertising, that which appeals chiefly to well-to-do people and investors."

Above: Abraham Lincoln making his first address in New York in February 1860. The bearded man seated behind him is Post *Editor in Chief William Cullen Bryant, who introduced the speaker that night. (Illustration from Post 100th Anniversary supplement)*

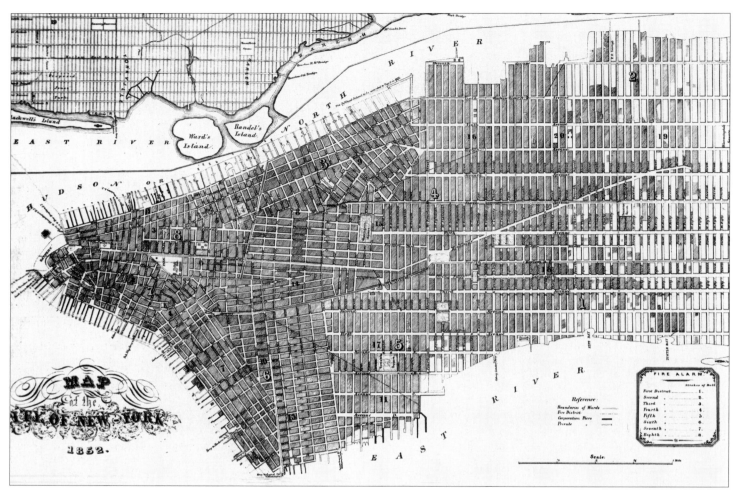

Slavery Outrage

Three years before Lincoln's speech at Cooper Union, the *Post* railed against one of the major events in the nation's long debate over slavery. The Supreme Court's Dred Scott decision of 1857, which ruled that all people of African ancestry, whether slave or free, could never become citizens of the United States. This prevented blacks—including Dred Scott, whose case led to the ruling—from suing for freedom in the courts. The decision also stated that the federal government did not have the power to prohibit slavery in its territories. In response, the *Post* wrote:

> Hereafter, if this decision shall stand for law, slavery . . . is a Federal institution . . . the shame of all the States . . . the chain and the scourge—wherever our flag floats, it is the flag of slavery. If so, that flag should have the light of the stars and the streaks of running red erased from it; it should be dyed black, and its device should be the whip and the fetter.
>
> Are we to . . . consent that hereafter it shall be the slaveholders' instead of the freemen's Constitution? Never! Never!

" Are we to . . . consent that hereafter it shall be the slaveholders' instead of the freemen's Constitution? Never! Never! "

—EDITORIAL, 1857

New York Newspapers in 1851

Nineteen new daily papers were founded in the city between 1851 and 1860—including *The New York Times* (1851). Although the *Post*'s circulation was 4,664 in 1858, the paper was a success in both financial and journalistic terms. It prospered with expensive advertising rates and was considered the best-written evening newspaper of the time under the leadership of Editor in Chief William Cullen Bryant.

ABOVE: *Map of New York City, 1852. (New York Historical Society)*

CITY INTELLIGENCE.

ATTEMPT TO COMMIT SUICIDE.—A woman, named Ellen Byrnes, last evening jumped from one of the Catherine ferry boats into the East river, but she was rescued from drowning and taken to the 7th district police station-house.

§ § §

CHILD KILLED BY THE FALLING OF A CHIMNEY.—A chimney in 85th street fell on Saturday afternoon, burying two children. One was immediately taken out of the rubbish; the other, named Louis Eugene Sabbin, was instantly killed. An inquest was held yesterday, and the following verdict rendered: "That Moses Larkin is guilty of gross neglect in leaving said chimney standing unsupported and without being properly secured."

§ § §

BRUTALITY ON BOARD AN EMIGRANT SHIP.—Yesterday Coroner Hilton held an inquest on the body of Frederika Klinart, a child who died from eating improper food, given her on board the emigrant ship George Canning. It appeared in evidence that the deceased and her friends on board the ship, which is commanded by Captain Jacobs, were not treated according to agreement, and that no physician was employed.

Christina Klinart being sworn, said—I am mother of the deceased child . . . there were eighteen deaths on board the ship on her voyage; sixteen of those were among children; I complained to the captain that my child was sick . . . he, however, did not give my child any medicine. The cook made the coffee from the sea water . . . the water that was given us was bad.

§ § §

A DARING BURGLAR.—A man named Chas. Hawkins was arrested on Sunday morning, shortly before 12 o'clock. It appears that, in company with a confederate, he entered the house of Mr. James O'Beirne, who, not wishing to be disturbed, paid no attention to a knocking which he heard at his room door, but hearing a similar knocking at the opposite side of the hall, he became curious to know who the intruder was, and looking through the key-hole, saw two men force open the door with a crowbar. He then threw open his window and cried out, "Robbers, robbers." The villains immediately fled into the street. One, Hawkins, while running, was knocked down and secured by Officer Hill, of the 3d ward.

§ § §

UNRULY STAGE-DRIVER.—Alonzo Swan, driver of a stage belonging to Murphy and Smith's line, had a dispute yesterday with one of his passengers about change, and drawing his strap declared that no one should leave until his demands were satisfied. Another of the passengers offering his fare and being refused egress, cut the strap, when the whole party went out. A policeman standing by took the driver and his team to the City Hall.

§ § §

DROWNED WHILE BATHING.—A man named George Bryan was drowned last evening at the foot of 16th street. His body was soon after recovered.

§ § §

THE MYSTERIOUS BOAT CLAIMED.—Patrick McLaughlin and Owen Barry, residents of Nos. 84 and 187 Cherry street, yesterday appeared at the office and claimed the small boat that was found on Wednesday morning at the foot of 86th street, East river. They stated that the boat had been stolen from Peck slip. The impression still prevails among the police that a female was murdered on the East river during the previous night.

§ § §

TRIAL OF IRA B. EDDY.
By Telegraph. Times Office, Hartford. A special session of the County Court was convened this morning by Judge Phelps, on a writ of habeas corpus, for the purpose of commencing the trial of Ira B. Eddy, the well-known banker of Chicago, who was reported to have become spiritually insane.

Two witnesses . . . gave testimony to the effect that Mr. Eddy had formerly been regarded as a peaceable man, but that he had recently become a believer in the "spirit rappings."

Mr. Eddy himself certified pretty much to the same effect.

So far as appearances indicate, Mr. E. appears to be perfectly rational.

§ § §

ASSAULT WITH INTENT TO KILL.—Frederick White and Castor Dannis were arrested this morning . . . for attempting to kill Henry Bauge, by stabbing him in the back.

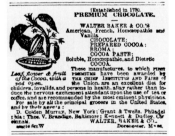

The Nation's First World's Fair

Manhattan's Bryant Park now stands on the site of the 1853–1854 "Exhibition of the Industry of All Nations," a world's fair housed in a spectacular iron-and-glass building called the Crystal Palace.

The Palace, containing approximately four acres of exhibit space, was topped with a dome described in the *Post* as "the largest as well as almost the only dome hitherto erected in the United States." The building was modeled after the Crystal Palace in London that had held the Great Exhibition in 1851. Newly elected President Pierce gave a speech at the opening ceremonies, the text of which was printed in full in the *Post*. He hailed New York City as "beyond all controversy, the commercial metropolis of our blessed Union," and continued:

> The rapidity with which New York has arisen to so commanding a position as one of the most important cities upon the globe, has no parallel in history. Already the enterprise of your merchants, the genius of your shipbuilders, the daring spirit of your vast trading marine, are beginning to make you first in the markets of the world.
>
> Who will set limits to your just ambition when the Atlantic is bridged with steamers to the shores of Europe, and united to the Pacific by the great thoroughfare that will eventually bind these states together as with hooks of steel? And . . . how can we fail to welcome those who come to us from the gray old nations of Europe? Let them come! There is room enough for all—room in the hearts and in the homes of the American people; and there is work and food enough for all.

BOOK NOTICES.

Illustrated Record of the Crystal Palace Exhibition.

G. P. PUTNAM & CO.
Publish this Day,

I.

THE ILLUSTRATED RECORD OF THE NEW YORK EXHIBITION OF THE INDUSTRY OF ALL NATIONS.

Edited by Professor B. SILLIMAN, Jr., and C. B. GOODRICH, Esq. aided by eminent writers in the several departments of Science and Art.

WITH NUMEROUS FINE ILLUSTRATIONS, Engraved from Original Designs, by the first Artists.

4to.   Numbers 1 and 2 together.   Price 25 cents.

II.

THE OFFICIAL HAND CATALOGUE OF THE NEW YORK EXHIBITION.

12mo., Paper covers, 25 cents.

₊ This work has been prepared expressly for the use of Visiters to the Crystal Palace, and is the only authorized and accurate account of the various objects on exhibition here.

The Inauguration of the Crystal Palace.

DESCRIPTION OF THE CRYSTAL PALACE.

RECEPTION OF THE PRESIDENT.

Theodore Sedgwick, the president of the Crystal Palace Association and a former *Post* associate editor, followed the president's speech with an address that introduced the goals of the exhibition:

> The great objects of our enterprise . . . are . . . to bring before our countrymen the choicest productions of the genius and skill of the Old World—to make a first exhibition on a national scale of the trophies of the inventive spirit and restless energy of our countrymen—on a national scale to collect . . . "The arts for luxury, the arms for strife/Inventions for delight and sight and sound" . . . to bind together the two hemispheres—to extend the area of commerce and the fraternity of nations.

Paintings, sculpture, industrial and agricultural products made up the more than 4,000 displays at the Crystal Palace. The *Post* reported the entrance fee receipts at the Palace on a regular basis throughout the run of the fair, such as this notice from July 23, 1853:

> —The cash receipts at the Crystal Palace, yesterday, amounted to $1,429.

New York would be the site of two more world's fairs in 1939–1940 and 1964–1965.

Illustration of the Crystal Palace from Post 100th Anniversary supplement.

Front-Page Formats in the Post's First 60 Years

In 1826, when William Cullen Bryant joined the *Post*, the front page (above) had increased to six columns from the original five. Small stock cuts of three-masted sailboats called attention to some of the shipping notices.

The *Post* went through extensive changes in the 1830s. The words "New York" were dropped from the flag in 1832, another column was added and the two outer columns were pulled up to create "ears" on the top. Note the absence of sailboat stock cuts. In an effort to clean up the appearance of the front page, acting editor William Leggett discontinued the use of the small art illustrations in the advertisements. Many customers dropped their ads as a result.

Ten years and another office move later, the *Post* expanded to nine columns. The "ears" became two-columns wide. Columns eight and nine were devoted to news stories, and the rest were filled with advertisements.

The paper had moved to new offices by 1840, and a new printing setup allowed for an additional, eighth column. A masthead was added to the top of column 1, listing both subscription and advertising rates. The paper reinstated the use of stock cuts of boats, horses, houses and other items for ads.

Headlines came to the *Post* during the Civil War. In the issue above, column 1's headline THE WAR is followed by eight decks (subheads). The front page was expanded to ten columns, and about half were given to news. In contrast, the *Post*'s biggest-selling rival papers, the *Tribune* and *Herald*, devoted the entire front page to news.

NEW YORK POST

Decade Seven

1861-1870

"They have given their lives in the noblest cause . . . for the great principles of human freedom and human justice," wrote the *Post* in honor of those who died in the battles of Vicksburg and Gettysburg in 1863.

The *Post* covered the war with reporters in the field such as William C. Church, who would later launch the *Army and Navy Journal*, Philip Ripley and Walter F. Williams. Managing editor Parke Godwin recalled that Walt Whitman "wrote a number of letters from Washington at the beginning of the war," but unfortunately there are no bylines from which to determine which reports were his.

Through this decade the *Post* covers a war, a president's assassination and a bloody riot in New York City unlike any in the nation's history.

The 17th New York Infantry on parade, ca. 1865. (National Archives and Records Administration)

"Fort Sumter On Fire!"

For four months the rebels have brought their best means and skill to the one object of dislodging eighty pale, patient, loyal soldiers from a federal fortress.

—EDITORIAL, 1861

CIVIL WAR!

BOMBARDMENT OF FORT SUMTER.

A DAY'S FIGHTING.

THE REBELLION CULMINATING.

Anderson Refuses to Surrender, and Makes a Brilliant Defence.

THE STORY OF FORT SUMTER.

At a late hour last night news was received of the commencement of hostilities at Charleston. During the entire day the telegraphic wires were in a disabled condition, so that no intelligence reached us up to the hour of putting to press the last edition of the EVENING POST. The reports of the attack upon Fort Sumter which have thus far been received must be taken with large grains of allowance, for they are evidently made in the interest of the rebels, who hold control of the wires. The damage inflicted by Anderson's fire is probably much greater than these statements admit, and it is also probable that the effect of the enemy's fire upon Sumter has been much less destructive than the traitors are willing to acknowledge.

"The cannonading is now going on fiercely. . . . The excitement in Charleston has reached fever heat. All business is suspended, and the citizens throng the wharves, watching the progress of the conflict with intense eagerness." With this breaking news on April 13, 1861, *Post* readers learned that the War Between the States had begun.

The editorial that day berated the traitors who vastly outnumbered the 80 soldiers at Fort Sumter, and called upon the government to "put down treason for ever . . . in the name of law and order, in the name of all that is dear to freemen." The editorial included the following:

The Confederate traitors have chosen war.

The long siege and the hasty attack are alike exemplars of southern chivalry. For four months the rebels have brought their best means and skill to the one object of dislodging eighty pale, patient, loyal soldiers from a federal fortress. They have spent thousands in the construction of bomb-proof contrivances, providing safety for themselves while spilling the blood of loyal men.

This is a day which will be ever memorable in our annals. To-day treason has risen from blustering words to cowardly deeds. They glory, in cowardly glee, in their thousands hunting to death the loyal eighty. They have learned the ignoble lesson in their blood-hound hunts of defence-less slaves.

With the demand for news of the battles, the paper's circulation rose during the war, and in 1862 it installed a new printing press to keep up with the demand. Fifty thousand dollars were spent on installing "the largest and most efficient eight-cylinder newspaper press that has ever been constructed."

ABOVE: *The* Post's *first front-page headline announcing the start of the Civil War, April 13, 1861.*

ORK, SATURDAY, APRIL 13, 1861.

POSTSCRIPT.

Two O'Clock.

THE WAR.

FORT SUMTER ON FIRE!

The Battle Resumed To-day.

FIERCE CANNONADING.

THE FLEET UNDER FIRE.

The Harriet Lane Reported Sunk.

CHARLESTON, April 13.—The attack upon Fort Sumter was resumed from all the batteries in the harbor at an early hour this morning.

The cannonading is now going on fiercely.

SECOND EDITION.

Half-past Two.

BY TELEGRAPH.

LATER FROM CHARLESTON.

THE SURRENDER OF SUMTER EXPECTED

DESPATCHES RECEIVED AT WASHINGTON.

[Special Despatch to the Evening Post.]

WASHINGTON, April 13.—Two or three private despatches have just been received in this city from Charleston.

The reports are conflicting, but one despatch from a high official in Charleston states that General Beauregard confidently expects to accomplish the reduction of Fort Sumter before night.

It is believed here that if the federal naval forces failed to reinforce Anderson's command under cover of the darkness last night, the fort will not long be

Still Later from Charleston.

WORSE NEWS!

ANDERSON IN DISTRESS.

HIS FLAG AT HALF-MAST.

His Officers' Quarters on Fire.

CHARLESTON, S. C., April 13—Half-past 10 o'clock A. M.—At intervals of twenty minutes the firing was kept up all night on Fort Sumter.

Major Anderson ceased firing from Fort Sumter at six o'clock in the evening.

All night he was engaged in repairing damages and protecting the barbette guns on the top of the fort.

He commenced to return fire at seven o'clock this morning.

Fort Sumter seems to be greatly disabled.

The battery on Cumming's Point does Fort Sum-

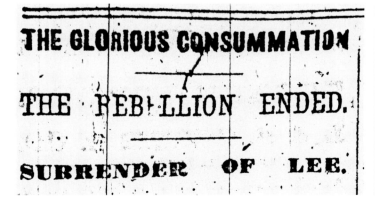

PROCEEDINGS OF CONGRESS.

SLAVERY ABOLISHED.

Final Passage of the Constitutional Amendment—The Vote.

THE GLORIOUS CONSUMMATION

THE REBELLION ENDED.

SURRENDER OF LEE.

Post's Civil War Coverage

During the course of the war, the *Post* kept readers informed through columns of headlines and articles derived from the latest telegraph wire reports.

Slavery ended with the passage of the 13th Amendment on January 31, 1865, and the news appeared on page 1 the following day under the headline: SLAVERY ABOLISHED. The article described the scene in the House chamber when the vote was announced: "Thereupon rose a general shout of applause. The members on the floor buzzed in chorus with deafening and equally emphatic cheers of the throng in the galleries. The ladies in the dense assemblage waved their handkerchiefs, and again and again the applause was repeated, intermingled with clapping of hands and exclamations of 'Hurrah for Freedom!' and 'Glory enough for one day!'"

The end of the war was announced on the front page on April 10, 1865, in an emotional tone: THE GLORIOUS CONSUMMATION: THE REBELLION ENDED. The official news contained reprints of the official dispatches of Lee's surrender. On page 2, William Cullen Bryant supplied a moving editorial about "the day of Peace" and the triumph of "universal liberty."

Gettysburg Address

The Dedication of the Gettysburg Cemetery.

The ceremony attending the dedication of the National Cemetery at Gettysburg, yesterday, was witnessed by an immense concourse of citizens. The military and civic display was very fine. The following is the dedicatory speech of President Lincoln:

"Fourscore and seven years ago our fathers brought forth upon this continent a new nation, conceived in liberty, and dedicated to the proposition that all men are created equal. [Applause.] Now we are engaged in a great civil war, testing whether that nation or any nation so conceived and so dedicated can long endure. We are met on a great battle-field of that war. We are met to dedicate a portion of it as the final resting-place of those who here gave their lives that that nation might live. It is altogether fitting and proper that we should do this. But in a larger sense we cannot dedicate, we cannot consecrate, we cannot hallow this ground. The brave men living and dead who struggled here have consecrated it far above our power to add or detract. [Applause.] The world will little note nor long remember what we say here, but it can never forget what they did here. [Applause.] It is for us, the living, rather to be dedicated here to the unfinished work that they have thus far so nobly carried on. [Applause.] It is rather for us to be here dedicated to the great task remaining before us, that from these honored dead we take increased devotion to that cause for which they here gave the last full measure of devotion; that we here higher resolve that the dead shall not have died in vain [applause]; that the nation shall, under God, have a new birth of freedom; and that governments of the people by the people, and for the people, shall not perish from the earth." [Long-continued applause.]

Extracts from Mr. Everett's oration are given on our first page.

THE EVENING POST.

MONDAY EVENING, APRIL 10, 1865.

GLORY TO THE LORD OF HOSTS.

The great day, so long and anxiously awaited, for which we have struggled through four years of bloody war, which has so often seemed to "stand tiptoe on the misty mountain tops," but which dawned only to go down in clouds and gloom; the day of the virtual overthrow of the rebellion, of the triumph of constitutional order and of universal liberty— of the success of the nation against its parts, and of a humane and beneficent civilization over a relic of barbarism that had been blindly allowed to remain as a blot on its scutcheon, in short, the day of PEACE, has finally come. It has come, as every wise lover of his country wished it to come, not as a weak compromise between the government of the people and its enemies, not as a concession to an exhausted yet vital power of revolt, not as a truce between two equal forces which lay down their arms for the time, to resume them as soon as they should repair damages and recover strength—but as the result of a stern, deliberate, unyielding determination to vindicate the supremacy of the organic law over the entire territory and people of the nation.

ABOVE: *Lincoln's Gettysburg Address, as reported and reprinted in the* Post *on November 20, 1863, the day after he gave the speech.*
LEFT: *The editorial of April 10, 1865, rejoices over the end of "four years of bloody war."*

CHARGE OF THE POLICE ON THE RIOTERS AT THE "TRIBUNE" OFFICE.

FIRST EDITION.

Half-past One,

THE RIOTS RESUMED TO-DAY.

GREAT CROWDS ASSEMBLING.

The Military Marching Through the Streets.

THE MOB FIRED UPON.

Continued Outrages Upon Persons and Property by the Rioters.

SPEECH OF GOVERNOR SEYMOUR.

RIOT!

In the third year of the Civil War, New York City witnessed four days of bloody rioting against the new draft—an event that remains the largest civil disorder in U.S. history. The first federal draft was called up in the city on July 11, 1863. This added fuel to the fury of poor Irish immigrants who had been facing job competition from black workers since the reading of Lincoln's Emancipation Proclamation. The Irish workers' rage grew the next day when they learned of a clause that allowed drafted men to buy a waiver for $300—a sum too high for any of them to pay. To them, it was another blow against the poor, who were now expected to give their lives for the war.

Anti-black and anti-war hatred exploded at dawn on Monday, July 13. A mob of dockworkers and other laborers attacked policemen and stormed up to the draft headquarters on Third Avenue and 46th Street. They smashed apart the draft selection wheel and set fire to the building, then moved on to three new targets. One group destroyed the armory on Second Avenue, a second ransacked a draft office on Broadway, and the third and largest mob burned down the Colored Orphan Asylum on Fifth Avenue.

ABOVE: *Draft rioters clash with police in July 1863. (New York Public Library)*

RESISTANCE TO THE DRAFT.

RIOT UP TOWN.

The draft was recommenced this morning at the headquarters of the Ninth Congressional district, corner of Third avenue and Forty-sixth street. The wheel had been revolving about twenty minutes when the building in which the officer was was attacked by a mob armed with clubs, stones, brickbats and like missiles, but no firearms. The building, a four-story brick house, the upper stories of which were occupied by families, was defaced, the windows broken, doors smashed and furniture destroyed.

The mob rushed into the enrolling office, seized all the machinery and papers, records, lists, &c., of the officers, except those contained in a large safe.

Throughout the day, smaller groups hunted down blacks and clubbed them to death.

The raiding, destruction and brutality continued until five regiments of the Union army made it to the scene, rushing north from Gettysburg. By nine p.m. on Thursday, the fighting was over.

Managing editor Charles Nordhoff was an eyewitness to much of the violence. During the mob scenes he kept rioters away from the *Post* building by manning a firehose attached to the steam boiler. He had not only the offices to protect, but an upper floor that had been outfitted as a makeshift hospital and was filled with wounded Union soldiers.

Ten days after the riots, Nordhoff wrote a long, detailed account of the horrifying events. Although the official death count was slightly over 100, Nordhoff was convinced it was actually closer to 400 or 500. He also suspected that the riots had been planned and instigated by anti-war activists rather than spontaneously erupting among angry workers. His narrative of the riots included the following:

The active rioters—nowhere more than a hundred in number—were followed here (as every where else) by numer-

THE STORY OF THE " FOUR DAYS."

THE MOB AND ITS LEADERS.

ous constituency of women and children, who took hold of depredation with a zest and pertness which showed that they were thieves the manner born.

Watches, bracelets, jewelry, valuables, and usables of every description, disappeared as by magic. In an hour the block was "gutted" and cleaned out.

Not far from the very time of the attack upon the Orphan Asylum a colored cartman had been murdered, mutilated, hanged and burned in Clarkson street under circumstances of atrocity without example . . .

On Wednesday the city cars were not running—the Hudson River road had also to discontinue its trips, the rails having been torn up uptown. The attention of the rioters was turned mainly towards the colored people, whom they persecuted wherever they could find a chance. A great many of their houses were plundered and destroyed, and several persons murdered. Some of the military were shot from windows while patrolling the streets, and numerous rioters who showed themselves were killed.

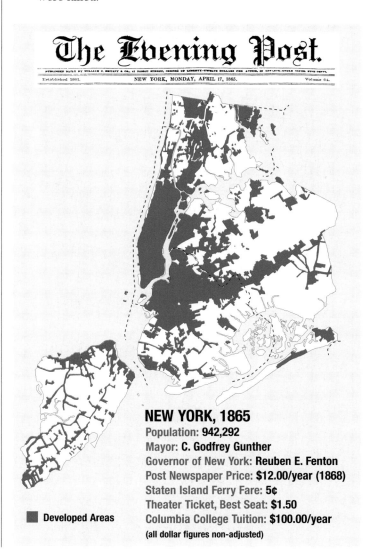

NEW YORK, 1865
Population: 942,292
Mayor: C. Godfrey Gunther
Governor of New York: Reuben E. Fenton
Post Newspaper Price: $12.00/year (1868)
Staten Island Ferry Fare: 5¢
Theater Ticket, Best Seat: $1.50
Columbia College Tuition: $100.00/year
(all dollar figures non-adjusted)

■ Developed Areas

AN APPALLING CALAMITY.

Assassination of the President.

TURDAY, APRIL 15, 1865.

SECOND EDITION.

Half-past Two.

THE GREAT CALAMITY.

LATER PARTICULARS.

Last Moments of Mr. Lincoln.

THE SURGEON'S REPORT.

The Remains of the President Taken to the White House.

Inauguration of Andrew Johnson as President of the United States.

BOOTH NOT YET ARRESTED.

A VIGOROUS PURSUIT ORDERED.

A Watch Upon the Canadian Frontier.

Secretary Seward's Wounds Not Mortal.

FREDERICK SEWARD STILL LIVING.

THE GRIEF OF THE NATION.

The following minutes, taken by Dr. Abbott, show the condition of the late President throughout the night:

11:00 o'clock— Pulse 44.
11:05   do.   do. 45, and growing weaker.
11:10   do.   do. 45.
11:15   do.   do. 42.
11:20   do.   do. 45; respiration 27 to 29.
11:25   do.   do. 42.
11:32   do.   do. 48, and full.
11:40   do.   do. 45.
11:45   do.   do. 45; respiration 22.
12:00   do.   do. 48; respiration 22.
12:15   do.   do. 48; respiration 21; ecchymosis in both eyes.
12:30   do.   do. 45.
12:32   do.   do. 60.
12:35   do.   do. 66.
12:40   do.   do. 69; right eye much swollen and ecchymosis.
12:45   do.   do. 70.
12:55   do.   do. 80; struggling motion of arms.
1:00   do.   do. 86; respiration 30.
1:30   do.   do. 95; appearing easier.
1:45   do.   do. 86; very quiet; respiration irregular; Mrs. Lincoln present.
2:10   do.   Mrs. Lincoln retired with Robert Lincoln to an adjoining room.
2:30   do.   President very quiet; pulse 54; respiration 28.
2:52   do.   pulse 48; respiration 30.
3:00   do.   visited again by Mrs. Lincoln.
3:25   do.   respiration 24, and regular.
3:35   do.   prayer by Rev. Dr. Gurley.
4:00   do.   respiration 26, and regular.
4:15   do.   pulse 60; respiration 25.
5:50   do.   respiration 28; regular; sleeping.
6:00   do.   pulse failing; respiration 28.
6:30   do.   still failing and labored breathing.
7:00   do.   symptoms of immediate dissolution.
7:22   do.   DEATH.

President Lincoln Shot

Lincoln's assassination hit the front page on April 15, 1865, with a poignant headline: AN APPALLING CALAMITY. "Abraham Lincoln was assassinated in Ford's Theatre in Washington at half-past nine o'clock last night . . ."

On page 3, another headline was underscored by 12 subheadings and the article included a minute-by-minute account of the president's dying hours. The doctor's notes included "growing weaker" at 11:05, "struggling motion of arms" at 12:55, "President very quiet" at 2:30, "pulse falling" at 6:00, "symptoms of immediate dissolution" at 7:00, and "death" at 7:22.

The assassin, John Wilkes Booth, had planned on kidnapping Lincoln and holding him for ransom, in exchange for Confederate prisoners of war. When that scheme failed, he formed a group of co-conspirators and planned Lincoln's assassination as well as the simultaneous murder of Vice President Andrew Johnson and Secretary of State William Seward.

CITY INTELLIGENCE.

Five Persons Drowned in Brooklyn.

Yesterday afternoon five persons lost their lives by drowning in a large pond situated between Fourth and Fifth avenues and Union and Douglass streets, in South Brooklyn.

About 2 o'clock p.m. three girls, named Margaret Dougherty, aged ten years, Mary Sullivan, aged nine years, and Ann Carroll, aged ten years . . . all went into the water to bathe, hand-in-hand, but had proceeded only a few paces when they stepped into a hole some ten feet deep, and being unable to extricate themselves, sunk beneath the surface and were drowned.

James McGee, a laborer, aged thirty-five years, who lives in a shanty on the Fifth avenue side of the pond, saw the girls struggling in the water and ran to their relief. He jumped in without divesting himself of his clothing, and getting beyond his depth, also sunk.

Mrs. Ann Dougherty, the mother of one of the girls, ran frantically from her house and plunged into the water for the purpose of saving the life of her child, and she too stepped beyond her depth and was likewise drowned.

Peter Conners, residing on the Fourth avenue side of the pond, seeing the unfortunates from a distance, ran to the spot, stripped and jumped in. Being a good swimmer he succeeded in bringing all the bodies to the shore.

The scene about the shanties was heartrending, the fathers, mothers, and children of the dead running frantically about, crying, and making the most violent demonstrations of grief.

§ § §

Runaway Accident.

A team of horses belonging to the Third Avenue Railroad Company ran away from the depot last night. The horses ran upon the sidewalk near Sixty-fifth street, knocking down and severely injuring a woman named Mrs. Currie. She was conveyed to her home in East Forty-seventh street.

§ § §

Careless Riding.

A man named H.J. Foster . . . while horseback riding last night carelessly ran over a boy named John Welsh, at the corner of Eighth avenue and Twenty-sixth street. The boy was much injured and was taken home by several citizens. Foster attempted to escape, but several police officers pursued him for several blocks, and finally succeeded in arresting him at the corner of Forty-fourth street and Eleventh avenue.

§ § §

Murder in Baxter Street.

On Saturday evening, Donato Magaldo, a blacksmith . . . quarreled with John Rilands, in Baxter street, and the former drew a large knife, with which he stabbed Rilands, the blade passing through his heart, and causing almost instant death. An alarm was given, and officer Mooney, of the Sixth precinct, started in pursuit of Magaldo, when the latter turned and attempted to stab the officer. Magaldo was secured and taken to the station house.

§ § §

First Elevated Railroad

The city's mass transit system began with horse-drawn railroads, also called streetcars, that carried passengers along several regular routes through the city and beyond. In the summer of 1868 the first elevated railroad appeared, replacing horses with engine horsepower. The *Post* announced the opening of this line on July 3 and noted that the modern version would cost "less than one-tenth that of running an ordinary horse railroad."

The "El" traveled 30 feet above the ground, supported by iron superstructures and pulled by a cable connected to a steam-powered generator. The elevated system expanded for the next several decades to include the outer boroughs, but in the depression of the 1930s they were torn down to increase property values. New York's ever-increasing need for speed brought about an electric trolley system in 1890 and the first subway line in 1904.

BELOW: *New York's El, ca. 1870. (New York Public Library)*

The Greenwich Street Elevated Railroad.

The directors of the West Side and Yonkers Patent Railway Company, this afternoon submitted their structure in Greenwich street to inspection by members of the press. It had been inspected by commissioners, and was approved yesterday by Governor Fenton. The effect of this action is to give the company full power to proceed with their railway from the Battery to Spuytin Duyvil.

The cars are propelled by a stationary engine, at an expense of less than one-tenth that of running an ordinary horse railroad. The structure will cost about $150,000 per mile.

Mr. Charles F. Harvey is the principal engineer, a self-educated man, and possessing great experience. The property owners are generally in favor of the enterprise; and as there is no serious engineering difficulty, it will probably be completed this year to Thirtieth street. The speed can be gained from five to fifteen miles an hour; and the trip can be made from Wall street to the Hudson River cars in fifteen minutes.

NEW YORK POST

Decade Eight
1871– 1880

After the Civil War the *Post* continued its fight against the corrupt city government run by Tammany Hall, the Democratic Party machine in New York City. "Never was the administration so ineffective, never was there so much corruption," railed an editorial about the leadership of William "Boss" Tweed. The *Post* demanded reform, and its constant attention to the issue helped expose the Tweed ring's system of kickbacks, corruption and waste.

City Hall in the late 1800s. (Illustration from Post 100th Anniversary supplement)

End of an Era

"Just as he was the first American poet to stand head and shoulders above the pack and was never surpassed during his own day except possibly by Poe and Whitman, he was the pre-eminent editorial writer of his era."

—CURTISS S. JOHNSON

The flags of New York were flown at half-mast the day William Cullen Bryant died. His death on June 12, 1878, was the result of a head injury from a fall he had taken three weeks earlier.

In a speech made after Bryant's death, his former associate editor John Bigelow summarized the hallmark of the editor in chief's 52-year career at the *Post:* "When the length of his career as editor is considered, it may be assumed that Mr. Bryant was one of the most voluminous prose writers that ever lived, and . . . one of the best."

In his biography of Bryant, Curtiss S. Johnson reflects that Bryant may not have been a newspaperman of the fame of Pulitzer or Hearst, but "to him must go the credit for pioneering the meaningful editorial page. Just as he was the first American poet to stand head and shoulders above the pack and was never surpassed during his own day except possibly by Poe and Whitman, he was the pre-eminent editorial writer of his era."

ABOVE: *William Cullen Bryant. (Illustration from Post 100th Anniversary supplement)*

Ribbons, Linens and Lawns

Advertisements from the 1870s

CITY INTELLIGENCE.

A Curious Case of Poisoning. Long Island. A singular poisoning case occurred at Mattituck on Saturday evening, when the whole family of Mr. Teed were suddenly taken ill at the supper-table, continuing sick during the night, with frequent vomiting. Mr. Teed believes that some kind of poison was placed in the butter used on the table, and a sample has been sent to a chemist for analysis.

§ § §

Mrs. Lizzie Pettit Cutler, the author of "Light and Darkness," "Household Mysteries" and other popular novels, will deliver a lecture at the Mott Memorial Room, Madison avenue, on Friday evening. The subject she has chosen is "Married Flirts."

§ § §

Murder and Suicide. Brooklyn Intelligence. Dennis Delaney, a sober man, aged thirty-five years, living at No. 382 Hicks street, killed his wife with an axe on Sunday morning, and then cut his throat with a razor, nearly severing his head from his body. He went home from his work in the evening at the usual hour perfectly sober. He had five children, and all the family slept in the same room. The oldest boy awoke at two o'clock, and saw his father standing by the bed beating his mother on the head with an axe. He was talking loudly. The boy did not hear his mother utter a sound, and it is probable that the first blow made her insensible. Delaney continued to beat her until convinced that she was dead, after which he killed himself.

It is thought, beyond doubt, that he was insane, and it is said by the neighbors that he had acted strangely at times before.

§ § §

The Coroner's Office. The inquest in the case of James Sylvester, the acrobat who was killed last night by a fall from a trapeze, will be held to-morrow morning.

Coroner Wiltman held an inquest to-day in the case of Ann Mangan, of No. 208 West Twentieth street, who died from the explosion of a kerosene lamp on Saturday night, during an altercation with her husband, both of them being intoxicated at the time. The jury returned a verdict of accidental death, and the husband, Hugh Mangan, was discharged.

§ § §

Terrible Death of an Actress. Miss Ada Noyes, a young actress, died at her residence, No. 166 Bleecker street, this morning, from hydrophobia. The unfortunate lady arrived in this city about a month ago from Charleston, S.C.: she had with

her a little pet dog, which bit her on the nose on the 20th of February.

But little notice of the occurrence was taken until Sunday last, when the dreaded symptoms presented themselves. The best medical aid was called in, but Miss Noyes grew rapidly worse, and died this morning in terrible agony.

§ § §

The Rev. Dr. Howard Crosby preached in the Fourth Avenue Presbyterian Church yesterday, on the depravity of drunkenness. He expressed himself as opposed to enforced total abstinence. He believed that Christ made and drank intoxicating liquor, and he could see no sin in the sale or in the moderate use of wine after such an example.

§ § §

The Temperance Movement. Women Already at Work in This City. As a result of the ten days' protracted meetings in the Seventeenth Street Methodist Episcopal Church, the temperance movement has there at last been put in practical working shape by the organization of a "Christian Women's League," at the head of which stands Mrs. W. H. Boole, the wife of the pastor of the church. Mrs. Boole submitted to a number of

Illustrations from Post 100th Anniversary supplement.

Christian women a plan of working in this city, the principal features of which are as follows:

A prayer meeting of women only. From this meeting bands of women will visit places where liquor is sold, and will make private appeals to the proprietors or the owners of the houses, and endeavor to induce them to sign pledges.

On the following day another visit will be paid to the same place, and these visits will be continued until a victory is ultimately achieved.

Mrs. Boole and two other ladies have visited several establishments on the west side, and already one prominent liquor seller . . . has given his word of honor that no more liquor shall be sold by him. His stock on hand has been disposed of and the establishment closed.

§ § §

Farrington, the Forger. The boy Joseph Farrington, who was arrested several days ago for forging certain money orders which he collected at the General Post Office, in this city, is a resident of Kings county, and has been in the employ of the Bible Publishing Company . . . for nearly two years. This statement is made at the request of the Postmaster, for the reason that there is a very worthy young man of the same name employed in the Post Office, and as the names have been confounded, Colonel James desires to correct the rumor to prevent future misconception.

NEW YORK POST

Decade Nine

1881-1890

Clockwise, from top left, Post *owner Henry Villard and the famous triumvirate of editors Horace White, E.L. Godkin and Carl Schurz. (*Post *100th Anniversary supplement)*

This decade began with a new owner of the *Post*, Henry Villard, a railroad magnate who had been a Civil War correspondent for Horace Greeley's *New York Tribune.* The *Post*'s distinguished editors in chief in this era were, consecutively, Carl Schurz, E.L. Godkin and Horace White.

Horace White's achievements in journalism included his role with the Associated Press. As managing editor of the *Chicago Tribune,* White was one of the founders of the Western Associated Press, which revolted against its ostensible New York–based affiliate and eventually broke the wire service monopoly. He was one of the driving forces that brought about a total reorganization and revitalization of the AP.

Carl Schurz' remarkable life story before joining the *Post* included serving as a brigadier general in the Civil War, as minister to Spain in Lincoln's cabinet, as U.S. senator from Missouri and secretary of the interior under President Rutherford Hayes. In addition to his role as editor of the *Post,* Schurz wrote for *Harper's Weekly* magazine. New York City paid tribute to Schurz with a park that bears his name, located directly across from Gracie Mansion.

Journalist E.L. Godkin was a war correspondent for the *London Daily News* during the Civil War and founded *The Nation,* the highly influential weekly journal of political opinion, before joining the *Post*. He sold *The Nation* to the *Post* in 1881 but stayed on as its editor. Godkin's leadership increased the paper's reputation as a voice of lively opinion.

Nation Joins Post

❝The Nation's *literary criticism has, for carefulness, evenness, justice and style, earned it the first place on this side of the water, and . . . put it on a par with the best authorities in any country.* ❞ —ADVERTISEMENT FOR THE NATION, 1880S

ABOVE: *A page of* The Nation *from January 1885.*

On July 1, 1881, the following announcement was made in the *Post:*

Beginning with the next number *The Nation* will be issued as the weekly edition of the *New York Evening Post.*

It will retain the name and have the same editorial management as heretofore, and an increased staff of contributors, but its contents will in the main have already appeared in the *Evening Post.*

This consolidation will considerably enlarge the field and raise the character of the *Evening Post*'s literary criticism and news. It will also add to its staff of literary contributors the very remarkable list of writers in every department with which readers of *The Nation* have long been familiar.

The Nation was founded in 1865 by E.L. Godkin, editor in chief of the *Post* from 1883 to 1899. The magazine quickly earned a reputation as one of the smartest publications in the country with excellent writing about politics and culture. Of Godkin's contributions to journalism, William James wrote: "To my generation, his was certainly the towering influence in all thought concerning public affairs, and indirectly his influence has certainly been more pervasive than that of any other writer of the generation, for he

influenced other writers who never quoted him, and determined the whole current of discussion." Godkin died in 1900, but *The Nation* lives on as America's oldest weekly magazine.

Post Publisher Pushed Out

Co-owner and publisher of the *Post* in the 1860s, Isaac Henderson hoped to gain major control of the paper and make it a family property. He had already installed his son-in-law as managing editor and was training his son, Isaac, Jr., to succeed him as publisher.

Henderson had been raked through the coals during the Civil War, however, on charges of profiteering. He was acquitted of the charges in federal court, but many were convinced that his actions had been dishonest and dishonorable. *Post* co-owner Parke Godwin was among those who remained suspicious of the publisher.

In 1881, when Godwin learned that Henderson planned to sell his shares of the paper to Jay Gould, Godwin arranged to sell the controlling shares of the *Post* to Henry Villard. Gould, one of the major "robber barons" of the 19th century, was considered a corrupt, ruthless scoundrel and was outcast from New York society. To Godwin, selling the *Post* to Gould was just one more piece of evidence that Henderson didn't care about the integrity of the paper. Godwin believed that selling the *Post* to Villard saved the *Post*'s reputation and its future.

THE BRIDGE!!

OPENING OF THE GREAT STRUCTURE TO-DAY.

Rejoicings in New York and Brooklyn.

THE MILITARY AND CIVIL PROCESSION.

Arrival of the President.

The Ceremonies on the Bridge and at the Brooklyn Approach.

FULL REPORTS OF ALL THE SPEECHES.

A General Suspension of Business.

Brooklyn Bridge Opens

For more than 80 years New Yorkers had dreamed of a bridge connecting Manhattan and Brooklyn. In an open letter to the New York state government, published in the *Post* on February 18, 1802, a writer stated the pressing need for a bridge to connect the city with surrounding areas via a bridge:

> The great and increasing population of the city of New York renders a daily supply from the country of the necessaries of life, almost indispensable, it has therefore become an object of great importance to the interest and welfare of those adjacent islands, that a bridge should be established between them, which may be so constructed as to answer all the purposes of intercourse, and at the same time be beneficial to the port and harbor of New York.
>
> Your petitioners humbly pray that the kind of Bridge to be built, and the place where it ought to be located, shall be determined by the Governor. . . .

"The height of Brooklyn's ambition—to be really a part of New York—was realized to-day, and the town across the bridge went wild with delight," wrote the *Post* in its lengthy coverage of the Brooklyn Bridge's opening ceremonies on May 24, 1883.

Designed by engineer John August Roebling, the steel suspension bridge spanned 1,595.5 feet between its towers and was revered at the time as the "Eighth Wonder of the World." Before work began, Roebling died in an accident while making observations to determine the exact location of the Brooklyn tower. His son, Washington Roebling, took over the project.

Twenty-six workers died during construction of the bridge. The greatest hazards came from below, where men built the foundations of the towers on the bedrock below the East River. They worked in immense, bottomless wooden boxes called caissons, and were constantly at risk of fire as well as the bends, or "caisson disease." In 1872, Roebling was struck with this decompression sickness while working 78 feet below the surface. Left paralyzed, partly blind, deaf and mute from the sickness, he supervised the building of the bridge from a window in his bedroom overlooking the East River. His wife, Emily Roebling became the surrogate chief engineer for the remainder of the project.

On opening day, spectators who couldn't find room on the packed sidewalks took to the rooftops to watch the parade and hear the speeches. Brooklyn Mayor Seth Low remarked on the significance and awesome achievement symbolized by the bridge:

> Fourteen years ago a city of 400,000 people on this side of the river heard of a projected suspension bridge with incredulity. The span was so long, the height so great, and the enterprise likely to be so costly, that few thought of it as something begun in earnest. The irresistible demands of Commerce enforced these hard conditions. But Science said, "It is possible;" and Courage said, "It shall be!"
>
> It must be a superlative moment in life when one stands on a structure as majestic as this, which was at first a mere thought in the brain, which was afterward a plan on the paper, and which has been transported hither from quarry and mine, from wood-yard and workshop, on the point of his pencil!
>
> Indeed, it is not extravagant to say that the future of the country opens before us, as we see what skill and will can do to overleap obstacles, and make nature subservient to human designs.

ABOVE: *Currier and Ives lithograph of the Brooklyn Bridge, 1885.* *(New York Historical Society)*

Lady Liberty

The lengthy, front-page *Post* coverage described the crowds that had come into the city for the historic day:

> The promenade was crowded with pedestrians, all hurrying to the metropolis. They were not the workers of every day. There were groups of entire families, father, mother, and a half-a-dozen youngsters; there were lovers by the hundreds, and small boys by the gross. Many of the young folk marched in military order, with banners and music . . . and gallant young officers with walking sticks for swords. Some of them were provided with big wooden boxes, which they carried all the way from Brooklyn, in order to have something to stand upon, so as to be able to see over the heads of taller sight-seers. The hurrying crowds were made gay by flashes of bright uniforms here and there. The red shirts of veteran firemen . . . to say nothing of the flags which flaunted themselves bravely everywhere.

A full military parade down Fifth Avenue, complete with President Cleveland in an open carriage; throngs of people lining the streets and the battery; 200 vessels steaming down the river in a naval parade (in spite of heavy fog); flags posted on thousands of homes, stores and boats; the dramatic unveiling of the French flag from the statue's head at three o'clock; gun salutes; bands and fireworks at three locations in the evening—these were only a few of the events that took place in the city on October 28, 1886, to celebrate the newly installed Statue of Liberty in New York Bay.

"How can we fitly frame in words the sentiments, the motives, the emotions which have filled and moved the hearts and minds of two great nations in the birth of the noble conception, the grand embodiment, the complete execution of this stupendous monument?" asked Senator William Evarts in the presentation address. France's gift was sculpted by Frédéric-Auguste Bartholdi, and Emma Lazarus' poem "The New Colossus" was added to the pedestal in 1903.

> *Give me your tired, your poor, Your*
> *huddled masses yearning to breathe free,*
> *The wretched refuse of your teeming shore.*
> *Send these, the homeless, tempest-tost to me,*
> *I lift my lamp beside the golden door!*
>
> —FROM "THE NEW COLOSSUS," BY EMMA LAZARUS, 1883

A photograph of the Statue of Liberty taken in the late 1880s, shortly after the statue was unveiled. (New York Historical Society)

LIBERTY'S STATUE.

The Unveiling Ceremonies To-day.

THE GREAT PARADE.

The Celebration on Sea and Shore.

SCENES THROUGHOUT THE CITY

Enthusiasm Unquenched by Rain.

THE MARCH PAST THE PRESIDENT.

Enormous Crowds in the Streets.

THE DAY ON BEDLOE'S ISLAND.

The First Lady on the Torch.

THE RECEPTION OF THE GUESTS.

Many anxious glances were cast skyward early this morning, and little consolation could be derived from the threatening aspect of the heavens.

The sky was still heavy with drifting clouds, the wind blew with abominable persistency from the northeast, and a mist veiled the Statue of Liberty and almost everything else in a most effective but dispiriting manner.

There was however one solid bit of ground for satisfaction. It was not raining. There was fog above and all around, and puddles below, but it was possible to be abroad without umbrellas, and this one fact was made the most of. It was plain enough from the earliest hours of the morning that the great mass of the people had made up their minds to celebrate the unveiling of the colossal statue of Liberty with something like a general holiday. The rush to New York from all quarters was wonderful. It was probably as great as it was on the memorable day of Gen. Grant's funeral. Excursion trains brought thousands of country visitors here yesterday and the day before, and the influx continued this morning. All local means of transportation were taxed to their utmost capacity. From New Jersey, Staten Island, Long Island, and the annexed districts trains, ferryboats, and horse cars poured in one vast tide of human traffic which flowed steadily toward the central line of Broadway. The East River Bridge cars carried tens of thousands of passengers as usual, and the promenade was crowded with pedestrians, all hurrying to the metropolis. They were not the workers of every day. There were groups of entire families, father, mother, and a half-a-dozen youngsters; there were lovers by the hundred, and small boys by the gross. Many of the young folk marched in military order, with banners and music — such terrible music — and gallant young officers with walking sticks for swords. Some of them were provided with big wooden boxes, which they carried all the way from Brooklyn, in order to have something to stand upon, so as to be able to see over the heads of taller sight-seers. The hurrying crowds were made gay by flashes of bright uniforms here and there. The red shirts of veteran firemen, the glitter of polished metal on some old hand-engine, the gold of epaulettes, and an occasional white feather all helped to give color to the scene, to say nothing of the flags which flaunted themselves bravely everywhere, in complete defiance of any attempt of the elements to dispirit them.

All along the line of the parade the sidewalks and the steps of buildings had become black with people far in advance of the time for the procession to move. In Madison Square and its neighborhood the crush was especially great, and many persons who supposed they had come there early enough to secure good positions were obliged to give up the attempt in despair, and go to some distant point. The piles of paving stones on the sidewalks in the part of Fifth Avenue just above the Square were early occupied by hundreds of men and boys. The section of the avenue between Twenty-sixth and Twenty-eighth Streets, being torn up in preparation for repaving, was fenced in at each end, and here the spectators did not gather, it being understood that the procession, having moved down Fifth Avenue from Fifty-seventh Street, would pass through Twenty-eighth Street to Madison Avenue, and thence through Twenty-sixth Street to Fifth Avenue again.

A number of buildings on the line of march were tastefully decorated. At the New York Yacht Club house, Madison Avenue and Twenty-seventh Street, the display was elaborate, a line of multi-colored flags and signals being stretched across the avenue. In Madison Square, the Hoffman House, the Albemarle Hotel, and the Hotel Bartholdi were adorned with many flags, the latter building being gay with a profusion of the colors of all nations. French and American flags were also shown on the Fifth Avenue Hotel, Delmonico's, and many other structures. The colors of the two great republics were exhibited on a number of private houses in the side streets as well as on Fifth Avenue.

The elevated railroads to-day carried great numbers of people both up and down town, and some of the horse-car lines also ran with densely crowded cars at certain hours of the day.

ALONG THE LINE OF MARCH.

If there was an oldest inhabitant who might have recalled greater crowds than lined the march of to-day's procession from Madison Square down to the Battery, he must have been laid up with rheumatism, for he was nowhere to be found along the line. Before nine o'clock people had begun to assemble, the greatest concourse being naturally in the neighborhood of Madison Square, but the three miles of line below that being well filled by the overflow, thousands of persons who found it impossible to obtain a foothold up town took the cars for the lower part of the city, so that they might obtain a place before it was too late. Along the line there was an evident disposition upon the part of shopkeepers to dress up their buildings in honor of the occasion, although in many instances the results gave evidence of a sincere desire to manifest enthusiasm rather than of any lavish expenditure of money. The north end of the Post-office building was gorgeous with bunting, and the City Hall has never looked better, notwithstanding the bedraggled appearance of the flags, damp and limp in the mist.

The vast number of Italians who thronged the east side of Broadway from Spring Street up to Bond was very noticeable, and gave old citizens a new idea of the swarm of Italians who have come here within the last ten years. The peanut venders, all of them Italians, were among the most active speculators in providing seats for people who would pay for them, and it was amusing to see the rapidity with which an entire Italian family, including many babies, guests of the proprietor, was dispossessed the moment a paying customer could be obtained. Notwithstanding the disheartening drizzle, which became more and more sensible as the morning wore on, there was general and marked good feeling evident in the crowd, and the only man who did not seem to enjoy himself was the soda-water vender who found his goods at a discount. One soda-water merchant utilized his row of useless cylinders by hiring them out as pedestals at 5 cents apiece. The great dry-goods houses utilized empty boxes by placing them along the curb and putting chairs on top of them, much to the indignation of people whose view of the procession was cut off; but as it was not a money-making speculation, no one was called upon to interfere.

SCENES DOWN TOWN.

In the early morning the crowds began to pour into the down-town streets. A continuous stream of people was coming off the bridge and elevated stations. Broadway and Park Row were rapidly filling up, and in spite of the drizzling rain which began to fall at about half past ten, well-dressed ladies were thronging the streets, and it looked as though there would be a good many ruined costumes. Every available space for sight-seeing was occupied, a good many of the steps of the building being actually impassable. In front of the Equitable building the staging was crowded. Rough seats had been placed there, and they were occupied by ladies and children. The windows along the route were crowded and the roofs held their army of spectators. The roof of the Field building was unoccupied save by a platform on which was stationed a signal officer.

The Battery Park was lined with lookers on. The crowd was standing ten deep along the seawall, waiting to see the naval parade, but as only a hundred feet from the shore was visible, owing to the heavy mist, it seemed worse than useless for them to stay, but they still held their places in the hope that the sky would clear and the fog lift. The route of the procession had been changed slightly, so that instead of passing through Mail Street the column moved along the plaza in front of the City Hall. The railing around St. Paul's Church was crowded, and in front of the Post-office the columns were occupied by small boys, the projections affording excellent footholds. The electric light poles were strung with small boys, the steps giving them good holding-places.

FORMATION OF THE PARADE.

At nine o'clock A. M. the first division of the parade began to form on Fifty-seventh Street and Fifth Avenue. The Fifth United States Artillery, commanded by Col. John Hamilton, and the Engineer Corps took their position in front of Secretary Whitney's house, No. 2 West Fifty-seventh Street, a few minutes after nine. Next came the Old Guard, who stood near a line of carriages waiting for the President and the accompanying members of his Cabinet to leave Secretary Whitney's residence, where they had passed the night. Promptly at ten o'clock President Cleveland, accompanied by the Secretary of State, Mr. Bayard, descended the steps and entered an open carriage. Following carriages were occupied by the Secretary of the Navy, Mr. Whitney, the Postmaster-General, Mr. Vilas, the Secretary of the Interior, Mr. Lamar, Private Secretary Lamont, Maj.-Gen. Schofield and staff, Rear Admiral Luce and staff, and Lieut.-Col. Whipple. The Old Guard preceded the carriages, and at a quarter past ten o'clock began the march down Fifth Avenue. Both sides of the avenue were crowded with people, who waved their hats and applauded loudly as the President's carriage passed. On all the side streets from Fifty-seventh down to Thirty-third the different military companies and civic organizations were formed.

The Seventh never did better marching. The men were in heavy marching order, without knapsacks. They paraded twenty commands of sixteen files front. Following them in line came the Sixty-ninth Regiment parading ten commands of twenty files, and then came the Eighth Regiment, with six commands of twelve files front. The Ninth Regiment, parading ten commands of twelve files front, also made a fine showing. Next came the Twelfth Regiment, with ten commands of sixteen files front. As they passed the reviewing stand the men marched in excellent form and received hearty applause. The Seventy-first, with nine commands of fourteen files, and the Eleventh, with six commands of twelve files, came next, and bringing up the rear of the foot soldiers of the National Guard came the Twenty-second Regiment, with ten commands of sixteen files, headed by Gilmore's band. As the regiment passed the reviewing stand the band and fife and drum corps played a medley composed of the Marseillaise and Yankee Doodle, and just as the band passed the President the tune was changed to "Hail to the Chief." The French guests and the spectators along the walk cheered heartily. The artillery of the First Brigade, composed of the First and Second Batteries, brought up the rear of the militia portion of the parade. The speakers' platform was handsomely decorated with flags and banners and presented a fine appearance. In the centre of the speakers' platform was an immense United States flag surmounted by a large banner on which was inscribed the name "A. Bartholdi" and the word "Liberty." On both sides was the tri-color of France. The platforms for the guests were all ready and the soldiers and police were on guard. At the last moment it had been decided to entrust the nominal task of preserving order to the police, and accordingly 200 members of the Metropolitan force were on duty under the command of Capts. Clinchy and Killilea. Military sentries were also posted on the ramparts. Below was Capt. Egan's Battery of six guns from Newport in readiness to fire the salutes. Lieut. Adams of the Fifth Artillery was in charge of the firing party. The troops on duty were from Fort Columbus, Fort Schuyler, and Governor's Island.

MR. PRESIDENT: Upon the recommendation of the President of the United States, Congress authorized and directed the President "to accept the colossal statue of Liberty Enlightening the World' when presented by citizens of the French Republic, and to designate and set apart for the erection thereof, a suitable site upon either Governor's or Bedloe's Island, in the harbor of New York; and upon the completion thereof shall cause the same to be inaugurated with such ceremonies as will serve to testify the gratitude of our people for the expressive and felicitous memorial of the sympathy of the citizens of our sister Republic.

The statue on the 4th of July, 1884, in Paris, was delivered to and accepted by this Government, by the authority of the President of the United States, delegated to and executed by Minister Morton. To-day, in the name of the citizens of the United States, who have completed the pedestal and raised thereon the statue, and of the voluntary Committee who have executed the will of their fellow citizens, I declare in your presence, and in the presence of these distinguished guests from France, and of this august assemblage of the honorable and honored men of our land, and of this countless multitude, that this pedestal, and the united work of the two republics, is completed, and surrendered to the care and keeping of the Government and people of the United States.

The ceremony of unveiling the statue of Liberty then took place, and was followed by a salvo from all the guns in the harbor. After music President Cleveland formally accepted the statue. An address was then made by the representative of the republic of France, Le Minister Plenipotentiare et Delegué Extraordinaire, A. Lefaivre. There was more music by Gilmore's Twenty-second Regiment Band, and then Mr. Chauncey M. Depew delivered the commemorative address. "Old Hundred" was played by the band, and the assembly joined in singing the Doxology. The ceremonies were closed with the benediction, pronounced by the Rt. Rev. Henry C. Potter, D. D., Assistant Bishop of the Diocese of New York. A national salute was then fired simultaneously by all the batteries in the harbor, afloat and ashore.

The programme provides for this evening an illumination of the statue, with fireworks on Bedloe's and Governor's Islands, and the Battery.

A dinner in honor of the French guests will be given at Delmonico's this evening by the Chamber of Commerce.

Blizzard Blocks Broadway

It began just after midnight on March 12, 1888. In the next 24 hours, 21 inches of snow would fall on the city and form huge drifts driven by winds as high as 60 miles per hour. All the roads and highways were blocked when New Yorkers woke up that Monday morning, and walking or riding a horse were nearly impossible. "The average New Yorker is a man not easily surprised," wrote the *Post* on the front page, "but thousands of them were surprised very thoroughly this morning, and must have wondered when they arose from their beds and looked out of their windows whether some malignant wizard had not transported them during the night to the land of blizzards."

Those who ventured out were struck by a wind that "hurled the snow in their faces like thousands of fine needles," and everyone was in danger of "swinging signs and shutters, as they were

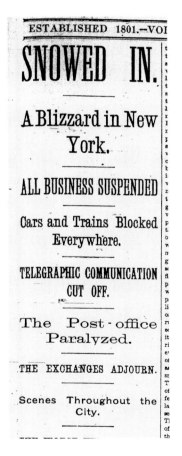

Front-page headlines from days 1 through 4 of the storm.

OPPOSITE: *Telegraph wires blown down on Wall Street by the blizzard. (New York Historical Society)*

very liable to [come] . . . crashing down on the sidewalk." The most dramatic sign of the storm's strength was the tangle of telegraph and telephone poles and wires down on the ground or hanging at crazy angles into the streets. This dangerous situation led to a new city policy the following year, ordering that all wires be placed underground—a transformation that was badly needed for safety as well as aesthetic reasons.

When cleanup started on Wednesday, another front-page article noted that able-bodied men, in true New York entrepreneurial style, were hiring themselves out to the railroad companies for shoveling for 40 to 60 cents an hour. The paper considered this "extortion," adding that "almost any one can get $1 for clearing a sidewalk."

In New York, property damage from the blizzard was estimated at $20 to $25 million. The "Nor'easter" also paralyzed Washington, Philadelphia and Boston, and a total of 400 lives were lost.

Wheat, Wine and Weights

Advertisements from the 1880s

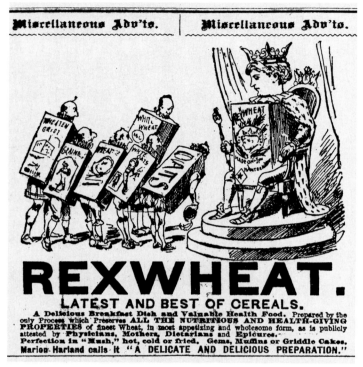

Post: 1; Tammany: 0

Post Causes a National Sensation Covering City Corruption

In 1890, the *Post* stepped up its war efforts against Tammany Hall, the Democratic Party machine in New York. Under Editor in Chief E.L. Godkin, the paper waged new battles on Tammany that included a famous, nine-column exposé that profiled each of the 28 men on the Executive Committee. This article, from April 3, 1890, contained biting profiles of each man's background and a list of crimes and occupations that colored their personal and professional histories. The list began: "Professional Politicians, 28; Convicted Murderer, 1," and included "Former 'Toughs', 4"; and "Sons of Liquor-Dealers, 2."

The *Post*'s incentive for delivering this bold report came from a recent article in *Harper's Weekly* praising the new Tammany mayor and announcing that a "New Tammany" had done away with its shady dealings and corruption. *Post* editors were baffled that *Harper's* could fall for such shrewd PR work on the part of the mayor—especially since it had made such strides against Tammany in recent years by publishing Thomas Nast's cartoons about Boss Tweed. By bringing the real story to the public, the *Post* started a wave of public awareness that ultimately resulted in the fall of Tammany's power. The April article gave New Yorkers the inside story on those who controlled the purse strings of the city, a motley group of boxers ("pugilists"), liquor dealers, gamblers and convicted felons.

The first biographical sketch described the mayor, "Hughy" Grant, as a man who "claims to be a lawyer," who "followed the race-tracks" and "was brought up by his guardian, a pawn-broker." The profile revealed that as sheriff, Grant accepted illegal money and had been found by a grand jury to run an office that was "mercenary, slovenly, and wholly indecent."

The article caused a sensation. Half of the important newspapers of the East reprinted it within the next few days. Editor in Chief Godkin remarked that Tammany politicians were suddenly coming out of their dark little holes, "squealing and showing their teeth," because the three things a Tammany leader dreaded most were the penitentiary, honest industry and biography.

A few of the men profiled in the article tried to sue the paper, but each case was dismissed or never even made it to the grand jury. Tammany officials did their best to make Godkin's life miserable—he was constantly receiving summonses and, at the height of the fiasco, was arrested three times in one day.

The deep roots of the city's corruption could not be pulled out

Two excerpts from the eight-column attack on Tammany Hall leaders published by the Post *on April 3, 1890. The article was picked up by dozens of leading papers and helped raise national awareness about the rampant corruption in New York City's government.*

THE "NEW TAMMANY"

Interesting Biographical Sketches of Its Leaders.

The government of Tammany Hall is exercised by its Executive Committee of twenty-seven members. Twenty-four of them are the leaders of the Tammany organizations in the Assembly districts of the city. Three of them are members *ex-officio*, because of being chairmen of sub-committees of the Tammany Hall General Committee. At present these three are Richard Croker, Tammany's chosen leader, Bourke Cockran, and Thomas F. Gilroy. They, with Mayor Grant, constitute the so-called "Big Four," who exercise almost supreme control over the Executive Committee. These twenty-eight men form, therefore, the council which, through Tammany Hall, is ruling the city and supplying it with officials. We give careful biographical sketches of all of them, compiled from the best obtainable data, verified by examination of official and court records, and believed to be trustworthy in every respect.

---

overnight. But the *Post* article did an enormous service by making the idea of a "New Tammany" something to laugh at, and the problems at City Hall became clear to everyone. In the city elections of 1894, Tammany lost two crucial posts. The new Republican mayor, William M. Strong, and recorder, John W. Goff, launched reforms that significantly improved the lives of New Yorkers.

Decade Ten

1891-1900

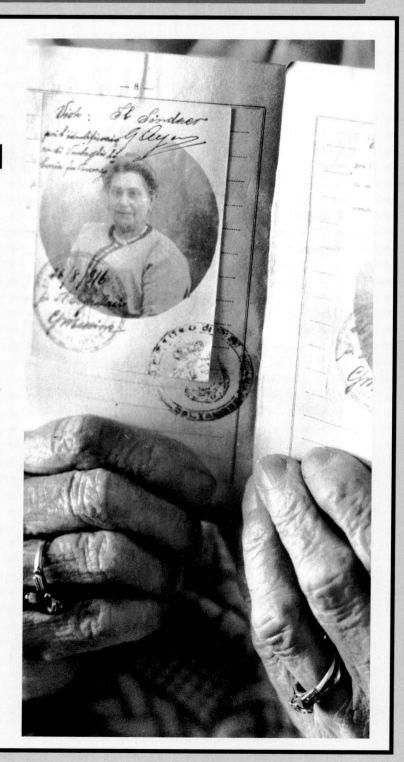

O n December 31, 1897, New Yorkers had more than New Year's Eve to celebrate. At the stroke of midnight, Manhattan and the surrounding communities officially joined together to become the City of Greater New York, the second biggest city in the world. The Industrial Revolution exploded in the dockyards and industrial sections of Brooklyn, and Manhattan was the business center of the United States. With consolidation, building and shipping and doing business in general became more organized and efficient.

Millions of the immigrants who wanted to make a new life in the United States took their first steps in the new land on Ellis Island, site of the immigration center that opened in this decade.

Anna Pasquale, 87, holds the passports her grandmother and she presented at Ellis Island when they emigrated from Italy. (Post photo by Charles Wenzelberg)

Gotham Grows

LAST NIGHT OF OLD NEW YORK

CELEBRATION FOR THE NEW YEAR
AND NEW CITY TO-NIGHT.

Carnival Parade, Flag-Raising, Choral Singing, Bomb-Firing, Chime-Ringing, and a Solemn Religious Service.

VIEW OF THE
CITY OF NEW YORK
AND VICINITY.
AUGUST R. OHMAN
Geographical Publisher
NEW YORK

By the late 1800s, 40 local governments made the running of New York's harbors and industry a bureaucratic nightmare. The city's leading merchants, led by Andrew Haswell Green, created a plan to connect all the boroughs and therefore streamline the city's shipping, railroad and utilities industries.

On January 1, 1898, great New York became the City of Greater New York as Manhattan, Brooklyn, Queens, the Bronx and Staten Island officially joined together under one city government. On New Year's Eve before consolidation, a celebration was held at City Hall in Manhattan with bands and fireworks. At the stroke of midnight, New York's population jumped from 2 million to 3.2 million, making it the second largest city in the world, next to London. From that moment, New York was a city encompassing 360 square miles, crossed by nearly 3,000 miles of streets.

Melding dozens of departments was a major challenge of the new year. In an article of January 1, entitled "Shifting the Policemen," the *Post* reported that "the commission had a long discussion over the best method of bringing about immediate organization of the Greater New York police. The trouble about the status of some of the policemen in the outlying districts, where appointments were made in November and December, is causing a hitch in effecting an immediate organization." Questions over new jurisdictions in the court system and other problems were outlined on the same page under the heading "Consolidation Complications."

ABOVE: *Map of Greater New York, published six years after the consolidation of Manhattan, Brooklyn, Queens, the Bronx and Staten Island. (New York Historical Society)*

LOCAL JOTTINGS.

Held for Selling Liquor to a Child. John Smith, barkeeper for John Neally, proprietor of the saloon at No. 2274 Eighth Avenue, who was arrested Monday night for selling liquor to a ten-year-old girl, was arraigned before Justice Kelly in the Harlem Police Court this morning, pleaded not guilty and was held in $300 bail for General Sessions.

§ § §

Fire Set by Boy Tramps. Patrolman Tarpey stopped John Fantry and William Voight, who were running past him at Sixty-seventh Street and Amsterdam Avenue at 3:30 o'clock this morning. They said they were "not doing nothing," but he took them back and discovered and sent an alarm for a fire, which they had caused in the cellar of the tenement No. 125 Amsterdam Avenue. The fire was put out before much damage was done, but the tenants were greatly disturbed. The boys told Magistrate Flammer that they built the fire to keep warm. They have homes. They were sent to the workhouse.

§ § §

Risked His Life for a Dog. The Rescue of Mrs. Dorney's Pug in a Boarding-house Fire. The boarding-house kept by Mrs. Laura Decew at No. 141 West Fifteenth Street was visited by a fire at 1:30 o'clock this morning, which caused much excitement among the inmates who were driven into the street. The fire broke out in a back room on the second floor occupied by two boarders named Reardon and Brown. They had gone out leaving the light burning, and a window open. A gust of wind blew the lace curtain against the gas jet, and in an instant the place was ablaze.

The front room in the second floor is occupied by Mr. and Mrs. Richard Dorney. Mrs. Dorney has a valuable English pug dog which she brought over from England a few weeks ago, and when they were driven from their apartments neither thought of the dog. Mrs. Dorney offered ten

dollars to any one who would bring out the dog. Edward Owens, a young nephew of Mrs. Decew, accepted the offer. By this time the flames were burning across the hall on the second floor, and the undertaking was dangerous. The room occupied by Mrs. Dorney was filled with smoke, but young Owens found the pug, who was crouching under the sofa, dragged him out, put him under his coat, and retraced his steps. He dashed through the flames in the hall and made his way down stairs. Young Owens sustained severe burns on the hands and face, and went to the New York Hospital.

§ § §

An Insane Man's Foot Crushed. Patrolman Hughes saw a man standing at Forty-second Street and Third Avenue shouting at the top of his voice at four o'clock this morning. Going up to the man, the policeman saw that his shoe had been torn and his foot was crushed. "A Wagon jumped on me, and then flew away," said the man. The policeman summoned an ambulance from Flower Hospital, but the man refused to allow his foot to be dressed, saying: "I'm a millionaire, and I won't allow any ambulance surgeon to attend my foot!" The ambulance returned to the hospital, and the man, taken to the station-house, began to talk about flying-machines falling on him, and gave other symptoms of insanity. The sergeant summoned another ambulance. Again the man resisted aid, but he was put in a strait-jacket, and carried off to Bellevue Hospital.

§ § §

A Girl's Suicide. Kate Breen, twenty-four years old, living at No. 2123 Eighth Avenue, committed suicide this morning by swallowing a large dose of carbolic acid. The police of the One Hundred and Twenty-fifth Street Station notified the Coroner.

The young woman was employed in a book-bindery as forewoman, and earned $15 a week. She was the sole support of a mother and elder sister, with whom she lived. Last night she appeared to be in her normal condition, but this morning she complained of a severe headache, and at seven o'clock went to the drugstore . . . to buy some medicine. She bought fifteen cents' worth of carbolic acid and drank it on her way home.

§ § §

George Ulsblom, twenty-four years old, of Westfield, N.J., went to the Mulberry Street Police Station at 5:50 o'clock this morning bleeding from a slight pistol-shot wound in the back. He said that he was coming through Elizabeth Street and was shot by some unknown person. An ambulance surgeon from St. Vincent's Hospital dressed the wound and he left for home.

Broad Street, 1890s. (Post *photo*)

Top Hats and Timepieces

Advertisements from the 1890s

No Tonic can rival
NICHOLSON'S

Most Popular and Palatable.

LIQUID BREAD

Most Nutritious and Invigorating

An absolutely pure MALT EXTRACT.

Baking Powder.

ROYAL BAKING POWDER

Absolutely Pure

Kennedy 12 Cortlandt St.

BEST HATS YET

The perfection of the Hatter,' art at first hands, saving middlemen's profit.

50 Styles, the regular $2.50 kind..	$1.90
The regular $3.00 kind, lined or skeleton	$2.35
A Derby worth $4.00, lined or skeleton	$2.90

Sl'k Hats $4.89, worth $7.00.

Hello! Hello!

Have you heard of **H-O** the Perfect Oatmeal?

THE H-O CO'S FLOUR IS TOO GOOD FOR BREAD.

Veuve Clicquot Champagne.

Yellow Label "Sec"
Gold Label "Brut"

The house of Veuve Clicquot supplies but one quality, THE VERY FINEST.

PELHAM BAY FRANCHISE REPASSED.

The Evening Post.

LAST EDITION · LAST EDITION

ESTABLISHED 1801—VOL. 94. · NEW YORK, MONDAY, APRIL 8, 1895. — TWELVE PAGES. · PRICE THREE CENTS.

NEW YORK, 1895

Population: 3.4 million
Mayor: William L. Strong
Governor of New York: Levi P. Morton
Post Newspaper Price: $9.00/year (1898)
Staten Island Ferry Fare: 10¢
Theater Ticket, Best Seat: $1.50
Columbia College Tuition: $150.00–$200.00/year

■ Developed Areas

(all dollar figures non-adjusted)

MACY'S

BOTH SIDES OF 14TH ST. (Running through from 13th to 15th Street).
SIXTH AVENUE.

CLOCKS AND BRONZES.

Our CLOCK and BRONZE DEPARTMENT has been moved to enlarged quarters on Second floor, Sixth Ave. side, where we are displaying a MAGNIFICENT line of goods specially adapted for HOLIDAY PRESENTS, comprising:

**Clocks, Bronzes,
Cabinets,
Library Tables,
Statuary,
Antique Hall Clocks,**

MANTEL CLOCKS (see cut), style Second Empire, marbleized, worth $7.50, choice... **2.99**

HANGING CLOCKS, in Swiss carved wood (see cut) with cuckoo.... **3.98**

EASEL CLOCK (see cut), Ansonia movement, brass with gold finish...... **1.79**

MANTEL CLOCKS (see cut), delft and floral decorations, 8 day movements **2.99**

CHINA CLOCKS (see cut), over two hundred distinct styles, from $3.66 down to medium size.................. **1.98**

MANTEL SET (see cut), French Gilt, comprising two four-light Candelabras and Clock, illuminated dial, 8 day French movement, worth $25.00 per set.................. **15.49**

SPECIAL VALUE—TABLE (see cut), brass finish, 8 inch Mexican Onyx top. LAMP with globe to match, burner and chimney ready for use, both pieces complete for.................. **3.94**

3.98

1.79

2.99

1.98

15.49

3.94

2.99   **15.49**   **3.94**

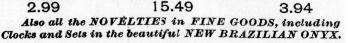

Also all the NOVELTIES in FINE GOODS, including Clocks and Sets in the beautiful NEW BRAZILIAN ONYX.

Ellis Island Immigration Center Opens

ABOVE: *Ellis Island, 1890s.* BELOW LEFT: *Immigrants arriving at Ellis Island.* (Post *photos*)

Between January 1, 1892, and 1924, 16 million immigrants passed through the rooms of the federal immigration center located on tiny Ellis Island in Upper New York Bay. The central French Renaissance–style building that stands today replaced the original wooden buildings that were destroyed by fire in 1897. Many more buildings were built over the years as the huge number of immigrants overwhelmed the existing space. The government had to increase the size of the island itself—with landfill—to accommodate more buildings.

A NEW POLICE BOARD.

MESSRS. ROOSEVELT, GRANT, AND PARKER SWORN IN.

Teddy Roosevelt and the NYPD

Among Mayor Strong's reforms in the 1890s was the hiring of a new president of the Police Commission—Theodore Roosevelt. A native of the city, graduate of Harvard, former state assemblyman and member of the city affairs committee, Roosevelt had earned a reputation as an energetic fighter of corruption and a reformer in his own right. In the *Post*'s front-page article announcing the new police board, Roosevelt was quoted: "We will lose no time . . . in taking charge of the Police Department."

The new commissioner received national press attention for original tactics such as his "midnight rambles," in which he would take to the streets to see if policemen were at their posts and to check city crime firsthand. He also made it policy that police must attend target practice, a rule that was the forerunner of establishing a police academy, one of the first in the United States.

Roosevelt was elected Governor of New York in 1898 and chosen as the vice presidential candidate for McKinley two years later. When McKinley was assassinated in office in September 1901, Roosevelt became the 26th President of the Untied States. He was overwhelmingly re-elected for a second term in 1904.

OPPOSITE: *Theodore Roosevelt, New York City Police Commissioner, at his desk ca. 1895. He would later become Governor of New York and the 26th President of the United States.* (Photo: Theodore Roosevelt Collection, Harvard College Library)

Part III
1901–1950

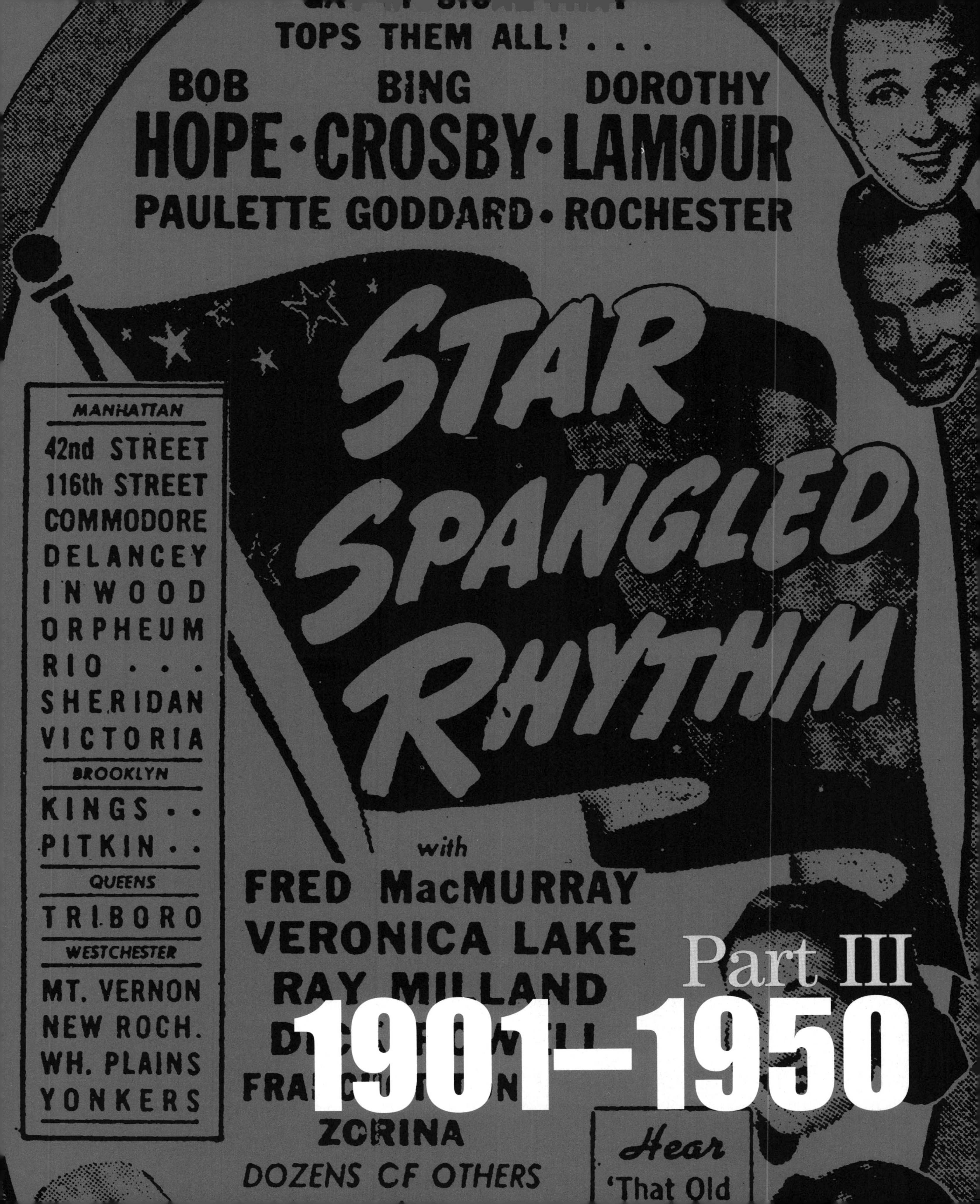

NEW YORK POST

Decade Eleven

1901-1910

Greater New York's population boomed to more than 4.7 million by 1910, and the city answered the need for quick transportation within and between the boroughs with the opening of the first subway line in 1904.

A small story that would one day have enormous historic impact appeared in 1903 under the heading BOX-KITE FLYING MACHINE, a three-paragraph narrative about the first test flight of a flying machine by an aviator named Wilbur Wright.

This was also the time of the nation's first big modern crime story—the assassination of President William McKinley. The close-range shooting spurred the formation of a new, full-time force to guard the president, the Secret Service.

Subway Premieres

Urbanites Go Underground

Even with the elevated trains that had arrived in the late 1860s, New York's overcrowded streets called for a more speedy public transportation system like the underground trains that opened in London in 1863. New York's first experiment with a subway came in 1870, when a "pneumatic tunnel" beneath Broadway near City Hall was presented to the public. Merely 312 feet of track, the project never got beyond the prototype stage and three decades would pass before the city opened its first real subway line. On October 27, 1904, the Interborough Rapid Transit Company (IRT) began service on the line running from City Hall to the central Bronx. A second line was approved to connect Brooklyn to the city via a tunnel underneath the East River. The entire system was in place by 1908. The New York City subway stood out from London's by having four tracks that provided both express and local service in both directions.

The system expanded in Manhattan, Brooklyn, Queens and the Bronx through the 1940s with ridership reaching a peak in 1947 with 2,050,000 straphangers. After this, with many trains falling into disrepair, the system began to decline in funding and ridership. The number of passengers using the subway fell drastically in the 1960s and 1970s with rising unemployment and a tide of movement to the suburbs. Heavy crime, panhandling, graffiti and homelessness added to the system's problems. In the early 1980s, the Metropolitan Transit Authority received a huge budget increase and began a major overhaul including the addition of thousands of new and refurbished cars, air-conditioning in every car and improved stations and tracks. The Transit Police was also expanded, which helped reduce crime and entice riders underground. The New York City subway covers more area than any other system in the world, with 722 miles of track, and is the transportation of choice for a majority of those who work in Manhattan.

NYC Subway Fare History	
1904	.5¢
1948	.10¢
1953	.15¢
1966	.20¢
1970	.30¢
1972	.35¢
1975	.50¢
1980	.60¢
1981	.75¢
1983	.90¢
1984	$1.00
1990	$1.15
1992	$1.25
1995	$1.50

OPPOSITE: *Photo of Broadway in 1901, from the Post 100th Anniversary supplement.* ABOVE AND RIGHT: *The first New York City subway opened in 1904, and construction continued on new lines extending through Manhattan, Brooklyn, Queens and the Bronx. These Post archive photos show aboveground and underground subway construction in 1928.*

ESTABLISHED 1801.— VOL. 100.

HOPE FOR McKINLEY

No Serious Symptoms Yet.

X-RAYS MAY BE USED

Bullet to Be Extracted if Found.

Assassination!

President William McKinley Shot

Vice President Teddy Roosevelt was hunting in the Adirondack wilderness when the news came. The president, who had been shot one week before but was reportedly on the road to recovery, had suddenly taken a turn for the worse and died. Roosevelt rushed to the scene in Buffalo, New York.

Before the shooting on September 6, 1901, the president had just finished his address at the Pan-American Exhibition in Buffalo and was shaking hands with members of the audience. Making his way to the front of the crowd, the assassin, Leon Czolgosz, fired two shots with a .32 revolver at close range. He confessed to planning the killing for days and described himself as an anarchist. The shooter was executed for his crime.

One bullet failed to penetrate, but the other lodged in the president's abdomen, and in emergency surgery the doctor failed to find the bullet or clean the wound. This led to a gangrenous infection of the intestines that ended the president's life. The first medical report hinted at the possible problems of infection that could arise: "The further course of the bullet could not be discovered, although careful search was made. The abdominal wound was closed without drainage. No injury to the intestines or other abdominal organ was discovered."

McKinley's assassination compelled the new president to step up security measures, as the old policy had called for only minimal, part-time protection of the president. The Secret Service was officially launched during Theodore Roosevelt's first term. The McKinley assassination was the first big crime of the modern era, and presidents and their families would never again travel or greet the public unguarded.

LEFT: *President William McKinley.* (Post *archives*)

BOX-KITE FLYING MACHINE.

First Flight

"A flying machine" made its first successful flight on December 17, 1903, according to this article that appeared in the *Post* on the following day. "The idea of the box kite has been adhered to in the basic formation of the flying machine," says the article, which introduced readers to the names Wilbur and Orville Wright for the first time.

Norfolk, Va., December 18.—A successful trial of a flying machine is reported to have been made yesterday near Kitty Hawk, N. C., by Wilbur and Orville Wright, of Dayton, Ohio. The machine, it is said, flew for three miles in the face of wind blowing at the registered velocity of twenty-one miles an hour, and then descended to earth at the spot selected by the man in the navigator's car as a suitable landing place. The machine has no balloon attachment, but gets its force from propellers worked by a small engine.

Preparatory to its flight the machine was placed upon a platform near Kitty Hawk. This platform was built on a high sand hill, and when all was in readiness the fastenings to the machine were released and it started down an incline. The navigator, Wilbur Wright, then started a small gasoline engine which worked the propellers. When the end of the incline was reached the machine gradually arose until it attained an altitude of sixty feet. In the face of the strong wind blowing it maintained an even speed of eight miles an hour.

The idea of the box kite has been adhered to in the basic formation of the flying machine. A huge frame work of light timbers, thirty-three feet wide, five feet deep and five feet across the top forms the machine proper. This is covered with a tough but light canvas. In the centre is the navigator's car, and suspended just below the bottom plan is a small gasoline engine which furnishes the motive power for the propelling and elevating wheels. There are two six-bladed propellers, one arranged just below the centre of the frame so gauged as to exert an upward force when in motion, and the other extends horizontally to the rear from the centre of the car, furnishing the forward impetus. Protruding from the centre of this car is a huge fan-shaped rudder of canvas, stretched upon a frame of wood. This rudder is controlled by the navigator and may be moved to each side, raised or lowered.

> *"The navigator, Wilbur Wright, then started a small gasoline engine which worked the propellers. When the end of the incline was reached the machine gradually arose until it attained an altitude of sixty feet. . . . it maintained an even speed of eight miles an hour."*
>
> —ARTICLE, DECEMBER 1903

BELOW: *The Wright brothers and their flying machine, 1903. (New York Public Library)*

Lights, Liners and Literature

Advertisements from the 1900s

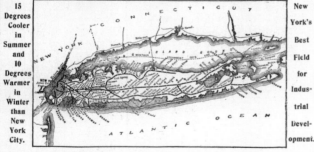

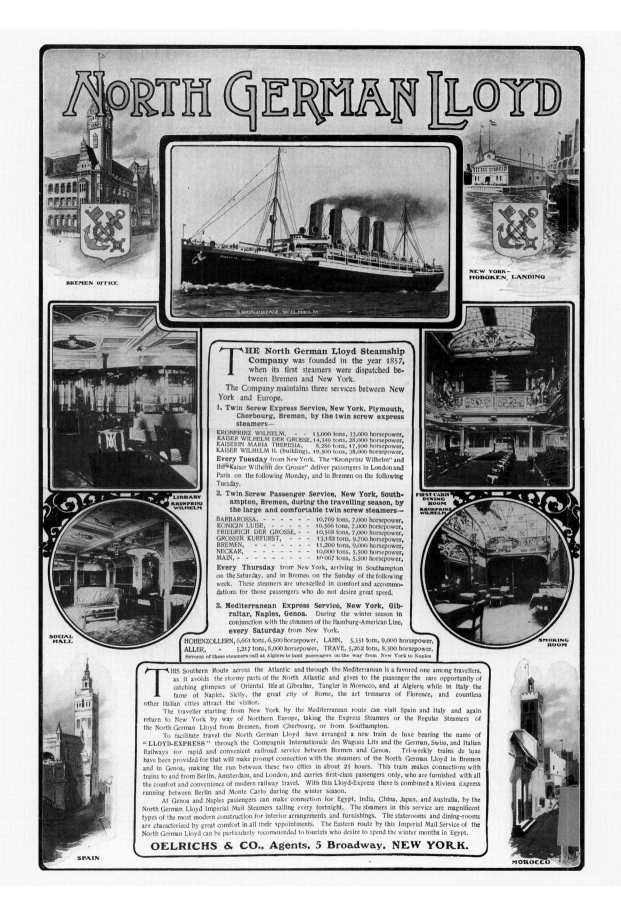

NORTH GERMAN LLOYD

BREMEN OFFICE

NEW YORK–HOBOKEN LANDING

KRONPRINZ WILHELM

LIBRARY KRONPRINZ WILHELM

FIRST CABIN DINING ROOM KRONPRINZ WILHELM

SOCIAL HALL

SMOKING ROOM

THE North German Lloyd Steamship Company was founded in the year 1857, when its first steamers were dispatched between Bremen and New York.

The Company maintains three services between New York and Europe.

1. **Twin Screw Express Service, New York, Plymouth, Cherbourg, Bremen**, by the twin screw express steamers—

KRONPRINZ WILHELM, - - - 15,000 tons, 33,000 horsepower,
KAISER WILHELM DER GROSSE, 14,349 tons, 28,000 horsepower,
KAISERIN MARIA THERESIA, 8,286 tons, 17,500 horsepower,
KAISER WILHELM II. (building), 19,500 tons, 38,000 horsepower,

Every Tuesday from New York. The "Kronprinz Wilhelm" and the "Kaiser Wilhelm der Grosse" deliver passengers in London and Paris on the following Monday, and in Bremen on the following Tuesday.

2. **Twin Screw Passenger Service, New York, Southampton, Bremen**, during the travelling season, by the large and comfortable twin screw steamers—

BARBAROSSA, - - - - - 10,769 tons, 7,000 horsepower,
KONIGIN LUISE, - - - - 10,566 tons, 7,000 horsepower,
FRIEDRICH DER GROSSE, - 10,568 tons, 7,000 horsepower,
GROSSER KURFURST, - - - 13,182 tons, 9,700 horsepower,
BREMEN, - - - - - - - 11,200 tons, 9,000 horsepower,
NECKAR, - - - - - - - 10,000 tons, 5,500 horsepower,
MAIN, - - - - - - - - 10,067 tons, 5,500 horsepower,

Every Thursday from New York, arriving in Southampton on the Saturday, and in Bremen on the Sunday of the following week. These steamers are unexcelled in comfort and accommodations for those passengers who do not desire great speed.

3. **Mediterranean Express Service, New York, Gibraltar, Naples, Genoa.** During the winter season in conjunction with the steamers of the Hamburg-American Line, **every Saturday** from New York.

HOHENZOLLERN, 6,661 tons, 6,500 horsepower, LAHN, 5,351 tons, 9,000 horsepower,
ALLER, - 5,217 tons, 8,000 horsepower, TRAVE, 5,262 tons, 8,500 horsepower.
Several of these steamers call at Algiers to land passengers on the way from New York to Naples

THIS Southern Route across the Atlantic and through the Mediterranean is a favored one among travellers, as it avoids the stormy parts of the North Atlantic and gives to the passenger the rare opportunity of catching glimpses of Oriental life at Gibraltar, Tangier in Morocco, and at Algiers; while in Italy the fame of Naples, Sicily, the great city of Rome, the art treasures of Florence, and countless other Italian cities attract the visitor.

The traveller starting from New York by the Mediterranean route can visit Spain and Italy and again return to New York by way of Northern Europe, taking the Express Steamers or the Regular Steamers of the North German Lloyd from Bremen, from Cherbourg, or from Southampton.

To facilitate travel the North German Lloyd have arranged a new train de luxe bearing the name of "LLOYD-EXPRESS" through the Compagnie Internationale des Wagons Lits and the German, Swiss, and Italian Railways for rapid and convenient railroad service between Bremen and Genoa. Tri-weekly trains de luxe have been provided for that will make prompt connection with the steamers of the North German Lloyd in Bremen and in Genoa, making the run between these two cities in about 25 hours. This train makes connections with trains to and from Berlin, Amsterdam, and London, and carries first-class passengers only, who are furnished with all the comfort and convenience of modern railway travel. With this Lloyd-Express there is combined a Riviera Express running between Berlin and Monte Carlo during the winter season.

At Genoa and Naples passengers can make connection for Egypt, India, China, Japan, and Australia, by the North German Lloyd Imperial Mail Steamers sailing every fortnight. The steamers in this service are magnificent types of the most modern construction for interior arrangements and furnishings. The staterooms and dining-rooms are characterized by great comfort in all their appointments. The Eastern route by this Imperial Mail Service of the North German Lloyd can be particularly recommended to tourists who desire to spend the winter months in Egypt.

OELRICHS & CO., Agents, 5 Broadway, NEW YORK.

SPAIN

MOROCCO

Post Helps Launch NAACP

In 1909, a small group of New York political reformers, shocked by recent racist riots in Abraham Lincoln's hometown of Springfield, Illinois, resolved to launch a national conference to discuss the national status and treatment of African-Americans that would "move the country." Their efforts would result in formation of the NAACP, the nation's oldest and most prominent civil rights organization.

Mary White Ovington, a politically active settlement house worker and organizer, decided to hold the mass meeting on February 12, 1909—the 100th anniversary of Lincoln's birth. To write a national call for action, she turned to *Post* owner Oswald Garrison Villard, who "received our suggestions with enthusiasm and aided us in securing the co-operation of able and representative men and women."

Villard was no stranger to the cause of civil rights: His grandfather, William Lloyd Garrison, had been America's most famous abolitionist in the period before the Civil War and had published the nation's leading anti-slavery newspaper, *The Liberator.*

"It was he who drafted the Lincoln's Birth Call" that was the NAACP's founding document "and helped give it wide publicity," White later wrote. Villard would soon become founding co-treasurer of the new organization and eventually chairman of the board of directors; he also provided the group with offices in the *Post* building at 20 Vesey Street.

The text of Villard's historic call follows:

The celebration of the Centennial of the birth of Abraham Lincoln, widespread and grateful as it may be, will fail to justify itself if it takes no note and makes no recognition of the colored men and women for whom the great Emancipator labored to assure freedom. Besides a day of rejoicing, Lincoln's Birthday in 1909 should be one of taking stock in the nation's progress since 1865.

How far has it lived up to the obligations imposed upon it by the Emancipation Proclamation? How far has it gone in assuring to each and every citizen, irrespective of color, the equality of opportunity and equality before the law, which underlie our American institutions and are guaranteed by our Constitution?

If Mr. Lincoln could revisit this country in the flesh, he would be disheartened and discouraged. He would learn that on Jan. 1, 1909, Georgia had rounded out a new confederacy by disenfranchising the Negro, after the manner of all the other Southern states. He would learn that the Supreme Court of the United States, supposedly a bulwark of American liberties, had refused every opportunity to pass square upon this disenfranchisement of millions, by laws avowedly discriminatory and openly enforced in such manner that the white men may vote and that black men be without a vote in their government; he would discover, therefore, that taxation without representation is the lot of millions of wealth-producing American citizens, in whose hands rests the economic progress and welfare of an entire section of the country.

He would learn that the Supreme Court, according to the official statement of one of its own judges, has laid down the principle that if an individual state chooses, it may make it a crime for white and colored persons to frequent the same marketplace at the same time, or appear in an assemblage of citizens convened to consider questions of a public or political nature in which all citizens, without regard to race, are equally interested.

In many states Lincoln would find justice enforced, if at all, by judges elected by one element in a community to pass upon the liberties and lives of another. He would see the black men and women, for whose freedom a hundred thousand of soldiers gave their lives, set apart in trains, in which they pay first-class fare for third-class service, and segregated in railway stations and in places of entertainment; he would observe that state after state declines to do its elementary duty in preparing the Negro through education for the best exercise of citizenship.

Added to this, the spread of lawless attacks upon the Negro, North, South and West—even in the Springfield made famous by Lincoln—often accompanied by revolting brutalities, sparing neither sex nor age nor youth, could but shock the author of the sentiment that "government of the people, by the people, for the people, shall not perish from the earth."

Silence under these conditions means tacit approval. The indifference of the North is already responsible for more than one assault upon democracy, and every such attack reacts as unfavorably upon whites as upon blacks. Discrimination once permitted cannot be bridled; recent history in the South shows that in forging chains for the Negroes, the white voters are forging chains for themselves.

A house divided itself cannot stand; this government cannot exist half-slave and half-free any better than it could in 1861.

Hence we call upon all the believers in democracy to join in a national conference for a discussion of present evils, the voicing of protests and the renewal of the struggle for civil and political liberty.

Among the many prominent signers of the document were two other *Post* figures: Editor in Chief Horace White and former muckraking reporter Lincoln Steffens.

ABOVE: *The NAACP logo.*

The Stanford White Murder

Reporting on one of the most sensational crimes in New York's history, the *Post*'s front-page article of June 26, 1906, read, "Harry K. Thaw, of Pittsburgh, was lodged in the Tombs this morning for the murder of Stanford White, the well-known architect, on the Madison Square Roof Garden last night."

The 52-year-old architect was shot in the head by his stalker, Thaw, an eccentric young millionaire who had married one of White's former mistresses. White's affair with the very young Evelyn Nesbit, a model, Gibson girl and actress, was one of the highly publicized stories that helped carry the era known as the Naughty Nineties into the next decade.

Evelyn Nesbit had carried on a long affair with White, but ended it before marrying Thaw. Crazed with jealousy over the fact that Evelyn had lost her virginity to White, Thaw became obsessed with following White's every move. On the evening of June 25, White went to Madison Square Garden at Madison Avenue and 26th Street—one of his own famous buildings—to attend a musical at the open-air theater on the roof. Both Evelyn and Harry Thaw were at the same performance. White had been warned by several friends about the mad millionaire, and Harry looked more peculiar than ever that warm evening in his long, heavy black coat. During the performance, he walked up to Stanford White's table and shot him three times with a pistol.

Evelyn Thaw stuck by her husband, as described in the *Post*'s retelling of the murder:

What Thaw Said After Shooting
Paul Brudi, a fireman detailed to duty in the Garden, said that he had noticed the strange figure in a long overcoat which appeared so unusual that he had kept an eye on the man. He heard only two shots. Then he followed Thaw and took the revolver from him. Asked by the assistant district attorney if Thaw had said anything, he responded, "Yes, he looked at me with big staring eyes, and said, 'He ruined my wife.'"

Warner Parson, the chief engineer of the Garden, who was in charge of the elevator, said that he had seen the shooting and afterward he had seen Thaw when he was taken down the elevator. There were others in the car including a woman, whom the witness had supposed to be Mrs. Thaw. This woman said to Thaw: "See what a fix you are in now." Thaw replied: "I've probably saved your life."

Lionel Lawrence, stage manager of the summer show at the Garden, said he had heard the first shot and turned in time to see the other two fired.

"Did you hear Mrs. Thaw say anything to her husband?"

"She said: 'Never mind, Harry, I'll stick to you through thick and thin.'"

Patrolman Anthony L. Debes, who arrested Thaw in the elevator, testified that Mrs. Thaw was in the elevator, and, according to Debes, she kissed her husband and asked: "Why did you do it that way?" to which Thaw replied: "Don't worry. Everything will be all right."

Harry Thaw was convicted and sent to Matteawan State Hospital for the Criminally Insane.

Stanford White's renowned buildings and structures in New York City included the second Madison Square Garden, Madison Square Presbyterian Church, the New York Herald Building, the Arch in Washington Square, and the Century Club, of which only the last two still stand.

Arctic Explorer

American black explorer Matthew Henson was a member of Robert E. Peary's expedition to the North Pole in 1909. Peary, Henson and four Eskimos were the first men to reach the North Pole and make exploration history. Henson had worked on ships since age 12 and was working in a store in Washington, D.C., when Peary met him. He was hired as Peary's valet, then joined the famous explorer on seven Arctic expeditions, including the one to the North Pole for which he and the other members of the expedition were awarded the Congressional Medal.

In 1913, one year after Henson published his memoir, *A Negro Explorer at the North Pole*, President William Howard Taft appointed him a clerk in the U.S. Customs House in New York City. Settling down at last, he held that post for 23 years until his retirement in 1936. Henson died in New York in 1955, and in 1988, on the 79th anniversary of the North Pole expedition, he and his wife were reinterred in Arlington National Cemetery and a special monument was erected in his honor.

ABOVE: *Stanford White. (New York Public Library)* RIGHT: *Matthew Henson accompanied Robert E. Peary to the North Pole in 1909.* (Post *photo*)

NEW YORK POST

Decade Twelve

1911-1920

New York sent thousands of soldiers to Europe when the nation entered World War I in 1917. The city faced its own battles in this decade, too, including a terrorist bomb on Wall Street and a deadly flu epidemic.

In 1918, the *Post* received journalism's highest honor, the Pulitzer Prize, for a series of articles that exposed the medieval horrors of the state prison at Trenton. These dramatic pieces not only brought the inhumane conditions of the prison to light, but ignited prison reform in New Jersey.

Early in the decade, one of the most famous disasters of all time occurred in the icy Atlantic, 1,150 miles from the port of New York. *Post* coverage of the *Titanic* story began with eerie hints from the first vague telegraph messages and culminated in powerful firsthand stories of the survivors.

Titanic Hit Berg

TITANIC HIT BERG

All Safe on Board, and She May Not Sink

PASSENGERS ON WAY TO HALIFAX

Five Other Steamships Rushed to Rescue in Response to Wireless "C. Q. D." Calls — The Virginian Was the First to Answer—Then Olympic and Baltic Turned Toward Scene, but Carpathia and Parisian Arrived First — Line's Spokesman Here Says Ship Is Unsinkable— Late Wireless Call Described as "Blurred" — Confidence Expressed in Ultimate Safety of the Vessel.

1,320 WENT DOWN

800 Titanic Passengers on Carpathia

VESSELS SEARCHING FOR BODIES.

The Biggest Ship Ever Launched Sank at 2:20 A. M., Yesterday, Four Hours After Hitting an Iceberg — She Was Then 1,150 Miles from this Port, to Which She Was Speeding on Her Maiden Voyage with 2,120 Persons on Board—Survivors Are Expected to Reach this Port on the Cunarder on Friday —Both Allan Line Ships Parisian and Virginian Have Reported That They Have No Survivors on Board.

The first news that came in over the telegraph wires about the great ship's accident was alarming but didn't explain the real scope of the tragedy. The *Post*'s headline on Monday, April 15, 1912, stated: TITANIC HIT BERG: ALL SAFE ON BOARD, AND SHE MAY NOT SINK: PASSENGERS ON WAY TO HALIFAX.

White Star line management in New York City received the same spotty information from the wires. The article of that first day gave the sketchy facts and included statements from the company's vice president, P.A.S. Franklin:

Out of the ice-strewn seas off the Newfoundland Banks, terse flashes of the wireless telegraph told to-day how the White Star liner Titanic, largest steamship afloat, had struck an iceberg on her maiden voyage to New York and was crawling or being towed slowly toward Halifax . . .

Vagueness, the shadowy vagueness of the open sea and illimitable distances, shrouded the story, which, even in its sketchiest outlines, loomed up as one of the most dramatic incidents of trans-Atlantic annals.

"We place absolute confidence in the Titanic," Franklin declared early in the day, in spite of the

OPPOSITE: Post *photo of a crowd celebrating the end of World War I in City Hall Park, November 11, 1918.*

alarming reports. "We believe the boat is absolutely unsinkable, and although she may have sunk at the head, or bow, we know that the boat would remain on the water. . . . We are not at all worried about the loss of the ship, but we are extremely sorry for the annoyance and inconvenience to our passengers and the traveling public."

The grim truth came out the next day. 1,320 WENT DOWN reported the *Post* headline. The article narrated the shocking facts:

Thirteen hundred and twenty persons were lost, and 800 were saved when the steamship Titanic, the biggest vessel ever launched, went to the bottom after collision with an iceberg, at 2:20 o'clock on Monday morning . . . 1,150 miles from this port, to which she was speeding on her maiden voyage.

The sea where this $10,000,000 fabric of the shipyards, this newest and most luxurious, and "safest," of ships, this "unsinkable boat," found her grave is two miles deep. The spot was only thirty miles south of where she had received the death blow from the ice.

After the survivors arrived in New York, the paper was filled with firsthand accounts of their experiences. On

Friday, an entire page was devoted to stories from women passengers including Miss Madeline Newell, who said:

> The shock was not sudden, but was more like that of an earthquake. The ship trembled, but I was not greatly alarmed, as I had perfect confidence in the great new ship, and the crew assured us that there was no danger.
>
> When I went on deck, it seemed to me that we had struck the iceberg almost head-on, but more to the right side of the bow. I believe that the side of the ship was ripped away.
>
> I left the Titanic in a boat about 2:15 o'clock—that was about a quarter of an hour before the ship sank. Many had refused to leave the big ship, and the men, Col. Astor and Major Butts, President Taft's aide, and the others, stood back and let the women get into the boats first. They were the most chivalrous men in the world.

Miss Hilda Slater, a passenger in the last boat to put off, told the *Post* that the orchestra members who kept playing until the very end were the most heroic men of the day. "There was a steady round of lively airs," she said. "It did much to keep up the spirits of every one and probably served as much as the efforts of the officers to prevent panic." She also recalled the selfless acts of two men:

> There were many touching scenes as the boats put off. I saw Col. John Jacob Astor hand his wife into a boat and then ask an officer whether he might

WOMEN IN BOATS

Their Story of How the Titanic Was Sunk

ORDER AND CHIVALRY THE RULE

Experiences of Those Who Were Aroused When Ship Struck Iceberg —Thought at First There Was No Danger and Were Allowed to Dress Without Hurrying — Boats Manned Without Much Disorder and the Few Cowards Were Kept at Bay by Officers with Revolvers.

also go. When permission was refused, he stepped back and coolly took out his cigarette case. "Good-bye," he called, as he lighted a cigarette, and leaned over the rail. "I'll join you later." Another man, a Frenchman, I think, approached one of the boats about to be lowered. He had with him two little boys. An officer waved him back sternly. "Bless you," he said, "I don't want to go, but for God's sake take the boys. Their mother is waiting for them in New York." The boys were taken aboard.

Two columns were filled with the dramatic story of Robert W. Daniel, a passenger who leapt into the frigid water two minutes before the ship went down and swam for an hour before being picked up by a lifeboat. Just after he jumped, he looked up at the captain who was still at his post:

> I saw Capt. Smith on his bridge. My eyes seemingly clung to him. The deck from which I had leaped was immersed; the water had risen slowly, and was now to the floor of the bridge. Then it was at Capt. Smith's waist.
>
> I saw him no more. He died a hero. The bow of the Titanic was far beneath the surface. It was all over in an instant.
>
> Until I die, the cries of those wretched men and women who went down clinging helplessly to the Titanic's rail will ring in my ears. Groans, shrieks, and sounds that were almost inhuman came across the water.

"The War to End All Wars"

BELOW: *A front-page headline in 1917 reports America's entry into World War I. The article highlighted the congressional debate that took place before the vote, stating: "More than a hundred speeches were delivered. . . . Proponents of the measure calmly and seriously declared that as a result of German violations of American rights a state of war really existed. Opponents pleaded that Germany's war . . . was forced by the British blockade, which was as much a violation of American rights as submarine warfare."*

[COPYRIGHT 1914. BY NEW YORK EVENING POST CO.] PRICE THREE CENTS.

MARTIAL LAW PROCLAIMED IN THE BOSNIAN CAPITAL

MAY CALL FOR STATE POLICE

Sheriff, Powerless to Restrain Strikers at Westinghouse Plant, May Appeal to Governor.

PITTSBURGH, June 29.—Disorder broke out among the striking Westinghouse employees in East Pittsburgh to-day. Pickets surrounded all entrances to the electric works and prevented persons from entering. Office men, foremen and

Anti-Servian Demonstration in Sarajevo

ASSASSIN'S AIM WAS UNERRING

HOUSE VOTE FOR WAR EARLY THIS MORNING

Resolution Passed with No Amendment

VOTE, 373 FOR TO 50 AGAINST

Final Action Came Soon After 3 o'Clock A. M., After Seventeen Hours of Debate—Party Lines Disappeared in the Division — The Democratic Floor Leader, Mr. Kitchin, and Miss Rankin, of Montana, Among Those Who Voted "No"—No Attempt Made to Limit Debate — House Adjourned Until Monday.

ABOVE: *The assassination of Archduke Ferdinand in Sarajevo, which ignited the war, reported on the front page on June 29, 1914. "For an instant after the attack," the article stated, "Field Marshal Pollorek thought the Archduke and the Duchess, seated opposite him, had again escaped. Neither uttered a sound, but a moment afterward the blood gushed from their mouths and throats, and it was seen that they had been mortally wounded."*

RIGHT: *Archduke Ferdinand, his wife and children.* FAR RIGHT: *An early World War I political cartoon.* (Post *archives*)

99

ABOVE: *American soldiers manning heavy artillery on a European battle-field. (Post archives) Over 116,000 Americans were killed during the war and more than 200,000 wounded.*

OPPOSITE: *Armistice Day— throngs of New Yorkers flooded onto Fifth Avenue to rejoice at the end of the war on November 11, 1918. (Post photo)*

The Evening Post

COMPLETE FINAL ★★★★★ TWELVE PAGES

DO NOT COMPILE FROM THIS PAPER FINAL ★★★★★

FOUNDED 1801.—VOL. 117. NO. 305. [MEMBER OF THE ASSOCIATED PRESS] NEW YORK, MONDAY, NOVEMBER 11, 1918. [COPYRIGHT 1918 N. Y. EVENING POST INC] 2 CENTS. In Greater New York and Within Commuting Distance—Elsewhere THREE CENTS.

GERMANY SURRENDERS; LOSES POWER TO RENEW WAR; GOES BACK ACROSS THE RHINE; GIVES UP MANY SHIPS; MAKES REPARATION; HER WAR TREATIES MADE VOID; PRESIDENT ANNOUNCES THE TERMS; CITY HAILS PEACE

CITY'S NOISY GREETING TO DAWN OF PEACE

Paraders Throng Streets,

COLOGNE CROWD FIRED ON STATUE OF KAISER

PARIS, November 11.—During the revolutionary disorders at Cologne a crowd tried to demolish with machine-gun fire a statue of Wil-

KING OF SAXONY HAS BEEN DETHRONED

Upheaval Involves Most

FAIR WEATHER PREDICTED.

LOCAL FORECAST.—Fair to-night and to-morrow, slightly warmer Tuesday. Fresh northeast winds, becoming southerly. Minimum temperature last night, 32 degrees.

ARMISTICE SIGNED AT DAWN TO-DAY

Hostilities Ended at 6

ARMISTICE TERMS BRIEFLY STATED

Following is a summary of the more important armistice terms granted to Germany:
Immediate evacuation of Bel-

ALLIED PRISONERS FREED; VAST SUPPLIES GIVEN UP

Book Pages

The Saturday book section of the 1920s, edited by Royal J. Davis, included long and short reviews and plenty of ads from New York publishers. An E.P. Dutton ad from January 1920 shows a strong interest in all things psychic, including *How to Speak with the Dead*, long before the arrival of John Edwards on national TV.

Our Military Heroes

"Heroes of the Army in America." By Charles Morris. Philadelphia: J. B. Lippincott Co.

A BOY'S book which has met with success in the past, as one of a series which brings out the part of history that appeals most strongly to youth—the exploits of individuals—has been brought up to date by the addition of a brief account of General Pershing's career. It is well that American youth should be made familiar with Putnam, and Stark, and Marion, and Light-Horse Harry, and Sam Houston, and the dashing soldiers of the Civil War on both sides, and Crook and Miles with their Indian exploits, by books like this. The other volumes in the series treat of the heroes of the navy, of discovery and of progress.

Selections from the Book Review section of January 17, 1920, and an illustration from a fashion column of the same year.

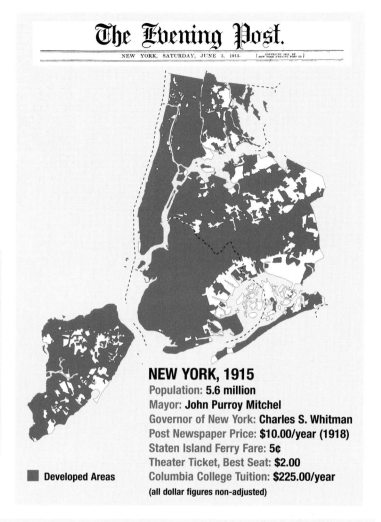

NEW YORK, 1915
Population: **5.6 million**
Mayor: **John Purroy Mitchel**
Governor of New York: **Charles S. Whitman**
Post Newspaper Price: **$10.00/year (1918)**
Staten Island Ferry Fare: **5¢**
Theater Ticket, Best Seat: **$2.00**
Columbia College Tuition: **$225.00/year**
(all dollar figures non-adjusted)

Hot Wheels and Deals

On January 7, 1920, the *Post* highlighted the New York Automobile Show and three of the new models being displayed. The article mentioned that one of the most popular exhibits was that of a "convertible roadster. The rear compartment of this car can be raised and folded over, converting the roadster into a comfortable five-passenger touring car."

The first New York Automobile Show was held in Madison Square Garden in 1900.

MUDDLED MANAGING SYSTEM TO BLAME FOR PRISON EVILS

Pulitzer Prize for Post

P*ost* writer Harold A. Littledale won the Pulitzer Prize in 1918 for his hard-hitting prison series that ran in January 1917. These articles revealed the horrible conditions at the New Jersey State Prison at Trenton, providing firsthand evidence that the prison blatantly violated the state law that "cruel and unusual punishments shall not be inflicted."

The series ran on the front page with powerful headlines such as THREE MEN SHACKLED IN THE TRENTON PRISON DUNGEONS and CONTRACT LABOR, ABOLISHED BY LAW IN 1911, EXISTS IN TRENTON. In the article published on January 13, Littledale described secret dungeons lying deep beneath the prison grounds. The tiny cells had no toilets or beds, just a chain joined to a shackle on the wall, and a man shackled in the cell could neither sit or lie down. Littledale visited the cells himself:

One of the worst, most vicious, most degrading features of the New Jersey State Prison at Trenton are the dungeons. Of these, there are fifteen in all. Eight of them are on the ground level, but they might as well be underground, for they are pitch black, and have no windows. Seven actually are underground—twenty feet underground. There is no doubt as to the existence of these, for, while ordinarily shown to no visitor, a reporter for the *Evening Post* got access to them. They are there. The writer has been in them. He has seen the ring-bolt in the wall and the chain that hangs down from that ring-bolt, the chain with which men have been shackled.

Twenty steps lead down to these seven separate hells.... At the twentieth step your boot hits cement. You feel this must be the bottom, but it is dark, and you are not certain ... In one wall, some seven feet above the floor of the dungeon, is a small window. but to give light and air to the State's wards incarcerated here would be too humane, indeed, far too humane, and so an iron shut-

ter has been made which completely excludes the light that brings only happiness and can do no harm.

You feel your way around the walls. Your foot strikes something. The grim, metallic ring of a chain resounds. You stoop to investigate. Your hand touches a cold, dank, rusted chain. In horror you let it fall. Then you take it again in your hand and feel along the links—one, two, three, four—until you find some eight inches above the level of the floor the ring-bolt in the wall to which it is fastened. You are now standing on your feet, your body bent over double, so that your head is within two feet of the ground, your arms stretched down. And it was so that men were chained, their wrists manacled, a handcuff

CONVICTS IN TRENTON COMPLAIN FOOD IS BAD

They Are Fed at Cost of 17 Cents a Day

NO DINING HALL FOR 1,300 MEN

Breakfast and Supper in Their Cells

COOKING SAID TO BE AT FAULT.

Charge that the Stew Is Mostly Water and Little Meat, that the Coffee is Undrinkable, that the Molasses Is Like Axle-Grease, the Fish Bad, and the Apples Black, Denied by Prison Officials—Cries of Men in Protest Often Heard by Those in the Streets—They Save Scraps of One Meal to Eat at the Next.

EDGE SOUNDS CALL FOR PRISON REFORM

Governor Tackles Problem in First Message

CONTRACT-LABOR EVIL TO END

Upon Occasion of His Inauguration at Trenton State Executive Asserts that System of Contract Labor Should Not Be Permitted to Remain Under Present Subterfuge — Believes Reform Lies in the Way of Penal Farms and Road Work for Convicts — He Will Call a Conference to Consider Prison Conditions.

TRENTON, January 16.—In his message to the Legislature upon the occasion of his inauguration to-day, Gov. Walter E.

binding fast the wrist-shackle and the chain. . . . The posture caused excruciating agony. Men screamed in their great pain. But their screams were of no avail, for each one of these dungeons, and each one of the eight other dungeons, is fitted with two doors, an inner door of wood and an outer door of sheet iron, made so that they fit exactly, and imprison in this tomb not only the man but the screams of that man.

The next article exposed the prison's illegal practice of hiring out convicts for contract labor. Even worse, they neglected to pay the convicts the pennies per day they were due. Prisoners who refused to work were sent to the underground cells, as detailed in the article of January 19:

In the underground dungeons of the New Jersey State Prison here lie three wretched men. In the midnight darkness of three separate hells they lie shackled to ring-bolts in the wall. They are there. The writer has seen the men and the shackles that are on them. Their names are James L. Green, James E. Hughes, and John Gerhardt.

Now, in the *Evening Post*'s exposures it has been said that these dungeons were not in use, that they have not been in use for months. And only two days ago Richard P. Hughes, the Warden of the prison, asserted that never again while he was in charge would these dungeons be used. But to-day these men are there. All last night they were there. All yesterday afternoon they were there. And all that time they have been in total darkness. All that time they have been shackled. All that time they have had nothing to eat but bread and water.

COMMITTEE TO INVESTIGATE NEW JERSEY STATE PRISON

Joint Resolution Provides for Body of Three Citizens — Edge Gets Consent of William S. Dicksen, of Montclair, to Act.

[Special Dispatch to The Evening Post.]

TRENTON, January 19.—Investigation of the *Evening Post's* charges against the New Jersey State Prison here will begin immediately.

THREE MEN SHACKLED IN THE TRENTON PRISON DUNGEONS

Seen To-day in Cells Far Underground

JERSEY CONVICTS GO HALF BLIND IN SHOP

HAD REBELLED AT THE FOOD

Worked Without Remorse by Contractors

Warden Had Said Dungeons Were Never Used

WHAT "REASONABLE OUTPUT" IS

How is it that these men are in these separate hells? The facts are that yesterday at noon lamb stew was served. Twice a week the convicts have stew. On Tuesday it is beef stew. On Thursday it is lamb stew. But in the stew yesterday some one found a cake of soap. And so the trouble began. There is some doubt as to how that soap came to be in the stew. Some say that the soap, which is used in cleaning the kitchen utensils, fell into the stew by accident; others insist that some convict put it there. Either story may be true. But, at any rate, there was the soap, and instantly all was in an uproar.

They shouted their protests at the top of their voices, and if you have never heard convicts shout you cannot have any idea of what a noise they make. . . . The warden took a spoon and tasted the stew, and he decided that there was no taste of soap in the stew. Then he left. . . . After the meal, two by two, these men in gray were led out to their toil in the contract shops. But the trouble had only begun. Once in the shops, Green and Hughes and Gerhardt and two others refused to work. . . . Warden Hughes . . . threatened the dungeons and the men jeered, until the keepers were called. Then two of them relented and returned to work, but the three, whom the horror of these dungeons could not break, were led away. They were placed in dungeons 3, 4, and 5.

To-day the writer saw these men. Down the twenty steps that lead to the dungeons that are underground he went, with the Warden leading, the lantern lighting the way.

Then a voice, as if from the tomb . . . "Some one came down the steps. They're going to take us up."

The hearts of these men were raised. Out of the tomb they were to come, they thought, for it was not yet time to get a slice of bread and a cup of water. For what reason would men come underground but to let them up?

Again the voice: "I done nothing. Just kicked at the rotten food, and here I am."

In the silence a chain rattled. A man had moved. And then a new voice, the voice of the third man: "Friends. Friends. I'm sitting on my bucket. My back's still bent over some, but it is not so bad as it was."

Littledale and the Warden spoke with the prisoners and returned to the prison office, where the Warden made a promise to the writer:

The Warden insisted that the men had dared him to put them there, and . . . [that] he had ordered them down into the dungeons he had declared he would never use again.

"But I promise you they will be brought out again today," he said. "And I promise you that never while I am here will those dungeons again be used."

And that Mr. Hughes will keep his promise the writer firmly believes, for Mr. Hughes is a man of honor, and not a hardened, brutal official.

The next day the paper's front-page headline declared: SHACKLED MEN FREED FROM TRENTON DUNGEONS. The article stated: "True to his word, Richard P. Hughes, Warden of the New Jersey State Prison, yesterday released from the underground dungeons of the prison James L. Green, James E. Hughes, and John Gerhardt, convicts, who were placed there because of a disturbance in the contract shops."

Littledale's series ignited a state investigation and the newly elected governor made prison reform a priority during his inauguration speech. "If New Jersey is to perform its duty to its criminal charges and itself, the prison problem must be solved," he said on January 16.

Harold Littledale's exposé received journalism's highest award and, more importantly, made a difference in the lives of prisoners in New Jersey.

CONTRACT LABOR, ABOLISHED BY LAW IN 1911, EXISTS IN TRENTON

Work of Convicts Farmed Out for a Pittance

MEN BROKEN IN TRENTON, SAYS BOYD

FAMILIES OF MANY IN WANT

"Place of Nightmare and Nervous Horror"

What Happens When Convicts Go on Strike

HE SERVED ONE YEAR THERE

"Gods of Ill Health": 1918 Flu Epidemic

"The present death-rate of New York is the greatest recorded in the annals of the city, a condition resulting from the epidemic of influenza and pneumonia," said the *Post* on October 16, 1918. "The total number of deaths last week was 3,808, and of these 979 were due to influenza."

The worldwide flu epidemic of 1918 was the worst in history, taking the lives of 15 to 21 million. The article excerpted above was published about six weeks into the epidemic, and the worst was yet to come. The New York City Board of Health hoped that the disease had reached its peak by that time: "Officials of the Board of Health are hoping that the 1918 outburst of the gods of ill health will recede after the third week." Their hopes were not fulfilled. By that date, 2,296 New Yorkers had died from the flu. Large daily figures would continue and, at the end of the outbreak, the New York death toll would be more than 12,000.

4,403 NEW CASES OF INFLUENZA REPORTED

Decline Since Figures of Yesterday

Pneumonia Record Also Shows Falling Off—Need for Nurses Throughout City Persists.

The increase in the number of new influenza cases reported to the Board of Health yesterday was not repeated to-day. Instead, the number dropped from 5,390 to 4,403, thus tending to bear out the official explanation yesterday that the record number of new cases was not due to an increase in the epidemic, but to the fact that a number of doctors happened to send in at the same time delayed reports of the disease. There was also a marked decrease in the new cases of pneumonia to-day—758, as against 852 recorded yesterday.

Deaths both from influenza and pneumonia showed a falling off. To-day's report was 443 from influenza and 316 from pneumonia in contrast to 461 and 390 yesterday.

The report of influenza and pneumonia by boroughs for the past twenty-four hours follows:

	New cases Infu.	Pneum.	Deaths Infu.	Pneum.
Manhattan	1,716	306	181	142
The Bronx	578	66	42	40
Brooklyn	1,027	269	163	107
Queens	294	92	43	22
Richmond	188	25	14	5
Total	4,403	758	443	316

CITY'S DEATH-RATE AT HIGHEST POINT

Most Virulent of All Influenza Epidemics

5,113 New Cases Are Reported To-day, the Highest Total Yet Reached.

Headlines and lists of new cases from October 1918 show the epidemic proportions of the flu outbreak.

The influenza and pneumonia record for the twenty-four hours ending at 9 A. M., to-day, follows by boroughs:

	New cases Infu.	Pneum.	Deaths Infu.	Pneum.
Manhattan	2,252	304	150	127
The Bronx	849	123	33	41
Brooklyn	1,419	84	101	124
Queens	400	56	22	17
Richmond	213	18	11	7
Total	5,113	585	317	316

A WORD of APPRECIATION

WHEN THE INFLUENZA EPIDEMIC was at its height, so many of our operators were absent that it was impossible to handle promptly all the telephone calls that were offered.

KNOWING that a word of explanation to the New York public would relieve the situation, we stated our case and asked our patrons to assist us by restricting their use of the telephone to necessary calls.

THE RESPONSE, as we expected, was immediate. Citizens' associations of all kinds, individual users both large and small, public telephone agents, in fact all classes of the telephone-using public gave us splendid cooperation.

THIS HELP was given cheerfully and willingly and the inconveniences were accepted with a good humor that greatly cheered those operators who were working so ably to carry the load during the absence of their fellow-workers.

WHILE MANY of our operators are still away and some restriction is still necessary on the general use of the telephone, the worst of a bad situation is now passed and we take this opportunity of expressing our appreciation of your kindly help.

THANK YOU!

NEW YORK TELEPHONE COMPANY

RIGHT: *A polite announcement from the telephone company thanks New Yorkers for cooperating during the epidemic when many operators were out sick.*

Collars, Caps and Colgate

Advertisements from the 1910s

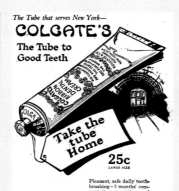

Ru-stella
The Phonograph with the master made horn

A Potent Influence in the Home

For Mother

Nothing is too good for Mother

After the home cares during the day, could an evening be spent better than with Music—with Ru-stella? Her happiness consists of two things—first seeing "her brood" happy and secondly being herself happy. If you would make mother profoundly happy— If you would see her radiant smile all the time— —if you, yourself, would be sincerely happy in seeing her happy— Buy her a

Ru-stella

The Only Phonograph Sold on a Strictly Cash Basis a truly great distinction.

Model A $184.00		Model C (Illustrated). $129.00
Model B $159.00	Model E $42.50	Model D $89.50

Representing a saving to you, of $35.00 to $100.00 on machines sold elsewhere on "convenient terms."

PAY CASH AND SAVE THE DIFFERENCE!

Macy—Music Dept., Fourth Floor, 34th Street, East.

R. H. Macy & Co
HERALD SQUARE   Inc.   NEW YORK

If moving this Spring, please tell us at your earliest convenience, that we may promptly disconnect the old and connect the new service

The New York Edison Company
At Your Service

General Offices: Irving Place and 15th Street

District Offices
where Electrical Appliances of all kinds are on display

Open Until Midnight

—HARPER BOOKS—

The Big Novel of 1920

THE MAN
of the
FOREST
By Zane Grey

A 250,000 Novel

Est. **HARPER & BROTHERS,** 1817

The Tube that serves New York—

COLGATE'S
The Tube to Good Teeth

Take the tube Home

25c
LARGE SIZE

Pleasant, safe daily tooth-brushing—3 months' commutation, morning and night. 100 round trips from "Good Teeth" to "Good Health."

COLGATE'S
RIBBON DENTAL CREAM.

DRY COLD STORAGE FOR FURS

Expert Care Reliable Insurance Prompt Service

Revillon Frères

5th AVE. at 53rd ST.
T E L E P H O N E

360
CIRCLE

Hats With Dash—

Formerly $8.50   Now   **$4.49**

Outclass all trimmed hats selling elsewhere at that price

On sale Friday.

Full of style—full of wear: our

Chauffeurs' Outfits

The photographs show their smart, trig lines. To realize what splendid service they give one must wear them. Offered in gray pure wool whipcord.

We're also displaying Palm Beach Outfits for Summer wear:

Suit	$22.50
Duster	$21.50
Cap	$3.50
Complete Outfit,	$47.50

Write or call for Chauffeurs' Apparel Chart and booklet picturing various outfits.

Brill Brothers
Broadway at 49th St.

Coat and Trousers..	$45.00
Overcoat....	$62.50
Cap	$4.00

ARROW COLLARS

WHEN you buy an Arrow you get the best that there is at the price you are asked to pay. That is the one big fundamental reason for the preference shown for Arrows.

Cluett, Peabody & Co., Inc. Troy N. Y.

Makers of Arrow Shirts and Gotham Underwear

Home Edition
The Weather
Fair to-night and Friday

The Evening Post

EXTI

FOUNDED 1801—VOL. 119, No. 256.   MEMBER OF THE ASSOCIATED PRESS.   NEW YORK, THURSDAY, SEPTEMBER 16, 1920.   COPYRIGHT 1920 N.Y. EVENING POST, INC.   THREE CENTS

EXPLOSION IN WALL ST. NEAR MORGAN'S OFFICE
FIFTEEN PERSONS KILLED, MANY BADLY INJUR

$5,500,000 More Needed to Finish Passaic Sewer

Estimated Cost of $11,500,000 Is Raised Now to $21,000,000

Boycotts in Ireland Futile; Drive Nation Nearer Civil War

Refusal to Buy Goods as Sectarian Reprisal Has Little Economic Effect—Special Constables Aggravate Situation

By Henry Clay

BELFAST, August 28.—Conditions in Ireland to-day fully justify the fears expressed at the Irish Peace Conference. Last week end six police-

Primary Results in Illinois Await Complete Count

Thompson Faction's Vote in Chicago Offset Through State

Ousted Socialists Look to Members of Other Parties

Expect Resentment Against Sweet Will Return Them to Albany

Wall Street Thrown Into Panic Exchange Closed For the Da Down Town Manhattan R

> *"Soon after the explosion there was a number of small boys running down Broad Street holding on to their heads, with the blood coming out between their fingers. . . ."*
>
> —ARTICLE, SEPTEMBER 1920

Bomb!

At noon on Thursday, September 16, 1920, an explosion behind the Stock Exchange building rocked the Wall Street district, killing 33 people, injuring hundreds and smashing all the windows in the area "to atoms."

The front-page article stated: "Soon after the explosion there was a number of small boys running down Broad Street holding on to their heads, with the blood coming out between their fingers. . . . The streets were soon packed with people watching the gruesome sight as the injured, many of them seriously so, were taken away from the scene of the disaster."

The next day the paper reported that the explosion was most likely caused by a bomb. Evidence of this came from iron fragments found at the site as well as gouging and pitting on the surface of the buildings. To this day, scars from the explosion can be seen on the Morgan Guaranty Trust building. "So far as the public is permitted to know," wrote the *Post* on the 17th, "mystery deep and devious shrouds the disaster." The investigation came up with one significant clue, the remains of the cart that held the bomb, but mystery still surrounds the bombing of 1920—the terrorists were never found.

RIGHT: *A* Post *photo of Wall Street in the early 1900s. The culprits who bombed it in 1920 were never found. (Post 100th Anniversary supplement)*

Decade Thirteen

1921-1930

The onset of Prohibition in 1920 ushered in a new era of mobster life in New York, with highly organized gangs ruling the liquor trade. Speakeasies, such as the famous 21 Club in Midtown, became the underground hangouts of celebrities, politicians, doctors and lawyers, and were the first public places in which women were seen smoking.

In 1922 the *Post* was sold to a syndicate headed by *Post* editor Edwin F. Gay, former dean of the Harvard Business School. This consortium of 34 members included future President Franklin D. Roosevelt, *Chicago Sun* publisher Marshall Field, former U.S. Attorney General George Wickersham and General Electric Company Chairman Owen Young.

The group had no central management and proved to be an unwieldy arrangement, so in December 1923 they sold the *Post* to Cyrus Curtis, best known as publisher of the *Saturday Evening Post* and other magazines.

Gangsterland

Prohibition Leads to Lawlessness

When Prohibition went into effect across the country at midnight, January 16, 1920, the last of New York's legal bars closed up. In that day's edition, the *Post* wrote: "National prohibition—the thing that so many regarded as the great impossibility—is at hand. Immediately after the stroke of twelve tonight the remains of John Barleycorn will be laid away out of sight, if not out of mind, in all parts of the United States. Thereafter the nation which has undergone various stages and degrees of dryness in the past few months will become, so far as the prohibition enforcement officials are able to make it, absolutely and permanently bone dry."

Alcohol consumption did not stop in New York but went underground under the control of a new breed of criminal—the gangster rumrunner. The Mob boomed during Prohibition with illegal supply networks run by such characters as Lucky Luciano, Meyer Lansky, Bugsy Siegel and Jack "Legs" Diamond.

Veteran New York mobster Arnold Rothstein knew that the market for high-quality whiskey during Prohibition was a liquid gold mine. He sought out up-and-coming Lower East Side toughs with real Mob potential, Lucky Luciano and Meyer Lansky, to run a complex distribution system that included importing grade-A scotch from Scotland. Customs officials and every other level of law enforcement had to be paid off, but whiskey running still paid off in a big way. A fifth of bootleg whiskey from the supplier cost about $2.20 and sold on the street for about $30.

New York's liquor supply was expensive but always

OPPOSITE: *Notorious mobster Jack "Legs" Diamond.* (*Post photo*)

Nation 'Bone Dry' at Midnight

Prohibition Officials Will Watch Late Diners Closely

Attempts May Be Made at Some Cafes to "Bury John Barleycorn" With Ceremony

National prohibition—the thing that so many regarded as the great impossibility—is at hand. Immediately after the stroke of twelve to-night the remains of John Barleycorn will be laid away out of sight, if not out of mind, in all parts of the United States. Thereafter the nation which has undergone various stages and degrees of dryness in the past few months will become, so far as the prohibition enforcement officials are able to make it, absolutely and permanently bone dry. This includes New York city. The

---

flowing thanks to mobsters like Bugsy Siegel and Meyer Lansky, the "Bugs and Meyer" Mob; Jack "Legs" Diamond, who earned his nickname early in his career for his ability to outrun the cops; and Lucky Luciano, former stickup man turned celebrity gangster. After Prohibition, the New York mobsters who survived the gang wars moved on to gambling, racketeering and other ventures.

One of the nation's most outspoken opponents of Prohibition, Congressman Fiorello La Guardia of New York, outlined the damage being done by the "great experiment" in a Senate hearing in 1926. His speech, excerpted here, presented the hard, cold facts of Prohibition's utter failure and denounced the new wave of corruption and crime that it bred:

It is impossible to tell whether prohibition is a good thing or a bad thing. It has never been enforced in this country.

At least 1,000,000 quarts of liquor is consumed each day in the United States. In my opinion such an enormous traffic in liquor could not be carried on without the knowledge, if not the connivance of the officials entrusted with the enforcement of the law.

I will concede that the saloon was odious but now we have delicatessen stores, pool rooms, drug stores, millinery shops, private parlors, and 57 other varieties of speak-easies selling liquor and flourishing.

I have heard of $2,000 a year prohibition agents who run their own cars with liveried chauffeurs.

ABOVE LEFT: *A police lineup photo from the* Post *archives shows four gangsters from the Prohibition era and their current status in 1926: left to right, Eddie Diamond, "Dead"; Legs Diamond, "Dead"; Joseph Walsh, "Dead"; and Lucky Luciano.*

OPPOSITE: *Lucky Luciano (center) began his gangster career as a member of New York's Five Points Gang, where he met future Mob stars such as Johnny Torrio, Al Capone and Frankie Yale.*

NEAR LEFT AND ABOVE: *Liquor-trafficking mobster Meyer Lansky, photographed by* Post *photographer Arty Pomerantz.*

FAR LEFT: *Jack "Legs" Diamond, another Mob gangster who earned fame and fortune running liquor during the Prohibition. (Post photos)*

New York Evening Post

HOME EDITION

HOME EDITION
With Opening Prices
Five Sections   60 Pages

FIVE 5 CENTS   FOUNDED 1801   MEMBER OF THE ASSOCIATED PRESS   SATURDAY, MAY 21, 1927   COPYRIGHT, 1927, N. Y. EVENING POST, INC.   FIVE 5 CENTS
VOL. 126, NO. 158   Published daily except Sunday   Entered as second-class matter at the Post Office, New York, N. Y.

REPORT LINDBERGH OVER ERIN

Post Talent Launches Saturday Review

When *Post* owner Cyrus Curtis discontinued the paper's Saturday literary section in 1924, the editors of that department left the *Post* and formed a new literary review. These men of letters were former Yale and Cambridge professor Henry Seidel Canby, Pulitzer Prize–winning poet William Rose Benét, and poet and novelist Christopher Morley. Their journal reviewed the major new works of the day and featured writing by some of literature's biggest names including T.S. Eliot and Ezra Pound.

Spirit of St. Louis Launches from New York

Charles Lindbergh made history at age 25 when he departed from Roosevelt Field, Long Island, on May 20, 1927, in the *Spirit of St. Louis* and landed 33 1/2 hours later at Le Bourget Field near Paris. He was the first aviator to make a nonstop trans-Atlantic solo flight.

Eight years previously, New York City hotel owner Raymond Orteig had offered a prize of $25,000 to the first pilot who could make the trans-Atlantic trip. Several flyers attempted, resulting in both injuries and deaths, but by 1927 none had succeeded. Lindbergh, who graduated as the best pilot in his class from U.S. Army flight training school and flew mail between St. Louis and Chicago for a private company, believed he could make the flight with the right plane. He persuaded nine St. Louis businessmen to finance the design and building of the *Spirit of St. Louis*.

Cramped inside his small plane with four sandwiches, a bottle of water and a simple compass as his only navigating equipment, Lindbergh flew 3,610 miles to Le Bourget Field and was greeted by a tumultuous welcome of 100,000 French people. While in Paris, Lindbergh was the guest of American Ambassador Myron Herrick and his wife. In a letter to President Calvin Coolidge, Herrick described Lindbergh as "modest, unassuming, gracious and with all the unmistakable spirit of a genius! . . . Had we searched all America we could not have found a better type than young Lindbergh to represent the spirit and high purpose of our people."

Cramped inside his small plane with four sandwiches, a bottle of water and a simple compass as his only navigating equipment, Lindbergh flew 3,610 miles to Le Bourget Field and was greeted by a tumultuous welcome of 100,000 French people.

THE PLAYBILL

Critical Success

During the Roaring Twenties, Broadway lovers turned to the *Post* to read theater reviews by soon-to-be theater icon Russel Crouse. After writing for the *Post* from 1924 to 1929, Crouse teamed up with playwright Howard Lindsay in 1933 to write *Anything Goes*, the first of their extraordinary collaborations. Their 1939 drama, *Life With Father*, ran for nearly eight years and was followed by *State of the Union*, for which they received the Pulitzer Prize for drama. The pair also wrote the libretto for *The Sound of Music*.

ABOVE: *Russel Crouse (left) and Howard Lindsay.* (Post *archives*) ABOVE RIGHT: *Theater listings from the 1920s.* RIGHT: *A poster from the Lindsay-Crouse collaboration of 1939.* (New York Public Library)

WINTER GARDEN Eves. 8.25. Matinees Tues. Thurs. and Sat.
ARTISTS AND MODELS PARIS EDITION
18 GERTRUDE HOFFMANN GIRLS

44th ST. THEA., West of B'way. Eves. 8.30
Matinees Wed. and Sat. at 2.30
AL JOLSON in his Greatest Success "BIG BOY"

SHUBERT Theatre, 44th St. West of B'way
Eves. 8.30. Mats. Wed. & Sat. 2.30
THE CONTINENTAL REVUE GAY PAREE

Have you ever seen an "Angel"?
—Consult "THE BUTTER AND EGG MAN" with GREGORY KELLY
at the LONGACRE, W. 48th St.

VANDERBILT 48 St. E. of B'way. Eves. 8.30
Matinees Wed. & Sat. at 2.30
"BEST OF MUSICAL COMEDIES"—News
Merry Merry with MARIE SAXON
The Vanderbilt Specialty Girls—And HARRY ARCHER'S ORCHESTRA

PLAYHOUSE 48th. E. of B'way. Eves. 8.30
Matinees Wed. & Sat. at 2.30
ALICE BRADY in 'OH! MAMA'

BROADHURST 44th St. W. of B'way. Eves. 8.30. Matinees Thurs. & Sat.
A. H. Woods Presents
"The GREEN HAT" By MICHAEL ARLEN

MOROSCO West 45th St. Eves. at 8.30
Matinees Wed. and Sat. at 2.30
BRIDGE OF DISTANCES with MARY NEWCOMB and ULLRICH HAUPT

JOLSON'S THEATRE, 59th St. & 7th Ave.
Eves. 8.30. Mats. Thurs. & Sat. 2.30
THE STUDENT PRINCE with HOWARD MARSH and
353rd TIME TONIGHT ILSE MARVENGA

BIJOU THEA., 45th St. West of Broadway
Eves. 8.30. Mat. Saturday at 2.30
HELEN MacKELLAR in "THE MUD TURTLE"

CENTURY | SAN CARLO GRAND OPERA
Tonight 8.20. FAUST, Roselle. Tafuro. Interrante; Fri. LUCIA DI LAMMERMOOR; Sat. Mat., BUTTERFLY; Eve. AIDA; with Pavley-Oukrainsky Ballet. Prices 50c to $3.

TIMES SQUARE Thea. 42d St. W. of B'way
Matinees Thurs. and Sat.
A. H. WOODS Presents "The PELICAN"
with MARGARET LAWRENCE, FREDERICK KERR and HENRY STEPHENSON

RITZ THEATRE, 48th St. West of B'way
Eves. 8.30. Matinees Wed. and Sat.
The KISS IN A TAXI
with Arthur Byron—Janet Beecher

49th ST. THEA. West of B'way. Eves. 8.30
Mat'nee Wed. and Sat. at 2.30
COURTING "Better than 'Binty Pulls the Strings'"
Special Midnight Performance Today

CHANIN'S Just W. of B'way
Eves. 8.15. Mats. Wed. and Sat. 2.30
46th ST. THEATRE
10th MONTH—LAUGH SENSATION! "IS ZAT SO?"

CASINO Thea., 39th St. & B'way. Eves. 8.30
MATINEES WED. AND SAT. 2.30
RUSSELL JANNEY'S MUSICAL SENSATION!
THE VAGABOND KING
Founded on McCarthy's "If I Were King"
MUSIC BY RUDOLF FRIML

Rachel Crothers presents
THE BOOK OF CHARM
By John Kirkpatrick
COMEDY THEA., 110 W. 41 St. Eves. 8.30
LAST MAT. TODAY at 2.30
Last Perfce. Fri. Eve. Opens in Chicago Oct. 4

NEIGHBORHOOD PLAYHOUSE
466 Grand St. Drydock 7516. Evs. 8.30. Mat. Sat.
Prices All Performances—Orch. $2; Balc. $1.50
"THE GRAND STREET FOLLIES"

OSCAR SERLIN presents

Clarence Day's

LIFE WITH FATHER

Made into a play by

HOWARD LINDSAY and RUSSEL CROUSE

Directed by BRETAIGNE WINDUST · *Setting and Costumes by* STEWART CHANEY

WITH

HOWARD LINDSAY and DOROTHY STICKNEY

Closing Market Prices, With Complete Bid and Asked, in This Edition

FINAL SPORTS
SEVENTH RACES
Wall Street Closing Prices
Cloudy, colder tonight; Tuesday rain (See Page 27).

New York Evening Post

FINAL SPORTS
★ ★ ★ ★ ★
Wall Street Closing Prices
Complete Bid and Asked

THREE 3 CENT' | FOUNDED 1801 VOL. 128, NO. 291 8 Published daily except Sunday | MEMBER OF THE ASSOCIATED PRESS | MONDAY, OCTOBER 28, 1929 | COPYRIGHT, 1929, N. Y. EVENING POST, INC. Entered as second class matter at the Post Office, New York, N. Y. | THREE 3 CENTS

LAUREL FEATURE TO CROSSBONES BY SHORT NOSE

McLean Juvenile Beats Ned O.,
Paying $18 — Candy Pig
Takes Fourth Event

FESTIC COMES FROM BEHIND TO WIN 3D RACE

Two Bad Spills Mar Steeple-
chase, Won by Wayfair as
Leaders Fall

By J. B. SNODGRASS

Staff Correspondent of Evening Post

LAUREL RACETRACK, Md., Oct. 28.
—E. B. McLean's Crossbones, bay son
of Colin and Black Flag, won the fifth
race here today from a field of candidates for the Jenkins Stakes to be run
on Wednesday in which ten high-class
juveniles started. The six furlongs was
run in 1:13 1-5. G. W. Foreman's Ned
O. was second, beaten a nose. Jimmy
Moran was third. The winner paid $18
for $2.

The favorite entry comprising Chio
Boy and Yarn was out of the money.
H. P. Whitney's Skiri was the con-
tender to the sixteenth, when he lost

LA GUARDIA HITS TIGER BANK BOOKS

Names "Everybody From
Curry Down"—Ex-
cludes Smith

DENIAL BY WALKER

By RICHARD F. WARNER

Pounding on his desk with his fist,
Congressman Fiorello H. La Guardia,
Republican candidate for Mayor, this
morning charged that many Tammany
Hall politicians would not "dare" to
have their bank accounts examined.
His accusation, and the tart reply it
drew from Mayor Walker: "I am not a
Tammany leader, but my bank account
will stand any scrutiny," were the high-
lights of the political situation today.
The Mayor delivered his answer immediately when Mr. La Guardia's statement was brought to his attention.
Meanwhile District Attorney Banton
came to the defense of his record
against the charges of Frederic R.
Coudert Jr., Republican candidate for
his office, that 596 murders have gone
unpunished under the Tammany regime,
and Mr. Coudert amplified his state-

JOHN F. CURRY.

ment with the assertion that Thomas
C. T. Crain, former Justice of the Supreme Court and the Democratic
aspirant for Mr. Banton's job, would di-
no better than his predecessor if elected.
Mr. La Guardia's charge was made this
(Continued on Page Three)

Laurel Results

By the Associated Press

FIRST RACE—Mary Eloise, 12.70, 8.80, 5.40; Zahn, 17.10,
7.10; St. Tuscan, 3.40.
Scratched—Fair Dawn, Wandering Gold, Frances St. L.

WARDER SEEKS TO BLAME AIDS; STATE RESTS

Submits Order to Show He Directed City Trust Examination Long Before Crash

COURT REFUSES MISTRIAL AFTER PROSECUTION RESTS

Court Bars From Records Ex-
Bank Head's Early Friend-
ship With Ferrari

By CEDRIC WORTH

James I. Cuff, the attorney conduct-
ing the defense of Frank H. Warder,
former Superintendent of Banks, began
his case for the former official this
afternoon after the State had rested in
a trial for bribery. Mr. Cuff presented
evidence by which he meant to show
that the City Trust Company would
have been found insolvent when examined last November if the bank ex-
aminers had carried out the orders of
the department.
He introduced an order to the exam-
iners in which they were told to verify
foreign balances listed as assets by
banks. He then called to the stand
Samuel Rauch, examiner in charge of

MARKET CRASHES WILDLY WITH LOSSES UP TO 47; MORGAN BANK POOL MEETS

Mitchell, Wiggin, Potter
Confer With Morgans
on Crisis

2 EXCHANGES REFUSE
TO DISCUSS MEETINGS

Pool Action Called Unnecessary
Earlier in Day Before Final
Stock Tumble

Bankers participating in the big pool
which was formed to protect the stock
market after Thursday's sensational
crash met at the offices of J. P. Morgan
& Co. again this afternoon following
today's drastic break.
Those present, in addition to mem-
bers of the Morgan firm, were A. H.
Wiggin, chairman of the Chase National
Bank; Charles E. Mitchell, chairman
of the National City Bank, and W. C.
Potter, president of the Guaranty
Trust Company.
It had been rumored around noon

Confer on Stock Emergency

Best Industrials, Public
Utilities Sag Under
Heavy Pressure

A. T. & T. DROPS 34,
GEN. ELECTRIC 47½

9,212,800 Shares Traded in
Day—Break More Severe Than
That of Thursday

By FRANK J. WILLIAMS

A drastic decline in stocks, even more
serious than occurred last Thursday,
caused the greatest anxiety in Wall
Street today. Prices of the country's
leading industrial, railroad and public
utility securities melted away under
public liquidation only slightly less
heavy than the record-breaking day last
week.
The market closed this afternoon
without the slightest rally, with stocks
selling at the lowest prices of the day,
some 5 to 7 points a share lower.

The Crash Heard Round the World

The high times and heavy borrowing of the Roaring Twenties came to a crashing halt in October 1929, when the stock market took its deepest dive in history. On Monday, October 28, the market dropped 38.33 points, and the next day, Black Tuesday, dropped another 30.57 points. The nation's entire economy took a severe blow: fortunes were lost, banks were closed, businesses went bankrupt and the nation slid into a devastating depression.

LEFT: *The anxious crowd that gathered in front of the New York Stock Exchange on the next day, Black Tuesday.* OPPOSITE: *An unemployed New Yorker sells fruit on a street corner during the depression that followed the crash.* (Post photos)

Decade Fourteen

1931-1940

Prohibition ended in 1933, offering a cause for celebration in the cities, towns and rural areas struggling to survive the Great Depression. A group of prominent New York lawyers was largely responsible for organizing the state convention process that led to the repeal, as well as the pro-repeal platform of newly elected President Franklin Delano Roosevelt.

In spite of the crumbling economy, construction began on the Empire State Building soon after the Wall Street Crash of 1929 and was completed—in all its glory—in 1931. The tallest building in the world raised the skyline and the spirits of New York.

The Great Depression

Herbert Hoover had been in the White House for just over seven months when the stock market crashed in October 1929. To stem public alarm, the president chose a new word to describe the economic disaster, moving away from the previous terminology of the "Panic of 1873" and the "Panic of 1893." He referred to the sudden economic downturn as a depression, but in spite of the softer term the economy continued its devastating downward spiral and the nation—as well as other industrialized countries throughout the world—fell into the Great Depression.

During this severe crisis, stock market prices decreased by 87 percent between 1929 and 1932. Thousands of banks throughout the nation closed. At the depth of the depression, 16 million people—one-third of the labor force—were unemployed. More than two million high-school students dropped out to try to find work and help their families. With the loss of jobs came foreclosures on homes and farms, and in some cities the homeless built settlements of cardboard shacks called "Hoovervilles" in reference to the president's inability to turn the tide. In the cities long lines of men waited in breadlines and former businessmen stood on corners selling pencils or fruit.

OPPOSITE: *Waiters in a New York restaurant stand ready to serve mugs of beer on April 7, 1933, the first day beer was legal in more than a decade. Prohibition would be repealed completely in December, allowing all types of alcohol to flow freely.* ABOVE: *President Herbert Hoover.* (Post *archives*)

President Hoover lost his re-election race to Franklin Delano Roosevelt, and in the new president's inaugural address of March 4, 1933, he promised the American people a "New Deal" for battling the depression and assured them that "the only thing we have to fear is fear itself."

Roosevelt's New Deal included relief programs to provide financial support for the unemployed and public works projects to create new jobs. In 1933, the director of the Federal Emergency Relief Administration sent investigators to several cities and towns to uncover firsthand how the depression was affecting American lives. In one report from New York, an investigator wrote: "No improvement in New York. Situation very bad and continually worse. No new jobs except very infrequently. Morale of the people is bad. . . . Jobs is the cry everywhere, and I can't over-emphasize this point. All agree that this is the one solution, and with no jobs in private business, they must be created by the government. There is no stigma attached to work relief jobs, but there is a growing hatred of home relief."

The string of New Deal legislation that came out of Congress between 1933 and 1938 greatly expanded the role of the federal government, and some were fiercely opposed to Roosevelt's "welfare state" solutions. President Roosevelt's vow to "wage a war against the emergency" did result in economic recovery, however, as evidenced by the declining unemployment rate and healthier gross national product. But the nation would not fully pull itself out of the depression until its entry into World War II in 1941.

World's Tallest Building, 1931

Like a giant arm thrust into the sky to signal hope and strength in the throes of the depression, the Empire State Building was an engineering wonder that employed thousands after the Wall Street Crash of 1929. The building was the world's tallest until the 1970s, and continues to dominate the skyline of Midtown Manhattan.

The *Post* covered the opening ceremonies on May 1, 1931, which featured a speech by New York Governor Franklin D. Roosevelt and a banquet for 200 VIPs on an upper floor.

The Empire State Building launched the modern skyscraper age and, completed ahead of schedule and under budget, demonstrated the amazing advances made in modern engineering. The building remained partially empty of tenants during the depression and throughout World War II, which caused some to call it the "Empty State."

"The Crowded Street"

By 1930, Greater New York was a city of 6.9 million. Pictured above is bustling Herald Square in 1936, and below is an excerpt of *Post* Editor in Chief William Cullen Bryant's poem "The Crowded Street."

> Let me move slowly through the street,
> Filled with an ever-shifting train,
> Amid the sound of steps that beat
> The murmuring walks like autumn rain.
> How fast the flitting figures come!
> The mild, the fierce, the stony face;
> Some bright with thoughtless smiles, and some
> Where secret tears have left their trace.

FRIDAY, MAY 1, 1931

PRESIDENT AND SMITH OPEN EMPIRE STATE, MIGHTIEST BUILDING

EMPIRE STATE

FDR and the New Deal

Franklin Delano Roosevelt, native New Yorker and two-term governor, was elected the 32nd President of the United States in 1932. Among his New Deal policies to put people to work during the depression were several programs that assisted New York City. The Works Progress Administration (WPA) provided work for the city's actors, artists, musicians and writers, and the construction of the Triborough Bridge that connects Queens, Manhattan and the Bronx was funded by the Public Works Administration (WPA).

A *Post* editorial published in the 1930s pointed out one of the city's most enduring and disturbing issues—the tenements—and expressed the need for a "great pioneer project" like Roosevelt's Tennessee Valley Authority to be applied to city housing needs:

What are we going to do about the slum?

Can Mr. Roosevelt let it be said that the New Deal is leaving us just where we were before in housing—two generations behind England and Belgium and Holland and the great cities of Central Europe?

The East Side of New York City is an example of how the poor continue to live in this country. A survey of vacant apartments showed three out of four without hot water, four out of five without steam heat, three out of five served by water closets in the hall.

Is it any wonder that, under such circumstances, tuberculosis death rates average 113 per 100,000 in New York slum areas, as compared with 27 per 100,00 in non-slum areas?

A comprehensive program of cheap money, tax exemption and partial subsidy is needed to provide low-cost housing for the poor, to avoid a mere shift of slum dwellers from one section to another.

The Roosevelt Administration made the Tennessee Valley the scene of a great pioneer project in public power production.

The *New York Post* suggests that the Administration make New York City the scene of a similar undertaking in public housing.

Fantastic land values, obsolete financing methods, vested interests that block new construction methods and materials, irresponsible concentration on profit making, rotten condemnation methods—these must be swept aside to make low-cost housing possible.

Will the Federal Government tackle the task?

A long-range comprehensive housing program could be a trail blazer for the rest of the country—the cornerstone of a New Deal.

ABOVE: *Franklin D. Roosevelt, President of the United States, 1933–1945, was the only president to be re-elected three times. He ran for president after serving as Governor of New York, 1929–1932, and promised a New Deal for the American people to combat the Great Depression.* LEFT: *Plowing a garden in the Bronx as part of one of FDR's New Deal work programs. (Post photos)*

THE RED TRADE MENACE

Post's Second Pulitzer

*P*ost readers learned the inside story of the Soviet Union's Five-Year Plan in a series of articles written by H.R. Knickerbocker in 1930. The correspondent's excellent coverage earned him the Pulitzer Prize. The paper announced the award on May 5, 1931: "For the best example of foreign correspondence from an American newspaper man in the year 1930 the Pulitzer Prize has been awarded to Mr. H.R. Knickerbocker of the Berlin bureau of the New York Evening Post."

The paper introduced the lengthy series with the following introduction:

> The Evening Post today begins publication of a series of twenty-four articles on "The Red Trade Menace" in an attempt to answer the question, "Can the Soviet's Five-Year Plan Succeed?"
>
> With the economic interests of Soviet Russia and the United States in almost daily conflict through charges of convict labor, short selling and "dumping," The Evening Post sent H.R. Knickerbocker, chief of its Berlin Bureau, into Russia for a two months' survey—not the conventional hand-conducted tour through Moscow, but an impartial eyewitness exploration throughout the length and breadth of Russia.

In the first installment, the author writes that the Soviet Union is "a land at war" for industrialization that holds Russia "in a feverish

grip." He summarized this conflict and the subject of his two-month study as follows:

> It is a war that, according to the Plan, will come in October, 1933, not to an end but to a brief moment of stock taking. That year will mark the formal close of the first period of the most gigantic economic project in history . . . an attempt over night to industrialize the most backward land in Europe, to make of vast Russia a self-contained entity, an impregnable fortress for Communism.

ABOVE: *H.R. Knickerbocker, chief of the* Post's *Berlin Bureau, won the Pulitzer Prize for a 24-part series on the Soviet Union published in 1930.* LEFT: *Knickerbocker's Pulitzer Prize.*

Crime of the Century

New York Evening Post

NIGHT EDITION
Wall Street Closing Prices

THURSDAY, MARCH 3, 1932

CLUE PUTS BABY NEAR LINDBERGH

Post photo of aviation hero Charles Lindbergh.

On the evening of March 1, 1932, Charles and Anne Lindbergh's 20-month-old baby boy was kidnapped from the nursery in their New Jersey home. A note demanding a $50,000 ransom was left at the scene. In spite of Lindbergh's compliance with the kidnapper's demands over the next agonizing weeks, the remains of the baby's body were found on May 12 about two miles from their home.

The American aviation hero had moved his family to the isolated New Jersey estate to keep some semblance of privacy, but the tragic kidnapping story brought them into the global spotlight once again. With the arrest, trial and conviction of Bruno Richard Hauptmann, a German immigrant living in the Bronx, the kidnapping story reached epic proportions. A bill from one of the ransom payments had led to Hauptmann, and during the investigation more than $14,000 of the ransom money was found hidden in the walls of his garage. He was executed for the crime in 1936.

New York Evening Post

NIGHT EDITION
Wall Street Closing Prices

WEDNESDAY, MARCH 2, 1932

THREE 3 CENTS

LINDBERGH BABY HUNTED IN NEWARK

Mrs. Lindbergh Lists the Diet Of Ill Baby in Plea to Kidnaper

Mrs. Anne Lindbergh, mother of the Lindbergh baby, today appealed to the kidnapers to take care of her child who has been ill and whose recovery depends on the treatment it gets, especially in its diet.

The anxious mother issued to the press the strict diet she has been following since the baby fell ill. She did this in the hope the kidnapers would read the story and be humane enough to guard the child's health.

Here is the diet:

One quart of milk during the day.

Three tablespoonfuls of cooked cereal morning and night.

Two tablespoonfuls of cooked vegetables once a day.

One yolk of egg daily.

One baked potato or rice once a day.

Two tablespoonfuls of stewed fruit daily.

Half a cup of orange juice on waking.

Half a cup of prune juice after the afternoon nap.

And fourteen drops of medicine called Viosterol during the day.

New York's mayor for three terms from 1933 to 1945, La Guardia is immortalized as one of the greatest leaders in the city's history. In addition to modernizing and improving the city administration, La Guardia went to the top—the White House—to secure billions of dollars for city improvements including parks, highways, hospitals, schools, bridges, tunnels, airports and health facilities. Admired for his honesty and boisterous personality, one of his most memorable media stunts was reading comic strips over the radio for children during a newspaper strike.

THIS PAGE: *Fiorello La Guardia, Mayor of New York, 1933.*
(Post *photo*)

King Kong Takes Radio City

An illustration in the entertainment section of March 4, 1933, announced the opening of the new film *King Kong* starring Fay Wray, showing at the sumptuous Radio City Music Hall.

Some prominent members of the cast of "King Kong," the prehistoric animal fantasy now showing at the music Hall and RKO Roxy Theatre in Radio City. The lady in the tree is reported to be Miss Fay Wray.

THE TRUTH ABOUT HITLERISM

Nazis Jail 40,000 Political Foes; Reds Shot 'Attempting to Escape'

Concentration Camps Being Built—Centrists Among Prisoners

SOCIALIST DEPUTY DESCRIBES TERROR

Arrests Diminishing—Friends Say Dictator Disapproves of Excesses

(Continued from Page One)

revolver shots, one of which took fatal effect."

All prisoners shot "attempting to escape" are Communists.

It may be that some part of the foreign world has been impressed by the campaign of the National Socialists against Communism. That was its purpose. The Japanese, invading Manchuria, proclaimed they were protecting the world against the Soviet threat—and sat back waiting for applause. The National Socialists, abolishing all civil liberties and suppressing all campaign activities of the Socialists—comparable in this country to liberal Democrats in America—as well as of the Communists, proclaimed they were protecting Europe against Communism.

The burning of the Reichstag, the alleged Red plot for bloody revolution were the occasions for the Terror and the suppression of the activities of the opposition parties. Who stood behind Van der Lubbe, the alleged Dutch Communist, who accommodatingly retained in his pocket his passport and party card as he was arrested in the flaming Reichstag may never be known. Certain is the fact, and admitted by National Socialists, that Van der Lubbe deserves much credit for the National Socialist clean-up of Germany.

Communist Chances Diminished in Reich

It cannot be denied that the Nazi campaign against the Communists has diminished to vanishing point the chances of Communism in Germany, until and unless war comes. But how

Above, police holding back crowd at Potsdam celebration that marked inauguration of Hitler Reichstag. Below, left to right, Ernest Thaelmann, head of German Communist Party, now in jail with other opponents of Nazi regime; Heinrich Himmler, chief of Nazi "Defense Squads," who is organizing concentration camps for political prisoners, and Dr. Curt Melcher, until a few weeks ago police chief of Berlin.

Associated Press Photo

Kill or Cure   By Sykes

Prewar Menace

A series published in 1933 entitled "The Truth About Hitlerism" informed *Post* readers about Hitler and his Nazi regime. The excerpt on this page states that Heinrich Himmler was responsible for organizing "concentration camps for political prisoners." A political cartoon from April 10, 1933, reflects upon the tactics of the German leader.

Prohibition Ends with Bloated Beer Fest

In the first step toward repeal of Prohibition, President Roosevelt called for a revision of the Volstead Act that would legalize 3.2 beer. Congress complied, and 21 states—including New York—ratified the policy. The day before the new law went into effect, the front page of the *Post* shouted the glad news: BEER AT 6 A.M. TOMORROW. On April 7, 1933, beer flowed in New York's restaurants, cafes, bars and drugstores.

The front page included a photo of beer trucks hauling barrels into the city. "America tasted its 3.2 percent beer today—tasted it and found it good," wrote Lindesay Parrott in the accompanying article. "In restaurants, hotels and drug stores, in railroad trains and lunch counters, the nation tasted, smacked its lips and ordered more."

Lunch hour turned into an overcrowded, jostling festival as everyone tried to get a taste of the weak but legal brew:

> In New York, where the delivery of beer began at 6 A.M., the lunch hour found a few dispensaries drunk dry already of the small deliveries they had been able to obtain.
>
> New York liked the stuff. The only trouble was there wasn't quite enough, what with 500,000 barrels in the breweries and time and trucks both lacking to distribute it as fast as the thirst grew.
>
> There was some cheering here in New York, in Pittsburgh, Philadelphia, Chicago and St. Louis and points west.
>
> In Washington 800 people stood out in the rain and shouted as the first beer truck made a delivery at the White House for the president who made beer possible.

Newspaper front page:

APRIL 6, 1933 — COPYRIGHT, 1933, N. Y. EVENING POST, INC. Entered as second-class matter at the Post Office, New York, N. Y. — THREE 3 CENTS

BEER AT 6 A.M. TOMORROW; THOUSANDS WAIT IN LINE IN JAM OVER LICENSING

Waiting for Those Beer Licenses

City Issues Permits on Fire Department Blanks

1ST OUT AT 1:50 P. M. CONFUSION IS GREAT

Ban on Midnight Deliveries Holds—Half Million Barrels Ready Here

Developments today in the beer situation were:

New York Health Department issuing permits for sale of 3.2 beer; thousands apply.

Governor Lehman signs Buckley bills, taxing beer $1 a barrel and setting special election for repeal convention on May 23, State to choose 150 delegates at large.

Nineteen States and the District of Columbia permit sale of Beer tomorrow, unofficial prohibition extended until 6 A. M. in several.

Lineup of applicants for beer licenses before the main office of the Health Department at 139 Centre Street today. — *Evening Post Photo*

Total Eclipse — **By Sykes**

Woman's Page editor Ruth Seinfel wittily pondered the consequences of beer drinking in her column that day:

> Well, and here we are drinking beer again. Drinking it and, I hope, enjoying it, in a nice ladylike way. Perhaps there won't be time today to think about what beer will do to change our lives, but one of these days, between sips, we are going to have to think about a few serious matters.
>
> How are we going to settle down and relax and not worry about the pounds that come with beer and especially with the substantial sandwiches and the variety of cheeses that are indispensable companions to beer?
>
> I'm sure it will be a pleasanter world to live in, when we make these changes in ourselves, but it is going to be pretty hard for some of us. Perhaps there will have to be a transition stage, in which the less hardy nervous systems will succumb to cases of "beer jitters" as a result of trying desperately to relax.
>
> But whatever happens, I'm for beer. . . . After all, it's another case of the survival of the fittest, and may the best beer-drinker win.

Prohibition was fully repealed when the 36th state ratified the 21st Amendment on December 5, 1933. New Yorkers were free at last to resume the civilized ritual of the cocktail hour—with real cocktails.

APRIL 7, 1933 — COPYRIGHT, 1933, N. Y. EVENING POST, INC. Entered as second-class matter at the Post Office, New York, N. Y. — THREE 3 CENTS

CITY IN EAGER BEER RUSH; DRINKS 3.2 FASTER THAN TRUCKS CAN SUPPLY IT

Big Brew Parade Starts

Hotels, Restaurants and Stores Call Frantically for More

MANY TURNED AWAY IN LUNCH HOUR JAM

Crowds Cheer at Breweries as Flow Starts—License Rush Continues

By LINDESAY PARROTT

America tasted its 3.2 per cent beer today—tasted it and found it good.

In restaurants, hotels and drug stores, in railroad trains and lunch counters, the nation tasted, smacked its lips and ordered more.

In New York, where the delivery of beer began at 6 A.M., the lunch hour found a few dispensaries drunk dry already of the small deliveries

Beer trucks leaving Ruppert's brewery for delivery. — *Evening Post Photo*

OPPOSITE: *A group of young women sample the 3.2 beer—just legalized—at a drugstore counter on April 7, 1933.*

"Little Eva" Fries

Eva Coo's grisly crime committed in upstate New York on June 14, 1934, led to her execution in the electric chair at New York's Sing Sing Prison in 1935. After taking out several life insurance policies on Harry Wright, her handyman, bordello madam Eva Coo and her accomplice, Martha Clift, planned Harry's murder. They took him to a remote spot outside Oneonta and Eva clubbed him on the head with a mallet. She then ordered Martha to drive over the body so that it would appear to be a hit-and-run accident. They dumped the body by a highway before returning home.

Post writer Joseph Cookman attended the execution at Sing Sing and shared his experience with readers on June 28, 1935. Here is an excerpt of his compelling piece:

Mrs. Eva Coo Bids
the World Good-Bye

You had to keep reminding yourself that "Little Eva" deserved everything that was coming to her—if any one ever deserved a cold-blooded killing.

Every now and then in those few but interminable minutes before you entered the execution chamber you had to think of that pitiable cripple, murdered because he had no better sense than to let a buxom and fortyish keeper of a bucolic bordello take out $10,000 worth of insurance on his life.

That woman whose hard face you had seen in newspaper pictures hadn't been a softy when she hit the limping Gimpy over the head with a mallet on a lonely road on Crumhorn Mountain. Mercy wasn't in her when she waved to her girl friend, Mrs. Martha Clift, to run her automobile over Gimpy's unconscious body and back up to do it all over again—and again.

You had to remind yourself of these things, because otherwise you couldn't watch what you were gong to watch in the way of business—a business that you had selected for yourself and a business that a lot of people thought was interesting.

The shirt-sleeved keepers let you in through those steel bars after looking over your credentials with a suspicious eye.

With no ceremony whatsoever, you were half pushed into a waiting room, where you sat on a greasy bench or stood and looked out of the window through the bars and galvanized netting.

And there you waited. And waited for some more, remembering that Eva Coo was a—well, whatever she was.

So then you find yourself in Warden Lewis E. Lawes's office—nice, with autographed pictures of President Roosevelt, Governor Lehman, ex-Governor Al Smith and some attractive children playing with ponies and pups.

There you find Mrs. Coo's latest set of lawyers, David Slade and Joseph Klein, red-eyed, exhausted and very earnest. They are anxious to tell you and the rest of the newspaper men that Mrs. Coo is innocent, that such and such and so and so indicates it perfectly—which it does if you accept it, although the time-tested rules of evidence didn't.

It is now ten minutes to eleven and the young man comes in and directs you down a long cream and brown corridor to a door.

Almost before you know it you are in a bare room. The walls are like the corridors, brown up to the wainscot level and a dull cream above. Silver pipes run along the ceiling and there is a silver painted grille under a sky light. Four rows of benches stand along the wall to the right as you enter and the keepers signal you to take a seat on one of them.

In the middle of the room is a chair.

Just plain wood, with a back piece that looks like a piece of leather, except that you know it isn't.

You note with surprise that the thing is the electric chair. You know it's deadly, but it doesn't look it; you wouldn't think much about it if you hadn't known.

So, feeling a little sick, you sit down. You don't have to wait. Before you have the chance to get a good idea of what the room looks like you hear murmurs off-stage.

They make your hair rise.

You know they are the voices of persons stating death—not discussing it.

And three women appear.

The one in the middle is the one going to die. You have been trying to imagine what she will look like after those hours of waiting. You have been told that she was a platinum blonde whose hair was really gray, that she was sallow and sagging when not painted.

But you see a woman whose hair has the sheen of youth and is brown.

Her face is pale, but her body is taut and strong. Not for years need she worry about the passing of her youth. One of the attending women is black. The other is white.

Hovering in the background is a bottle-shaped man.

You see Mrs. Coo as she enters, as she sits in the chair like a child told to sit down. And then your sight is blocked out. You see the bottle-shaped man and broad backs of the two matrons.

A muffled voice says:

"Goodby my darlings."

There is a moment of silence.

Then a smothered "Oh."

An electric sound makes you rise in your seat.

Then there is the intermittent sizzling noise that you can hear and feel although you can't see through the broad backs of the three persons who serve as a shield.

But you can see the backs of the two matrons shudder as one after another the shocks from the hidden executioner go through the woman who is being killed.

It only takes a minute. You see the men standing around the walls, leaning there with affected nonchalance, come bolt upright. Two doctors go forward and apply stethoscopes to the woman's breast.

Dr. C.C. Sweet, chief doctor of the prison, announces in a sepulchral but impersonal voice:

"I pronounce this woman dead."

It is as simple as that. The woman that you saw a couple of minutes ago walk into the room as a woman might walk in, hesitantly, to a strange tea party, is dead.

Very dead. As two men pick up the body you note that her face has twisted into a mask of agony. Her dead lips are blue. Her left leg where the electrodes have penetrated is burned from the ankle to the knee.

You find that you are on your feet. Some of the blue-shirted men indicate by their looks that you are violating the proprieties.

It was a beautiful opportunity to write a story exemplifying the virtues of capital punishment.

While she was in the death cell two women from Cooperstown, N.Y., came to see her. One woman knew nothing about her plight. The other wore the clothes that she, then in the death house, had intended to wear this summer.

"I don't want my family bawling around here," said Mrs. Coo in her last hours, "but the only thing that woman had on which wasn't mine was shoes. I always wear tan shoes."

Mrs. Coo was executed in black shoes and tan stockings.

The Post by Any Other Name . . .

In 1934 the *New York Evening Post* became the *New York Post*. Approximately 100 years previously, a similar change had been made on the flag when the words "New York" were deleted, leaving the front page to read: "Evening Post."

In 1948 the paper was renamed the *New York Post & Home News*, then the *New York Post Home News*. On November 14, 1949, it returned to the name the *New York Post*.

Decade Fifteen

1941-1950

With the surprise attack of Pearl Harbor in December 1941, America entered another war-torn era. During World War II, the *Post* was filled with news from European and Pacific fronts as well as articles dealing with the effects of war at home.

Pearl Harbor, Hitler's marches through Europe, gripping Pacific air- and sea-campaigns, the A-bomb—this was one of the bloodiest and most dramatic decades in U.S. history. The *Post* goes through its own sensational changes in this period, too, under the direction of new owner Dorothy Schiff, who switched the paper to tabloid format in 1942. Schiff bought the paper and named her husband, George Backer, publisher and president. When Backer resigned, she assumed his titles and became the first woman newspaper publisher in New York.

Post publisher and president Dorothy Schiff, New York's first woman newspaper publisher. (Post photo)

World War II

Eleven Extra Pages of War News, Including 4 Pages of Maps and Pictures

New York Post

CONGRESS VOTES WAR, 470--1
Jap Bombers Reported Off Oakland—Schools Shut

1,500 AMERICANS DIE IN BATTLE

From the beginning of the United States' entry into World War II in 1941 to the Japanese surrender in 1945, nearly 900,000 New Yorkers served in the armed forces. The dark realities of war, reported in the casualty lists and overseas reports of the newspapers, existed side by side with the positive new changes at home, where industry boomed with the building of ships, planes, munitions and other materials of war and lifted the economy out of the Great Depression.

A *Post* editorial from June 1943, in the middle of the war years, discussed the twists and turns of Germany's idealism as the war rolled on:

> One thing that strikes people who follow closely what the Germans have to say is that they have stopped talking about ideas.
>
> When the war was going all their way, when they were feeling cocky and sure of victory, they were full of talk about the Herrenvolk and the world it was going to make.
>
> They fizzed with ideas about Lebensraum and the government of peoples—which peoples were going to be allowed to survive and under what conditions . . . and so on.
>
> Now that the Germans have had their ears pinned back in Russia and North Africa they appear to have sickened of ideas. Now they talk of . . . the inhumanity of bombing, the effectiveness of the U-boat campaign. . . . Now their tune is that they are fighting for survival and to defend themselves against the terrible vengeance of their enemies.

When news of the German death camps reached the outside world, opinions varied on how to deal with the victims. In a 1943 editorial entitled "Can We Do Less?" the *Post* suggested that the least the United States could do is treat the Jews as humanely as we treated the thousands of prisoners of war held within our borders:

> Both Rumania and Bulgaria, to cite two cases, have offered to surrender a number of their Jews to us if we would take them. At this point our State Department has always gotten very technical about visas and passports and documents. . . . We have so far been unable to come to any other conclusion than that it's just too bad, but . . . they'll have to get along the best they can. Getting along the best they can has come to mean a gas chamber in a Polish forest or maybe a bite from a typhus-infected louse in the Warsaw Ghetto.
>
> We want to save some lives. . . . If Bulgaria and Rumania are willing to surrender just a few thousand of the four million Jews still alive in Europe, let's take them.
>
> Can our conscience allow us to do any less for the unfortunate victims of Fascism than we do for the Fascists themselves?

More than 1.6 million residents of New York State entered the military during the war, and 31,215 of them lost their lives in Europe, the Pacific Islands or at sea. At the southern end of Manhattan, the East Coast Memorial in Battery Park is dedicated to the servicemen who died in the Atlantic during World War II. President John F. Kennedy dedicated the memorial at its unveiling in 1963.

ABOVE: *America's entry into World War II began after the Japanese attack on Pearl Harbor on December 7, 1941. The* Post's *headline of the following day announced both the attack and the declaration of war.*

ABOVE: *Troops approaching the Normandy coast in the D-Day invasion of June 6, 1944.* (Post *archives*)

Hero from the Bronx

A native of the Bronx, Roscoe Brown, Jr., was a squadron commander of the "Tuskegee Airmen," the black pilots of the Army Air Force who were trained at a remote base near Tuskegee, Alabama, during World War II. This famed group flew more than 1,500 missions in Europe and proved to the armed forces that blacks could fly combat aircraft. Their success led the way to full integration of the U.S. military.

Captain Brown was awarded the Distinguished Flying Cross for his service, and after the war he earned a doctorate in education and became a professor at New York University's School of Education, a position he held for 25 years. During his tenure he founded the university's Institute on Afro-American Affairs.

LEFT: *Roscoe Brown, Jr., one of World War II's famed "Tuskegee Airmen."* (*Photo courtesy of Dr. Roscoe Brown*)

RIGHT: *: The now-classic* Post *casualty list of April 13, 1945, opened with the name of President Franklin D. Roosevelt, who died the previous day.*

Today's List of Casualties

Washington, Apr. 13.—Following are the latest casualties in the military services, including next-of-kin.

ARMY-NAVY DEAD

ROOSEVELT, Franklin, D., Commander-in-Chief, wife, Mrs. Anna Eleanor Roosevelt, the White House.

Navy Dead

s Anthony, Fireman 1c. abeth Decker Metz, 16 cord, S. I. Norton, Lt. Mother, Mrs. iler, Fifth Av. Bank. lfred Harold, Ensign. Mrs. Harold Giles Staind., Brooklyn.

Navy Missing

SMITH, Thomas Hoy, Chief Carpenter. Wife, Mrs. Virginia Barbara Smith, 2165 E. 33d St., Brooklyn.

Army Dead—European Area

COHEN, David D. S., Cpl., son of Harry A. Cohen 1900 Quenten Rd., Brooklyn.
COWARD, Louis C., Sgt., son of Mrs. Eloise Coward, 545 Warren St., Brooklyn.
DI GRUGILLERS, Clement C., Sgt., son of Louis Di Grugillers, 732 E. 137th St.
DI MAURO, John T., Pfc., son of Mrs. Josephine Di Mauro, 306 Haven Av.
DRUCKER, Simon, Pfc., brother of Morris Drucker, 721 Van Sicklen Av., Brooklyn.
DUDEK, William S., Pfc., brother of Mrs. Helen Reitz, 147-08 105th Av., Jamaica.
FIRENZA, Frank J. Cpl., son of Mrs.

Nancy Firenza, 2423 Bathgate Av., The Bronx.
GELLER, Seymour L., Lt., c/o H. Cohen, 85 McClellan St., The Bronx.
HOLCOMB, Charles N., Capt., husband of Mrs. Barbara H. Holcomb, 44 E. 78th St.
JOHNSON, William N., Pvt., husband of Mrs. Dorothy B. Johnson, 7022 18th Av., Brooklyn.
JUCHTER, George H., Pfc., son of Mrs. Frieda E. Juchter, 201 E. 82d St.
LAQUIDARA, Emilo C. Pvt., son of Mrs. Anna P. Laquidara, 27-01 24th Av., Astoria.
LIPPMAN, Seymour, Pfc., cousin of Leo Weinrich, 178-10 Jamaica Av., Jamaica.
LUNETTA, Salvatore J., Pfc., son of Mrs. Mary M. Lunetta, 1463 84th St., Brooklyn.
McCULLOUGH, James A. Sgt., husband of Mrs. Elizabeth McCullough, 1719 Jarvis Av., The Bronx.
McDONALD, John J. Jr., Lt., husband of Mrs. J. J. McDonald Jr., 107-53 113th St. Richmond Hill.
McPIKE, Owen, Pfc. brother of Mrs. Mary O'Dell, c.o. McKnight, 1792 Washington Av., The Bronx.
MERINGOLO, Palmieri D., Pfc., son of Frank Meringolo, 2910 Av. D. Brooklyn.
MICHEL, George W., Pfc., husband of Mrs. Dorothy Michel, 1345 Decatur St., Brooklyn.
MILLER, Felix E., Cpl., son of Mrs. Mary Miller, 2737 Gifford Av. The Bronx.
MULLER, William R., Sgt., son of William V. Muller, 3410 Kingsbridge Av., The Bronx.
MURTHA, James J., Pfc. son of Thomas Murtha, 1669 Park Av., The Bronx.
NUTTALL, Harold P., son of Mrs. Dora Park, 1111 Washington Av. The Bronx.
PELLECCHIA, Raymond W., Sgt., son of Carmine Pellecchia, 32-16 107th St., Corona.

RODGRIGUEZ, Milton. Sgt., son of Mr Narcisa R. Rodriguez 619 W. 140th St.
ROSA, Nicholas J., Pfc., son of Mr Carmela Rosa, 37-50 104th St., Corona.
ROUX, Robert J., Pfc., son of Mrs. Bett Piano, 763 Courtland Av., The Bronx.
RUBIN, Dave, Pfc. husband of Mr Frances Rubin, 199 E. Second St., Brookly
SAGLIANO, Nicholas A., Pvt., husband Mrs. Edith Sagliano. 959 E. 89th S Brooklyn.
SARKIES, Michael, Pvt., husband Mrs. Jane Sarkies, 448 W. 167th St.
SHEEHAN, Eugene H., Pvt., brother Miss Dorothy Sheehan, 50 Granite S Brooklyn.
SIMONE, Peter F., S'Sgt., son of Mr Frances Simone, 55 Beaver St., Brookly
STEINTHAL, Morton H., Pfc., son Mrs. Lillian Steinthal, 900 West End Av.
TURNER, Edward P., Pfc., son of Mr Alice Turner, 1481 Castleton Av., Ric mond, S. I.
WEXLER, Joseph, Pfc., husband of Mr Doris Wexler, 1914 W. 6th St. Brooklyn
WUPPESAHL, William T., Pfc., son Mrs. Meta Miller Wuppesahl, 184 Sixth A Brooklyn.

Army Dead—Pacific Area

DI MURO, Salvatore J., Pfc., son of Mr Mary Di Muro. 1737 Zerega Av., The Bron
LICITRA, George J., Pfc., son of Phili Licitra, 2073 W. Eighth St., Brooklyn.
O'DWYER, Joseph P., Pfc., son of Mr Mary R. O'Dwyer, 641 Grand Av., Broo lyn.
RUBENSTEIN, Arthur, 2d Lt., son Mrs. Estelle Rubenstein, 1125 Sheridan A The Bronx.
RUGGIERO, Michael J., Pfc., brother Mrs. Lena Latello, 125-16 Sutter Av., Ozor Park.
WARREN, William T., Pfc., son of Wi liam Warren, 368 Chauncey St., Brooklyn

ARMY-NAVY DEAD

ROOSEVELT, Franklin, D., Commander-in-Chief, wife, Mrs. Anna Eleanor Roosevelt, the White House.

BELOW: *War ends in Europe when Germany agrees to an unconditional surrender on May 7, 1945. War in the Pacific continues with major U.S. bombing raids on Japan later that month and in July.*

COMPLETE NEWS—MAGAZINE SECTION—COMIC FEATURES

5¢ IN NEW YORK CITY AND SUBURBS
10¢ ELSEWHERE IN THE UNITED STATES

New York Post

7 FINAL LATE NEWS PAGE

FOUNDED 1801. VOLUME 144. NO. 143. COPYRIGHT, 1945, NEW YORK POST CORPORATION.

TWO SECTIONS   NEW YORK, MONDAY, MAY 7, 1945   32 PAGES

EXTRA

AP REPORTS: NAZIS QUIT!

No Official Confirmation, Says SHAEF
But British Set V-E for Tomorrow

Story on Page 3

COMPLETE NEWS—MAGAZINE SECTION—COMIC FEATURES

5¢ IN NEW YORK CITY AND SUBURBS
10¢ ELSEWHERE IN THE UNITED STATES

New York Post

7 FINAL LATE NEWS PAGE

FOUNDED 1801. VOLUME 144. NO. 144. COPYRIGHT, 1945, NEW YORK POST CORPORATION.

TWO SECTIONS   NEW YORK, TUESDAY, MAY 8, 1945   32 PAGES

TRUMAN PROCLAIMS VICTORY

WARNS JAPAN TO GIVE UP

Story on Page 3

President Calls for Prayer on Mother's Day

"For the triumph of spirit and arms which we have won, and for its promise to peoples everywhere who join us in the love of freedom, it is fitting that we, as a nation, give thanks to Almighty God, who has strengthened us and given us the victory.

"Now, therefore, I, Harry S. Truman, President of the United States of America, do hereby appoint Sunday, May 13, 1945, to be a day of prayer.

"I call upon the people of the United States, whatever their faith, to unite in offering joyful thanks to God for the victory we have won and to pray that He will support us to the end of our present struggle and guide us into the way of peace.

"I also call upon my countrymen to dedicate this day of prayer to the memory of those who have given their lives to make possible our victory."

FULL TEXT OF THE PRESIDENT'S PROCLAMATION ON PAGE 14

We're All in This Together

Advertisements from the 1940s

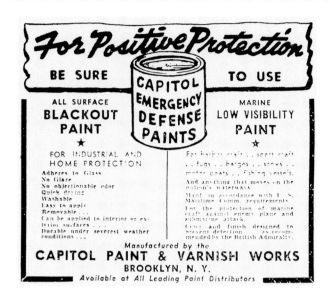
FOOD WILL WIN THE WAR

—Edited by Agnes Adams—

Good Food for Good Health

Classification	Week's Units Required	Today's Menu Provides	This Week Total Units Provided
Total Calories	19,614	2,766	2,766
Protein Calories	2,324	446	446
Vitamin A	35,000	14,000	14,000
Vitamin C	11,200	1,600	1,600
Vitamin B1	4,430	575	575
Vitamin G	3,850	1,700	1,700
Niacin	105	17	17
Calcium	5.6	1.6	1.6
Iron	91	19	19

THE POST MENUS, which give you an appetizing variety of meals
from day to day, achieve a complete scientific balance for the average healthy adult every week. Follow this chart. The week ends
with Monday's menu published each Saturday.

In this solemn moment let us give thanks to God for
the victory and for the lives of our men who have been spared.
To the memory of those who will not return, let us dedicate
ourselves to the end that war may not come again to the earth.

Macy's *closed all day today and tomorrow*

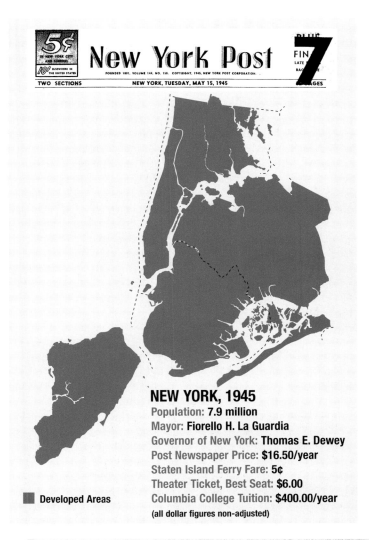

NEW YORK, 1945
Population: **7.9 million**
Mayor: **Fiorello H. La Guardia**
Governor of New York: **Thomas E. Dewey**
Post Newspaper Price: **$16.50/year**
Staten Island Ferry Fare: **5¢**
Theater Ticket, Best Seat: **$6.00**
Columbia College Tuition: **$400.00/year**

(all dollar figures non-adjusted)

■ Developed Areas

BABE HELPS—WITH $50,000

BABE RUTH today bought another $50,000 worth of U. S. defense bonds—he bought a like amount some time ago—and remarked: "This is one way of knocking Hitler and Mikado out of the box." He is shown at the Treasury Dept.'s defense savings staff office at 1270 Sixth Av.

Mankind Will Curse His Memory

DEAD
SAYS NAZI RADIO

London, May 1 (AP)—The Hamburg radio announced tonight that Adolf Hitler was killed this afternoon in his command post at the Reichs Chancellery in Berlin.

The Hamburg radio broadcast said Adm. Karl Doenitz, commander of the German fleet, is his successor.

The Soldier

In a Hospital

In Prison

The Nazi Leader

Adolf Hitler is dead, according to the Hamburg Radio. This may or may not be true. In any event, it hasn't been confirmed by Allied sources. Nevertheless, the world knows that, dead or alive, Hitler is through. The Post, therefore, presents his obituary.

The death of Adolf Hitler prompted an obituary in the *Post*, complete with a photo-montage of the chancellor and his parents. In true *Post* style, the headline and article carry a passionate tone in describing the life and death of Hitler in all his "evil glory." This article was published on May 2, 1945.

COMPLETE NEWS—MAGAZINE SECTION—COMIC FEATURES

New York Post

5¢ IN NEW YORK CITY AND SUBURBS
10¢ ELSEWHERE IN THE UNITED STATES

7 FINAL LATE SPORTS AGE

FOUNDED 1801, VOLUME 144, NO. 219. COPYRIGHT, 1945, NEW YORK POST CORPORATION.

TWO SECTIONS   NEW YORK, MONDAY, AUGUST 6, 1945   **36 PAGES**

EXTRA

ATOM BOMB
(2,000 Times as Powerful As Any Ever Made Before)
DROPPED ON JAPS

Story on Page 3

IMPEACH BILBO, VETERANS DEMAND

Story on Page 5

—THIS IS OFFICIAL

WATCH IT, SAM!

OPPOSITE: *On August 6, the* Enola Gay *drops an atomic bomb on Hiroshima. Three days later, the U.S. drops an atomic bomb on Nagasaki. The Soviet Union declared war on Japan on August 9.* ABOVE: *A political cartoon of August 15 acknowledges peace, but is followed by a cautionary cartoon that warns Uncle Sam to keep an eye on the Japanese.* RIGHT: *With news of the Japanese surrender, 2 million flag-waving New Yorkers jammed Times Square for "the longest and greatest celebration New York has ever seen."*

Paris Post

In 1945, believing that the *Post* could have a global impact, editor Ted Thackrey convinced his wife, publisher Dorothy Schiff, to begin a Paris edition. The four-page (eight on weekends) afternoon tabloid, published in English and edited by Paul Scott Mowrer, went head-to-head with the Paris edition of the *New York Herald-Tribune*, the only other American newspaper in the city, which had resumed publication the previous December.

The paper copied the *New York Post*'s layout as closely as possible and included many *Post* features from home: political columns by Samuel Grafton and Victor Riesel, gossip by Leonard Lyons and sports news from Leonard Cohen. Run on a shoestring budget, it faced multiple problems, including shortages of ink, newsprint and qualified journalists. Still, it managed to hold on until 1948, when Mrs. Schiff pulled the plug. All she would say about the paper in her authorized biography was, "It didn't survive."

Orson Welles' Column

Actor, director, producer, artist and writer Orson Welles contributed a column in 1945 entitled "Orson Welles' Almanac." This collection of facts and observations appeared on the back page and covered Welles' thoughts on everything from theater to politics to the war.

LEFT: *This 1943 photo appeared in the* Post *under the caption: "Smoked cigars at ten."*
RIGHT: *Orson Welles' column from March 8, 1945.*

The Legendary Ted Poston

In 1936, Ted Poston joined the *New York Post* and began an illustrious 36-year career with the paper. The first black reporter on a major American newspaper, Poston covered the famous "little Scottsboro" case in 1949, in which three young black men in Florida were accused of raping a white housewife and for which Poston endured daily attempts on his life. He covered many major events of the 1950s and 1960s including integration in Little Rock, Martin Luther King, Jr., and race riots, and by the time of his retirement in 1972 was considered the "dean of black journalists."

In Ted Poston's obituary of January 11, 1974, the *Post* described him as "a city room presence and city room legend . . . [who] wrote with the flair, the speed, the seeing eye, the sources, the insights that pump life into the facts."

ABOVE: *Ted Poston at the* Post. *(Post photo)* RIGHT: *Ted Poston with Martin Luther King, Jr., 1957. (Post photo)*

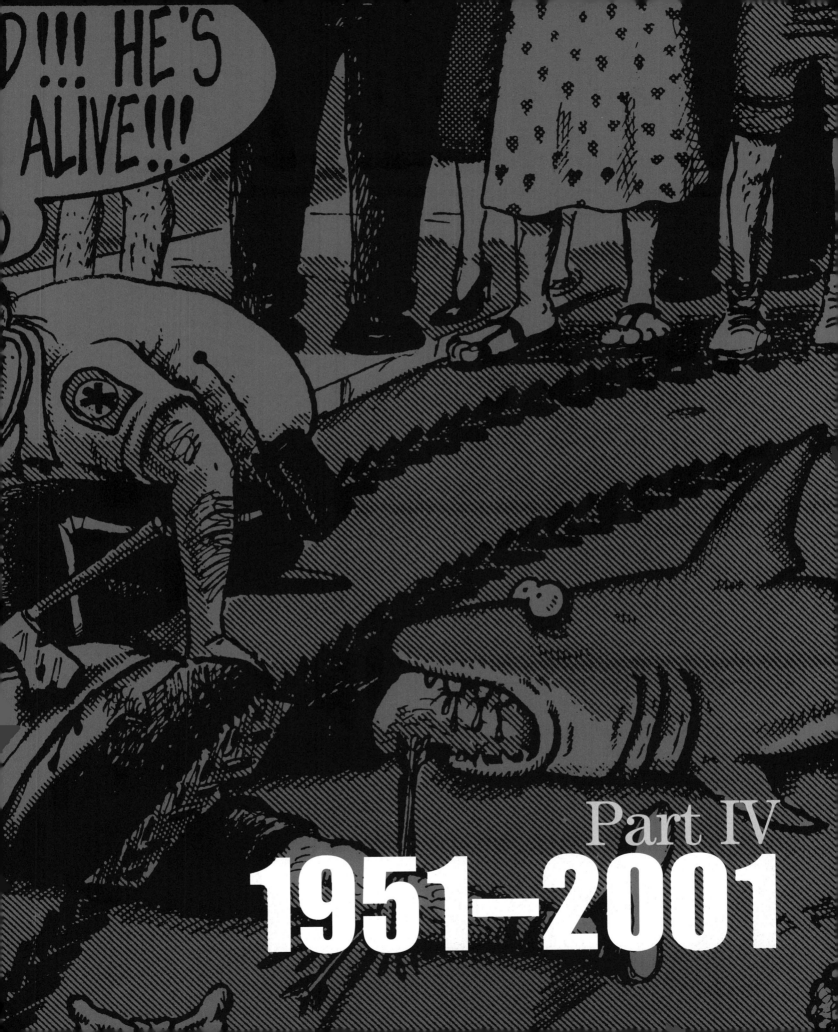

Decade Sixteen

1951-1960

In this Cold War decade two American citizens, man and wife, were tried, convicted and executed in Sing Sing Prison's electric chair for spying. Julius and Ethel Rosenberg, the "atom spies," gave atomic bomb secrets to the Soviets during World War II. The Cold War era was also the setting for the beginning of the space race between the U.S. and the Soviets, covered with great pride and competitive fire in the press.

Fifties' prosperity boosted tourism in New York, with thousands taking the elevators to the top of the Empire State Building every day to see the breathtaking view, such as the girl in the *Post* photo, right. On a clear day, the pay-binoculars offer a view of fifty miles.

A girl takes in the view from the top of the Empire State Building, ca. 1955. (Post photo)

38th Parallel

On June 30, 1950, President Harry Truman authorized General Douglas MacArthur to lead American troops into Korea following North Korea's invasion of South Korea. The *Post*'s front page of July 2 reported America's entry into the Korean Conflict. By mid-September North Korean forces controlled all but the southeastern corner of the Korean peninsula.

In November General MacArthur's United Nations forces mounted a successful counterattack that drove the North Koreans back behind the 38th parallel. In late November the Chinese entered the conflict and staged a counter-offensive into South Korea, followed by the UN forces' final counterattack in early 1951. This drove the Chinese and North Koreans back to the 38th parallel, and the fighting continued.

The conflict, which lasted until a cease-fire agreement was signed on July 27, 1953, ravaged the Korean peninsula and took the lives of approximately 2 million civilians. North Korean military deaths were put at 215,000, South Korean at 47,000, Chinese estimated at 400,000 to 1 million, and American deaths over 54,000. Little territory changed hands as a result, and Korea remained divided at the 38th parallel.

High Court Ruling Today Decides On Life or Death for Rosenbergs

Atom Spies

Sing Sing Prison, June 19, 1953. "The minutes of the Rosenbergs' extra day of life passed slowly, slowly today as their fate was being decided by nine black robed men. Julius and Ethel Rosenberg, their outward calm masking what must be an incredible agony of suspense, may not know until virtually the last minute whether they will die tonight—or tomorrow—or perhaps in a week or so."

They did die that night, in the electric chair.

The Rosenbergs, convicted of giving atomic bomb secrets to the Soviet Union during World War II, spent two years in prison after the trial while their death sentence was sent to the Supreme Court and the president for appeal. Protests went up throughout the United States and Europe from those who declared they were innocent. The Supreme Court rejected the cases, as did President Eisenhower.

"Atom spies Julius and Ethel Rosenberg will be buried today in a quiet corner of the land they betrayed," wrote the *Post* on Sunday, June 21, 1953.

A small article appeared on page 26 that day entitled "Why Rosenberg Died First," explaining why the husband was taken to the chair before the wife. The warden told the *Post*, "If Mrs. Rosenberg had gone first, she would have had to pass her husband's cell on her way to the death chamber. We saw no reason to make the end harder for either of them, so we took him first."

From the East Side to Sing Sing ... They Never Looked Back

(A member of The Post staff, Oliver Pilat has covered many aspects of the Rosenberg case and is the author of a book on it, "The Atom Spies.")

By OLIVER PILAT

Julius and Ethel Rosenberg did not start out to be atom spies. Obviously not; nobody starts out to betray his own country.

This pair of East Side New Yorkers, rather frail physically, bookish but not particularly intelligent, began with socially acceptable goals somewhat beyond their reach.

Ethel wanted to be a singer, operatic if possible, night club if necessary; she lacked the physical appearance, charm and voice for either role. Julius was destined in youth to be a rabbi, though he had no real religious calling.

Out of frustration, idealism and to some extent self-interest, for reasons inherent in their social background as well as their psychological makeup, Ethel and Julius were converted as adolescents to communism.

As Communists, they repudiated their families, non-party friends, their neighborhood, their religion and their country. They went through three stages, never looking back.

First they were outer-party members, full of the noisy flubdubbery of petition-signing, resolution-presenting, circular-distributing, oratory, propaganda and recruitment.

Williamsburg Bridge; Ethel on Sept. 28, 1915, and Julius, on May 12, 1918.

Harry Rosenberg, Julius' father, was a union operator in women's clothing, who brought home a comparatively good wage, dominated his family and had considerable standing in the community.

An extremely patriotic man, like many other immigrants, Harry Rosenberg used to give lectures on American history and government to the family after dinner. He was determined to make his oldest son a rabbi, so Julius dutifully attended Hebrew school, the downtown Talmud

glass, was an immigrant from Austria.

Ethel, small, sallow and dark-haired, was graduated from high school at the age of 15. She went to work as a clerk. She tried professional singing on the side, without success. She also thought of herself as a poet, though she wrote with no particular distinction.

As a stenographer, in 1934, Ethel joined the CP, thereafter focusing all her energies on party work. It was through the party that she met Rosenberg when he was still a CCNY student, backing American Student Union and

ETHEL AND JULIUS ROSENBERG
The road led to the chair

OPPOSITE: *Ethel and Julius Rosenberg in New York's Sing Sing Prison, 1953, and an article about the execution proceedings.* (Post *archives*)

Why Rosenberg Died First

Ossining. N.Y., June 20 Warden Denno of Sing Sing explained today why Julius Rosenberg was put to death before his wife.

"If Mrs. Rosenberg had gone first." he said, "she would have had to pass her husband's cell on her way to the death chamber. We saw no reason to make the end harder for either of them, so we took him first."

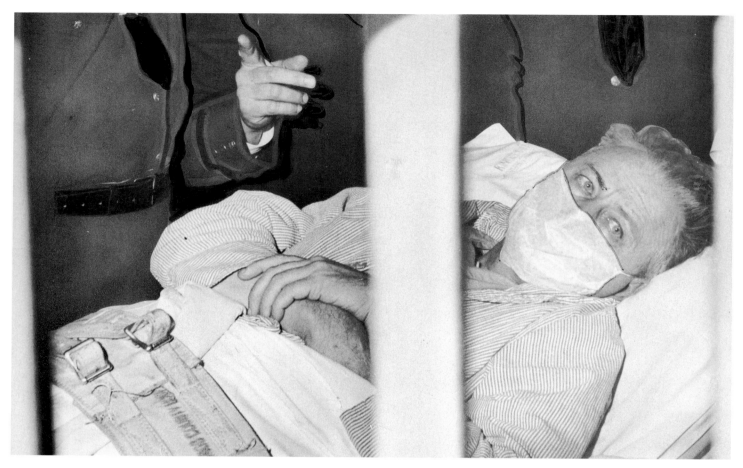

New York City's Mad Bomber

For sixteen years a mystery bomber planted his devices in public places around New York, including the public library and the Brooklyn Paramount Theater. The mysterious bomber took a hiatus during World War II as a patriotic gesture (not adding to the nation's woes), but returned to his crimes in March 1950 by placing one in Grand Central Station. Like many of his bombs, this one did not detonate. Fortunately, no one was killed by his bombs over that span of years, and only fifteen people were injured.

The Brooklyn movie theater blast on December 2, 1956, seriously injured three people. At his wits' end to solve the long-standing case, Police Inspector Howard Finney called on a psychiatrist, Dr. James Brussel, to create a profile of the criminal to help in the search for what the police called the Mad Bomber. In addition to delivering the detailed profile of a 50-year-old male, paranoid, not married, neatly dressed, probably a disgruntled former employee of Con Edison (the power company that had received the first bombs and many hate letters), Brussel urged the police to publicize the case in the press and the media. He was convinced that the bomber, who was undoubtedly angry that none of his letters were put in the papers, would be tempted to come forward and admit to the brilliant crime spree everyone was talking about.

The investigators agreed to create a media blitz. As expected, crackpots from all over the city called in to confess or to implicate a relative. The case was cracked when the investigation turned up an old Con Ed personnel file that nearly matched Dr. Brussel's profile point by point. Name of the suspect: George Metesky.

On January 21, 1957, Inspector Finney went to the Metesky home in Connecticut and arrested the mild-mannered bachelor. Metesky admitted to planting 32 bombs in New York City.

In a sanity hearing, a Bellevue psychiatrist described Metesky as "one of the most dangerous and psychotic I have ever seen." The Mad Bomber was committed to the Matteawan Hospital for the Criminally Insane.

TOP: *Strapped onto a cot, the captured Mad Bomber gets a sanity hearing at Kings County Hospital in April 1957 while also being treated for tuberculosis.* ABOVE CENTER: *The bomb squad takes a bomb found in the New York Public Library to the beach to detonate it in December 1956.*

Post Scoops Quiz Show Fraud

The TV quiz show scandal of the late 1950s might never have happened had it not been for the *Post*. Indeed, nearly all of the stories attributed in the movie *Quiz Show* to congressional investigators actually were broken by the *Post*.

On August 18, 1958, *Post* reporter Jack O'Grady reported exclusively that the highly rated CBS quiz show *Dotto* had been suddenly yanked from the air. The reason why, according to O'Grady, was that a former contestant was charging that one of the winners had been pre-fed the answers.

O'Grady had good reason to know what was going on: Three weeks earlier, that contestant—Eddie Hilgemeier—had told O'Grady how the program was fixed. O'Grady got Hilgemeier to write out a sworn affidavit, which the reporter then sent to a contact at the Federal Communications Commission, which then launched an investigation.

Two things happened as a result of the *Post* story: First, Manhattan District Attorney Frank Hogan opened his own grand jury probe, which ultimately uncovered the widespread fraud. And O'Grady's story prompted Herbert Stempel

Charles Van Doren. (Post photo)

to step forward and tell the DA what he knew.

Nearly 18 months earlier, Stempel had contacted the *Post* and told reporter David Gelman how, while appearing on the NBC quiz show *Twenty-One*, he had been ordered to lose to the popular Charles Van Doren. He also charged that Van Doren, a Columbia University professor, had been given answers in advance. But Gelman couldn't get the kind of corroboration that would make the story libel-proof, and it was never published.

Even after Stempel's story became public, the producers of *Twenty-One* continued to deny any wrongdoing, and NBC stuck with the program—until O'Grady and *Post* colleague William Greaves found out about James Snodgrass. He'd won $4,000 on the show until he was ordered dumped. But he had more than his word to go on: He took copies of the answers and stage directions that he'd been given and sent them to himself by registered mail before he appeared on the show.

The *Post* broke his story on September 26, 1958. Three weeks later, *Twenty-One* was off the air for good.

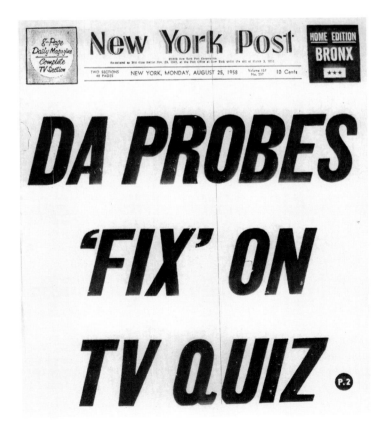

Move Over, Sputnik

Four months on the blinking heels of Sputnik, the United States launched its first Earth satellite, Explorer 1. The rocket that carried it into space on January 31, 1958, was built by the Army under the direction of Dr. Wernher von Braun, and the satellite was designed by the Jet Propulsion Laboratory (JPL) of the California Institute of Technology. (NASA was not formed until October 1958.)

The launch of Russia's Sputnik 1 and 2 in late 1957 ignited high anxiety about the Soviet Union's technological strength. The space race was on.

Post coverage of Explorer 1 reveals the competitive aura surrounding the event. Explorer's stats were presented side by side with Sputnik's, and the article was filled with bravado about American superiority: "Last night's spectacular success was no surprise to the Army, which claimed it could have done the job long before the Sputniks if it had been given the chance."

Explorer 1 carried instruments that gave scientists new information about cosmic rays in space. This information led to the discovery of the belt of charged particles known as the Van Allen Belt—considered the first great discovery of the Space Age.

ABOVE TOP: *A political cartoon published the same day ponders the nation's obsession with the satellite.*

Post Blasts Harriman

In the race for New York Governor in 1958, the *Post* initially backed the incumbent, Democrat Averell Harriman. During the last week of the campaign, however, Mrs. Schiff heard Harriman on a radio program in which, she said, he implied that opponent Nelson Rockefeller was pro-Arab because of his family's oil interests. In the final edition of the last issue before Election Day, Mrs. Schiff ran the following personal notice—unprecedented in modern journalism—which covered the *Post*'s entire front page:

> TO POST READERS: Gov. Harriman's recent snide insinuation that Nelson Rockefeller is pro-Arab and anti-Israel should not be condoned by any fair-minded person. Rockefeller, far from being anti-Israel, has been a liberal contributor to the United Jewish Appeal for 12 years. It is deplorable but true that in political campaigns, lower echelons on both sides indulge in vile demagoguery. But when the head of the ticket repeats such libels, he should be punished by the voters. If you agree with me, do not vote for Averell Harriman tomorrow. Dorothy Schiff, Publisher.

Rockefeller won the election by 550,000 votes in large part because he cut Harriman's 1954 margin in New York City in half. To his death, Harriman never forgave Mrs. Schiff and the *Post*, who he insisted had cost him the election and launched Rockefeller's electoral career.

ABOVE: *New York Governor Averell Harriman. (*Post *photo)*

Robert Moses: Big Apple's Friend or Foe?

By the time he resigned from city government in 1960, Robert Moses had connected every borough of the city with 35 roads and expressways and 12 bridges and tunnels—thoroughly outfitting the city for the modern age of the automobile. He also transformed the urban landscape by clearing slums and replacing them with scores of public housing projects.

Moses' 45-year reign of absolute power in city construction was filled with controversy, primarily when one of his freeways or housing projects meant the displacement of thousands of poor residents. Many resented Moses' high-handed tactics, and the *Post* joined the public outcry with articles and editorials.

Post reporters Joe Kahn and William F. Haddad spent months probing his Title I slum-clearing program—and found a cesspool of corruption. They then trained their sights on Moses' Triborough Bridge and Tunnel Authority, and uncovered incompetence and favoritism. Moses biographer Robert Caro called Kahn "one of the shining journalists of his generation."

ABOVE: *Robert Moses.* RIGHT: Post *editor James Wechsler, who was called before Sen. Joe McCarthy's hearings after criticizing the senator's anti-communist crusade.* (Post *photos*)

McCarthyism and the Post

When Sen. Joseph McCarthy began his anti-communist crusade in 1950, the *Post* was among the first to condemn his activities. "There were a few others in the same camp," wrote editor James Wechsler about the press's attitude at the outset, "but it was a painfully small contingent, and not until McCarthy had set the stage for his own disaster did any considerable body of newspaper opinion begin to make itself heard."

As a result of his furious editorials against McCarthy, Wechsler himself was hauled in to the hearings. One *Post* editorial stated that McCarthy's rants against the press "demonstrated that his contempt for the right of newspapers to say what they think about public officials is equalled only by his contempt for truth," and another: "We are, of course, always honored by McCarthy's denunciations; we interpret them as evidence that our fight to expose the McCarthy fraud has not been in vain."

Convinced that McCarthy was hoping he would refuse to answer questions about his youthful fling with communism and thus risk a contempt citation, Wechsler faced a political dilemma: He could defy McCarthy and face possible imprisonment, or answer questions about his past activities and open himself to political scorn. Fearing that McCarthy's ultimate intent was to silence him, he chose to cooperate.

Reflecting on this era in his autobiography, the editor stated, "I often feel a sharper contempt for the able-bodied, full-grown men in politics and the press who bowed to him, pampered him and fled from him than I do for the crazy mixed-up man who was Joe McCarthy."

Decade Seventeen

1961-1970

By 1967, *New York Post* circulation skyrocketed when it became the only afternoon paper in the city—its day-time rivals left the scene to merge with the morning paper, the *Herald Tribune*. Big stories of the decade included super cool Joe Namath and the Jets' Super Bowl win in 1969, a big party up in Woodstock and a moonwalk for two American astronauts. The dark side of the sixties, from a slew of bloody assassinations to the Vietnam War, touched every-one's life. And New York was literally in the dark for 13 hours in November 1965 when electricity shut down in the biggest blackout in history.

President John F. Kennedy, Jr., victim of the first of four assassinations of the 1960s on November 22, 1963. (Post *archives*)

Dark November

" Most of all it is the strength that one remembers. Not the strength of size or bigness, but of purpose, of intensity, of lean, compact force. . . . He made use of every ounce of energy and every moment of consciousness that was granted him. "

—Washington Correspondent William V. Shannon

President John F. Kennedy was 46 years old when he was assassinated in Dallas on November 22, 1963. Two days after the tragedy, Washington correspondent William V. Shannon offered a personal reminiscence of his 12 years in the press corps while Kennedy was in Congress and the White House. In the full-page article entitled "The JFK I Knew," he wrote that he first met Kennedy in the House of Representatives:

One's first impression of him remained intact and unchanged. He was quick and alert; there was never anything slack or careless about him. He moved with grace; from the cut of his clothes to the tilt of his jaw, he had style. And he was strong.

Most of all it is the strength that one remembers. Not the strength of size or bigness, but of purpose, of intensity, of lean, compact force. He never let up on himself. He made use of every ounce of energy and every moment of consciousness that was granted him.

He had a hard life because he would not permit himself to have an easy one. So many of the big moments of his life, as one thinks back on them, were moments of pain or of intense stress.

For an emotionally reserved man, Kennedy was always exceptionally candid with us, sometimes startlingly frank. He gave us his honest assessments of other public men, and he would sometimes volunteer a fascinating run-down of what was going on inside a legislative committee. To the day of his death, no reporter seriously violated his confidence.

There were moments of high triumph despite the tragic shadows. The happiest was a little over a year ago on that Sunday afternoon in October when he walked slowly out of the White House and headed for his country house in Virginia. A few hours earlier, the definitive cable had come from Nikita Khrushchev announcing the Russian government's decision to withdraw its missiles from Cuba. The most terrible week in the world's history since the end of World War II was at an end. Nothing could be surer proof that the pressure was off than the sight of the departing, young President that afternoon.

John Kennedy had met the greatest test a President could face, and he had won. He had shown courage under crushing pressure, great calmness and steady mature judgment. He had justified the people's confidence in him.

Shannon had last spoken to Kennedy at a state dinner in the White House, when the president volunteered a completely unexpected compliment to the *Post:*

"Oh, I see your husband's columns," he told my wife. "They're like those letters Ken Galbraith writes me from Cambridge—always taking me up on something and telling me how I should have done better.

"But I wish there were a hundred *New York Posts* across the country," he continued.

Thinking of how often our editorials and my fellow columnists on this paper criticized him, I suggested he was not serious.

"Yes, I am," he insisted.

Then for the next several minutes, he gave an impromptu analysis of the political situation of the country, relating the strongholds of political enlightenment to the presence of good newspapers.

John F. Kennedy on his last birthday, May 29, 1963. He was 46.

New York Post

Shecter
On Page 38

40   NEW YORK, SUNDAY, NOVEMBER 24, 1963

Buckshot
On Page 36

Sports Pays Tribute

The following events have been postponed or cancelled:

Racing

Aqueduct
Roosevelt
Narragansett
Caliente

Football

Pro

All AFL Games

College

Harvard at Yale
Dartmouth at Princeton
Boston U. at Boston C.
Columbia at Rutgers
Penn State at Pitt
Notre Dame at Iowa
Colgate at Brown
Oregon St. at Oregon
Wisconsin at Minnesota
Purdue at Indiana
Air Force at Colorado
N. Carolina at Duke
SMU at Baylor
UCLA at USC
California at Stanford

High School

Brooklyn Tech-Boys
New Utrecht-New Rochelle
Bayside-Far Rockaway
Stuyvesant-Clinton
John Jay-Madison

Basketball

Friday NBA Games

Boxing

Thomas vs. Peralta

Golf

Cajun Classic

Hands tightly clasped, Mrs. Jacqueline Kennedy and Attorney General Robert Kennedy watch the casket of husband and brother placed in ambulance at Andrews AFB.

Malcolm X

The first of three more assassinations that shook the nation in the sixties was that of Malcolm X. The front page of February 22, 1965, the day after he was shot in New York City, carried a picture of his widow and the opening of Thomas Skinner's eyewitness account of the shooting. The reporter was seated four rows away from the assassins:

> Bespectacled and dapper, in a dark suit, his sandy hair glinting in the light, Malcolm said: "Brothers and sisters . . ." He was interrupted by two men in the center of the ballroom, about four rows in front and to the right of me who rose and, arguing with each other, moved forward. Then there was a scuffle in the back of the room and, as I turned my head to see what was happening, I heard Malcolm X say his last words:
>
> "Now, now brothers, break it up," he said softly. "Be cool, be calm."
>
> Then all hell broke loose.

ABOVE: *Malcolm X in 1964.* (Post *photo*)

BELOW: *With the nation still in shock two months after the assassination of Dr. King, another shooting blasted into the headlines. Sen. Robert F. Kennedy, 42 years old, was shot by Sirhan Sirhan in Los Angeles. The issue shown here was the first* Post *edition to sell 1 million copies. In 1964, following the assassination of his brother, Robert Kennedy resigned as U.S. Attorney General and moved to New York City. He ran for the U.S. Senate that year, won the election and focused heavily on urban issues that affected New York's poorest citizens, such as housing. Kennedy was also outspoken against several of President Lyndon Johnson's policies including the escalating war in Vietnam.*

NEW YORK POST, SUNDAY, MAY 19, 1963   MAGAZINE PAGE FOUR

By MARTIN LUTHER KING

A Letter From Birmingham Jail

(newspaper article text)

MARTIN LUTHER KING
'Just as the Apostle Paul...'

ABOVE: *Martin Luther King, Jr.'s now-classic "Letter from Birmingham Jail" was published for the first time anywhere in the* Post *in May 1963.*

Letter from King

In April, 1963, four months before delivering his "I Have a Dream" speech in Washington, Martin Luther King, Jr., wrote a now-classic document known as the "Letter from Birmingham Jail." The *Post*, continuing its commitment to report on the Civil Rights Movement, was the first newspaper in New York—or anywhere—to publish the letter.

King was imprisoned in Birmingham, Alabama, after leading peaceful protests about the city's segregated department store facilities and unfair hiring practices. The police had responded to the thousands of black marchers with beatings, hoses and attack dogs. While in prison, King read a published statement in the newspaper by a group of eight white Alabama clergymen who denounced his work, criticizing it as too extreme, "unwise and untimely." In response, he penned a passionate letter in the margins of the newspaper and any scrap of paper he could find to express his anxiety and moral concern over the nation's racial divide. An excerpt of the letter reads:

In your statement you asserted that our actions, even though peaceful, must be condemned because they precipitate violence.

The question is not whether we will be extremist but what kind of extremist will we be. Will we be extremists for hate or will we be extremists for love? Will we be extremists for the preservation of injustice—or will we be extremists for the cause of justice? In that dramatic scene on Calvary's hill, three men were crucified for the same crime—the crime of extremism. Two were extremists for immorality, and thus fell below their environment. So, after all, maybe the South, the nation and the world are in dire need of creative extremists.

Dr. Martin Luther King was gunned down in Memphis on April 5, 1968. James Earl Ray was convicted of the crime.

Close Call for Lady Liberty

With the help of an undercover New York cop, the NYPD and FBI caught a group of terrorists who were planning to blow up the Statue of Liberty and other national monuments in 1965. The pro-Castro group, three of whom lived in New York City, were called the Black Liberation Front.

Officer Raymond Wood, who was promoted to detective after the would-be terrorists were arrested, learned that the group was planning to blow up the Statue of Liberty, the Liberty Bell and the Washington Monument in a sabotage campaign. In the *Post*'s article, the police commissioner said that the group's goal was to make a statement. "It would merely have been symbolic," he said.

OPPOSITE: *Anti-war and other politically motivated riots of the 1960s in New York included the Columbia University protests of April and May, 1968. In response to the school's decision to allocate a gymnasium to students rather than residents of Harlem, protesters organized massive rallies, held three university officials hostage, occupied buildings and tore down fences at the gymnasium construction site. In this photo, students climb through a window into President Grayson Kirk's office on April 28, 1968. They tore the room apart while other students held a dean and two other officials captive in another campus building. (Post photo)*

Nat King Cole:
HOW THEY REMEMBER HIM
See Ted Poston on Page 23, News Story on Page 5

WEATHER
Fair, 40s.
Tomorrow:
Partly cloudy,
upper 30s.

New York Post
©1965 New York Post Corporation

Vol. 164
No. 77   NEW YORK, TUESDAY, FEBRUARY 16, 1965   10 Cents

COMPLETE MARKET
FINAL
LATE SPORTS

PLOT TO BLOW UP STATUE OF LIBERTY

FBI Nabs Woman, 3 Men, Cache of Dynamite

LEFT: *New York Mayor John Lindsay fakes a dive from the Manhattan Bridge, held back by actors Jack Lemmon, center, and Peter Falk, 1966. This photo op occurred during a promotion for the movie* Luv, *which was being filmed in the city. Lindsay served in Congress before being elected mayor in 1965. He was re-elected for a second term in 1969. (Post photo)*

Kennedy vs. Wagner's Men —Open Clash in Albany

Story on Page 4

WEATHER
Sunny, mild, 50, chance of rain tonight.
Tomorrow: Cloudy, rain, 40s.
SUNSET: 5:26 P.M.

New York Post

FINAL
LATE
SPORTS

COMPLETE MARKET
P. 25-13

Vol. 164 No. 73   NEW YORK, THURSDAY, FEBRUARY 11, 1965   10 Cents

Stocks Take Sharp Drop

Story on Page 3

BIGGEST U.S. RAID

150 JETS HIT VIET REDS

Stories on Pages 2 and 3

Vietnam

More than 58,000 Americans died in the country's longest and most unpopular war. For all the death, all the conflict it inflicted at home and all the illusions lost about America's role to defend freedom everywhere, South Vietnam fell to communism at war's end in 1975.

The front page shown at left appeared just after the start of the U.S. bombing campaign, Operation Rolling Thunder, in 1965. The front page below covered the start of the evacuation of Saigon in late April 1975.

RIGHT: *A casualty list published on September 14, 1970.*

Week's War Dead

Following is a list of American servicemen killed in action in Southeast Asia during the last week as announced by the Defense Dept.

ARMY

SGT. J. Duckworth, Hanceville, Ala.
SSG. J. W. Fenton, Frescott, Ariz.
SP/4 R. E. Koonce, San Diego, Cal.
PFC. E. G. Mathern, Corona, Cal.
PFC. D. P. Zerba, Napa, Cal.
SSG. M. E. Quick, Wauconda, Ill.
SP/4 J. L. Ervin, Springfield, Ill.
PFC. S. K. Rankins, Chicago, Ill.
PFC. R. A. Scarbrcugh, Dixon, Ill.
1/LT. H. C. Inman, III, Lousiville, Ky.
SGT. M. C. Bates, Jr., Baltimore Md.
SP/4 N. C. Stefanich, Tower, Minn.
PFC. C. A. Schmitz, Kirkwood, Mo.
SP/4 H. B. Thomas, Phila., Pa.
SP/4 J. Luna Jr., Azusa, Cal.
PFC. D. G. Chaney, Michigan, Ky.
PFC. G. R. Metz, Adrian, Mich.
PFC. R. H. Von Der Hoff, Traverse City, Mich.
SP/4 R. E. Dew, Raeford, N.C.
SP/4 L. Fox, Nashville, N.C.
SP/4 C. P. Hutton, Tulsa, Okla.
PFC. W. O. Cody, Wynne, Ark.
PFC. C. G. Wehrhelm, Chicago, Ill.
SP/4 W. D. Thorpe, Jesup, Iowa.
CW/2 D. W. York, Tulsa, Okla.
PFC. J. M. Ginn, Alexandria, Va.
SGT. R. A. Bowers, St. Long Beach, Cal.
SP/4 R. L. Lloyd, Sterling, Ohio

"WE SEEM TO HAVE THAT PAPER TIGER IN OUR TANK"

Beame's New Tax Plan — Page 3

NOW! **SUPER POST-O** $5000 IN CASH PRIZES EVERY GAME — SEE PAGE 15

WEATHER
Tonight: Cloudy, 40s.
Tomorrow: Cloudy, 60s.
Cloudy Thursday.
Air: Good
SUNSET: 7:58
SUNRISE TOMORROW: 6:14

New York Post

FOUNDED 1801, THE OLDEST CONTINUOUSLY PUBLISHED DAILY IN THE UNITED STATES.

FINAL
6 RACES

CLOSING MARKET

Vol. 174 No. 138   NEW YORK, TUESDAY, APRIL 29, 1975   20 Cents

PULLOUT

- ## Last Airlift Is On
- ## Panic in Saigon
- ## Reds Moving In

By George Esper

SAIGON (AP)—Dodging bullets from bitter South Vietnamese troops and fighting off desperate civilians, Americans fled Saigon today in an armada of 81 helicopters guarded by 800 marines and U.S. fighter planes roaring overhead.

Communist-led troops, meanwhile, pressed closer to Saigon and President Duong Van Minh maneuvered in search of a ceasefire.

The helicopters landed at Tan Son Nhut airport and on rooftops at the U.S. Embassy to compound to pick up most of the 800 to 900 remaining Americans and many Vietnamese.

The Pentagon said in Washington that 4,500 persons had been evacuated six hours after the operation began at 6 a.m. EDT and that about 600 were still awaiting pickup at the embassy. The evacuees were ferried to aircraft carriers in the South China Sea.

Senate Minority Leader Scott (R-Pa.) put the total number of South Vietnamese evacuated up to that time at 45,000. This compares with the 129,000 originally set as the goal. There was no estimate of how many of the 50,000 whose lives were believed at risk had gotten out.

[Another 50,000 persons, most of them presumably Vietnamese, fled from Saigon's port of Vung Tau in boats of all sizes. Some were picked up by American, South Korean, Japanese and Taiwanese vessels 10 miles off the port, destined for the main U.S. fleet farther out in the South China Sea, Reuters reported.

[Two boats carrying the U. S. consul general from the Mekong Delta town of Can Tho, 700 Vietnamese, 6 U.S. marines and 16 other Americans were fired on by helicopters with South Vietnamese markings. U. S. Navy planes answered their May Day call and rescued the passengers.]

The Viet Cong and North Vietnamese moved closer to Saigon with the heaviest fighting reported along Highway 1 less than 10 miles from the western edge of the capital. One officer said Saigon forces could hold out only a *few days* at best.

He said the American evacuation had caused panic among military men as well as civilians. America's 30-year involvement in the Indochina war was ending in wild and tragic scenes with U.S. marines and civilians using pistol and rifle butts to smash fingers of Vietnamese trying to claw their way over the 10-foot wall of the embassy.

At the airport, angry Vietnamese guards fired at busloads of evacuees and shouted: "We want to go, too." U.S. fighter-bombers flew air cover high over the city for the evacuation.

The Pentagon, which earlier reported only slight ground fire, said one outbound helicopter had been hit. No injury to the crew was reported.

The Pentagon said the evacuation had been delayed about an hour because of an unexploded

Continued on Page 5

LEFT: *Cartoon that appeared on February 11, 1965, after the start of Operation Rolling Thunder.*

OPPOSITE: *A Vietnam veteran at the memorial in Washington, D.C.* (Post *photo*)

Blackout of 1965

At the height of rush hour on November 9, 1965, the plug was pulled on New York City and most of the Northeast in the biggest power failure in U.S. history. The culprit was a power relay failure in Ontario. The blackout lasted 13 hours, but instead of igniting panic it created a giddy, school's-out attitude. Skyscrapers were illuminated with a milky glow from the full moon and those who were not trapped in elevators or the subway took to the streets to walk home or, if out-of-towners, wander and take in the sight. Restaurants stayed open and some businesses—including the *Post*—worked by lamp- and candlelight.

An article on the 10th described the scene of the previous day:

Darkness at dusk downtown . . .

THE STREETS were choked with cars going home when the traffic lights blinked out. And then the street lights, suddenly.

THE BUILDINGS soared up into the gray blue dusk, their windows blazing with light one second, then flickering, then out. In the cavernous lobbies, thronged with people on the way home, the darkness came down like a black shade. Worse the elevators stopped, instantly, without any explanation, and the passengers hung somewhere in the silent shafts—in pitch darkness.

THE PEOPLE said nothing at first. It happened so fast. It was worst in the elevators, in the rush-hour-jammed subway trains and in the stations. The light simply vanished. . . . No one had any idea what to do.

Out on the streets, the wind was blustery and raw, the shadows dark and unfamiliar. The skeins of cars moving along Broadway and its tributary streets began—with the traffic signals gone—to tangle together. The horns honked behind the headlight beams—the only illumination anywhere.

Another article listed what New Yorkers had experienced:

- Nearly 600,000 passengers were caught underground in 600 stalled subway cars when the power failed at 5:28 p.m., the height of the rush hour. Thousands were trapped for hours and hundreds for as long as eight hours.
- Several thousands were trapped in more than 200 elevators that jammed between floors in apartment and office buildings. At the Empire State, firemen had to bust through a wall to rescue three women.
- Untold thousands were left stranded at Penn Station and Grand Central. unable to get hotel rooms—even Bowery flea bags were sold out—they milled about in the dark, catnapped on steps, slept sprawled out on the floor under a blanket of newspapers.
- At Bellevue Hospital alone, the emergency ward treated 145 patients for injuries blamed on the blackout—broken arms and limbs from falls, car-accident victims and some heart cases.
- Looters smashed some 100 windows in Harlem, Bedford-Stuyvesant, South Bronx and East Bronx. Fifty-nine persons were arrested in connection with those lootings which police described as "very light."
- The Transit Authority put 3,500 buses, practically its whole fleet, into service. They didn't make a dent in pedestrian traffic. Cabs did peak business. Thousands of hikers walked up Eighth, Park and Fifth Aves. and across the bridges to Brooklyn and Queens to get home.

To everyone's amazement, the crime rate actually went down that night. "The city's astonishing aplomb in the face of a major crisis had a remarkable impact on police statistics," stated one article. "Commissioner Broderick reported that both the crime and casualty rates for the night were below normal."

Subway riders entertain themselves in a stalled subway car during the blackout. (Post *photo*)

BLACKOUT EXTRA

WEATHER
Fair, around 50. Cloudy tonight.

Tomorrow: Cloudy, 50s.

New York Post

© 1965 New York Post Corporation

FINAL BLUE

Vol. 164
No. 302

NEW YORK, WEDNESDAY, NOVEMBER 10, 1965

10 Cents

Gross On
Namath: P. 68

New York Post Sports

Race Results,
Entries: P. 62

72   NEW YORK, MOONDAY, JULY 21, 1969

'. . In Peace for All Mankind'

NASA via Associated Press Wirephoto

WEATHER
Tonight:
Cloudy, 60s.
Tomorrow:
Partly
Cloudy, 80s.
SUNSET: 8:22 P.M.
TOMORROW:
SUNRISE
5:42 A.M.

New York Post

© 1969 New York Post Corporation

Vol. 168
No. 207

NEW YORK, MOONDAY, JULY 21, 1969

10 Cents
15c Beyond 50-mile Zone

LATEST
NEWS
FINAL
7
RACES

Moonday

The dateline running along the borders of the *Post* read, "Moonday, July 21, 1969." The day after man first stepped on the moon, and the day the lunar module blasted off to bring them home.

Those who weren't home on Sunday, July 20, 1969, flocked to storefront window televisions to watch the moonwalk. "When Columbus landed in the New World, Spain's Queen Isabella didn't hear about it for six weeks," wrote the *Post*. "Through the magic of television, an estimated 500 million people around the world had a ringside seat at man's greatest adventure."

Astronauts Neil Armstrong and Buzz Aldrin uttered eloquent phrases during the exciting hours of *Apollo 11:*

ONE HOUR IN JUAREZ
THE JET DIVORCE
Start His Series in the Magazine
New York Post
HOME EDITION
BRONX
GLENN IN ORBIT

As Armstrong planted his left foot on the powdery surface at 10:56 p.m. yesterday, he said, "That's one small step for man, a giant leap for mankind."

The camera trained on Aldrin as he stepped on the far shore 20 minutes later and exclaimed: "Beautiful! Beautiful! Magnificent desolation."

There were other memorable utterances during the day of high adventure.

There were Armstrong's and man's first words from the moon's surface after touchdown at 4:18 p.m.: "Houston . . . Tranquillity base here. The Eagle has landed."

And when Aldrin, a deeply religious man, relayed this message to the world shortly after the landing: "This is the LM pilot. I'd like to take this opportunity to ask every person listening, whoever, wherever they may be, to pause for a moment and contemplate the events of the past few hours and to give thanks in his or her own way."

They unveiled a stainless steel plaque bearing the words: "Here men from planet earth first set foot upon the moon, July, 1969, A.D. We came in peace for all mankind."

The theme was carried through when President Nixon placed an extraordinary radio call to Armstrong and Aldrin as they strolled the surface.

ABOVE: *Seven years before the moonwalk, John Glenn made history as the first American to orbit the earth.* OPPOSITE: *"One small step for man . . ."*

Peace and Love, Baby

"Getting there was more than half the problem but for those who stuck it out there were compensations at the Woodstock Music and Art Fair," stated the *Post* on the second day of the three-day rock festival in August 1969. Four hundred thousand people made their way to the 600-acre site, a sloping meadow that created a natural amphitheater. Twenty-mile traffic jams, rain, lack of facilities, overcrowding and a health crisis didn't stop Woodstock from becoming a colossal love fest and defining event of the sixties. Those who gathered there to hear the music came from all backgrounds, from "crew-cut college students as well as pilgrims bearing the colors of the freak scene."

Jimi Hendrix, Joan Baez, Arlo Guthrie, The Who, Janis Joplin, the Greatful Dead, Jefferson Airplane, Santana, Sly and the Family Stone and many more took the 40-acre stage. The rain came the first day, during Ravi Shankar's sitar performance.

Bad weather was not expected. On Friday, "there were no signs of rain in the skies and the only clouds to cast an early pall over the festival came from marijuana smoke. State police and Sullivan County Sheriff's officials reported at least 51 arrests for possession of hashish and marijuana by 8 this morning," said one article. On Saturday, doctors were flown in to help the 20 on hand when the health situation got out of control. "'We simply can't cope with the medical needs of what amounts to a large city packed into a field,' said Dr. William Abruzzi. He said that many of the persons taken to hospitals were suffering from drug overdoses. Abruzzi said that his staff had treated diabetics in comas as well as epileptics."

Overall, the problems built up a sense of camaraderie and goodwill in the crowd. To the vast majority it was worth it, because it was all about the music.

ABOVE: *Music fans flock to Woodstock in August 1969.* (*Post* photo)

NEW YORK POST

Decade Eighteen
1971-1980

A president resigns; a serial murderer stalks women in three boroughs; a rock icon is shot dead in front of his Upper West Side building; a spree of Mob killings bloody the streets of Little Italy . . . and the nation throws its biggest 200-year birthday party in New York City.

The 1970s also brought a major shift to the *Post* with the arrival of new owner Rupert Murdoch. Owner of London's biggest tabloid, the *Sun*, as well as several other papers, Murdoch gradually turned Dorothy Schiff's liberal paper into a conservative one. He broadened the scope of readership by highlighting stories that concerned a diverse, working-class audience and ushered in the era of the *Post*'s now-legendary headlines such as HEADLESS BODY IN TOPLESS BAR.

Millions celebrated the jubilant bicentennial spectacles in New York on July 4, 1976. (Post photo)

Nixon Resigns

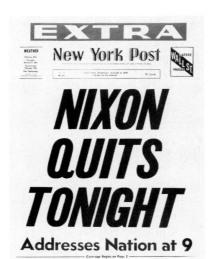

EXTRA

WEATHER

New York Post

NIXON QUITS TONIGHT

Addresses Nation at 9

The page-2 article of June 19, 1972, hinted at a possible court suit against a Nixon campaign committee member, but no one in the newsroom realized where the story would lead. "Court Action Over Dem Break-In?" would become part one in the chronicle of the Watergate scandal that rocked Washington and culminated in President Nixon's resignation two years later.

The president admitted to manipulating how the break-in investigation was handled and, faced with impeachment, became the first president to resign from office. At 9 p.m. on August 8, 1974, he addressed the nation from the Oval Office and announced, "I shall resign the Presidency effective at noon tomorrow."

The news went up in lights in Times Square on the streaming Allied Chemical tower. "President Nixon says he will resign tomorrow" flowed above the gathering crowd for five minutes.

The next day, in an article entitled "How New Yorkers Took the News," the *Post* reported that "small knots of people gathered in midtown to read the momentous news that the nation's 37th president . . . had become the first Chief Executive to choose to leave office. But, for the most part, the city seemed unmoved. None of those questioned was unhappy to see Nixon leave office, but none was ecstatic that he did." Theatergoers attending a performance of *Good Evening* at the Plymouth Theater on Broadway watched a TV in the lobby during intermission. "Subdued applause greeted Nixon's announcement that he would leave office. When the President was finished, the show went on."

"History came and went, but New Yorkers just went on and on," wrote William T. Slattery in his article.

LEFT: *The resigned president takes a lonely stroll along the ocean.* (Post *photo*) ABOVE: *News of President Nixon's resignation in August 1974.*

1970s: City Nears Bankruptcy

The fiscal crisis of the early 1970s fell heavily upon Mayor Abraham Beame, a Democrat elected in 1973. He staved off bankruptcy with massive city employee layoffs and by halting maintenance and other expensive yet necessary municipal projects. Working with the state and the federal government as well as with banks and unions, the mayor averted total disaster but the SEC accused him of faulty money management and an emergency city financial board was formed to restrict his power.

Recalling the financial crisis, former Editor in Chief Roger Wood told author Steven Cuozzo in *It's Alive* that the New York papers in that decade—except the *Post*—were not focused closely enough on the city. "Where the *Post* really scored, I felt, was that New York papers were seeing themselves as national newspapers— what was going on nationally or internationally was more important than what was going on in New York." He added that attention given to city matters by all New York papers in the 1990s would never allow a similar situation to escalate: "Do you think it would be possible to get into the same kind of mess [former Mayor] Abe Beame did with the kind of scrutiny that goes on now?"

ABOVE: *Abe Beame, Mayor of New York during the finance crisis–stricken 1970s.* ABOVE RIGHT: *Rupert Murdoch, who purchased the* Post *in 1976.* (Post *photos*)

Murdoch's Post

In late 1976 the *Post* was purchased by Rupert Murdoch, the Australian-born owner of newspapers in Australia, the United Kingdom and Texas *(San Antonio Express-News)*. Rupert Murdoch brought a conservative voice to the traditionally liberal New York newspaper scene as well as a new team of Australian and British reporters and editors to the offices on South Street.

In *It's Alive*, Steven Cuozzo writes: "Murdoch envisioned transforming the stodgy Post into a popular organ of news and entertainment appealing to large numbers of people. He told an advertising forum, 'Our entire editorial thrust at the Post will be to provide New Yorkers with brighter, shorter, more clearly understood stories and to marry the words with better and sharper pictures.' The crusade was on to make the paper more easily readable, and to sell more copies with punchier front pages."

Murdoch, who ventured into television and electronic media and built a multibillion-dollar media empire, would be forced to sell the *Post* 11 years later due to an FCC cross-ownership ruling. In 1993 he obtained a waiver to the ruling and reacquired the paper.

Lights Out! Looting!

Unlike the relative calm and giddiness of the Blackout of 1965, the massive shutdown that hit the city on July 14, 1977, erupted into arson, looting and violence. Shortly after 9:30 that night, generators throughout greater New York shut down as a result of power shortages caused by three lightning strikes in Westchester County.

The sudden darkness on that hot night instigated total anarchy, from fires, looting and sniper fire to a prison riot in the Bronx. Police took to the streets with shotguns and made mass arrests, but through the night mobs crashed through storefronts and destroyed millions of dollars' worth of property.

ABOVE: *A police officer orders two looters to give up their bags filled with stolen items in the Bushwick section of Brooklyn.* (Post *Photo*)
RIGHT: *The* Post's *blackout headline of July 15, 1977.*

NEW YORK POST FINAL
CLOSING MARKET
FRIDAY, JULY 15, 1977. 25 CENTS

DAILY PAID CIRCULATION FOR JUNE
603,517

24 HOURS OF TERROR

Carey fears a new blackout
See Page 5

- Several thousand looters and arsonists ran wild in parts of four boroughs during yesterday's blackout. It was the worst outbreak of rioting in the city's history and more than 3400 were arrested. See Page 3.

- The blackout and the violence that went with it will cost uncounted millions of dollars. New York's disaster adds up to most expensive man-made one the nation has ever seen. See Page 17.

- Inspectors fanned out through the city today in a massive sweep of stores and restaurants to guard against the sale of food spoiled after refrigerators and freezers were knocked out. See Page 7.

- The blackout started because lightning struck three times — not in the same place, but close enough to trigger a crisis. It lasted 24 hours due to the enormous technical problems involved in restoring service. See Pages 4 and 13.

- Con Edison is under heavy criticism on many levels as both the state and federal government begin investigations. See Page 5.

- It was a time for heroes as well as villains. Some of the greatest benefactors were those involved in the life-and-death drama of the hospital emergency wards. See Page 4.

- New York's long nightmare. See Editorial, Page 44.

Grand Central Terminal is crippled
See Page 7

BLACKOUT SPECIAL

"Sam told me to do it"

Serial killer David Berkowitz shot six persons dead and wounded seven others in 1976 and 1977, instigating one of the most dramatic manhunts in New York history. A task force of 100 detectives worked on the case which finally resulted in the arrest of the paranoid schizophrenic in August 1977. Five of the six victims Berkowitz shot with his .44 caliber pistol were pretty young women he stalked in Queens, Brooklyn and the Bronx; the sixth was a male companion in a car with one of the women.

After his arrest, Berkowitz told detectives he was following orders from a demon named Sam. "I was out to kill. It was my job.

ABOVE: *David Berkowitz arrives for booking at the 84th Precinct in Brooklyn* (Post *photo by Terence McCarten*)

Sam told me to do it. Sam sent me on an assignment. I had to do what I had to do. I had my orders. Sam sent me."

Under a headline reading, LET MY DAUGHTER BE THE LAST ONE of August 2, eight days before Berkowitz was caught, the mother of the serial killer's last victim begged the madman to stop. *Post* writer Steve Dunleavy's interview with the mother of Stacy Moskowitz quoted her plea to the unknown killer: "I know what I have lost and I just don't want anyone to lose in the same way." Stacy and her boyfriend had been shot while they sat in a parked car in Bensonhurst, Brooklyn. Her boyfriend survived, but was blinded by the bullet that hit his face.

Investigators discovered bizarre writing on the walls of Berkowitz's filthy studio apartment in the Bronx after his arrest. Scrawled next to a fist hole: "Hi. My name is Mr. Williams and I live in this hole. I have several children who I'm turning into killers. Wait til they grow up."

Berkowitz pleaded guilty, but quickly switched to an insanity plea. He later confessed to FBI agents that he made up the story about a demon commanding him to kill. In his insanity plea, Berkowitz claimed that his orders came from a 3,000-year-old demon living in a dog owned by his neighbor, Sam Carr. In spite of this crazy story, the prosecutor's forensic psychiatrist said, "While the defendant shows paranoid traits, they do not interfere with his fitness to stand trial . . . the defendant is as normal as anyone else. Maybe a little neurotic." With that, Berkowitz was found fit to stand trial and ultimately sentenced to 365 years at Attica Prison.

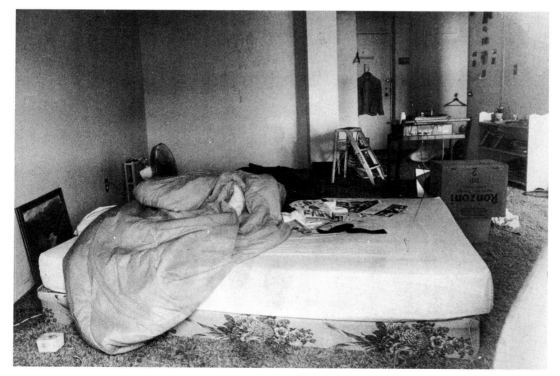

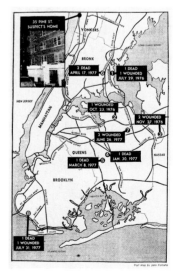

ABOVE: *Son of Sam victim map.*
LEFT: *View of Berkowitz's $265-a-month studio apartment in Yonkers.* (Post *photo by Robert Kalfus*)

TODAY
Partly Cloudy, 85-90
TONIGHT
Partly Cloudy, low 70s
TOMORROW
Sunny, 90s
Details, page 2

TV: PAGE 34

NEW YORK POST

METRO
TODAY'S RACING

THURSDAY, AUGUST 11, 1977   25 CENTS   Vol. 176, No. 225   © 1977 The New York Post Corporation

DAILY PAID
CIRCULATION
2D QUARTER 1977   **609,390**

CAUGHT!

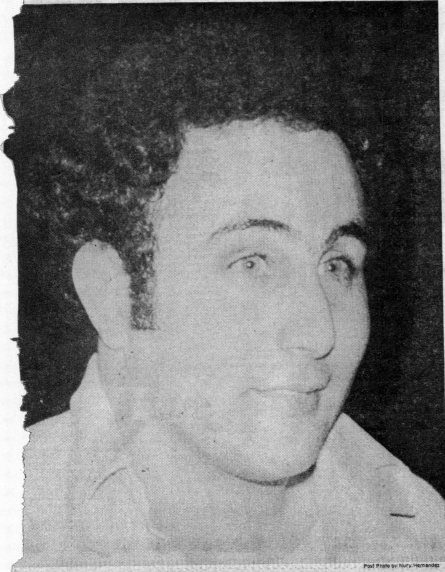

Post Photo by Nury Hernandez

Son of Sam was on way to kill again

'I wanted to go out in a blaze of glory'

By CARL J. PELLECK

The man police say is the Son of Sam was on his way to claim more victims when he walked into the arms of waiting detectives.

David Berkowitz, 24, had already written a letter—his third—addressed to Suffolk County and New York police and the press. He was going to leave it alongside his latest victim. It had no stamp on it.

In questioning after his arrest last night, Berkowitz said he hadn't quite made up his mind whether to stalk his next victims in Riverdale or in the Hamptons.

And he told police that he wanted to "go out in a blaze of glory" because he felt the cops were closing in on him. Sources said the letter made a similar claim.

'DID IT FOR SAM'

A pleasant-looking, slightly chubby young man, Berkowitz remained calm throughout the many hours of questioning at Police Headquarters.

He gave no reason why he started his killing spree on July 29, 1976 other than "I was doing it for Sam . . . Sam can do anything . . . I was driven to do it by Sam."

He gave cops the answer they had long been seeking: Sam is a man who lives in a building behind Berkowitz' Yonkers apartment house.

He identified the man as Sam Carr of 316 Warburton Av.

When Berkowitz was grabbed, he had the dreaded .44-caliber pistol with him. He had two dozen extra bullets in a brown paper bag he had

Continued on Page 2

Full coverage: Pages 2, 3, 4, 5, 7, 32, 33.

POST WEEKEND
SPORTS

FRIDAY, JULY 13, 1979 25 CENTS

YANKEES
CRUSH
SEATTLE;
GOOSE
RETURNS
●
Race probe zeroes in
on 'crime kingpin'
●
SPORTS BEGINS ON P. 79

U.S. Government Report:
Carlton
is lowest.
Box or Menthol:
Ten packs of Carlton
have less tar than
one pack of...

'There's no mafia, it's all baloney.
Killings happen. It's a way of life'

CARMINE GALANTE TALKING TO THE POST IN DANBURY CORRECTIONAL CENTER, NOV. 3, 1978.

The end of Godfather Carmine Galante is marked inglorious
from the restaurant where he ate his last meal. The moment
Galante's cigar smoldered on, clamped tightly in his teeth,

DC-10s going back in the air: Page 9

NEW YORK POST

FINAL
LATEST PRICES

FRIDAY, JULY 13, 1979 25 CENTS

DAILY SALES
NOW EXCEED 620,000

TV: Page 28

GREED!

Mob chiefs
killed the
Godfather
for grabbing
too much

INSIDE
● Expert crime reporter Carl Pelleck
tells the whole story of how and why
the national Mafia bosses ordered
the killing of Carmine Galante. P. 3
● Exclusive account of the shootings
from the boy who survived. P. 4
● Godfather's last interview: he was a
"political prisoner." P. 5
● Galante's respectable facade — the
cleaning shop, the ranch house, P. 5
● Dragnet out for his bodyguards, who
saw the triple murder. P. 3

ANOTHER PHOTO: BACK PAGE

tsly as a detective covers him with a bloodstained tablecloth
t of truth — his left eye shot out — was so brutally instant,
long after his life, notable only for cruelty and greed, ended.

Mob Wars

On a summer night in 1979, Mafia boss Carmine Galante was enjoying a cigar after dinner in Joe and Mary's Italian restaurant in Brooklyn when an unknown gunman walked in and shot him. The *Post* caption for a set of gruesome crime-scene photos read:

> The end of Godfather Carmine Galante is marked ingloriously as a detective covers him with a bloodstained tablecloth from the restaurant where he ate his last meal. The moment of truth—his left eye shot out—was so brutally instant, Galante's cigar smoldered on, clamped tightly in his teeth, long after his life, notable only for cruelty and greed, ended.

Galante had earned the wrath of New York's other bosses with his bloody campaign to become the boss of all bosses, a strategy that included killing off eight top Mafiosi in 1978.

After Galante's execution the *Post* published an exclusive series about the Mob's hold on New York. The first article revealed the shocking power of underworld control throughout the city:

> Who owns New York? According to the Mob they do— and yesterday's slaying is just one more part of proving that. Top detectives who have spent the past 20 years investigating the Mob's activities say they brandish not only an influence but, in many cases, control a very large chunk of New York's industry and commerce—which also means America.
>
> If the city's five crime families ever conspired to paralyze the city, they could halt the movement of virtually every car, cab, bus, truck, train, ship in the harbor, and passenger and cargo plane.
>
> With such potential power over the people in New York's five boroughs and millions more in surrounding suburbs, the underworld can also shut down literally thousands of retail and wholesale businesses.

In spite of a force of 1,000 officers working in the NYPD's Organized Crime Control Bureau and another 400 federal cops involved in the war against the Mob, battles were not being won:

> Law enforcement has spent billions trying to stem the tide of underworld infiltration . . . but the effort has been almost a total failure . . . gambling, narcotics, pornography, prostitution, murder-by-contract, hijacking, robberies, embezzlements, burglaries, and strongarming are in a healthier state of illegality today than ever.

The *Post* explained that Carmine "The Cigar" Galante was executed for his greed, since the heads of New York's other four crime organizations got fed up with his push for complete control. In 1979, the five main crime families were as follows:

CRIME FAMILY	BOSS
Gambino	Paul Castellano
Bonanno	Carmine Galante
Genovese	Frank "Funzi" Tieri
Luchese	Anthony "Tony Ducks" Corallo
Colombo	Carmine "The Snake" Persico

Retired NYPD police officer and organized crime expert Ralph Salerno wrote the *Post* Mob series with *Post* writer George Carpozi, Jr., another Mafia expert and author of 40 books. In the article that appeared on July 18, 1979, they reported on the Mob's role in New York's garment industry. Unlike other spheres of influence where one family would dominate, all five crime families were involved in the clothing industry housed in the 40-block neighborhood around Fashion Avenue. In addition to owning many of the businesses and the trucking firms that deliver the goods, the Mob ran loansharking operations for dress manufacturers and other companies. A company may have cash flow problems until it receives payments from its buyers. Before the big checks come in, the company must pay salaries and the electric bill. When banks judge him a bad risk, the owner turns to a Mob loanshark. It's a costly decision, explains the *Post* writers:

> A $25,000 loan isn't an uncommon advance. Nor is the vigorish or Vig—in slang—meaning the interest. It's 3 to 5 percent. More often 5. That compares with, say 11.5 percent to the banks.
>
> The difference is that the Mob's interest isn't yearly, but weekly.
>
> Thus the borrower of that $25,000 must come up with $1250 every seven days.
>
> The Mob doesn't care about getting back its principal. All it wants is the vigorish. Because if the dress man-

ABOVE: *Mafia don Joseph Colombo, who ironically created an organization that rallied against the stereotype that all Italian-Americans are connected to organized crime. His execution was covered in award-winning articles by* Post *writer Judith Michaelson. (*Post *photo by Vic DeLucia)*

NEW YORK POST, WEDNESDAY, JULY 18, 1979   17

THE MOB'S DEADLY HOLD ON NEW YORK

Where you'll find the best-dressed mobsters in town

The Mob has penetrated all facets of daily life. The Post continues its special investigation of crime's control of the Big Apple with this report by former New York policeman Ralph F. Salerno and prize-winning Post author George Carpozi Jr. Today, Part 5 of the series examines the underworld control of the life of Fashion Avenue.

NOWHERE in New York does the Mob have greater power than in the garment business. The 40 blocks around Fashion Avenue crawl with Mafia hoodlums and other unsavory denizens of the underworld.

The syndicate has its finger in every level of the apparel industry:

● From ownership of large manufacturing firms to silent but sovereign partnerships in other dress houses;

● From involvement in the cut-

Louis (Lepke) Buchalter, left, infiltrated Seventh Avenue for the Mob. Today's top cats include Joe (Stretch) Stracci, right, and Joseph Rosato, below. Ruby Stein, below right, was on the Avenue until he landed in Jamaica Bay.

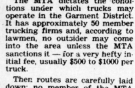

The MTA dictates the conditions under which trucks may operate in the Garment District. It has approximately 50 member trucking firms and, according to lawmen, no outsider may come into the area unless the MTA sanctions it — for a very hefty initial fee, usually $500 to $1000 per truck.

Then routes are carefully laid down; no member of the MTA ever encounters a competitor's tire tracks crossing its designated delivery zones.

An MTA trucker may never fear losing a route to a competitor, so long as he pays his dues to the association.

So what, you ask, has the MTA to do with the Mob? Hear this: a police undercover agent, who bought into a garment business and found himself with a strike threat on his hands, was visited by one of Funzi Tieri's emissaries, Matthew (Matty the Horse) Ianiello, who informed him that all his problems could be solved if he put a couple of MTA friends, Larry Paladino and another, on the pad for $200 a week.

Of course, they would no be required to work for that stipend. They would merely service the undercover man with their influence — and muscle if ever needed.

One of first benefits of that arrangement was an end to the threatened strike.

That was worked out, as an undercover tail discovered, when Ianiello met an unidentified underworld emissary in Ferrara's Restaurant in Little Italy then returned to nearby Umberto's Clam House.

(Umberto's, owned by Ianiello's brother, is the place where Joseph "Crazy Joe" Galio bled to death when blasted with a fusilade of bullets during a late night dinner.)

---

ufacturer encounters a problem in collecting for this new line, he rides along the $1250-a-week interest payment for as long as he's in the hole.

Those who can't cough up the interest have two options:

Historically, organized crime has never been known to have patience with slow payers. Unsightly weed-grown lots, the waterways around the city, and many of our concrete highways hold the remains of borrowers who failed to eliminate their indebtedness to the Mob.

But the garment manufacturer has an alternative to giving up his life. He can just give over his business.

And that's mainly why so many Mob figures are owners and partners in dress firms.

One of the most sensational Mob hits in the city was the shooting of Mafia don Joe Colombo. In one of Mob history's most amazing twists, Colombo was the founder of the Italian-American Civil Rights League, an organization dedicated to eradicating the stereotype that all Italian-Americans are connected to organized crime.

Colombo's highly publicized rallies did not sit well with the rest of the Mob, and in 1970 Carlo Gambino decided he'd finally had enough. Colombo was shot in the back of the head at his second annual Italian-American Civil Rights League march on June 27. The attempted execution did not immediately kill Colombo; he remained in a coma for the next seven years.

Post writer Judith Michaelson covered the shooting with her story "I Was with Him," and her reporting won her the 1971 Front Page award for best general news story from the Newspaper Women's Club of New York and the 1971 Byline award for writing against a deadline from the Newspaper Reporters' Association of New York City.

OPPOSITE: *In 1972, a rash of Mob hits included the death of Joe "Crazy Joey" Gallo at Umberto's Clam House on Mulberry Street. In the early morning hours of April 7, 1972, after a night out at the Copacabana, Gallo of the Colombo crime family was dining with five others, including his wife and her 10-year-old daughter at the Little Italy restaurant. A gangland shooter walked in, stepped up to his table and shot him.*

The Gallo shooting was the third Mob execution that week. On April 5, mobster Bruno Carnevale was shot in the head in Queens, and the next night Tommy Ernst was shot down in Staten Island.

New York Post

FOUNDED 1801. THE OLDEST CONTINUOUSLY PUBLISHED DAILY IN THE UNITED STATES.

AFTERNOON MARKET OPENING

Vol. 171
No. 121

NEW YORK, FRIDAY, APRIL 7, 1972
© 1972 New York Post Corporation

15 Cents

WEATHER

Light rain, 40.
Tonight: Chance of snow, 30s.
Tomorrow: Cloudy, 40s.
Clear and cool Sunday.

SUNSET: 6:27
SUNRISE TOMORROW: 5:29

JOE GALLO SLAIN

Reds Push On, Open 4th Front

By George Esper

SAIGON (AP)—North Vietnamese troops today opened a fourth front in their nine-day-old offensive with more than a dozen attacks on towns and bases in the Mekong Delta to the south.

U.S. warplanes, meanwhile, hammered North Vietnamese forces in North and South Vietnam and neighboring stretches of Laos with more than 600 strikes. Two Navy fighter-bombers and a big rescue helicopter were shot down, the U.S. Command said, and six Americans were missing.

The district town of Loc Ninh, 75 miles north of Saigon, fell after fighting so close that an air spot-ter overhead reported that the defending South Vietnamese were calling artillery fire in on their own positions.

The U. S. Command announced the first casualties in the renewed air attack on the North that began yesterday. It said two Navy A7s were downed by surface-to-air missiles near Dong Hoi, 45 miles north of the DMZ. It also reported a big rescue helicopter shot down south of the DMZ and said enemy shore batteries slightly damaged the destroyer Lloyd Thomas as it was shelling the coast.

Six Americans were missing in the air crashes, one flier was rescued and

Continued on Page 5

By Carl J. Pelleck and Cy Egan

Joseph (Crazy Joe) Gallo was shot to death by an apparent gangland assassin early today in a restaurant in the heart of Manhattan's Little Italy.

The 42-year-old Brooklyn gang leader was cut down by three bullets as he sat eating with a party of five other persons, including his bride of less than a month, in Umbertos Clam House, 129 Mulberry St.

Witnesses told police the shots were fired by a short, stocky man in a brown suit who entered the restaurant and started shooting without a word.

One bullet struck Gallo in the left buttock, a second shattered his left elbow and the third ripped into his left shoulder and apparently traveled downward, striking his heart.

Gallo was rushed to Beekman Downtown Hospital in a police car. He was dead on arrival.

His death came nine months after the attempted assassination of rival Brooklyn gang leader Joseph Colombo Sr. at an Italian - American Civil Rights League rally in Columbus Circle last June 28.

There have been repeated hints that the attempted killing had been engineered by Gallo with the approval of Carlo Gambino, the 73-year-old reputed overlord of the Brooklyn rackets.

Just recently Gallo turned up on the Broadway scene and announced

See Earl Wilson story on Page 5.

that he was through with the underworld and would write his life story now.

There were reports that Gallo had gone early today to Umbertos—a recently opened restaurant on the northwest corner of Mulberry and Hester Sts.—for a birthday celebration.

With him were the former Sina Essary, 30, a dental assistant whom he married on March 16; her daughter, Lisa, 10; his sister, Carmella Fiorello, of Howard Beach, Queens; a friend, Peter Diapioulas and the latter's companion, Edith Russo, about 23, of 3006 Av. L, Brooklyn.

Police said Gallo lived at 7 W. 14th St.

Gallo and his party took seats in the heavy captain's chairs around one of the butcher block tables that are a feature of the restaurant — which specializes in scungilli, fried shrimps and other Italian fish delicacies.

The restaurant was due

Continued on Page

Post Photo by Tim Boxer

Joe Gallo and his bride, Sina after they were married last March 16 in the apartment of actor Jerry Orbach.

ON THE INSIDE

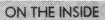

Winning Lottery Numbers, Page 2

NEW YORK POST

Decade Nineteen
1981- 1990

An entrepreneurial New Yorker hawks pieces of the Berlin Wall on Fifth Avenue. (Post photo by Don Halasy)

The *Post*'s new emphasis on classic headlines and sizzling crime coverage built it into the nation's fourth largest daily newspaper by 1983. News doesn't stop on the weekends, so the 35-cent Sunday *Post* hit the streets in 1989.

In 1988 a new congressional bill forced Rupert Murdoch to sell the *Post*—newspaper owners like Murdoch, who owned television stations as well as print media in the same market, would no longer be granted permanent waivers from cross-ownership rules. Thus began a tumultuous period of new owners and rollicking changes during which the city—and the world—doubted the *Post* would survive.

The world cheered the fall of the Berlin Wall in November 1989, heralding the close of the Cold War era and followed two years later by the dissolution of the Soviet Union. The most notorious crimes of the eighties included those of Bernhard Goetz, the subway gunman who took the law into his own hands; Robert Chambers, the preppie murderer; John Gotti, the Mafia boss who lost his status as the "Teflon Don" with a big conviction; and the mysterious case of the Zodiac killer.

Striking Back

On the afternoon of December 22, 1984, four young men surrounded Bernhard Goetz on the No. 2 train and demanded five dollars. In a move that earned him folk-hero status with some, Goetz pulled out a .38 from his waistband and started shooting. "When the smoke had cleared," wrote the *Post*, "four teenagers lay seriously wounded, one paralyzed for life." Goetz jumped out at the next stop and disappeared up the stairs.

The press dubbed Goetz the Subway Vigilante and the city was polarized with those who cheered him and those who felt he was a menace to society. Syndicated columnist Patrick J. Buchanan lauded the pro-Goetz camp as a "sign of moral health" in an article of January 1, 1985 in which he stated:

> The scene was played out thousands of times last year. Four young hoodlums, all with criminal records, armed with sharpened screwdrivers, moved boisterously into a subway car, and then selected their prey.
>
> In this instance, a slight, bespectacled 36-year-old man was sitting alone. Crowding around, they asked first for the time, then for a cigarette, then if he had $5. The shake-down was on.
>
> This time, however, the outcome was different. The fellow they had chosen to intimidate, to humiliate, to toy with and rob, was calm and gutsy.
>
> "Yes, I've got $5 for each of you," the prey replied to the predators.
>
> Then, he pulled out a silver-plated .38 and put a bullet into each of his tormentors, hitting two in the front and two in the back.
>
> Far from being a manifestation of "insanity" or "madness," the universal rejoicing in New York over the gunman's success is a sign of moral health.
>
> Swaggering storm troopers in sneakers commit 40 felonies a day; a reported 10,000 men, women and children were robbed, brutalized or assaulted in the first 10 months of last year alone.
>
> Why should there be such alarm at the healthy jubilation in the sheep pen, when the astonishing news arrives that one of our own has just ripped up four predator wolves and escaped unscathed?

Goetz turned himself in and was sentenced to six months in prison on the charge of weapons possession.

ABOVE: *Pope John Paul II greets a girl from the crowd during his visit to New York in October 1979. (Post photo)*

Pope John Paul II was circling St. Peter's Square as usual on May 13, 1981, waving to the crowd assembled for his traditional Wednesday audience. Gunfire ripped through the scene when Mehmet Ali Agca aimed at the pontiff and opened fire. One of the pope's bodyguards threw himself on the pope to protect him from further fire.

The pope was severely wounded and spent the next two months recovering in a Rome hospital. Two years later the pope visited his would-be assassin in prison and forgave him.

LEFT: *The freed Iranian hostages receive the biggest ticker tape parade in New York history on January 30, 1981. The parade wound through the Valley of Heroes on lower Broadway and used 1,262 tons of ticker tape. (Post photo)*

Coupons for Koch

In January 1982 the *Post* launched a campaign to drum up support for Ed Koch as a candidate for Governor of New York. The paper made the move on its own, and the mayor, then in his second term, was taken by complete surprise when he saw the Monday issue at the airport upon returning from a vacation in Spain. He quickly went with the idea, however, and announced he would run.

The Koch campaign included a coupon that readers could fill in and mail to the *Post* to show their support. Koch lost the primary election to Mario Cuomo, but was re-elected for a third term as mayor in 1985.

OPPOSITE: *The* Post *urged Mayor Ed Koch to run for governor in an article complete with a coupon Koch fans could mail in to show their support.* ABOVE AND LEFT: *Ed Koch, Mayor of New York from 1978 to 1989. This enormously popular, three-term Democrat was supported by both major parties in his run for his second term and was famous for stopping among a crowd to shout, "How'm I doing?" After losing his bid for a fourth term to David Dinkins, Koch wrote a bestselling memoir,* Mayor, *and contributed a column to the* Post *for five years. (*Post *photo)*

NEW YORK POST, MONDAY, JANUARY 25, 1982   R★★★★ 3

Ed Koch: *He combines long political experience and acumen with an awesome record of achievement.*

THE POST SAYS:

LET'S DRAFT ED KOCH FOR GOVERNOR

THE Post today publishes an editorial on Page 34 urging Mayor Koch to declare himself a candidate for the Democratic nomination for Governor of New York.

READ IT. IF YOU AGREE SIGN THE COUPON BELOW.

Cut it out and mail it to: Governor Koch P.O. Box 495 Knickerbocker Station New York, N.Y. 10002

The Post wants the Mayor to know how many New Yorkers agree that he should be the next Governor.

The more coupons are received from our readers, the bigger the response, the more it is possible that a "Draft Ed for Governor" movement will gather force and eventually sweep him to victory.

★ The Post believes

Mayor Koch is the right man for the tough job waiting in Albany when Governor Carey bows out at the end of this year.

MAYOR KOCH IS RELUCTANT TO PUT HIS NAME FORWARD.

He has a very real love for New York City and he has just been reelected with a massive vote of confidence to a second term.

But The Post believes he has larger obligations.

New York City needs him — but so does New York State.

Moreover, it is clear the City can never be entirely sound and secure unless the State itself is sound and secure.

★ Ed Koch combines long political experience and acumen with an awesome

record of achievement — a record explored in detail in today's editorial.

Mayor Koch is as familiar with the corridors of power in Washington as he is with the levers of power in Albany and the limits of power in City Hall.

It is no secret that the Mayor flies back from his vacation in Madrid today to increasing speculation that he should consider moving to Albany.

HELP MAKE UP HIS MIND.

Send your coupon in today. Encourage your friends to do the same.

★ Let's get Ed Koch to Albany — for the sake of the city — and the sake of the State.

High court showdown on ERA

WASHINGTON (AP) — The Supreme Court said today it will decide soon whether the proposed Equal Rights Amendment is dead.

But the timing of the court's review could prove a crushing blow to pro-ERA forces.

The justices, agreeing to speed up their deliberations, said they will review a ruling by a federal judge in Idaho that the proposed amendment died three years ago.

U.S. District Judge Marion Callister of Boise ruled Dec. 23 that Congress acted unconstitutionally when it extended the ratification deadline from March 22, 1979, to next June 30.

Callister's decision also said that state legislatures are free to rescind previous ERA ratification votes.

Although the judge's

ruling did not block the ratification process, feminist groups view it as a major psychological stumbling block to a final six-month ratification drive.

In today's brief order, the high court said it will decide whether Callister was right.

But the court's orders did not include any timetable for hearings. It was expected that the constitutional issues would not be argued before the justices until mid-April.

If ratified, the ERA would become the Constitution's 27th Amendment and ban discrimination based on sex.

The ERA ratification drive suffered setbacks

in the legislatures of three non-ratifying states — Georgia, Oklahoma and Illinois — in recent weeks.

Thirty-five of the required 38 states have ratified the ERA, but five of those states have voted to rescind previous ratifications.

The National Organization for Women rushed directly to the Supreme Court to challenge Callister's ruling.

The Reagan administration advised against any speedy decision on the constitutional issues, and instead suggested that the justices consider setting aside Callister's decision as legally premature.

ED KOCH FOR GOVERNOR

MAIL TO:

GOVERNOR KOCH, P.O. Box 495, Knickerbocker Station, New York, N.Y. 10002.

★ **I THINK** that Ed Koch should declare himself a candidate for the Democratic nomination for the Governorship of New York.

SIGN YOUR NAME HERE

Murder at the Steakhouse

At 5:25 p.m. on December 16, 1985, the sidewalks of East 46th Street were filled with shoppers and people coming home from work. A limo pulled up in front of Sparks, the upscale steakhouse frequented by wealthy East Siders and diplomats from the nearby United Nations Building. The driver got out and helped an older man out of the backseat. The passenger, 73-year-old Paul Castellano, head of the Gambino crime family, and his right-hand man, 45-year-old Thomas Bilotti, were late for a meeting inside. Before they got to the restaurant door, two men in trench coats rushed up and started shooting. Both mobsters were killed instantly with shots to the head and chest. The *Post* story described the scene:

Terrified pedestrians ran for their lives and ducked behind cars as the trio of trenchcoated killers—all armed with automatic weapons—approached the chrome-plated black limo, opening fire and ran off to a waiting getaway car.

Big Paul, the feared godfather of the Gambino crime family . . . tumbled onto the sidewalk, his head coming to rest on the limo's floor and his blood flowing in rivulets into the gutter. . . . His half-smoked, partially chewed cigar fell form his lips and was found on the curb alongside a piece of his skull the size of a ping-pong ball.

And blood was splattered over his elegant dark blue mohair suit, light blue shirt and $200 designer Italian loafers.

Bilotti fell beside the open driver's door of his 1986 black Lincoln Continental . . . a fat, gold pinky ring on his left hand shined in the street lights, and the keys to his car lay just inches from his outstretched right hand.

With the death of Castellano, up-and-coming mobster John Gotti was elevated to head of the Gambino clan. He had orchestrated the hit with a group of Gambino confidants, including his friend Sammy "The Bull" Gravano, who called themselves the Fist.

This killing would come back to haunt seasoned hitman John Gotti, but not before he became the most famous wise guy in the world. Acquitted in two high-profile cases in the late 1980s—in which he paid off jury members—Gotti became known as the Teflon Don, whom the law couldn't seem to touch. Admired by the media as well as movie stars who attended his trials, he basked in the limelight and fearlessly walked the streets in flashy suits and silk ties.

ABOVE: *The famous Gotti-ordered hit of Mob boss Paul Castellano.* LEFT: *Gotti arriving for trial at 111 Centre Street in January 1990. This time the "Teflon Don" would not beat the charges.* OPPOSITE: *Gotti in cuffs, 1990.* (Post *photo*)

Gotti held court at the Ravenite Social Club in Little Italy and, on the weekends, at the Bergin Hunt and Fish Club in Queens. Intimidating witnesses and paying off jurors had made him feel invincible, but in late 1990 his luck ran out. Gotti, Gravano and two others were arrested for the slaying of godfather Paul Castellano back in 1985 as well as 13 other charges. This time the trial didn't go Gotti's way. FBI wiretaps had nailed Gotti's incriminating conversations, and Sammy the Bull made a deal with the prosecutors to testify against his onetime Mob *fratello* in the sensational trial. On April 2, 1992, the jury delivered guilty verdicts on all 14 counts, and Gotti received multiple life sentences without parole.

An American Tragedy

The final words from the space shuttle *Challenger*, reprinted on January 28, 1986:

Mission Control: Challenger, go at throttle up.
Smith: Roger, go at throttle up. [Fireball occurs]
Mission Control: We're at a minute 15 seconds, velocity 2900 feet per second, altitude 9 nautical miles, range distance 7 nautical miles.
[A long silence]
Mission Control: Flight controllers are looking very carefully at the situation. Obviously a major malfunction. We have no downlink.

Crowds of spectators at Cape Canaveral and the national television audience watched in horror as the shuttle exploded and disintegrated into plumes of smoke that spiraled into the Atlantic. All seven crew members were killed, including schoolteacher Christa McAuliffe.

In his address to the nation that evening, President Ronald Reagan expressed his sorrow and quoted from John Gillespie Maggee's poem "High Flight":

The crew of the space shuttle Challenger honored us by the manner in which they lived their lives. We will never forget them, nor the last time we saw them, this morning, as they prepared for their journey and waved goodbye and "slipped the surly bonds of earth" to "touch the face of God."

Pieces of the shattered shuttle trail smoke and fire across the Florida sky today as the doomed ship explodes — only 75 seconds after blastoff.

Final words from Challenger

The Preppie Murder

On a warm summer night in 1986, two teenagers strolled into Central Park for a tryst after having drinks at Dorrian's, an Upper East Side bar popular with the private-school crowd. But only one of them left the park later that night. In September, a grand jury indicted Robert Chambers for the murder of 18-year-old Jennifer Levin. They didn't buy the handsome college dropout's story that Jennifer lured him into kinky sex and initiated the tragic, accidental outcome.

Mel Juffe's article, "A Chilling View of the Preppie World," pointed out the contrasts between hardworking Jennifer Levin, a graduate of the Baldwin School who was working at a restaurant to save money for college, and Chambers, two-time prep school dropout who was kicked out of Boston University after one semester. The article described them both as "well-bred products of America's most exclusive prep schools" and summarized the case:

They seemed to live in a fast lane paved with all the instant gratifications that trust funds can buy.

At first Chambers, now 21, denied he was even with Levin at the time she died. Every time the cops caught him in a lie he changed his story, creating about a half dozen versions.

Finally Chambers came up with a lurid story of kinky sex in Central Park, saying Levin used her panties to tie his hands behind his back—and then painfully squeezed his testicles.

Chambers—a brawny six-footer—claimed in effect he was a rape victim defending himself.

Killing the slender Levin was just an accident, he insisted.

The 12-week trial ended when Chambers pleaded guilty to first-degree manslaughter. The charge carried a five- to 15-year jail sentence. The jury had deliberated for nine days on the two counts of second-degree murder charged against him, but were nowhere close to a verdict. From one day to the next they leaned toward conviction, then acquittal. "The plea he copped was probably the least serious charge he would have gotten," a juror told the *Post* after the trial.

As part of the plea agreement, Chambers had to spill the truth to the judge. It didn't come easily for him:

It took Robert Chambers three tries before he finally admitted he meant to seriously hurt Jennifer Levin when he killed her in 1986.

The 21-year-old preppie shook his head violently throughout the state Supreme Court proceeding yesterday and cried after he pleaded guilty to first-degree manslaughter in a plea-bargain deal.

"Is it true that on Aug. 26, 1986, you intended to cause serious physical harm to Jennifer Levin and thereby caused her death?" Judge Howard Bell asked Chambers as the defendant entered the plea.

"Looking back on everything, I have to say yes," Chambers said in a barely audible voice. "But in my heart, I didn't mean it."

Asst. District Attorney Linda Fairstein leaped to her feet and rushed to the bench after Chambers spoke.

"I want you to ask him about his mind and his hands—not his heart," she told Bell loudly before returning to her table.

The judge repeated his question.

This time Chambers sighed, looked at the ceiling and said, "Yes, Your Honor"—but he shook his head firmly from side to side as he uttered the words.

After another heated discussion at the bench, Bell again repeated his question.

"You did intend to cause serious physical injury to Jennifer Levin, didn't you?" he asked. "There's no question in your mind?"

Chambers finally—and unemotionally—said, "There's no question, Your Honor."

And when the defendant pleaded guilty to a second-

degree burglary charge, he again appeared violently opposed to entering the plea.

Shaking his head hard from side to side, he stood as both his lawyers put restraining hands on his shoulders.

When Bell asked him if he had broken into a doctor's apartment in 1985, Chambers appeared cornered.

He threw both arms wide into the air, let them flop to his sides, and gave a hopeless "Yes" in reply as he again shook his head.

He then bent his head in defeat and wiped his eyes repeatedly.

When Chambers entered the courtroom at 5:05 p.m., it was filled to capacity with an expectant crowd.

When he had to stand up to enter his plea, he looked over his right shoulder at his mother, Phyllis, and father, Robert, and gave an untroubled, reassuring smile.

But as the proceedings continued and Bell began asking specific questions about what he intended to do, Chambers' demeanor changed.

He shifted from foot to foot, shook his head almost continuously and stared at the ceiling while keeping his hands clasped in front of him.

Chambers told the judge, "I want to thank you for being as fair as you possibly could. I appreciate it for my family and myself."

And then he cried.

ABOVE: *Robert Chambers was charged with two counts of second-degree murder for killing 18-year-old Jennifer Levin during a sexual tryst in Central Park.* LEFT: *Chambers walking investigators through the scene of the crime in Central Park.* (Post *photos*)

Tycoon Donald Trump told the Post *that he saw the crash coming in preceding weeks and had pulled his entire $500 million stock portfolio out before the crash.*

"Wail Street"

Overpriced stocks, rising interest rates, a weak dollar against foreign currencies and fears of potential war with Iran were all factors in the stupendous Wall Street Crash of October 19, 1987. In the biggest drop since 1929, the Dow Jones index plunged 288 points by 3:00 in the afternoon. Although minor by today's standards, a drop of even 200 points was very significant in 1987.

Tycoon Donald Trump told the *Post* that he saw the crash coming in preceding weeks and had pulled his entire $500 million stock portfolio out before the crash. "I'm a great believer in history," he said. "So when I saw the market go up 200 points in a day . . . it reminded me of 1929." By putting his money elsewhere, he ended up about $200 million richer on October 19.

UNAWARE OF THE MARKET'S REBOUND, YUPPIE BROKER COMMITS HARA-KIRI AT HIS FAVORITE SUSHI BAR.

TOP: *A young Wall Street broker drowns his sorrows on October 19, 1987, after enduring the worst stock market drop since 1929.* ABOVE: *An editorial cartoon that appeared two days after the crash.* OPPOSITE: *Reading the grim news on Wall Street.* (Post *photo*)

The Zodiac Killer

In 1990, New York police were faced with one of the most baffling cases in the city's history.

On June 6, the *Post* received a cryptic letter describing three deaths that occurred in March and May. An exact duplicate of the letter was sent to the CBS television show *60 Minutes*. The writer, using the signature "Faust," wrote:

> This is the Zodiac the twelve sign
> will die when the belts in the heaven
> are seen
> the first sign is dead on march 8 1990 1:45 AM
> white man with cane shoot on the back in the street
> the second sign is dead on march 29 1990 2:57 AM
> white man with black coat shoot in the side in front of house
> the third sign is dead on May 31 1990 2:04 AM
> white old man with can shoot in front of house
> Faust
> no more games pigs
> all shoot in Brooklyn with .380 RNL or 9mm
> no grooves on bullet

The letter contained hand-drawn illustrations of the astrological signs of Gemini, Taurus and Scorpio as well as a circle with in a cross. The *Post* and *60 Minutes* forwarded the chilling letters to the police, who looked up the dates and descriptions of the shootings listed in the letter. They discovered that the crimes did occur, but were not fatal. The victims were alive. The *Post* printed the letter two weeks later when the police decided to go public with their investigation into the suspect wanted for the three attacks.

The most shocking fact about the three who had been shot involved the astrological signs in the mystery letter. The birth signs of the victims matched up exactly with the signs given by the writer. Therefore, the attacker knew the birth dates of his victims and planned his attacks.

The gunman attacked again on June 21, shooting a homeless man in Central Park. A note left beside the victim correctly named his birth sign—Cancer. The Zodiac sent a second letter to the *Post* the next day, describing the Central Park shooting and angrily insisting that he was the infamous Zodiac killer who had struck in San Francisco in the 1960s. Police were certain that this attacker was not the original San Francisco killer but a copycat who could easily have learned details of the 20-year-old killings in a popular book that had been written on the subject.

The Zodiac attacker became the Zodiac killer when one of his victims, 78-year-old Joseph Proce, died from his wound on June 24.

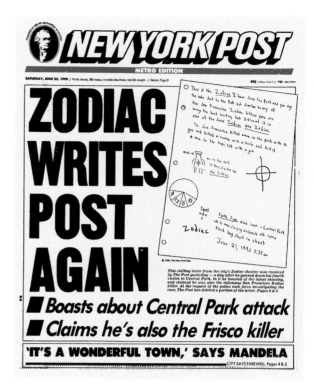

The second letter described a Central Park shooting that had occurred the day before. The shooter insisted he was the same Zodiac who terrorized San Francisco in the 1960s.

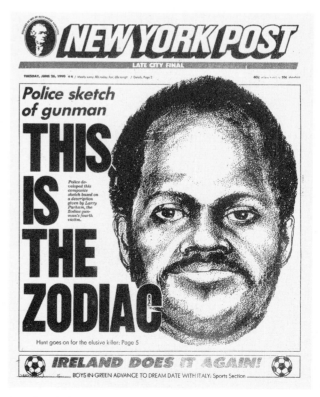

Based on descriptions given by his victims, the Zodiac killer's composite sketch was distributed by the police on June 26.

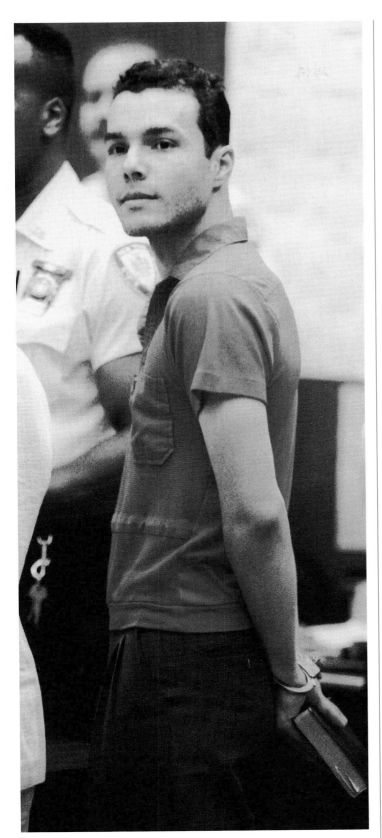

Heriberto Seda, 26, was caught and confessed to the Zodiac crimes in 1996. (Post photo)

"Cheers at Checkpoint Charlie"

The most prominent symbol of the Cold War broke open on November 9, 1989, with Berliners gleefully dancing on top of the wall that had divided Germany since 1961. East Berliners walked and drove back and forth through the gates, no papers required.

"What joy!" This is the best thing that happened in 100 years!" yelled a West Berlin man as he crossed into what once had been forbidden territory.

Many hugged and kissed total strangers, while cars packed with East Germans and others paraded down the streets of West Berlin in a carnival-like atmosphere.

"It's crazy! It's crazy!" yelled one young man as he sat in the back seat of a car with his parents after a brief trip through the once-impenetrable Berlin Wall.

His parents said they just wanted to see the West—and then drive back.

The next day, citizens began chipping away and pulling down the wall. By December 1991, the sweep of independence in Eastern Europe that began in the 1980s culminated in the disintegration of the Soviet Union.

185

NEW YORK POST

Decade Twenty

1991–2001

The new millennium in the Capital of the World was celebrated with dozens of sparkling events—and an atmosphere of good will that completely overshadowed a possible Y2K disaster. Just over a year later the world would focus on the city as the World Trade Center was destroyed by terrorists.

In the decade leading up to the new millennium, major stories included the scandal surrounding President Clinton and his impeachment, bombing the World Trade Center, the deaths of Princess Di and John F. Kennedy, Jr., a subway series and controversial presidential election.

At the *Post*, nothing in the paper's history matched the day-to-day white-knuckled drama of its near demise and ultimate survival in the early 1990s. The story behind the headlines covers ownership, staff revolts and the amazing surprise return of Rupert Murdoch.

A Times Square crowd of more than two million usher in the year 2000. (Post photo by Jim Alcorn)

DESERT STORM

The United Nations Security Council had authorized the use of "all means necessary" to drive Iraq out of Kuwait, and when Saddam Hussein ignored the U.N.'s deadlines to retreat, Allied forces began bombing Iraq. The war began in the early hours of Thursday, January 17, 1991.

After a 38-day air campaign, the ground offensive of Operation Desert Storm began. After a mere 100 hours of combat, the war-weary Iraqi army was crushed. Soldiers surrendered by the thousands, and a cease-fire was declared on February 28.

The following excerpt is from an article by Pete Hamill that appeared on the first day of the Gulf War:

"Here It Comes Again"

And so the killing and the dying have begun. We sat down for dinner. We walked into theaters. We set out upon dates or searched the tube for basketball and suddenly, irrevocably, here it was again: war.

The planes came in the night, as they almost always do, and from a great height dropped their exploding metal upon the place beneath.

Last night, that particular place was called Baghdad, on the Tigris river in Iraq, where what we laughingly call civilization had its beginnings. It was not the first city to be bombed in this awful century and won't be the last. This time, we stared at CNN (for this is the CNN war) and sipped coffee and knew that all the sketchy words, all the sounds of airplanes and the rumbling of bombers meant that people were being slaughtered.

We also knew that while men die, we will be drowned in a swamp of euphemism. We will hear the words "surgical strike" many times in the next week, along with "pinpoint accuracy." They will be used to disguise the horror of charred flesh, destroyed bodies, exploded faces. We will hear about "the enemy," too, but it will be awhile before we can turn over a body and see a young Iraqi soldier's dead face and find his woman's picture in a wallet, smiling from the unretrievable past.

"The liberation of Kuwait has begun," said Marlin Fitzwater from the safety of the White House press room. George Bush told us that, soon, "Kuwait will once again be free." They might even mean this, although the words "liberation" and "free" obviously mean nothing when connected to the oil-can despots who ran Kuwait until Saddam Hussein took it away at gunpoint.

If our young men are to die so the emirs can go back into the oil business, then they will die for many reasons, but liberation will not be one of them. Still, we will hear a lot about liberation in the coming weeks, and freedom, but almost nothing about oil.

We are in another war. That's all. It's what we do. Men will die. And women. And children. They will die in the most disgusting ways. Saddam Hussein might even die, too, but that would be unlikely.

But we know a few things now, as the wars of this century go on and on and on. The most important is that nobody wins wars from the air. You can cause extraordinary damage and much death; we did it to Germany and Japan and to North Vietnam.

But unless you use the atom bomb, you must eventually send in the infantry. And, almost certainly, that will be the heart of the war in Iraq. At some point, this will become a war of foot soldiers. Their grunts against our grunts. Some will die instantly. Some will be crazy brave. . . . What they will go through will be dirty and ugly. And if they live they will carry the memory through all of their lives.

FOUNDED IN 1801 BY ALEXANDER HAMILTON

NEW YORK POST

LATE CITY FINAL

SATURDAY, FEBRUARY 27 / SUNDAY, FEBRUARY 28, 1993 / Mostly sunny, 30s today; clear, low 20s tonight / Details, Page 2

50¢

BOMBED

A gasping woman is helped to safety after the massive explosion. More than 650 people were injured in the noon horror yesterday.

World Trade Center blast kills at least 5

FULL COVERAGE OF HORROR PLUS MORE PHOTOS BEGIN ON PAGE 2

NEW YORK POST, THURSDAY, NOVEMBER 13, 1997

4 ★★R

Two more terrorists convicted in World Trade Center blast

By AL GUART

A jury yesterday convicted Ramzi Yousef and an accomplice of bombing the World Trade Center as part of an evil scheme to terrorize the United States for its policies on Israel.

The anonymous panel of seven men and five women deliberated three days in Manhattan federal court before finding Yousef and Eyad Ismoil guilty on all counts of conspiring to blow up the twin towers.

They are the sixth and seventh men convicted in the attack.

Yousef, 29, sat stoically and never glanced at the panel as he was pronounced guilty 10 times on charges related to the February 1993 bombing, which killed six people and injured 1,000.

During deliberations, the panel made 15 requests for evidence and legal guidance, apparently deadlocked over whether Ismoil, 26, knew the van he drove into the trade center's underground garage was packed with explosives.

After sending a note asking when Ismoil confirmed his flight out of New York, which was for the day of the blast, the panel sent a note stating it had reached its verdict.

Ismoil betrayed no emotion as the verdict was read, but at least one juror looked over sympathetically at his mother as she sobbed quietly.

"I wonder if they [the jury] understood the need to find beyond a reasonable doubt that he knew there was a bomb in there," said Ismoil's lawyer, Louis Aidala, who had argued Yousef led his client to believe the van was filled with cleaning chemicals.

Yousef's lawyer, Roy Kulcsar, vowed an appeal and insisted his client's confession was not credible.

The panel heard from more than 100 witnesses, saw numerous photographs and reviewed phone logs during the four month trial. Bank records revealed the attack cost between $8,000 and $12,000.

"The message is you can run, but you can't hide," New York FBI head James Kallstrom said after the verdict. "We're going to put the resources in to get you and we're going to continue to do that."

Manhattan U.S. Attorney Mary Jo White said: "This prosecution and the ones before it show our joint resolve to pursue terrorists wherever they may be and whatever their role may have been.

"This case and investigation will never be over in a sense until we track down every single person who had any conceivable role in this type of terrorism."

The convictions mark the last trial of any terrorists directly involved in the scheme who have been captured. Four others were previously convicted in the attack. Another was convicted of driving one of the terrorists, who was his brother, to the airport. Abdul Rahman Yasin, who remains a fugitive, is accused of mixing bomb chemicals and providing a mail drop for the plotters.

Yousef and Ismoil will face life in prison when they are sentenced Jan. 8 and Feb. 12, respectively. Yousef also faces life for a previous conviction in a plot to blow U.S. commercial jets out of the sky in the Far East.

GUILTY! Eyad Ismoil (left) and Ramzi Yousef react stoically to their convictions in Manhattan federal court yesterday.   Reuter

Towering Justice

Six died and more than 1,000 were wounded in the World Trade Center bombing. In the trials that followed, six terrorists were convicted in the attack and will spend the rest of their lives in prison.

The mastermind of the bombing, Ramzi Yousef—whose plan fell short of its goal to topple one tower onto its twin amid a cloud of cyanide gas—was sentenced to 240 years in solitary confinement.

Post coverage included a gripping firsthand account by staff photographer Michael Schwartz (excerpted at right), who had been on assignment nearby at City Hall Park and was among the first on the scene.

NEW YORK POST, SATURDAY, FEBRUARY 27, 1993

3

TWIN TOWERS TERROR

BOMB HORROR

TEARS: *Evacuee cries with relief as she leaves.*

BLOOD: *A garage worker staggers from scene.*

NOW YOU SEE IT . . . *Blast destroyed wall that stood between vending machines at rear and rest of World Trade Center's PATH station.*

HELP! *An EMS worker calls for assistance as a smoke-inhalation victim fails to come round.*

It was a hell of a day at work for survivors

By SETH KAUFMAN, JIM NOLAN, RICHARD STEIER, KAREN PHILLIPS and BILL HOFFMANN

Vito DeLeo was one of the first to know

DeLeo, 32, an air-conditioner mechanic from Staten Island, was on his lunch break on a B-2 underground level office about 12:15 p.m. He was with about 75 other building workers when a brilliant flash ripped through a nearby parking lot.

"I saw the flash coming toward me and I bent down, and my desk somehow landed on top of me. The desk went up and threw me underneath," he said.

"I thought I was dead because everything went black," DeLeo said from New York Downtown Hospital, where he was treated for a punctured ear drum and cuts and bruises.

"There was furniture up in the air, the concrete walls were down. We crawled out. It's just terrible down there."

"We thought a helicopter hit the building," said Gwen Maddox, a 41-year-old dispatcher for New Jersey Transit, who was on the 58th floor with a friend.

On the B-1 underground level below 1 WTC, where the Port Authority police command post is located, Lt. Herman Gabora, 41, was putting on his jacket to go to lunch when the ceiling collapsed on him.

Covered in plasterboard, he still managed to get up and help others get out.

"Police are trained in emergency situations," the 19-year veteran said later, after getting five stitches in his head. "Their instincts are to survive."

When the explosion rocked level B-3, between 1 WTC and 2 WTC, Ken Olsen, 34, a pipefitter from Hicksville, L.I., said, "All hell broke loose."

"All the water pipes ruptured. Luckily we stayed together," Olsen said.

The workers used their flashlights to pick their way to the nearby entrance to the PATH tracks, where they hopped over the third rail, onto the platform and up the stopped escalator to safety.

Asked if he was concerned going over the third rail, Olsen laughed. "At that point you didn't care if you got hit by a train."

In one of the day's most dramatic moments, a police helicopter hovered about 50 feet above 2 WTC while emergency personnel low-

See HELL *on Page 10*

See HELL on Page 10

"I ran after [the emergency vehicles] to the World Trade Center . . . to get a first-hand look at the damage. It was terrifying. Walls were blown out, huge slabs of jagged concrete littered the floor. Thick, black smoke hung heavy in the air . . . cops passed me, shouting that a man was trapped in fiery rubble in the upper parking lot. Suddenly, I heard the trapped man's screams and followed them. The fire illuminated the horrible scene. Doing this crazy job for 10 years, I've seen a lot of dead people, a lot of blood and a lot of destruction. You almost get used to it. But not this scene. This was a true, true nightmare."

—POST *PHOTOGRAPHER* MICHAEL SCHWARTZ, FEBRUARY 27, 1993

MUTINY ON SOUTH STREET

Timetable/article that appeared on March 30, 1993:

Day-by-Day Tale of the Rescue

The following are key events that led up to the triumphant return of Rupert Murdoch to the *New York Post*.

JANUARY

20 Bankers Trust, which controls the paper's finances, cuts off publisher Peter Kalikow's credit. The bank expresses dismay that the *Post* failed to pay the government $3.3 million in taxes withheld from 700 employees.

23 Kalikow meets with union leaders, who agree to 20-percent pay cuts.

24 Despite the cuts, Bankers Trust still refuses to extend the line of credit. Kalikow prepares to suspend publication. But debt-collection tycoon Steven Hoffenberg suddenly comes to the rescue.

27 Securities and Exchange Commission says it is investigating Hoffenberg's debt-collection company, Towers Financial Corp.

FEBRUARY

1 *Daily News* owner Mort Zuckerman raids the *Post*, luring away several editors and columnists. Hoffenberg vows Zuckerman's attempt to destroy the rival *Post* will not succeed.

10 Hoffenberg names columnist Pete Hamill as new editor in chief.

11 Federal Judge Whitman Knapp temporarily bars Hoffenberg from pumping any more funds from Towers into the *Post*.

17 Hoffenberg agrees to allow a court-appointed trustee to oversee operations of Towers—until a federal suit against him alleging securities fraud is settled.

19 Federal bankruptcy Judge Burton Lifland approves the sale of the *Post* to Hoffenberg.

21 Hoffenberg brings in eccentric parking-garage magnate Abe Hirschfeld—and Hirschfeld's $3 million—and makes him chairman of the board.

MARCH

11 Hoffenberg and Hirschfeld have a falling-out.

12 Federal bankruptcy Judge Francis Conrad ends Hoffenberg's two months at the helm of the *Post*. The zany Hirschfeld is given operational control and the right to buy the paper. He immediately fires Hamill. Gerard Bray becomes interim editor.

14 Hirschfeld hires *Amsterdam News* publisher Wilbert Tatum as co-publisher and editor of the *Post*. He also demands list of 272 *Post* employees he wants to fire. Bray resigns as editor in protest.

15 Turmoil caused by Hirschfeld, plus effects of big weekend Storm of the Century, result in the paper failing to publish Monday editions. Unions join top management to resist Hirschfeld takeover.

16 The mutiny on South Street erupts with a classic edition of the *Post*. On page 1, Alexander Hamilton weeps for the paper he founded in 1801. Inside, on page after page, staffers blast Hirschfeld and Tatum. Employees take over paper, ignoring Hirschfeld.

17 Hamill returns in triumph to newsroom to take charge of the rebellion.

18 Hirschfeld says he is firing Tatum and wants Hamill to be editor again.

ABOVE: *Rupert Murdoch, far left; Pat Purcell, publisher of the* Boston Herald; *and Murdoch's new editor, Ken Chandler.*

19 Judge Conrad works out truce under which Hirschfeld would write the business checks while Hamill would resume editing the paper.

22 Hirschfeld bars four of the *Post*'s top editors and columnists from the building.

26 The *Post*'s creditors ask Judge Conrad to end Hirschfeld's management contract because he failed to pay bills. Australian-born tycoon Rupert Murdoch makes a purchase offer.

28 Hamill "respectfully" declines Murdoch's "generous" offer to stay on as editor-at-large.

29 Judge Conrad grants Murdoch control of the *Post*. The new prospective owner is welcomed at the *Post* by cheering employees.

4   NEW YORK POST, MONDAY,

LOOKS LIKE IT'S POST TIME AGAIN FOR RUPERT

By COLIN MINER

Media mogul Rupert Murdoch is poised to take possession of the New York Post today for a historic second time.

Murdoch and interim publisher Abraham Hirschfeld reached an agreement over the weekend that would return control of The Post to Murdoch.

The agreement — described by insiders as "a done deal" — is scheduled to be presented before federal bankruptcy Judge Francis Conrad in an 8:30 conference call this morning.

The deal provides for Murdoch to assume immediate control of the editorial and financial operations of the paper.

"We will devote every effort possible to restoring The Post as a strong, professional and competitive newspaper," Murdoch said through his spokesman, Howard Rubenstein.

"For it to have been silenced would have been a great loss to New York and the nation," Murdoch continued.

Rubenstein added: "Mr. Murdoch is pleased to return to what he considers his home."

One of Murdoch's first tasks if he takes over the paper will be to name a new editor to replace Pete Hamill.

Hamill's attorney, Richard Emery, said late yesterday that Murdoch had made Hamill a "lucrative offer to write a Post column and do other work for the Murdoch media empire," but Hamill respectfully turned it down.

"It was not what Pete is interested in doing. He leaves with great respect for Murdoch and thanks him for jumping into the breach and saving The Post," Emery said.

At today's hearing, the third in the past five days, Murdoch will present his proposal to operate the paper for 60 days. He has not set any limit on how much he will spend.

It was unclear late yesterday what, if any, personnel changes would be made by the media mogul.

"Overall, this is a good agreement," said attorney Robert Miller of Berlack, Israels & Liberman.

"We are hopeful we will be able to iron out the remaining problems by morning."

Miller was retained by a coalition of Post non-union employees to represent them in bankruptcy proceedings after Hirschfeld put the paper under Chapter 11 protection from creditors.

Hirschfeld entered the roller-coaster story of The Post when he was brought in by another wannabe owner, Steven Hoffenberg.

Hoffenberg joined the fray

RUPERT MURDOCH
Second go-around.

as The Post's white knight, coming up with the cash needed to run the paper after owner Peter Kalikow threatened to close it down in late January. But Hoffenberg's debt-collection company, Towers Financial, is itself in trouble. It is battling the Securities and Exchange Commission, which has frozen Towers' assets, alleging the firm bilked investors out of hundreds of millions of dollars. Towers declared bankruptcy last week.

Kalikow purchased The Post in March 1988 when Murdoch was forced by federal regulation to sell either the paper or WNYW-TV / Channel 5, which he had purchased two years earlier.

Murdoch, who bought the paper in 1977, was forced to sell it because of a Federal Communications Commission regulation that prohibits anyone from owning both a broadcast station and newspaper in the same market.

In recent days Murdoch has been given assurances he will be granted the waiver needed to own both The Post and Channel 5.

Murdoch chairs News

Corp., an international media conglomerate and the third-largest media company in the United States, behind Gannett and Time-Warner.

In 1992, News Corp. had worldwide sales of $7.6 billion with a net profit of $385 million.

Fortune magazine estimates Murdoch's personal wealth at $2.6 billion.

The Post would be operated by NYP Acquisitions Corp., a subsidiary of News America, the U.S. arm of Murdoch's empire.

Gov. Cuomo, credited with being instrumental in helping bring the deal together, called Murdoch "the only realistic hope for long-term survival of the Post."

During the next 60 days, Murdoch will work on obtaining the waiver to the FCC cross-ownership regulation.

The agreement calls for Murdoch to have the 60-day window extended to 90 days, if necessary.

Friday, the judge directed Murdoch, Hirschfeld and the other "interested parties" to hammer out an agreement.

The extraordinary Friday session — which took place in a conference call to the judge's office in Vermont — was prompted by Hirschfeld's refusal the day before to pay $366,000 in bills necessary for the paper's continued operation.

After the conference call, Hirschfeld went up to Murdoch's office on Sixth Avenue at 49th Street and the two men met face to face to iron out details of Murdoch's takeover.

The agreement requires Murdoch to become responsible for Hirschfeld's remaining financial obligations to the paper.

"It's Good to Be Home"

Villains. Heroes. Angry bankers. Eccentric millionaires. The tumultuous first months of 1993 at the *Post* were the stuff of grand opera—complete with dramatic surprise ending.

Post owner and real-estate developer Peter Kalikow had been hit by a double blow of financial setbacks by early 1993. The New York real-estate market had bottomed out and the *Post*'s bank had cut off his credit. Kalikow declared personal bankruptcy in 1991 and planned to shut down the paper in January 1993. For the next three months, as outlined on the timeline on page 190, the paper miraculously continued to make it to press each day due to a sweeping parade of people and events.

No one dreamed of the solution that would ultimately walk through the doors on March 29: Rupert Murdoch, who had been forced to sell the *Post* five years earlier due to an FCC cross-ownership rule. With the help of Governor Cuomo and others, he was promised a waiver of that rule.

2 ★★   NEW YORK POST,   TUESDAY, MARCH 30, 1993

New York Post: David Rentas

COMEBACK KID: *Rupert Murdoch addresses Post staffers yesterday in a rousing return. Murdoch threw down the gauntlet to the competition, describing The Times as "elitist," The News as "static," and Newsday as "impotent."*

WELCOME HOME!

Murdoch takes over Post, names Chandler editor

By COLIN MINER

Media mogul Rupert Murdoch yesterday returned triumphant to the New York Post — for the second time taking the helm of the country's longest continuously published newspaper.

"It's good to be home," Murdoch told his staff as he entered the newsroom just after 3 p.m. to thunderous applause.

Murdoch said his return to the jubilant newsroom was a "very emotional" experience.

"I want to recognize all the real heroes of the past few weeks — all of you," Murdoch told the packed newsroom.

"What has happened to the Post recently has been very tragic," said Murdoch, who owned the paper from 1976 to 1988.

"The staff has been caught in the throes of some very difficult times and has come through it with great courage."

Murdoch singled out Pete Hamill, the paper's inspiring editor-in-chief during its tumultuous struggle to survive.

On Sunday, Hamill "respectfully" declined what he described as Murdoch's "generous" offer to remain at the paper as a columnist and editor-at-large.

"I wish Pete Hamill very well in whatever he choses to do," said Murdoch. "I certainly respect him."

Joining Murdoch at The Post yesterday was Ken Chandler, whom Murdoch named editor.

> "I want to recognize the real heroes . . . All of you."
> RUPERT MURDOCH TO STAFFERS

Chandler, the Post's managing editor during Murdoch's first stint, was also roundly cheered by the staff.

"I expect Ken Chandler to put out the best paper ever," Murdoch said. "I know what he is capable of achieving, and he knows that I know."

Chandler, who recently ran Murdoch's Boston Herald and Fox-TV's "A Current Affair," See POST on Page 15

New York Post: David Rentas

NEW WAVE: *The Post's new editor, Ken Chandler, salutes the staff yesterday as the paper's new publisher, Patrick Purcell (left) looks on.*

191

A New Beginning: An Editorial

Today marks the start of a new day for The New York *Post*—a bright new day.

The return of Rupert Murdoch leaves all who labored to put out the *Post* during the last two nightmarish months with a sense of profound excitement, unmixed elation and unmitigated enthusiasm. . . . And so we forge ahead, determined to rebuild this newspaper into one which—as Murdoch himself promised yesterday—will dedicate itself to providing an "alternative voice" in the ongoing New York City public-policy debate.

The *Post* will continue to be different from the other dailies in this town. We will eschew the Politically Correct path. We will embrace the concerns and highlight the problems of working- and middle-class New York families.

To you—our readers—whose enormous outpouring of affection and support meant more to us than we can say, we offer our thanks.

—from the March 30, 1993, editorial

The Murdoch Team

RUPERT MURDOCH is chairman and chief executive of News Corporation, one of the world's largest media companies. A native of Australia, Murdoch began his career at the *Daily Express* in London after graduating from Oxford.

LACHLAN MURDOCH began his career as general manager of Queensland Newspapers in Australia in 1994. He is chairman and chief executive of News Limited and deputy chief operating officer of News Corporation.

MARTIN SINGERMAN was president and publisher of the *New York Post* from 1993 to 1999. He joined News America in 1973 when the Murdoch organization initially entered the United States and advanced to president and chief executive of News America Publishing, the U.S. magazine and newspaper publishing arm of News Corporation, in 1985. Singerman continues to work with News Corporation as an advisor on various projects.

ROGER WOOD was editor of the *Post* from 1975 through 1985. Following this he became editorial director of News Corporation for a brief period until joining *Star* magazine as publishing director. When the magazine was sold to the National Enquirer Group he was named president. He began his career as editor of the *Daily Express* in Manchester, Glasgow and London and spent five years as managing director of a magazine company in Australia.

KEN CHANDLER was appointed publisher of the *Post* in 1999 and was editor in chief from 1993 to 2001. Born in England, Chandler entered publishing as a copy editor at the Murdoch-owned *Sun* and first joined the *Post* in 1978.

ERIC BREINDEL was the *Post*'s editorial page editor from 1986 until 1997, then senior vice president of News Corporation until his death at the age of 42. Before joining the paper he worked as a legislative aide for Sen. Daniel Patrick Moynihan, one of his Harvard professors, and on the Senate Intelligence Committee. In the words of Rupert Murdoch, Eric Breindel "was a brilliant leader of the editorial page and one of the most influential people in New York." The National Eric Breindel Award was set up in 1998 with an annual $10,000 prize for journalists who carry on his good work.

COL ALLAN was named editor in chief of the *Post* in April 2001. Born in New South Wales, Australia, he came to the *Post* from the *Daily Telegraph* where he had been editor since 1992. Under Col Allan's leadership, Sydney's *Telegraph* developed into a daily with one of the highest circulations in the country.

ABOVE: *Lachlan Murdoch.* OPPOSITE: *Rupert Murdoch.* (*Post photos*)

O.J. VERDICT EXTRA
NEW YORK POST
P.M. SPECIAL
TUESDAY, OCTOBER 3, 1995 / Morning sun today, 74-79; becoming cloudy tonight, 60-65 / Details, Page 42   50¢

NOT GUILTY!

Jury clears Simpson in murders

Today's court coverage begins on Page 2

O.J. Simpson is cleared of murder charges in the final day of the trial of the century, October 3, 1995.

"Horror in the Sky"

A National Guard pilot was on patrol on July 16, 1996, the night TWA Flight 800 exploded. "You know what a comet looks like?" he said. "It was 100 times bigger than that."

Everyone aboard the Boeing 747 headed from Kennedy Airport to Paris was killed. Investigators spent the next 17 months recovering wreckage from the ocean floor and interviewing hundreds of witnesses. Even though many witnesses claimed to have seen what appeared to be a missile flying toward the plane, officials ruled out a missile or bomb. They knew for certain that the plane's nearly empty center fuel tank exploded, but not what ignited it. The most plausible explanation, according to the researchers, was an electrical problem that sparked the vapors in the fuel tank.

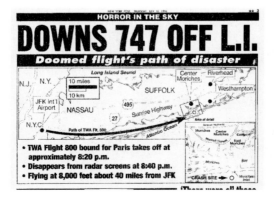

SPECIAL EDITION
NEW YORK POST
HOME DELIVERY 1-800-940-7678 CALL TODAY!
LATE CITY FINAL
THURSDAY, JULY 18, 1996 / Afternoon storms, 85-90; chance of showers tonight, 72 / Details, Page 30   50¢

FIREBALL

All aboard were killed when a TWA Boeing 747 airliner like the one above bound to Paris from Kennedy Airport exploded in midair, broke in two and crashed into the Atlantic Ocean off the south shore of Long Island last night.

JUMBO JET EXPLODES AND CRASHES OFF L.I.

All 229 aboard JFK flight dead

COVERAGE STARTS ON PAGE 2

Terrorism in the Heartland

The bomb that blasted the federal building in Oklahoma City on April 19, 1995, also destroyed the nation's belief that terrorism could not reach into the heartland. Timothy McVeigh was tried for the crime, convicted and sent to death row. The day after the tragedy, *Post* columnist Andrea Peyser wrote:

> Take a good look at Oklahoma City, for this is the battle-field in which we all live. This is the spot where the enemy made a preemptive strike—driving a stake of terror into the nation's heart.
>
> We thought we were safe here, deep in America. Now we know we were simply naïve. A beautiful, and perhaps uniquely American trait. Gone.

A related article, found under the headline MAYOR PUTS APPLE ON RED ALERT, described the stepped-up security in New York City the following day. Authorities sent extra police units to buildings that were possible targets, suspicious packages were investigated by bomb squads, bridge and tunnel security was increased and many office buildings instituted extra security. Mayor Rudy Giuliani's statement gave no false promises: "Human beings, unfortunately, devise horrible ways to harm other human beings," he said. "In New York City, we are fortunate to have, I think, the most effective response to this kind of thing any place. . . . And that's the very best you can offer."

ABOVE: *A grieving couple console each other in front of the Alfred P. Murrah Federal Building in Oklahoma City, 1995.* (Post *photo*)

MORE TEARS

JFK JR., WIFE AND HER SISTER PRESUMED DEAD IN PLANE CRASH

NEW YORK POST

HOME DELIVERY
1-800-552-7678
CALL TODAY!

LATE CITY FINAL

FRIDAY, JULY 23, 1999 / Mostly sunny and humid, 90 / Weather: Page 49 ★★   http://www.nypost.com/   · · · · 50¢

FAREWELL

JOHN F. KENNEDY, JR.
1960-1999

CAROLYN BESSETTE KENNEDY
1966-1999

LAUREN BESSETTE
1964-1999

A boy throws flowers into the waters off Martha's Vineyard yesterday as the ship carrying the families heads to the burial at sea.

Death of JFK, Jr.

The Piper Saratoga II airplane took off from Essex County Airport in Fairfield, New Jersey, at 8:38 on Friday night, July 16, 1999. Seated behind the pilot, John F. Kennedy, Jr., were his wife, Carolyn Bessette Kennedy, and her sister, Lauren Bessette. John and Carolyn were on their way to a cousin's wedding in Hyannis Port, Massachusetts, with a quick stop at Martha's Vineyard to drop off Lauren.

Weather conditions were hazy, with four to six miles' visibility, adequate but "marginal" for someone with John's flying experience of fewer than 100 hours.

They did not arrive at Martha's Vineyard, and by early Saturday were missing and presumed dead. President Clinton ordered the U.S. Navy to spare no expense in a massive search-and-recovery mission because of "the role of the Kennedy family in our national life."

After agonizing days of waiting, in which a piece of Lauren Bessette's luggage and airplane debris washed up on the coast of Martha's Vineyard, Navy divers discovered all three bodies in the broken fuselage of the plane at the bottom of the ocean. The plane had plunged into the Atlantic 7.5 miles west of the island.

ABOVE: *John F. Kennedy, Jr., and his wife, Caroline, at an awards dinner in New York in April 1998. The couple lived in a sprawling loft apartment in Tribeca.* (Post *photo by Susan May Tell)*

SUNDAY
NEW YORK POST

Sunday Victory

In early 1997 the *Post* launched a Sunday edition, giving New Yorkers a shorter Sunday alternative designed like a daily paper—right down to the newsstand price. The *Post* had unsuccessfully attempted a Sunday edition twice before, but the popular new version owes its success to the same components of quality writing and coverage that have made the *Post* one of the nation's most successful daily newspapers. Introducing something new—and making it work—makes the Sunday edition one of the *Post*'s major successes in the 1990s and the new century.

NYPOST.COM

The *Post*'s on-line edition was launched in 1997, giving instant global access to the paper. The site includes color photo sections; breaking news, columnists; business, cartoon, lifestyle, opinion, travel, traffic information and current weather sections; a free seven-day archive and article-for-fee archive that spans the past 90 days, and much more.

Millennium Capital of the World

New York celebrates in a big way, and ushering in the new millennium in a style worthy of the Capital of the World required extravagant plans. To begin, the city spruced up its New Year's Eve icon, the 500-pound rhinestone and halogen ball that descended at the countdown to midnight in Times Square. The artifact was retired in 1999 for a new glass ball designed by Waterford Crystal. The new ball, made in Ireland, consists of 540 handcrafted crystal triangles forming a transparent globe. The central circle represents the earth and a seven-pointed star represents the continents. Updating the Times Square ball tradition—which began in 1907—was one of the first items on the list of NYC2000, the official committee of the millennium celebration.

For some unlucky New York workers the evening was spent in the office, as many were assigned to keep a close eye on computer screens to watch for Y2K disasters—which never came. In Times Square, anti-terrorism measures were in place including sealed manholes and mailboxes, bomb-sniffing dogs and rooftop sharpshooters. The night was free of any terrorist acts, too.

The celebrations in Times Square were coordinated to line up with the events all over the globe, as the new millennium came in through each time zone.

Cops, FBI smash B'klyn terror ring

PAGE 5

Michael Abram

The madman who attacked George Harrison

PAGES 6-8

NEW YORK POST

ONLY 50¢

LATE CITY FINAL

FRIDAY, DECEMBER 31, 1999 / Partly sunny, 44 / Weather: Page 68 ★★   http://www.nypost.com/   • • • • **50¢**

The clock ticks down to new millennium

IT'S HERE!

New York Post: W.A. Funches Jr.

SPECIAL KEEPSAKE EDITION

A young reveler tries on her new millennium glasses in Times Square yesterday. **Coverage starts on Pages 2 & 3.**

ABOVE LEFT: *Hillary Rodham Clinton beats Republican Rick Lazio in one of the longest and most expensive Senate races in history. Her history-making win makes her the first first lady to be elected to political office as well as the first woman elected to statewide office in New York.* ABOVE: *Like many papers, the* Post *jumped the gun the day after Election Day by announcing Bush the winner. The official vote would not be announced for another month.* LEFT: *A Thanksgiving-week cartoon on Page Six.*

Election Chaos

36 Days of Chads
2000 Presidential Election Timeline Highlights

November 7
8 p.m.— Television networks project Gore winner in Florida.

10 p.m.— Networks retract Gore win in Florida and announce vote "too close to call."

November 8
12:10 a.m. — Bush and Gore tied with 242 electoral votes each.

2:17 a.m. — Networks announce Florida win for Bush, giving him the election.

2:30 a.m. — Gore congratulates Bush in phone call.

3:00 a.m. — Bush's lead in Florida drops.

3:30 a.m. — Gore calls Bush to retract his earlier concession.

4:30 a.m. — Networks announce Bush may not have Florida. Voters wake to find Gore ahead with 260 electoral votes and Bush 246. Florida conducts automatic recount of votes and voters in Palm Beach complain that the ballots are confusing.

November 9
Democrats ask for hand count of ballots in four Florida counties.

November 12
Republicans ask for halt of Florida hand recounts.

November 13
U.S. judge refuses to stop recounts. Florida Secretary of State Katherine Harris states that the 11/14 deadline stands for certifying the election results. Democrats state they'll take the deadline rule to court.

November 14
Florida judge upholds deadline but not all counties comply.

November 15
Harris asks Florida Supreme Court to halt recounts. Court rejects her application. Certified recount shows Bush ahead by 300 votes, but some counties still deliberating.

November 16
Democrats sue in Florida Supreme Court to continue manual recounts. Court rules Palm Beach can keep counting.

November 17
Court hearing on constitutionality of Palm Beach revote. Florida Supreme Court blocks Harris from announcing official vote certification.

November 20
Bush lawyers ask Florida Supreme Court to stop recounts; Florida judge rules he does not have constitutional authority to order a revote in Palm Beach County.

November 21
Florida Supreme Court allows recounts in three counties.

November 22
Bush lawyers file cases with U.S. Supreme Court. Miami-Dade County stops recounts and Democrats vow to take the issue to Florida Supreme Court. Dick Cheney, Republican vice presidential candidate, suffers heart attack. Harris declares Bush winner by 537 votes.

November 27
Democrats file legal challenges to outcome.

December 1
For the first time in history, the U.S. Supreme Court intervenes in a presidential election, hearing arguments on Gore's objection to certified results.

December 12
U.S. Supreme Court rules that the Florida Supreme Court ruling allowing manual recount was unconstitutional.

December 13
Gore concedes defeat and Bush proclaims win. Electoral votes—Bush: 271; Gore: 266.

P.M. Election Update

NEW YORK POST 25 CENTS

ELECTION EXTRA

WEDNESDAY, NOVEMBER 8, 2000 / Partly sunny, 65 / Weather: Page 56 ★★★★★ www.nypost.com · · 25¢

FLORIDA FIASCO

- Prez race recount in chaos
- Gore concedes, then retracts it
- Bush victory hangs in balance

SPECIAL ELECTION SECTION: ALL THE LATEST RESULTS / BEGINS ON P.2

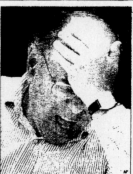

AIN'T OVER YET!

Bush 'victory' is yanked in Fla. squeaker

AY, AY, AY: Canvassing board member Judge Robert Rosenberg looks this way, that way and every other way as he examines a ballot in Broward County.

The Day Everything Changed

The Terrorist Destruction of the World Trade Center

On the morning of September 11, 2001, New York City faced a challenge unlike any in its history. Two commercial jetliners—in the early stages of transcontinental flights—were hijacked by terrorists and deliberately crashed into the twin towers of the World Trade Center. In Washington, a third jet destroyed part of the Pentagon, while heroic passengers aboard a fourth plane apparently sacrificed themselves in order to prevent the terrorists from claiming another target.

Less than two hours later, the most dominant feature of the New York skyline had collapsed in a mountain of rubble that devastated much of Lower Manhattan—and took thousands of innocent lives. It was the worst criminal attack America had ever seen.

The toll in human lives was incalculable. A week later, more than 6,000 people working in or visiting the World Trade Center were still missing. So were many New York City police officers and over 300 firefighters, most of whom had rushed to the Trade Center when the first plane hit and were buried under the rubble of the collapsing towers.

America and the world reacted first with shock and disbelief—then with a combination of grief and outrage. Even as New York tried to pick up the pieces and count the dead—hoping against hope for some miracle in which lives would be spared—the nation demanded action.

Many New Yorkers also came to understand, for the very first time, the true heroism of its police officers, firefighters, emergency services technicians and other rescue workers. The nation watched in awe as these giants combed through Ground Zero, even while mourning their fallen colleagues who had given their lives in order to save others.

Literally scores of millions of dollars were quickly donated to funds that would benefit the victims' families. The *Post*, through the full global resources of its parent company, News Corporation, mobilized behind the Twin Towers Fund established by Mayor Rudy Giuliani—who won praise worldwide for his steadying and reassuring hand throughout the disaster.

"Rudy Giuliani is a rock," said a *Post* editorial. "From the earliest moments of Lower Manhattan's agony, the mayor of the City of New York was—and continues to be—magnificent…. America and the rest of the world saw a visible symbol that New York had not been defeated by this horrific attack—that the city and its leaders remained on the job, making sure the instruments of government functioned."

In the same way, the *Post*'s editorial team worked around the clock to assure its readers that its information network would not be crippled by the terrorist attack. The *Post*'s pages were filled with the horror of the carnage at Ground Zero, the heartache of thousands of families vainly searching for their loved ones—and the incredible stories of courage, sacrifice and heroism that unfolded daily during the grim rescue effort.

"Words cannot express our sympathy for the tremendous loss so many people experienced," said Publisher Ken Chandler. "What the terrorists failed to count on was the resilience and determination of the people in this city. For both New York and the *Post*, this has been their finest hour."

ABOVE: *United Flight 175 hits the World Trade Center at 9:03 A.M., September 11, 2001. (* Post *photo by Tamara Beckwith)*

CLOCKWISE FROM ABOVE LEFT: *Ground Zero news conference, from left, Sen. Charles Schumer, Mayor Rudolph Giuliani, Governor George Pataki, Sen. Hillary Rodham Clinton, and City Council Speaker Peter Vallone.* (Post *photo by Robert Miller*); *Exhausted firefighter prays before returning to the rubble.* (Post *photo by Matthew McDermott*); *Rachel Uchitel searches for fiancé Andy O'Grady, who worked on the 104th floor of the south tower.* (Post *photo by Charles Wenzelberg*); *Police officer helps an injured woman to safety.* (Post *photo by Joey Newfield*); *President George Bush and Firefighter Bob Bechwith rallying rescue workers.* (Post *photo by Michael Norcia*)

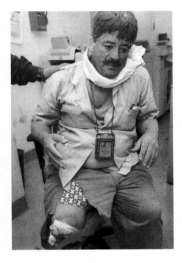

OPPOSITE: *Remains of the day. (*Post *photo by Don Halasy)* LEFT: *After the collapse a firewoman is taken out by stretcher; she survived. (*Post *photo by Bolivar Arellano)* ABOVE: Post *photographer Bolivar Arellano returns to* Post *headquarters after being injured covering the story. (*Post *photo by Michael Norcia)*

The Post at "Ground Zero"

Even as the horrifying events at the World Trade Center unfolded live on television, the *Post* sprang into action, despite initially limited resources: Most cityside reporters, scheduled to work late that night covering the city's primary election, had not yet arrived for work; political reporter Bob Hardt was on an elevated subway at Jamaica Bay, headed to the office, with a clear view of the Trade Center. He watched in horror as the second plane crashed into the tower.

Still, the paper quickly produced an "Extra" afternoon edition. The front page carried a heart-stopping photo of the second jet moments before it crashed into the south tower; the headline was an uncharacteristically understated TERROR.

Distributing the papers was more difficult; city officials, uncertain whether more attacks were under way, closed all entries to Manhattan. Still, the paper managed to distribute 75,000 copies. Ironically, the *Post* had just three weeks earlier stopped publishing papers at its longtime South Street plant; indeed, had the newspaper still been housed at its Lower Manhattan offices, publishing would have proved virtually impossible.

For veteran *Post* photographer Don Halasy, the World Trade Center was almost the last thing he ever saw. He was one of the two *Post* lensmen—Bolivar Arellano was the other—who nearly lost their lives in the destruction.

Although the first tower had already collapsed, Halasy remained just 200 feet from its crippled twin, shooting photos for

the Extra edition that the paper already was planning. Suddenly, he heard an unearthly roll of thunder in the air above him.

"As I turned to run," he wrote in the following day's *Post*, "a wall of warm air came barreling toward me. I tried to outrace it, but it swept me up and literally blew me into the wall of a building. By the time I regained my footing, a hailstorm of debris was falling from the sky."

In the days ahead, the *Post* performed superbly under the leadership of Editor in Chief Col Allan, Editorial Page Editor Bob McManus and Metropolitan Editor Jesse Angelo. For the next week, virtually the entire paper was given over to the coverage of the horrifying crime. The September 12 *Post*, carrying the front-page headline ACT OF WAR, sold over one million copies—the first time that had happened in nearly 20 years.

RIGHT: *The* Post *distributes a million "Wanted Dead or Alive" posters for prime suspect Osama bin Laden. (*Post *photo by Jim Alcorn)*

Part V

The Post Today

"An Oasis of Good Sense"

200 YEARS
NEW YORK POST

After 200 years in a changing city, the *Post* has evolved into the fastest-growing daily newspaper in the most competitive market in the country. New Yorkers—and a global Internet audience—turn to the *Post* for breaking news, in-depth stories on the city and politics, excellent gossip and entertainment coverage and outstanding sports. Through lively photo galleries and commentary, this chapter celebrates the *Post*'s news, entertainment and sports coverage.

As described by Harry Stein in the *City Journal*, "The Post, in its noisy, irreverent, often over-the-top way, stands out as an oasis of good sense. . . . [It is] a civic treasure. . . . What counts is that, with the culture in the balance, we never have an instant's doubt where the *Post*'s heart and mind are."

OPPOSITE: *New York Mayor Fiorello La Guardia (far right) and Sen. Robert Wagner (center, with raised hand) among cheering workers pleased to be working again on city housing projects in 1938. (Post photo by Barney Stein)* ABOVE: A Post *photographer delivers a King Kong view from the needle of the Empire State Building, looking down on three of the building's maintenance workers. (*Post *photo)*

The Post Is News

New York's Tabloid Treasure

HARRY STEIN, *City Journal,* Winter 2001

A friend of mine reports that a few days into the extended post-election agony, he found himself on a plane out of La Guardia beside a forty-fiveish Upper West Sider. Midway through the flight, his seatmate suggested they exchange papers, his *New York Times* for my friend's *New York Post.*

"I never buy it myself," remarked the guy, taking the tabloid, "but I get a kick out of the gossip and scandal stuff. The *Post*'s a guilty pleasure."

My friend looked from the Gray Lady's headline—BUSH SUES TO HALT HAND RECOUNT IN FLORIDA—to the one in the *Post:* STOP, THIEF! "And also an antidote to the *Times,*" he replied.

I say my friend had it just right. Though in the best (and worst) tabloid tradition, the *Post* is as subtle as a Vegas floor show—its tone more Bill O'Reilly than Alistair Cooke—we should stop making apologies for the paper and recognize it for what it is: a civic treasure. In a town whose other dailies celebrate every kind of diversity except the intellectual kind—and in an era when the meaning of morality is as flexible as a Clinton-Gore Democrat's concept of the rule of law—the *Post,* in its noisy, irreverent, often over-the-top way, stands out as an oasis of good sense.

For an increasing number of us, the *Post* is a daily essential, reflecting our attitudes and values in ways the holier-than-thou *Times,* obsessed with social and moral fashion, would scorn to do. Nor has the tabloid ever been so vital as in the ethical chaos of the Clinton-Gore years. "These days," as my friend puts it, "I actually flaunt my affection for the *Post.* What better way to tick off the terminally smug?"

It goes without saying that those on the other side of the political and cultural divide are clueless about the paper's appeal to anyone with an IQ north of 90. With a history of bizarre sensational

headlines stretching back to the seventies—HEADLESS BODY IN TOPLESS BAR, ran one classic—and with its continuing enthusiasm for stories featuring sex and mayhem, the *Post* is easy to caricature; and its detractors, including many who labor at more conventionally respectable media outlets, do so with reflexive relish. Across the city, the politically correct love to dismiss it as a sort of daily *National Enquirer*—only worse, for having an editorial side that's pre-Neanderthal.

Of course, some committed liberals do continue to read the *Post,* if only by force of habit. Most are holdovers from the pre-1976 days, when, under publisher Dorothy Schiff and editorial page editor James Wechsler, it was by far the most liberal paper in town, its opinion page for years home to Eleanor Roosevelt herself. But now, with an eye toward their blood pressure, these readers tend to navigate past the editorial pages, heading instead to the celebrity gossip on Page Six or the excellent sports section. For those inhabiting America's most politically correct precincts, today's *Post* is more than just a source of pitiless aggravation; it speaks the vilest kind of sacrilege, challenging—mocking—contemporary liberalism's guiding assumptions. In an era of rampant relativism, on issue after contentious issue—from the Brooklyn Museum's Sensation exhibition to bilingual education, from homosexual scoutmasters to feel-good multicultural history—the paper confidently makes the case for standards and the sustaining power of tradition, unapologetically asserting conservatism's claim to the moral high ground.

Little wonder that on the *Times* opinion pages, virtually every reference to *Post* proprietor Rupert Murdoch or his paper comes laced with venom. But of course what truly gets to the broadsheet's mandarins is that their fury is to so little effect. Indeed, as the *Times'* readership has continued to erode, the *Post* is the only daily in the nation whose circulation has actually risen (if usually only slightly) in every reporting period over the past six years.

That is, ever since Murdoch (who had owned the paper in the eighties and been forced to sell after acquiring a local TV outlet) was allowed to reassume control at the end of 1993, after a series of tragi-comic misadventures with would-be publishers had left the *Post* gasping for life. While much of the region celebrated the resurrection of the nation's oldest continually published paper, founded

OPPOSITE: *A Post* reader gets first news of the Simpson verdict on October 3, 1995. *(Post* photo)

Harry Stein is a contributing editor to the prestigious Manhattan Institute's City Journal *magazine. He is most recently the author of "How I Accidentally Joined the Vast Right-Wing Conspiracy: (And Found Inner Peace)."*

by Alexander Hamilton—even Mario Cuomo had played a key role in saving it, very likely to his regret—the very day Murdoch was back, the *Times* editorialized that "his purchase of the *Post* may save it as a daily, but there should be no illusions that he is a healthy influence on American journalism. . . . Mr. Murdoch's greatest sins have not been those against taste. His newspaper journalism has often been, at bottom, professionally and politically dishonest. He used his papers to grind the axes of his political buddies, to promote a reflexive conservatism and to make sensationalism rather than accuracy the animating principle of the news pages."

For Eric Breindel, then the *Post*'s lead editorialist, this was akin to a Margaret Dumont lob to Groucho. A more gifted thinker than the sober apparatchiks of the *Times*' editorial board and an infinitely better writer, Breindel clearly saw the attack as an opening skirmish in a welcome war. An "important message permeates this smug diatribe," he wrote the very next day. "Indeed, the *Times* provides a key clue to the genesis of its animosity when it decries Murdoch 'for using his papers to promote a reflexive conservatism.'

"Now, as it happens, Rupert Murdoch isn't 'reflexively' anything. But it is fair to say he doesn't hide his generally right-of-center

No. 40, Pine-Street.

Post Addresses: 1801–Today

1801–1831 . . . . . . .40 Pine Street
1831–1837 . . . . . .49 William Street
1837–1849 . . . . . .23-27 Pine Street
1849–1853 . . . . . .18 Nassau Street
1853–1875 . . . . . .55 Liberty Street
1875–1907 . . . . . .206-210 Broadway (at Fulton Street)
1907–1926 . . . . . .20 Vesey Street
1926–1970 . . . . . .75 West Street
1970–1995 . . . . . .210 South Street
1995– . . . . .1211 Avenue of the Americas

Only the last four buildings are still standing. Twenty Vesey Street is now known as the Garrison Building and is a designated historical landmark. Like the Broadway and West Street buildings, it was specifically built for the *Evening Post*. The South Street building was built by William Randolph Hearst to house the *New York Journal-American* (the building still has the Hearst eagles carved on the side). The William Street building was located directly across the street from Aaron Burr's law office.

NO. 49 WILLIAM-STREET

ideological orientation. And he's allergic by nature to that which is deemed Politically Correct.

"Interestingly—as the *Times* editorial demonstrates—the liberals and leftists who dominate the American media universe can't face the fact that they too are likewise animated by ideological considerations. Those folks actually think that they—and the newspapers they produce—are entirely non-partisan and non-ideological.

"By their lights, conservative journalists are—ipso facto—ideologues; liberal editors and writers, on the other hand, believe that they, somehow, manage to check their ideological baggage at the door and carry out their journalistic duties in an entirely apolitical fashion. . . .

"Americans are expected to accept this fantasy at face value."

Breindel remained in place another five years, his influence such that when he died at 42, in 1998, conservatives across the country felt his loss keenly. His funeral service was very much a *Post* event: mingling with Henry Kissinger, Rudy Giuliani, George Pataki and assorted former Harvard classmates of Breindel were a good number of ordinary readers. As each august eulogizer in turn stepped solemnly to the podium, one large, open-faced fellow in a ski jacket, carrying the *Star* as well as the *Post*, loudly asked from his seat a couple of rows behind the family, "Who's that?"

Though in Breindel's wake the *Post* remains a powerful redoubt of conservative thought and opinion, in fact it has never been quite as ideologically uniform as outsiders on both sides of the cultural divide assume. This being New York—and the journalism business—most of the paper's reporters and news editors tend to be, in their personal politics, decidedly liberal. One *Post* scribe, who confided in me that his dream job would be at *The New Yorker*, acknowledges he's often hesitant even to tell other journalists where he works. Another ruefully noted that when he applied for a job at the *Times*, "the first thing they asked was if I was hired pre- or post-Murdoch." Too bad for him: There are precious few holdovers from the Schiff days; the very last hire of the late liberal regime, conservative Eric Fettmann, is happily ensconced as one of the paper's top editorialists.

But you can make a strong case that, on both the news and editorial sides, the *Post* takes the task of airing alternative viewpoints at least as seriously as do publications that make a fetish of diversity. During the Elián Gonzalez business, notwithstanding the paper's strongly anti-Castro tilt, columnist Douglas Montero, a liberal who sees himself as a voice for the disenfranchised, was in Havana beating the drums for the child's return to Cuba with the zeal of Fidel himself: He actually filed stories that used Cuban government documents as reliable sources. Gossip mavens Liz Smith and Cindy Adams both use their daily allotment of space to push liberal themes, with Cindy laying it on particularly thick for her pal Hillary Clinton. Ditto TV critic Linda Stasi. During the post-election chaos, columnist Sidney Zion, a *Times* and *News* vet in the regular-

> 66 *Having Mr. Murdoch give the go-ahead and say 'Let's build a new plant' was an announcement to the whole New York community that the company was behind the* Post *completely and that there was no doubt about where we were going.* 99
>
> —MARTIN SINGERMAN, *POST* PRESIDENT AND PUBLISHER 1993–1999

Start the Presses!

In 2001, the *Post* begins a new era with the grand opening of its new printing plant at 900 East 132nd Street in the Bronx. This state-of-the-art plant brings the *Post* thoroughly into the 21st century.

For the first time, the *Post* has the capacity to print 64 pages in full color—the most color of any paper in New York. The plant is the first in the United States to incorporate laser-guided robots that take the paper to the four presses. It also features the latest "shaftless" printing technology and the most sophisticated press control system ever designed. Barry Mechanic, vice president of operations, who oversaw the building of the plant, adds that the presses are capable of producing 72,000 copies of the paper per hour, about twice the speed of the last presses.

On its 200th anniversary, the *Post* comes full circle with this bold advance in newspaper printing. When the *Post*'s first printer, Michael Burnham, produced the first editions of the paper in 1801, the style and appearance of the paper received wide acclaim. As related in the opening chapter, one newspaper described the look as "a style by far superior to that of any other newspaper in the United States." Exactly 200 years after launching the nation's most beautifully typeset newspaper, the *Post* greets its historic anniversary with the same dedication to superior printing.

ABOVE: *The* Post's *new printing plant in the Bronx.*

guy, street-smart Jimmy Breslin–Pete Hamill mode, could be found blasting away at the Bush team with all the snarly contempt of a West Palm oldster.

Still, let's not pretend: The *Post*'s ideological reputation is hardly unmerited. Day after day, in its news coverage as well as in the opinion sections, it offers a slant on events that goes against the usual media grain—occasionally enough to make a real difference. Think back on the paper's role in the controversy over the pro-homosexual "Children of the Rainbow" elementary-school curriculum in 1992; how, while the *Times* reflexively characterized curriculum opponents as unregenerate bigots, running pieces entitled BOOKS HELP CHILDREN OF GAY PARENTS and TEACHING ABOUT GAYS AND TOLERANCE, the *Post* gave a hearing to those, like District 24's Mary Cummins, who spoke to traditional religious beliefs and age appropriateness—which is to say, it covered the issue not only more equitably but with a far greater sense of

CELEBRATING 200 YEARS
NEW YORK POST
LATE CITY FINAL
MONDAY, MARCH 5, 2001 / Snow, 30 / Weather: Page 58 ★★
www.nypost.com

NEW YORK, 2001
Population: 8 million
Mayor: Rudolph W. Giuliani
Governor of New York: George E. Pataki
Post Newspaper Price: $134.68/year
Staten Island Ferry Fare: Free
Theater Ticket, Best Seat: $100.00
■ **Developed Areas** **Columbia College Tuition: $25,044.00/year**

nuance and sophistication. Only in the *Post* could you learn how deep and widespread among parents, including many minority parents, was the belief that to inflict DADDY'S ROOMMATE and HEATHER HAS TWO MOMMIES on six- and seven-year-olds was an assault upon their own most cherished values.

Then, too, just this past summer, none of the city's other papers, for all their ostensible concern with First Amendment issues, initially saw any news value in the MTA's summary rejection of pro-life ads for the subways. It was left to the *Post* to break and pursue the story, eventually leading to a lifting of the ban.

That, of course, is the dirty but increasingly blatant little secret in many newsrooms: that what's fit to print, and how to print it, is a highly subjective proposition. Many have drawn attention to the *Times*' strategic use of story placement—how, for instance, during the recent presidential campaign, even when a story bearing on Al Gore's ethical lapses managed to make it into the paper, it would get buried in the corner of page A23. Such tactics help explain why, even today, many who get their news exclusively from the paper of record or NPR, let alone the broadcast networks, have only the dimmest awareness that someone named Juanita Broaddrick lodged a highly credible accusation of rape against Bill Clinton or that the open-ended sexual harassment statute that brought on the president's troubles had been signed into law by Clinton himself.

Needless to say, the typical *Post* reader, in his way far less blinkered, is likely to know all that.

The *Post* gives its readers something else that *Times* followers don't get: gritty reporting on the street-level realities of metropolitan life. Its columns teem with stories of everyday crime and everyday heartbreak that *Times* mandarins would dismiss as mere sensationalism, vulgar and beneath contempt. But without knowing the human reality, the details of what people are actually doing to one another, who can gauge the city's social health?

In no area is this difference more apparent than in the two papers' treatment of violent crime, especially when committed by minorities. The *Times*, viewing certain kinds of criminality largely as a product of social forces beyond individual control, routinely strains to understand (and thereby prompt sympathy for) even the most predatory monsters. An opposite set of understandings relentlessly informs the *Post*'s coverage: that it is not the perpetrators of crime but those whose lives they've shattered who merit our concern; that in the ongoing war for the city's streets between cops and robbers (and murderers, rapists, child abusers and assorted lesser thugs), it is law enforcement that saves us from mayhem; and that those who smugly sow confusion in the public mind about who are the good guys and who are the bad abet evil.

The character of a news operation also shows itself in its choice of less weighty stories, even the most incidental items. Take, for instance, the following items that zipped across the wires over the past few months, further documenting the degree to

DOCTORS' VERDICT ON GEORGE BRETT BACK PAGE

NEW YORK POST FINAL CLOSING PRICES

TODAY Mostly sunny, near 80
TONIGHT Partly cloudy, near 70
TOMORROW Cloudy, mild, 70s
Details, Page 2

TV listings: P. 91   FRIDAY, OCTOBER 17, 1980   25 CENTS   © 1980 News Group Publications Inc. Vol. 179, No. 283   AMERICA'S FASTEST-GROWING NEWSPAPER   AVERAGE DAILY SALES EXCEED **700,000**

POST

Reagan for President

THE NEW YORK POST today endorses Ronald Reagan to be the next President of the United States.

The Post says President Carter has shown himself to be indecisive, incompetent and weak.

Under him we have had four years of decline. A declining economic base, a declining standard of living, a declining dollar, a decline in our great industries, a decline in our great cities and a decline in our power in the world.

It is a record of almost total failure.

The Post believes Reagan would bring a sense of decency, perspective and enterprise to the presidency, the nation's **leadership and to the country.**

Please turn to our Editorial on Page 32.

REAGAN TO MEET CARTER HEAD-ON

By STEVE DUNLEAVY

RONALD REAGAN agreed today to debate President Carter one on one, but said he still feels independent John Anderson should be included.

Carter quickly jumped at the chance to debate and the League of Women voters invited the two to meet in Cleveland on Oct. 28 — seven days before Election Day.

Reagan told reporters at LaGuardia Airport as he wrapped up a visit to New York.

"I'm eager to debate the critical issues of the presidential campaign with Jimmy Carter.

"I look forward to having

these matters raised in a face-to-face situation where Mr. Carter's views and mine will stand for all to see and judge."

Reagan *dropped his insistence* that Anderson *must be* included but added:

"Measured by his present support and resources, Congressman Anderson should be included in that debate.

"Mr. Carter should do what's right and fair and I will leave to his conscience and the judgment of the American people whether or not Mr. Carter should meet

Continued on page 9

POST ELECTION SPECIAL   STARTING MONDAY **GET THE POST FOR A QUARTER EVERY DAY THRU THE ELECTION** Details: Page 3

 NEW YORK POST

LATE CITY FINAL

FRIDAY, OCTOBER 28, 1994 / Sunshine today, 65; clear and mild tonight, 45 / Details, Page 24 **   50¢

A POST EDITORIAL

TIME FOR A CHANGE

Post endorses Pataki

Mario Cuomo's two decades of service to the people of the state of New York mark him as a man of integrity, discipline and intense dedication. The fact that we seldom agreed with the governor on policy questions during his 12 years in the Executive Mansion did not keep him from coming to the aid of this newspaper during its darkest hours and helping in a manner that cannot easily be overstated to ensure The Post's survival.

Beyond our abiding institutional gratitude to him for the part he played along

with other leaders of all persuasions in saving The Post, the entire episode, we believe, says a great deal about Mario Cuomo as a man of honor. But we've come to the view that in New York, as in the rest of America, it's time for new directions. Republican State Senator George Pataki pledges to take this state down a new path. We believe he has the ability to do so and we endorse Sen. Pataki.

Cuomo's rhetorical gifts have elevated the public policy discourse in this

Continued on page 26

George Pataki: New direction.

Full political coverage: Pages 2, 3, 16 & 17

The Post and Politics

With its purchase by Rupert Murdoch in 1976, the *Post* began a new era, politically as well as journalistically. Once the nation's preeminent liberal daily, its politics gradually began moving to the right; its dramatic front-page endorsement of Ronald Reagan for president in 1980 placed the *Post* firmly in the conservative camp.

Since then, the *Post* has become one of America's most important conservative dailies. Its early support of Al D'Amato for senator in 1980, Rudy Giuliani for mayor in 1993 and then little-known George Pataki for governor the following year energized their campaigns toward eventual victory. The paper's editorial support is eagerly sought by candidates on the national, state and local level.

The *Post* also won a strong core of loyal readers through its unflinching support of often-unpopular causes: At a time when the police were under constant attack from some segments of the community, the *Post* has been a strong champion of New York's Finest. And the paper is widely known as America's foremost journalistic defender of the state of Israel—a role it has played ever since that nation's founding in 1948.

Now, thanks to its Web site, nypost.com, the *Post*'s editorial and op-ed pages have won a nationwide following of readers and political newsmakers who look to the paper for the best in opinion journalism.

ELECTION EXTRA 25¢ SPECIAL

NEW YORK POST 25¢ SPECIAL

P.M. SPECIAL

WEDNESDAY, NOVEMBER 9, 1994 / Cloudy today, 66; cloudy then brightening skies tomorrow, 55/ Details, Page 26 ***   25¢

A NEW ERA

MAN AT THE TOP: Gov.-elect George Pataki celebrates victory last night at the New York Hilton.   New York Post: Michael Norcia

Pataki: I'll change New York

22 pages of election coverage begins on Page 2

Tidal wave! GOP sweeps House and Senate Pages 10-13

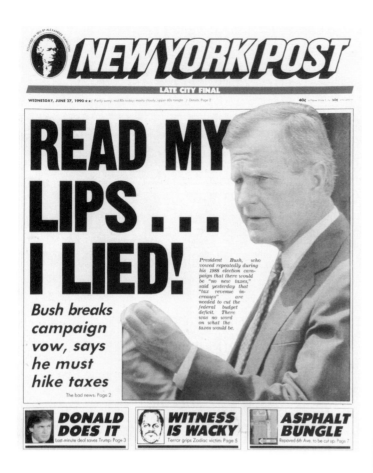

the nation's—capacity for cynicism and denial steadily grew. Yes, obviously the paper went after the sex and personal betrayal angles with wanton abandon—this is the *Post* we're talking about—and it also had its fair share of fun with the scandal, much of it at the hands of Sean Delonas, one of New York's most gifted editorial cartoonists. Indeed, Delonas's portrayal of Clinton as a self-serving libertine, wearing nothing but heart-festooned underwear and accompanied by Arkansas chickens who, post-Lewinsky, started appearing with cigars in their beaks, ranks up with Thomas Nast for hilariously savage mockery.

During that tumultuous year, even Page Six, where Delonas appears, jumped into the act, gleefully skewering "portly pepperpot" Monica and carrying on a joyous vendetta against arch-Clinton apologist Alec "Bloviator" Baldwin.

Still, in the most meaningful sense, throughout the long months of Clintonian evasion and spin, the *Post* took the scandal more seriously than most of its more liberal counterparts, never losing sight of the fundamental issues of law at the heart of the crisis, or the vital underlying matters of ethics and character. Leafing through the files I was keeping for a book I was doing at the time dealing in part with Clintonism's impact on the culture, I find more

which the P.C. epidemic has gripped the nation's campuses. While both items got a fair amount of play, neither saw the light of day in the paper of record. In the *Post*, however, each got full treatment, complete with photo.

• In the interest of highlighting its commitment to diversity, the University of Wisconsin had altered the cover photo on its recruiting brochure, turning a white student into a black one.

• The administration at SUNY Albany, faced with black activists' bizarre claim that the word "picnic" was derived from lynch mobs crying "pick a nigger," had decreed the word could not be used to describe an event honoring Jackie Robinson. Administrators ruled that, while the activists were mistaken, their sensibilities demanded respect. The *Post* writer also reported that, in deference to homosexual students, the school's Affirmative Action director had further forbidden the use of the word "outing."

This is where having the *Post* around really pays off. Askew as the world often seems these days, indifferent to what were once taken to be common sense and common decency, the brassy tabloid offers daily proof that one isn't crazy—or alone.

Never was that more true than during the Clinton scandals and impeachment saga. While the ostensibly high-minded press gave the president the kind of indulgence that only common interest and shared values can explain, with elite reporters and editorialists more and more brazenly echoing the party lines of "it's only sex" and "let's move on," the *Post*'s outrage at the president's—and

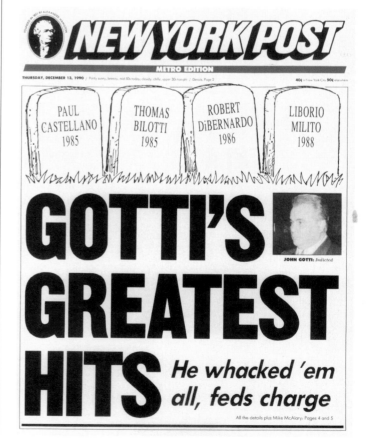

NEW YORK POST

LATE CITY FINAL

TUESDAY, MARCH 2, 1993 / Partly sunny, upper 40s today; partly cloudy, mid 30s tonight / Details: Page 2 — 50¢

WTC bomb probe zeroes in on three terrorist gangs

HOT ON THE TRAIL

A task force prober gathers evidence from the exit ramp of the garage at World Trade Center yesterday. Coverage begins on Pages 4 and 5.

Associated Press

SOCIAL SECURITY SWEEPSTAKES
PLAY HOTTEST GAME IN TOWN
Win your share of $60,000 in prizes: Page 21

TIMES SQUARE TERMINATOR
Schwarzenegger filming closes busy streets: Page 3

---

columnist George Will); MEDIA GANG OUT TO SMEAR HARRIS (Page Six gets in on the act); MORE SHAMELESS THAN BILL (Thomas Sowell). And of course, day after day, there was cartoonist Delonas. A typical effort had the president, in his heart-festooned boxers and smoking his cigar, in a golf foursome with O.J., Claus von Bülow, and freed baby killer Louise Woodward. "Don't worry," he blithely reassures them, "the justice system will sort this election mess out."

Yes, it was utterly partisan; but hardly more so than the broadsheets and broadcast outlets that pretend to neutrality even while savaging Ken Starr or Linda Tripp or, this time around, Katherine Harris.

To be sure, there have been changes in the paper over the years that some of us who read it closely regret. Personally, I very much miss ex-Timesman Hilton Kramer's scathing weekly critique of the mainstream media and would like to see a lot more of Kelly, Mona Charen and Paul Greenberg, among other compelling syndicated voices who've largely vanished from the opinion pages in favor of local writers on local themes.

Then, again, in the grand scheme of things—in a media universe that accepts as reasonable and fair the direction and tone set by the likes of Pinch Sulzberger and Howell Raines—these are quibbles. What counts is that, with the culture in the balance, we never have an instant's doubt where the *Post*'s heart and mind are.

"The liberalism in this city is so militant," as my friend Dreher puts it, "with the *Times* as its house organ, that for a lot of people the *Post* is more than a newspaper: it's an inspiration. I know that sounds hokey, but I see it all the time in my mail—'Thank God someone's defending religion or the Boy Scouts or the cops. Maybe the world hasn't gone completely mad, after all.'"

---

than 100 passionately written and argued pieces clipped from the paper. Indeed, if the good guys eventually prevail to write the story of our time, and Sexgate comes to be considered nearly as sorry a chapter in journalism's history as in America's, arguably only the *Wall Street Journal* will be seen as having brought to those events such visceral outrage as the *Post*.

And just post-election, with the nation's soul again at risk, there was the *Post*, back on the case. The edition my friend read on the plane that day launched a period of journalistic passion that surely equaled that of its most passionate reader. Here, truly, was Clinton's long-sought legacy in full bloom: a contempt for law and tradition never before imaginable on such a scale, and right in the glare of klieg lights! THE HIJACKING OF THE PRESIDENCY, proclaimed the *Post*'s appalled front-page editorial the following morning; and in the days to come, as the Gore legal team and Democratic hand-counters showed themselves to be ever more brazen, the paper's star columnists returned to the theme with renewed intensity. The titles of their pieces tell the story: SMEARING HIS WAY TO A WIN (John Podhoretz); NOT-SO-BLIND JUSTICE IS ON GORE'S SIDE (Rod Dreher); AL'S STOMACH-TURNING PIETY (syndicated columnist Michael Kelly); HOW DOES OUR CREEP VEEP SLEEP AT NIGHT? (Steve Dunleavy); HAS AL NO DECENCY? (Podhoretz again); OH, HOW I WISH THAT I'D NEVER VOTED FOR GORE (Andrea Peyser); GIVE IT UP, AL (Dick Morris); IT'S PURE OPPORTUNISM—CLOAKED IN OUTRAGE (syndicated

DON'T WORRY, THE JUSTICE SYSTEM WILL SORT THIS ELECTION MESS OUT

Studio strokes critic-fakers

Page Six.com

Richard Johnson

With Paula Froelich
and Chris Wilson

SONY Pictures' punishment of two execs for creating a fake movie critic to hype their flicks looks more like a pat on the back.

The two studio execs were suspended for running favorable quotes from critic "David Manning," who doesn't exist, of the Ridgefield Press, a Connecticut weekly which *does* exist, on ads for the **Heath Ledger** vehicle "A Knight's Tale" and "The Animal" starring **Rob Schneider**.

Junior marketing exec **Matthew Cramer** took the heat for the ploy, and was suspended for 30 days without pay, along with Cramer's boss, senior v.p. of creative advertising **Josh Goldstine**.

"That's the extent of what our investigation took us to," Sony spokesman **Steve Hagey** told us.

But since movie ads need approval from studio brass, those in the know say it's inconceivable that Cramer, if he even was respon-

sible, acted alone. If he had, he'd have been fired right away.

"There is no bleeping way the top people at Sony didn't know that David Manning didn't exist," one insider told PAGE SIX.

And as one rival Hollywood exec sniped to Inside.com, since most Tinseltown types have more than enough money but no time to spend it, a month off without pay sounds more like a perk than a penalty, joking, "I want to know what I have to do to get the same punishment."

At the Key Art marketing awards last Friday, "Animal" star Schneider joked that to make the penalty even more severe, Cramer and Goldstine should be forced to go on a two-week cruise.

Another Hollywood source howled to Inside.com that Sony's "investigation" into the misdeeds "reminded me of O.J. looking for the real killer."

Internet journalist **David Poland**, acting

on a tip from a Sony source, fingered Sony's head of motion picture publicity **Blaise Noto** as the real culprit in an e-mail bulletin, which was picked up and later retracted by **George Pennachhio**, a correspondent for L.A.'s ABC affiliate Ch. 7.

Meanwhile, others are wondering why the Ridgefield Press didn't raise a stink when "Manning" was quoted.

Marty Hersam, owner of the paper's parent company Hersam Acorn Newspapers, says that when they first saw the Manning quotes they assumed they came from one of the syndicated Cinema Source capsule reviews that the Ridgefield Press and many other papers publish, or else that it was another Ridgefield Press altogether.

"We didn't really pay that much attention to it," Hersam told us. "We didn't think it had anything to do with us, and we didn't really care." He does concede that as a result, "everyone" has now heard of his paper.

Sightings

"SURVIVOR" siren **Jerri Manthay** running out of a co-ed bathroom at a Stuff magazine-sponsored party at Crazy Girls strip club in L.A. after **Tommy Lee** unzipped and made an indecent proposal . . . **LAURA Ingraham**, the leggy blonde conservative with a syndicated talk radio show, lunching at the Palm in D.C. with Harvard president **Larry Summers**. The former commerce secretary is recently separated from his wife, but sources say he and Ingraham are "just friends."

Lucky dog

SCOTT Baio, a legendary ladies man since his years as Chachi on "Happy Days," isn't a hit with *all* the Playmates he meets at the Playboy Mansion. At a dinner organized by Jalouse magazine and transcribed in the July issue, Playmate **Nicole Wood** said of Baio, 39, "We call him the Playmate Lapdog. He just doesn't care . . . right after he broke up with **Pamela Anderson**, he was after any Playmate he could get, young or old, he was always there, and he didn't look good. Weathered."

Heavy traffic

GUESTS at the Plaza Athenee hotel are complaining about the constant crush of people coming in and out of **Michael Jackson**'s room. The pale-faced pop oddity, who checked into a suite under the name Bob Simpson, has "delivery people, lawyers, producers, caterers coming in and out of his room all day — it's really annoying," gripes one irritated guest. Jacko checked in to the hotel on 64th near Madison the other day with his children, who had towels draped over their heads to foil photographers.

NOW WHAT SEEMS TO BE THE PROBLEM?

MARRIAGE COUNSELOR

Monkey business

SLATE editor **Michael Kin**-

sley stands behind his web site's much-maligned "monkeyfishing" story, and he dares doubters to prove him wrong. "Nothing is

ever the final word, but after several days of accusations, there is no evidence that he [writer **Jay Forman**] made this stuff up, and a lot of evidence that he didn't," Kinsley writes. Kinsley accuses the Wall Street Journal's online op-ed page of launching an "ad hominem attack" on him by suggesting he lacked "street smarts" and was duped into printing Forman's first-person account of snaring simians on the monkey-infested island of Lois Key using fruit and fishing hooks. Forman insisted to PAGE SIX: "The monkeyfishing story is, unfortunately, true."

Christian Curry's paper losses

MAYBE **Christian Curry** didn't win so much money from Morgan Stanley after all. The handsome stockbroker who posed nude for Playguy reportedly pocketed $20 million from his wrongful dismissal settlement. But Curry is past due on a bill from a printer in Port Washington, L.I. "Christian owes me $940 plus $1200 in legal fees," said **Kenny Cummings** of Finer Touch Printing. Curry bought letterhead fax sheets, memo pads, envelopes and business cards. "He hasn't returned any of our calls since we delivered," Cummings said. "We took the problem to a collection agency in March." Curry, who claims he never received the stationery, mysteriously told PAGE SIX: "I only scratch my head when it itches, and I only dance when I hear the music . . . Everybody and their mother thinks I owe them money . . . I will only give money and help people who have helped me in the past and who deserve it, and they have been well taken care of, and anyone else who tries to suck me for funds will be viciously dealt with."

For the hottest celebrity photos on the web, go to **pagesix.com**

Just asking

WHICH handsome nephew of a big man in D.C. picked up a pretty young thing after a few drinks in the bar of the W Union Square? He got her upstairs to his room, but then proceeded to vomit all over the hapless honey.

Croaky crooner

ROCK star **Dave Matthews** (above) is apologizing to his fans for singing himself hoarse during his three-night stint at Giants Stadium. After his final gig Wednesday night, Matthews returned to his suite at the Peninsula and ran into The Post's **Brad Hamilton** at the bar. "I'm sorry, man," said Matthews, looking spent and massaging his taxed tonsils. "After three nights, my voice is very scratchy. I sound like **Joe Cocker**."

The Post Is Celebrities

New York's Favorite Guilty Pleasure

By ERIC FETTMANN, Associate Editorial Page Editor

It's said we live in the age of celebrity; a time, as the late Andy Warhol put it, when "everyone will be famous for fifteen minutes." But celebrity and notoriety have long driven American journalism—even before the first U.S. tabloid was founded in 1919. It is, in fact, one of the secret guilty pleasures of most newspaper readers.

The *Post* has covered the rich and famous with a no-holds-barred abandon that has both entertained and informed its readers and continually captures the fast-paced theatricality that is life in New York City.

Back in the days when society revolved around nightclubs like the Copacabana, the Stork Club, Toots Shor's and El Morocco, the *Post*'s Earl Wilson—who was given the title "Saloon Editor" and Leonard Lyons ("The Lyons Den") were second only to rival Walter Winchell as the kings of New York nightlife.

Fierce competitors, they invented the Broadway column, described by one biographer as "a look through the peep-hole which opens on the cosmos, a whisper of information that will make nations goggle. . . ."

Wilson's column, "It Happened Last Night," ran for 45 years in the *Post*. He called himself a specialist in "the three B's: booze, busts and behinds." At one time, he was the most popular syndicated gossip columnist in the country and had his own TV show. His nightly pub-crawling of the city's hot spots produced some major exclusives: It was Wilson, for example, who first told the world of the John F. Kennedy–Marilyn Monroe romance.

Wilson's celebrity contacts also provided him with non-entertainment exclusives. In 1954, he scored a 24-hour lead over the national press corps with word that Dr. Jonas Salk had invented a successful anti-polio vaccine. He got the tip from actress Lilli Palmer, who'd heard it from writer Anita Loos.

As for Leonard Lyons, his stories were so good that *Post* editors routinely plucked items out of his column and ran them in the paper's news section. According to one memoir of old Broadway, Lyons was "in a class by himself." Who else would think of bringing the poet Carl Sandburg as his guest to the Stork Club?

ABOVE: *Remorseful Yankee slugger Darryl Strawberry wipes a tear away while his wife, Charisse, looks on outside their New Jersey home in 1998.* (Post *photo*)

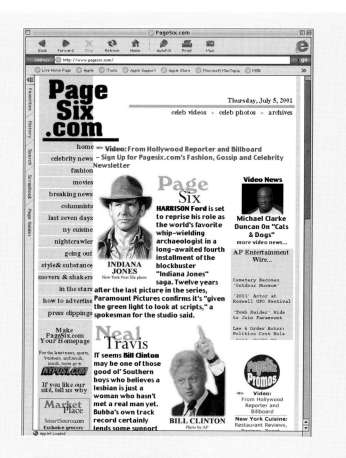

PageSix.com

Other celebrated *Post* gossip columnists of the past have included Aileen Mehle, who as "Suzy" chronicled the doings of the East Side upper crust. Also Elsa Maxwell, songwriter, actress and party hostess par excellence was the host of the celebrated radio show *Elsa Maxwell's Party Line* and made weekly appearances on the *Tonight Show* when Jack Paar hosted it.

Today Page Six is the touchstone of celebrity reporting in New York, the media and celebrity capital of the world. Created by Neal Travis in 1977, Page Six's must-read exclusives from the worlds of show business, politics and society are the first thing thousands of New Yorkers turn to every morning. Page Six's first reporter was the now-famous author Anna Quindlen.

Currently edited by Richard Johnson—past editors include James Brady and Claudia Cohen—the page is the nationally recognized trademark of celebrity journalism and has spawned its own highly successful Web site, PageSix.com.

The column has even enjoyed its own celebrity status: Melanie Griffith cites a Page Six item to Harrison Ford as the inspiration of her media merger deal in the hit 1988 film *Working Girl*. And Al Pacino, as a harried playwright escaping from police to the roof of his Greenwich Village town house in the 1982 flick *Author! Author!*, is asked by one of his children what he sees down below. "What do I see?" he replies. "I see myself on Page Six of the *Post*."

As it enters its third century, today's *New York Post* continues as the leader in entertainment journalism. It's an area that's a never-ending source of great stories because we all know celebrities, socialites or politicians will always make news and that we'll always want to read about them—whether those celebrities, socialites or politicians want us to or not.

It's just one of life's guilty pleasures that we all enjoy.

ABOVE: *Comedian and filmmaker Woody Allen and then-girlfriend (now wife) Soon-Yi Previn shop on Madison Avenue in 1996. (Post Photo)*

The *Post* has a long history of dishing up the best gossip in the city, from the pioneering columns of "Saloon Editor" Earl Wilson, Elsa Maxwell and Leonard Lyons to the current all-star lineup. PageSix editor Richard Johnson's stable of gossip and entertainment writers keep the entire nation informed about the movers and shakers that illuminate New York: Cindy Adams, Liz Smith and Neal Travis.

PageSix was formed when Murdoch purchased the *Post* and has evolved into an internationally recognized source of gossip. The on-line PageSix site, PageSix.com, contains columns by Cindy Adams, Liz Smith and Neal Travis and up-to-the-minute stories on celebrities, fashion, food, style, entertainment and media news.

Our First Sex Scandal

Alex Tells All

ALEXANDER HAMILTON *founded the Evening Post in 1801 in order to strengthen the Federalist party. The leading merchants of New York joined with him in raising the original capital. Hamilton wrote occasionally for the paper and often dictated or suggested editorials. The first editor was referred to as "Hamilton's typographer."*

News of Alexander Hamilton's adulterous affair with a married woman produced vicious personal attacks against him in the press that have never—even in today's tabloid press and television—been matched.

The affair began in Philadelphia in the summer of 1791, while Hamilton was secretary of the Treasury in what was then the nation's capital. His wife, Betsy, was spending the hot months in upstate New York with their children. Twenty-three-year-old Mrs. Maria Reynolds, a pretty woman-about-town, approached Hamilton with the story that her abusive husband had walked out on her and left her without means. The damsel in distress needed financial help to get to New York. Hamilton told her he would bring her the money. He visited her that night and commenced an affair that he would come to deeply regret.

In December, Hamilton received letters from both Mr. and Mrs. Reynolds. The husband demanded $1,000 to keep his mouth shut about the affair, and his wife expressed her sorrow for bringing the great and dear Mr. Hamilton so much trouble. Hamilton paid Reynolds off. One month later, the couple wrote to him again, the husband now saying that Maria desperately wanted to see Hamilton and that it was okay with him. The truth was clear: Maria was prostituting herself, her husband was her pimp and they were both blackmailers. In spite of this knowledge, Hamilton resumed the affair.

Hamilton's first confession came in December 1792 when he had to defend himself against accusations of corruption as secretary. Three congressmen, armed with statements by James Reynolds, met with Hamilton to get his side of the story. The secretary was overwhelmingly honest, explaining that his connection to Reynolds concerned not a financial scheme but his affair with

> **"[Hamilton's house is] a rendezvous of . . . whoredom."**

the man's wife. He pulled out a stash of love letters and proceeded to describe the affair in detail.

The affair came to national attention five years later when it was exposed in a series of pamphlets by muckraking newspaperman James Thomson Callender. *The History of the United States for 1796* claimed that Hamilton had used the affair as a coverup for corrupt dealings with Mr. Reynolds. In response, Hamilton published his own pamphlet, *Observations on Certain Documents . . . In Which the Charge of Speculation Against Alexander Hamilton, Late Secretary of the Treasury, Is Fully Refuted. Written by Himself.* Hamilton demolished the charges against him with rational arguments and offered an astonishing tell-all confession of his affair with Maria. He stated that the charges against him were for illegal financial dealing with James Reynolds, but that "my real crime is an amorous connection with his wife." He expressed regret for bringing pain to his wife and described how he felt about his behavior: "I have paid pretty severely for the folly and can never recollect it without disgust and self-condemnation."

Richard Brookhiser, author of *Alexander Hamilton, American*, writes that Hamilton's pamphlet "remains the frankest admission of adultery by any major American politician."

The newspapers would never let Hamilton hear the end of it. One paper wrote that he had made his house a "rendezvous of . . . whoredom," and another that the "frosts of America are incapable of cooling your blood." One of his enemies, John Adams, stated that Hamilton's ambitions sprang from "a superabundance of secretions which he could not find whores enough to draw off."

In the press, the political sex scandal had its heyday long before stories of cigars and stained blue dresses.

Silver screen heartthrob Rudolph Valentino, flanked by two unidentified beauties, in New York, 1924. (Post photo)

Charlie Chaplin, left, Mary Pickford and Douglas Fairbanks in New York, 1921. (Post photo)

A Youthful Suicide—and Its Lessons	Dorothy Dix	Urges Other Flappers to Beware Early Marriages

THE other day a girl of eighteen, tired of being what she called "a married slave," committed suicide. Investigation showed that her husband was a kindly, worthy young man, as far removed as possible from being a domestic tyrant and that the wife's slavery consisted merely in her having to take care of her home and her baby.

But she rebelled against doing this. She didn't want to be tied down with a child. She loathed cooking and sewing and mending and dusting and all household duties. She longed to be free to gad the streets and go joyriding with other youngsters. She wanted to spend her evenings going to movies and jazzing in cabarets instead of being a fireside companion to her husband and walking the colic. And because she couldn't devote all of her time to amusing herself life was worthless to her and she threw it away.

The tragedy of this poor, little silly girl has two lessons in it which I commend to the consideration of all other flappers. The first lesson is a warning against the folly of early marriage.

The girl who marries too soon almost invariably

Ask Dorothy Dix

One of America's most popular and highly syndicated columnists, Elizabeth Meriwether Gilmer (1861–1951), wrote under the pen name Dorothy Dix. The *Post* carried the advice of this writer who paved the way for "Dear Abby" and "Ann Landers." The excerpt shown here, offering marriage wisdom for young "flappers," appeared on November 4, 1925.

One of the columns readers wanted to see in print year after year was Dix's ten rules for happiness:

Dorothy Dix's Ten Dictates for a Happy Life

First. Make up your mind to be happy. Happiness is largely a matter of self-hypnotism. You can think yourself happy or you can think yourself miserable. It is up to you . . . learn to find pleasure in simple things. If you can't go to the opera, you can turn on the radio. Nail on your face the smile that won't come off, and after a bit you will find that it comes naturally.

Second. Make the best of your lot. Of course, you're not everything you want and things are not just right. Nobody is that lucky. Even the most fortunate have a lot of crumpled rose leaves under their forty mattresses of ease. There isn't a single human being who hasn't plenty to cry over, and the trick is to make the laughs outweigh the tears.

Third. Don't take yourself too seriously. Don't think that everything that happens to you is of world-shaking importance and that somehow you should have been protected from the misfortunes that befall other people. When death robs you of one you love, or you lose your job, don't demand to know of high heaven why this should happen to you and grow rebellious and morbid over your sorrow. We are never happy until we learn to laugh at ourselves.

Fourth. Don't take other people too seriously. They are not so much, anyway. Don't let their criticisms worry you. You can't please everybody, so please yourself. Don't let your neighbors set your standards for you. Don't run into debt trying to keep up with the Joneses, or bore yourself to death trying to be as intelligent as the Highbrows. Be yourself and do the things you enjoy doing if you want to be comfortable and happy.

Fifth. Don't borrow trouble. You have to pay compound interest on that and it will bankrupt you in the end. It is a queer thing, but imaginary troubles are harder to bear than actual ones. There are none of us who have not lain awake at night petrified with dread of some calamity that we feared might befall us and that we felt would shatter our lives if it should occur. Generally it never happened, but if it did, it was not so bad after all and we survived it without serious injury. Enjoy today and let tomorrow take care of itself.

Sixth. Don't cherish enmities and grudges. Don't keep up old quarrels. Don't remember all the mean things people have done to you. Forget them. Hate is a dreadful chemical that we distill in our own hearts, that poisons our own souls. It takes all the joy out of life and hurts us far worse than it does anyone else. There is nothing so depressing as having a grudge against someone. . . . So if you have an enemy, forgive him and kiss him on both cheeks, not for his sake but simply because it is to making you unhappy and uncomfortable to be stirred up in wrath against him.

Seventh. Keep in circulation. Go around and meet people. Belong to clubs. Travel as much as you can. Have as many interests as possible. Have hosts of friends. That is the way to keep yourself cheerful and jolly and thinking that this is the best of all possible worlds.

Eighth. Don't hold post-mortems. Don't spend your life brooding over the mistakes you have made or the sorrows that have befallen on you. What is done is done and cannot be changed, but you can have your whole future life in which to make good. Not all the tears can bring back those we have lost, but we can make life miserable for ourselves and those about us by our unavailing weeping. Quit beating upon your breast because you haven't as much money as you used to have. Don't be one of those who never get over things. Have the courage to take misfortune on the chin and come up smiling.

Ninth. Do something for somebody less fortunate than yourself. Minister to other people's trouble and you will forget your own. Happiness is a coin that we keep only when we give it away.

Tenth. Keep busy. That is the sovereign remedy for unhappiness. Hard work is a panacea for trouble. You never saw a very busy person who was unhappy.

High Society and Celebrity

Celebrity was an institution in New York City by the 1920s, and the *Post*'s society pages were filled with the names and faces of prominent local figures. The "Saturday Gravure" section featured photo collages of ladies' committees, famous citizens walking about town and lovely debutantes. This section also carried listings of social events, marriage announcements and the comings and goings of high society.

CLOCKWISE FROM LEFT: *Images from a "Saturday Gravure" section: Grace Vanderbilt strolling on Park Avenue; debutante Miss Mary Whitney; a grand ball committee.*

The Jimmy Walker Scandals

Flamboyant, tap-dancing New York Mayor Jimmy Walker turned the heads of even the most freewheeling Jazz Agers by openly flaunting his mistress in front of New York society, not to mention his wife. The mayor created scandal in both his personal and public life—his financial corruption launched the greatest investigation of municipal wrongdoing in the nation's history.

In 1931 the New York legislature formed a committee to investigate the city's finances and administration. The investigation exposed the large sums of money that had been deposited in Walker's personal account with no satisfactory explanation. By the end of the wildly publicized hearings, fifteen charges of corruption were aimed at Walker, and he resigned on September 1, 1932.

ABOVE LEFT: *Jimmy Walker.* ABOVE: *Humphrey Bogart and Lauren Bacall in New York in the 1940s.*

OPPOSITE: *An illustrated listing from June 1953 announces Brando's appearances in summer stock that season.*

BELOW LEFT: *George Gershwin in 1933, two years after the opening of his hit musical* Of Thee I Sing *and two years before the premier of his opera* Porgy and Bess. *The Brooklyn-born composer's extraordinary output spanned both popular music and concert works such as* Rhapsody in Blue *(1924) and* An American in Paris *(1928).* BELOW: *Marlon Brando in December 1955. (*Post *photos).*

Rural Theaters Begin New Season

Continued from Preceding Page

Burning"; July 20, "Island Visit"; Aug. 3, "The Show Off."

YARDLEY—Summer Theater, John Hurd, producer-director; 8-week season starts June 30 with "Hay Fever"; July 7, "Night Must Fall"; July 14, "The Chocolate Soldier"; July 21, "Dark Finale" (new); July 28, "The Skin of Our Teeth."

Massachusetts

CHATHAM—Monomoy Theater, Mary B. Winslow. Opens 10-week season July 1 with "The Importance of Being Earnest"; July 8, "The Great Big Doorstep"; July 15, "The Country Girl"; July 22, One-actbill; July 29, "An Invitation to a Murder"; Aug. 5, "Tony Draws a Horse."

COONAMESSETT—Falmouth Playhouse, Richard Aldrich, managing director. Starts 10-week season June 29 with Ezio Pinza in "The Play's the Thing"; July 6, Ella Raines in "I Am a Camera"; July 13, Marlon Brando in "Arms and the Man"; July

Dagmar opens her season's tour with Arthur Treacher in "Loco" Monday at the Niagara Falls Summer Theater.

20, Wally Cox in "Three Men on a Horse"; July 27, "The Frogs of Spring" (new).

DENNIS—Cape Playhouse, Richard Aldrich, managing director. Begins June 29 with Eva Gabor in "Sailor's Delight."

FALMOUTH—Highfield Theater. Nine-week season starts July 7 with "White Wings"; July 14, "The House of Bernarda Alba"; July 21, "The Beautiful People"; July 28, "The Sea Gull."

FITCHBURG—Lake Whalom Playhouse, Guy Palmerton, managing director. Currently play-

ing "Gentlemen Prefer Blondes."

HOLYOKE—Mt. Park Casino, Production manager, Dorothy M. Crane. 13-week season. Monday, "Affairs of State"; June 29, "The Velvet Glove"; July 6, "The Shop at Sly Corner"; July 13, "Sight Unseen"; July 20, "Happy Birthday"; July 27, "See My Lawyer."

HYANNIS — Cape Cod Music Circus, Richard Aldrich, managing director. Opens June 29, "Show Boat"; July 6, "Music in the Air"; July 13, "Gentlemen Prefer Blondes"; July 20, "Brigadoon"; July 28, "Call Me Madam."

JACOB'S PILLOW — Dance Festival, Ted Shawn, managing director. Nine-week season opens July 3 with Melissa Hayden, The Lester Horton Dance Theater, and La Meri; July 10, Choreographer's Workshop Program; July 16, Glen Tetley, "Games" and Iva Kitchell; July 23, Alicia Markova, Myra Kinch and La Meri and Di Falco.

MARTHA'S VINEYARD—East Chop Playhouse, Trio Productions, Thomas Clancy, director. Nine-week season opens July 2, "The Plough and the Stars"; July 13, "The Time of Your Life"; July 20, "S. S. Glencairn"; July 27, "Liliom."

MASHPEE — Oberlin College Gilbert and Sullivan Players, Dr. W. H. Boyers, director. Opens July 20 with "H. M. S. Pinafore."

NANTUCKET — Barn Stages, Vincent Y. Bowditch, managing director. Opens Monday with "Murder Without Crime."

NANTUCKET — Straight Wharf Theater, Vincent Y. Bowditch, managing director. Opens July 6 with "Candlelight."

PROVINCETOWN—Provincetown Playhouse, commences July 2 with "Dynamo."

SOMERSET — Playhouse. 12-week season starts Monday with "Gentlemen Prefer Blondes"; June 29, Barry Sullivan and Viveca Lindfors in "Bell, Book and Candle"; July 6, Dagmar and Arthur Treacher in "Loco"; July 13, Cedric Hardwicke in "Island Visit"; July 20, Magda Gabor in "The Play's the Thing"; July 27, Zachary Scott in "The Moon Is Blue."

STOCKBRIDGE — Berkshire Playhouse, William Miles, managing director. 11-week season

starts Monday with Elsie Ferguson in "And Two Make Four" (new); June 29, "The Moon Is Blue"; July 6, Leo G. Carroll in "You Never Can Tell"; July 13, "The Velvet Glove"; July 20, Katherine Alexander and Barbara Brady in "The Marquise"; July 27, Francesca Bruning in "Jane."

STURBRIDGE—Merry - Go - Round Theater, William Martin.

Marlon Brando takes "Arms and the Man" to four summer playhouses. Included is the Ivoryton, Conn., Playhouse, where he'll play the Shaw comedy during the week of July 27.

Manager; Howard Orms director. Opens Tuesday with "The Moon Is Blue." June 30, "The Male Animal"; July 7, "The Importance of Being Earnest"; July 14, "Our Town"; July 21, "The Indoor Sport" (new); July 28, "The Corn Is Green."

WESTBORO—Red Barn Theater, Sid Sawyer, manager. Tuesday, "Is Your Honeymoon Necessary?"

Maine

BAR HARBOR — Playhouse, Charles O. Carey, managing director. Starts June 30 with "Affairs of State."

BOOTHBAY—Playhouse, opens 10-week season June 30 with Fall River Little Theater in

Continued on Page ...

When Radio Ruled

D—DRAMA	**S—SONGS**	**T—TALKS**	**V—VARIETY**

LEFT: *Radio shows for June 5, 1944, included* I Love a Mystery *at 7:00 and* Ed Sullivan *at 7:15 on WABC,* Lone Ranger *at 7:30 on WJZ, and a fireside chat with President Roosevelt on all channels at 8:30.* ABOVE LEFT: *Frank Sinatra.* ABOVE RIGHT: *Louis "Satchmo" Armstrong.* BELOW: *Jackie Gleason in his dressing room for* The Honeymooners *TV series, which was filmed in New York in 1955–56. (Post photos)*

	3:00	3:15	3:30	3:45
WMCA	News; Love Songs	Ethel Colby	News	Glen Gray Orch.
WEAF	Woman of Amer.	D Ma Perkins	D Pepper Young	D Right to Happiness
WOR	Black Castle	D Sunny Skylar	S Food Forum	Food Forum
WJZ	Morton Downey	S Hollyw'd Star Time	Drama	Drama
WNYC	Symphonic Mat.	Symphonic Mat.	S Amer. Way	News; Rations
WABC	Mary Marlin	D Bob Trout	Now and Forever	D The Jubalaires
WHN	Bandstand	Bandstand; News	Bandstand	Bandstand
WNEW	Music Hall	Music Hall	News; Music	Music Hall
WQXR	Request Program	Request Program	Request Program	Request; News

	4:00	4:15	4:30	4:45
WMCA	News; E. Britt	Elton Britt	S News; Music	Music
WEAF	Backstage Wife	D Stella Dallas	D Lorenzo Jones	D Widder Brown	D
WOR	News; J. Gambling	John Gambling	Bob Stanley Orch.	Maritime Day
WJZ	Ethel & Albert	Don Norman Show	W. Van Voorhis	Sea Hound	D
WNYC	Four Strings	Four Strings	Four Strings	Reader's Almanac
WABC	B'way Matinee	V B'way Matinee	V Off Record; Songs	Raymond Scott Or.
WHN	Bandstand	Bandstand; News	Bandstand	Bandstand
WNEW	5 Shades of Blue	Music; Songs	News; Three Aces	Paula Stone
WQXR	Symphonic Matinee	Symphonic Mat.	Symphonic Mat.	Concert; News

	5:00	5:15	5:30	5:45
WMCA	News; Music	Popular Music	News	Steve Ellis, Sports
WEAF	Girl Marries	D We Love & Learn	Plain Bill	David Farrell
WOR	Uncle Don	Chick Carter	D Adven. of Tom Mix	Superman	D
WJZ	Terry & Pirates	D Dick Tracy	D Jack Armstrong	D Capt. Midnight	D
WNYC	Music	Music	Richard Harvey	S Talk; Musicale
WABC	Fun With Dunn	V Fun With Dunn	V Three Sisters	American Women
WHN	Bandstand	News	Dick Gilbert	Dick Gilbert
WNEW	10 Shades of Blue	Kathryn Cravens	News; Ballroom	Ballroom to 7:30
WQXR	Encore, Encore	E. Sternberger	Great Masters	Great Masters

	6:00	6:15	6:30	6:45
WMCA	News; Help Wanted	Movie; Sports	World News R'dup	Dr. Frank Kingdon
WEAF	Don Hollenbeck	Serenade to Amer	Music; B Stern	Lowell Thomas
WOR	Sydney Moseley	Imogen Carpenter	S Frank Singiser	Stan Lomax
WJZ	News; J. Kennedy	Hop Harrigan	D Stories; Songs	Henry J. Taylor
WNYC	U. Nations Music	U. S. Secret Serv.	U S Secret Serv.	News; Want Ads
WABC	News Analysis	Lyn Murray Or.	Arthur Godfrey	World Today; News
WHN	Dick Gilbert	Wm. Lang, News	Spotlight	Bob Howard
WQXR	Music to Remember	Music; News	Dinner Concert	Dinner Concert

	7:00	7:15	7:30	7:45
WMCA	News; Orchestra	Five Star Final	Johannes Steel	So the Story Goes
WEAF	Fred Waring Orch	Robt. St. John	Music; Revue	H. V. Kaltenborn
WOR	Fulton Lewis Or.	The Answer Man	Louis Sobol	Louis Sobol
WJZ	Horace Heidt Or.	Horace Heidt Or.	Lone Ranger	D Lone Ranger	D
WNYC	Masterwork Hour	Masterwork Hour	Masterwork Hour	Masterwork Hour
WABC	I Love a Mystery	Ed Sullivan	Blondie	D Blondie	D
WHN	Geo. H. Combs Jr.	Bert Lee	Congress Record	Voice of Experience
WNEW	Ballroom	Ballroom	News; Bruno Shaw	A.A.F. Newsreel
WQXR	Lisa Sergio	Operetta; News	Treasury of Music	Treasury of Music

	8:00	8:15	8:30	8:45
WMCA	News; Music	Jerry Lawrence	Pres. Roosevelt	Jerry Lawrence
WEAF	Cavalcade	V Cavalcade	V Pres. Roosevelt	Richard Crooks	S
WOR	Cecil Brown	The Smoothies	S Pres. Roosevelt	Sherlock Holmes	D
WJZ	News	Lum & Abner	Pres. Roosevelt	Blind Date	V
WNYC	Associated Hosp.	N. Y. Heroes	Pres. Roosevelt	News; Rations
WABC	Vox Pop	Vox Pop	Pres. Roosevelt	Nineties; B. Henry
WHN	Army Air Forces	Army Air Forces	Pres. Roosevelt	Music

Papa and Lenny: The Hemingway-Post Letters

For more than twenty years, novelist Ernest Hemingway corresponded with his longtime friend Leonard Lyons, the *Post*'s celebrity columnist. In his letter of October 22, 1955, Hemingway wrote, "Maybe you and I are the best friends we will either of us have." In 1996, the letters were discovered and auctioned off.

A letter dated May 22, 1952, explained why the novelist refused to write a guest column for the *Post*:

"I'll let you have three shots at me from ten paces rather than write a column. You do it so well and easily it must seem silly to think how impossible it would be for someone who has disciplined themselves into the kind of damn writing I try to do. . . . If you needed it to keep out of jail, or if you or Sylvia were ill I would be glad to write your column as well as I could and fill in for you. I would come to town and stay up all night and not drink and move around and write as good a column as I could. But if I write a bastard half-a-column for you down here which would have nothing but my name to recommend it then my name should not be worth much long.

In 1954 Hemingway received the Nobel Prize in Literature "for his mastery of the art of narrative, most recently demonstrated in *The Old Man and the Sea*, and for the influence that he has exerted on contemporary style." He confided in Lyons about his attitude toward the honor in a letter of December 1954:

Lenny that prize business is awfully hard on your work. No matter how valuable it is it does you more harm than good if you let it. No prize is worth interrupting a good book, so I'm going to stick to the same schedule now until I get the book done then have some fun and start working again.

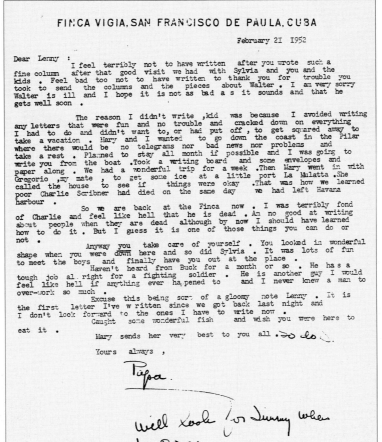

Leonard Lyons' column, "The Lyons Den," covered the lives and careers of movers and shakers in New York and the world. This excerpt is from April 16, 1947.

*Ernest Hemingway in the 1940s. (*Post *photo)*

In this letter, signed "Papa," Hemingway apologizes for not writing sooner and explains that he only had time to get out some crucial mail before leaving for a vacation in Cuba. (Photocopy from Post *archives)*

The Post*'s story about the newly discovered letters included a picture of the columnist and the novelist.*

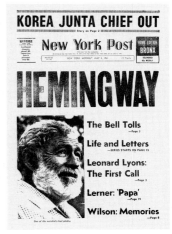

Coverage of Hemingway's death in 1961 included a personal note from Leonard Lyons, the first person to get the news.

227

LEFT: *Barbra Streisand hugs her poodle, Sadie, good-bye before jetting out of New York for London.* (Post *photo*) *Brooklyn-born Streisand starred in* Funny Girl *on Broadway in 1964 and won the 1968 Academy Award for Best Actress for her performance in the movie version. She first appeared on Broadway in 1962 in the musical* I Can Get It for You Wholesale, *for which she won the New York Drama Critics Award and received a Tony nomination.*

BELOW: *Opera diva Maria Callas backstage at New York's Metropolitan Opera House in the 1960s.* (Post *photo*)

OPPOSITE ABOVE: A Chorus Line *at the Schubert Theater, 1983. Broadway's "singular sensation," composed by Marvin Hamlisch with lyrics by Edward Kleban, closed in 1990 after more than 6,000 performances.* (Post *photo*)

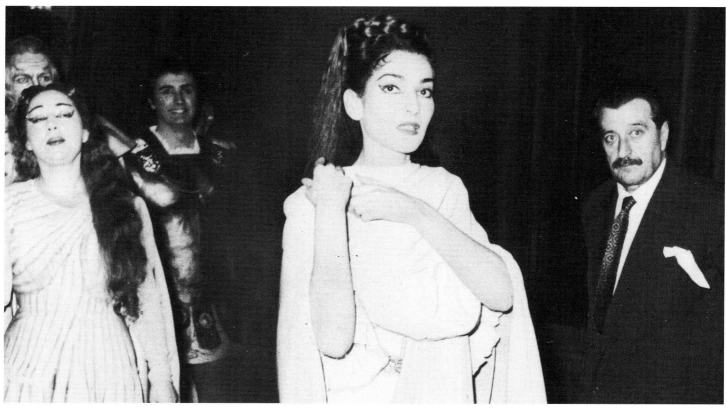

Royal Wedding

"This is the stuff of which fairy tales are made—the prince and princess on their wedding day," said the Archbishop of Canterbury in a homily after the wedding ceremony of Prince Charles and Lady Diana Spencer.

The wedding vows were spoken at 6:15 a.m. New York time, and television cameras inside St. Paul's Cathedral brought the event to the entire world.

The prince and princess had two sons, William and Harry, before the fairy tale began to unravel beyond repair. They separated in 1992 and divorced in 1996. The drama of "The People's Princess" came to a tragic end when she was killed in an automobile accident in Paris the following year.

Royal fact

The palace is unconcerned that Charles and his wife are related. Both claim four kings as ancestors — making them 16th cousins.

One of the ultimate photo ops of all time—shy young royal marries the future King of England. Post *coverage included trivia and a logo.*

Princess Diana in New York in December 1995 at the United Cerebral Palsy Awards Dinner, where she received the Humanitarian Award. (Post photo by Michael Alexander)

ABOVE LEFT: *Manhattan moguls Harry and Leona Helmsley.* (Post *photos*)

ABOVE RIGHT: *Ivana Trump shoulders her way through the paparazzi to her limousine.* (Post *photo*)

LEFT: *The front-page photo shows Princess Diana entering the Mercedes in which she and her boyfriend, Dodi Fayed, would die hours later. The couple and their chauffeur were killed in a high-speed crash in a tunnel along the Seine River in Paris. Paparazzi on motorcycles were following them in hot pursuit when the crash occurred.*

NEW CLINTON BOMBSHELL

WHITE HOUSE SEX COVERUP

NEW YORK POST
LATE CITY FINAL
WEDNESDAY, JANUARY 21, 1998 / Sunny, 35-39 / Weather: Page 59 ★★   http://www.nypostonline.com/   · · 50¢

President Clinton yesterday became the focus of allegations that he influenced a one-time intern to lie to Paula Jones' lawyers.

Whitewater lawyers to probe charges prez had affair with intern and got her to lie about it

STORY ON PAGE 3

HOME DELIVERY
1-800-940-7678
CALL TODAY!

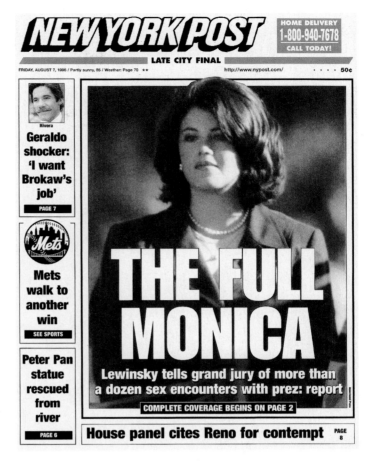

NEW YORK POST
LATE CITY FINAL
FRIDAY, AUGUST 7, 1998 / Partly sunny, 85 / Weather: Page 70 ★★   http://www.nypost.com/   · · · · 50¢

HOME DELIVERY
1-800-940-7678
CALL TODAY!

Rivera

Geraldo shocker: 'I want Brokaw's job'
PAGE 7

Mets walk to another win
SEE SPORTS

Peter Pan statue rescued from river
PAGE 6

THE FULL MONICA

Lewinsky tells grand jury of more than a dozen sex encounters with prez: report
COMPLETE COVERAGE BEGINS ON PAGE 2

House panel cites Reno for contempt PAGE 8

The bombshell dropped in January 1998, when reports of the president's affair with a White House intern appeared in the Washington Post. *The "Sexgate" scandal ultimately resulted in the president's impeachment, but the Senate needed a two-thirds majority to remove him from office. The vote fell far short of that margin, and the president survived. Throughout the scandal and trial President Clinton's popularity remained high with the public.* BELOW: *President Bill Clinton in New York, January 2001. (Post photo by Jennifer Weisbord)*

Nomo has shaky start in debut
METS FALL AT SHEA: SEE SPORTS

Death-case DA: I'll watch him die
ANDREA PEYSER: PAGE 4

MetroCard's days may be numbered
MTA HAS NEW PLAN: PAGE 2

NEW YORK POST
LATE CITY FINAL
WEDNESDAY, JUNE 10, 1998 / Cloudy, high 80s / Weather: Page 57 ★★   http://www.nypost.com/   · 50¢

HOME DELIVERY
1-800-940-7678
CALL TODAY!

Monica's new lawyers launch talks with Starr

LET'S MAKE A DEAL!

FULL STORY: PAGE 5

Former White House intern Monica Lewinsky may be closer to an immunity deal over her involvement in the Sexgate scandal.

231

The Post Is Sports

The Best Sports in Town

By GREG GALLO, Executive Sports Editor

Sports always have fueled the emotion-charged fires of the people of New York, who proudly root for their home teams in a passionate but knowledgeable way. It is with similar tabloid moxie that the *New York Post* connects with its sports readers.

Sports coverage in the *Post* blossomed when Babe Ruth arrived from Boston in that historic mistake by the Red Sox, who 81 years later are still looking for their first championship since the theft was made on January 3, 1920. The Yankees have won 37 American League pennants and 26 world championships, including the last three, since they stole the Babe for $125,000.

After Ruth came Lou Gehrig, Joe DiMaggio, Mickey Mantle, Roger Maris, Yogi Berra, Whitey Ford . . . and now there's Derek Jeter, making a mere $19 million a year. Over the years the *Post* has chronicled all the Pinstripe glory with its own powerhouse presentation.

As legendary as the Bombers and their Murderers' Row became, the *Post* had its own stable of sluggers who covered the Yankees' every move. None was better than Jimmy Cannon, whose columns about life and sports still grace the pages of the *Post*'s Sunday sports section 27 years after his death. During his 12 years at the *Post*, between 1946 and 1959, Cannon became recognized as the city's top sports columnist.

Cannon was at his best when he put his gifted hand to baseball and boxing. He wrote about the courage of Jackie Robinson back in 1947 when Branch Rickey made him a Brooklyn Dodger and the color barrier was broken, forever changing the game for

Jimmy Cannon Says:

the better. He later followed the legendary career of the Giants' spectacular centerfielder Willie Mays, predicting early on that the Say Hey Kid was destined for Cooperstown and the Hall of Fame.

Cannon entertained readers with famous tales of the great and colorful pugilists of the day . . . Joe Louis, Rocky Marciano, Floyd Patterson, Sugar Ray Robinson and New York's own Rocky Graziano.

Of the *Post*'s 25 Greatest Sports Moments, a celebration of New York's top sporting events of the century that appeared in the paper in 1999, Cannon banged out columns on an amazing eight of them. His great words made these special moments even better:

No. 1 Bobby Thomson's Shot Heard 'Round the World.
No. 3 Don Larsen's World Series perfect game.
No. 7 Jackie Robinson's call up to the Dodgers.
No. 8 Colts beat Giants in sudden death NFL title game.
No. 11 Dodgers win '55 Series, at last.
No. 19 Willie Mays' World Series catch off Vic Wertz.
No. 22 Giants and Dodgers leave New York for West Coast.
No. 23 CCNY wins NIT and NCAA titles in same year.

Cannon's brilliant skills were only just one example of the kind of sports writing that has always made this section special. We are proud that he was one of us and that the tradition has been carried on in a grand way.

Today's current lineup of byline stars on the pages of the *Post* Sports section carry the flaming torch of sportswriting excellence to our readers with the Best Sports in Town as they cover the new heroes of the day like Tiger, Jeter and Kobe. After all, this is our legacy, a tradition that is as rich and as brassy as the city of New York.

OPPOSITE: *The New York City Marathon, the city's ultimate sporting event, began in the mid-1970s as a race consisting of laps around Central Park. On October 25, 1976, the first Marathon as it is known today was run through the five boroughs of Staten Island, Brooklyn, Queens, the Bronx and Manhattan. Runners begin the 26.2-mile race on the Verrazano Bridge leading from Staten Island to Brooklyn. Approximately 30,000 runners—from Olympic athletes to professional runners to ordinary people from all over the world—wind through streets filled with cheering crowds toward the finish line in Central Park. (Post photo)* ABOVE RIGHT: *One of sports' greatest writers, Jimmy Cannon worked for the* Post *from 1946 to 1959. He became as popular as the celebrities he covered, and his writing is emulated by sportswriters to this day.*

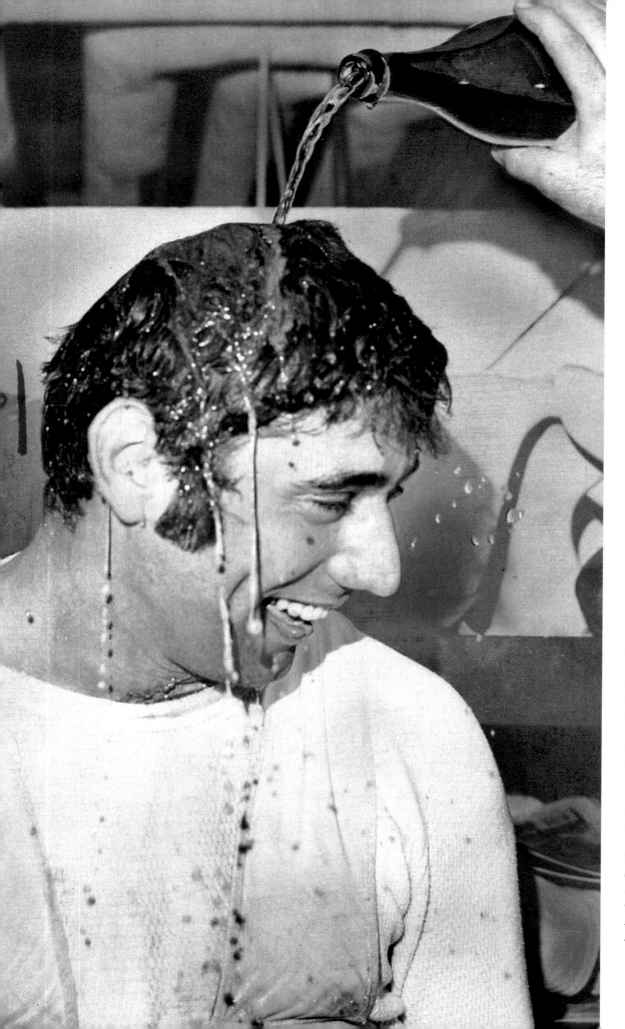

Broadway Joe

Times were changing in 1969. We put astronauts on the moon. We partied at Woodstock. Heck, we watched the Mets win the World Series!

Times were changing, and Jets quarterback Joe Namath decided to be bold.

"We're going to win Sunday," Broadway Joe assured everyone on the eve of Super Bowl III. "I guarantee it."

Namath's words were splashed all over the news, and Jets Coach Weeb Ewbank started to worry; his men were 18-point underdogs against the heavily favored Baltimore Colts.

But, hey, hadn't Namath heard Ewbank speak confidently to the team? Hadn't the coach been trying to get his players to believe the very thing his quarterback spilled to the press, anyway? Heck, the Jets could win this game, and they knew it. Namath just let the rest of us in on the secret.

He then went out and put his passes where his mouth was, completing 17 of his 28 throws, racking up 206 yards, and leading his team on four scoring drives in the 16-7 shocker.

Afterward, Namath ran off the field, his index finger thrust firmly in the air in the "We're Number One" salute. Bravado came easily to the man who predicted the biggest upset in Super Bowl history.

LEFT: *Joe Namath grins through a champagne shower after his three touchdown passes led the Jets to win their first American Football League championship in December 1968.*

Football

Post's 25 Greatest Sports Moments (created 1999)

1. Bobby Thomson's Shot Heard 'Round the World
2. Jets win Super Bowl III
3. Don Larsen's World Series perfect game
4. Joe D.'s 56-game hitting streak
5. Ali-Frazier I at Garden
6. Willis Reed limps out and Knicks win '70 title
7. Jackie Robinson called up to Dodgers
8. Colts beat Giants in '58 title game
9. Rangers win '94 Stanley Cup
10. Mets win Game 6 in '86 Series
11. Dodgers win '55 Series
12. Miracle Mets win '69 series
13. Lou Gehrig retirement speech
14. Reggie hits 3 homers to win Series
15. Secretariat wins Belmont by mile
16. Yankees buy Babe Ruth from Red Sox
17. Louis vs. Schmeling II
18. Maris/Mantle 1961 HR chase
19. Willie Mays' World Series catch
20. Bucky Dent slays Bosox
21. Wilt scores 100 points vs. Knicks
22. Giants and Dodgers leave NY
23. CCNY wins NIT and NCAA
24. Giants win Super Bowl XXV
25. Isles win fourth Stanley Cup

Jubilant coach Bill Parcells punches air with fist after his Giants trounced Broncos, 39-20, to win the Super Bowl.

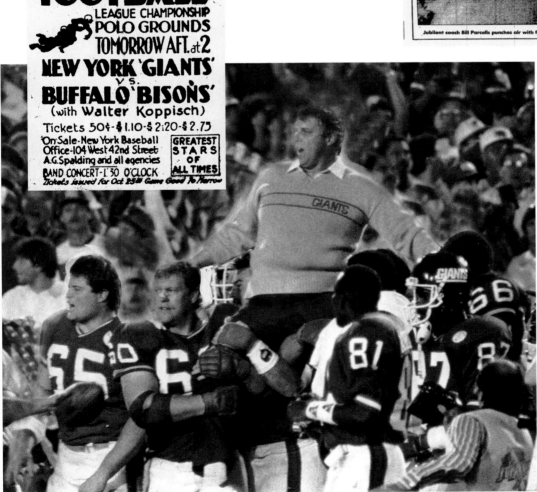

Giant Victory

The New York Giants won their first Super Bowl in 1987, beating the Denver Broncos with a score of 39 to 20. Quarterback Phil Simms was named Most Valuable Player for the game, and linebacker Lawrence Taylor earned the same for his performance in the regular season. The team went on to win Super Bowl XXV against the Buffalo Bills in 1991. The Giants played but were defeated in three more Super Bowls in 1994, 1997 and 2001.

ABOVE LEFT: *New York's NFL team, the Giants, was formed in 1925. This advertisement appeared in their first season of play in November of that year.* LEFT: *The New York Giants carry coach Bill Parcells off the field after their 1987 Super Bowl victory.*

235

Hockey

High-Ranking Rangers

The New York Rangers, also known as the "Broadway Blues," won the Stanley Cup in 1928—just two years after the team was founded. The exciting five-game championship of 1928 against the Montreal Maroons was played in Montreal, but the victors were given a party at Madison Square Garden upon their return to New York. After the Stanley Cup win, Leonard Cohen wrote in the *Post:*

Two years ago, the Rangers were a bunch of kids, regarded as a joke team which the National Hockey League hesitated to honor with a charter signifying membership in the highest professional hockey circuit. That was two year ago. Today they are the champions of the world, and proud possessors of the Stanley Cup. Such is the startling story of the sensational ascension to fame of the New York Rangers, as game an aggregation as ever skated on to the ice.

NEW YORK RANGERS OWED HIGH HONORS FOR RAPID SUCCESS

Unknown Two Years Ago, Hold World Title and Stanley Cup Today

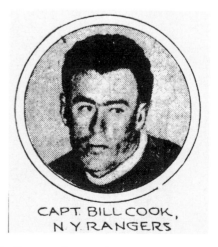

CAPT. BILL COOK,
N.Y. RANGERS

LEFT: *Detail of a Rangers photo on the sports page, 1930s.*

Rangers Champs!

The New York Rangers win their battle for the Stanley Cup on June 14, 1994. (Post photo)

237

Boxing

Dempsey

Boxing champ, giant sports icon, adopted New Yorker and restaurant owner Jack Dempsey had his first fight in the city in 1916. He learned the sport during his teens as an itinerant laborer traveling through the West on freight trains, camping out with hobos and rough characters along the way. He fought in hundreds of unrecorded matches in small towns before becoming a professional, developing a style that included scowling, crouching, baring his teeth and humming as he constantly moved toward his opponent.

Dempsey became the world heavyweight champion in 1919 and defended his title the following year at Madison Square Garden.

The crowd that night expected a big knockout early in the match, but Dempsey wasn't in his usual form. His challenger, Bill Brennan, "was fighting better and had more stamina than any one suspected," wrote *Post* sportswriter Harry Cross.

> In the twelfth round, Dempsey finally made a left punch to Brennan's stomach that brought him to his knees. "He dropped slowly and sadly to the floor. Then his head fell forward and he curled up on the canvas. For five seconds, as Referee Haukip counted over him, Brennan did not move. He tried to get up, but the count of ten had been made before he got on his feet.

To Dempsey's dismay, the crowd was still not on his side:

> Then followed a scene probably never before seen at a championship fight. Instead of being centered on the champion, the attention and sympathy of the crowds went to the fallen challenger. He was cheered as he got to his feet and went to his corner. He was cheered even louder when he was able to walk across the ring and shake Dempsey's hand.

Cross described the champ's unusual performance:

> That dynamic rush, the panther-like spring as his wicked flat shot to his opponent's jaw were missing last night. . . . To see the heavyweight champion of the world backing away from the attack of a challenger of Brennan's calibre was a far more surprising spectacle than the knockout.

Dempsey had good matches ahead, however. In 1923 he knocked out his challenger in the second round and in his career fought 69 professional fights with 47 wins by knockout. After retiring from boxing he opened a very popular restaurant on Broadway and 49th Street and became one of the city's most gentlemanly restaurateurs. He died in 1983 at the age of 87.

BELOW: *Jack Dempsey, left, and Joe Louis. Dempsey defended his heavyweight title twice at Madison Square Garden.* OPPOSITE: *Superstar Muhammad Ali in his dressing room, 1981.* (Post *photos*)

Baseball

Babe Ruth Joins the Yankees

On January 5, 1920, the Yankees bought Babe Ruth for $150,000—the most expensive purchase in baseball up to that date. The "Sultan of Swat" would hit 619 of his 714 career home runs for the Yankees and lead the team to seven pennants and four World Series championships. Babe Ruth's popularity guaranteed sellout crowds at Yankee Stadium, built in the Bronx in 1923. The first ballpark with a triple deck and the first to be called a stadium, Yankee Stadium held 67,244 fans—many of whom thronged to games to see Babe Ruth.

In the article of January 6 that announced the acquisition of Babe Ruth, Davis J. Walsh wrote: "Through the medium of what is undoubtedly the greatest one-man deal ever consummated in the

history of organized baseball, or any other kind, 'Babe' Ruth, the most illustrious long-distance hitter known to the civilized world, is now a member of the New York American League Club. . . . Every baseball follower in America, from Ban Johnson to the peanut vendor in the stands, is conceding the Yankees a better than even chance to head off the White Sox, Indians et al., at the wire."

ABOVE: *A Post photo of Babe Ruth from the early 1920s.* LEFT: *New York kids playing ball in the 1930s. The* Post *has been the leading source of sports coverage for fans, young and old, for decades. (Post photos)*

"Murderers' Row"

Considered one of the greatest single teams of all time, the 1927 New York Yankees opened the season with an 8-5 win over the Philadelphia Athletics and never looked back. They remained in first place throughout the season and swept the World Series in four games against the Pittsburgh Pirates. The Bronx Bombers scored over 100 more runs than any other team that year and held an astonishing .307 team batting average.

The team's lineup that year included five .300 hitters—Babe Ruth, Lou Gehrig, Earl Combs, Bob Meusel and Tony Lazzeri—appropriately dubbed "Murderers' Row." The championship season included Babe Ruth's record 60 homers, Lou Gehrig's 175 RBIs and Earle Combs' 231 base hits.

Adding to the fireworks were the Yankees' extraordinary pitchers including Waite Hoyt, whose 22 wins tied him for the league's top spot (with Chicago's Ted Lyons) and Wilcy Moore, who won 19 games and earned a 2.28 ERA—the best in the league. "They could easily have scored 100 less runs and won the pennant just as handily, so efficient was their pitching," wrote the *Post*'s Frederick G. Lieb on October 10, 1927.

All rolled into one team, these giants of baseball obliterated the competition to the very end, beating the Pirates in the World Series with scores of 5-4, 6-2, 8-1 and 4-3. "A new world's championship team has been crowned," wrote Lieb in the *Post*, "and one which is deserving of a place among the very greatest."

ABOVE: *Lou Gehrig, whose retirement speech at Yankee Stadium on July 4, 1939, remains one of the most memorable moments in sports.*

Joltin' Joe

Joe DiMaggio was a true matinee idol. Center fielder for the New York Yankees. Husband of Marilyn Monroe. How, people would ask, could you top that?

DiMaggio was arguably the greatest all-around player of his era—some would say of any era. With Joltin' Joe in the lineup, the Yanks won an amazing nine championships in 13 years during the '30s, '40s and '50s.

How valuable was Joe D. to his team? Ted Williams hit .406 in 1941 and didn't win the MVP. He lost to DiMaggio who hit in a still-unmatched 56 straight games.

When DiMaggio retired, he didn't leave baseball for good; he often returned to Yankee Stadium for Opening Day to throw out the first pitch, and always being introduced as "the greatest living ballplayer."

That title was abdicated in 1999 when Joltin' Joe passed on, and a nation finally turned its lonely eyes away.

ABOVE: *Sports icon Joe DiMaggio, left, who spent 13 seasons with the Yankees. (Post photos)*

BELOW RIGHT: *The New York Yankees followed up their historic 1927 season with another World Series sweep against St. Louis in 1928. The 1928 team is pictured here. Top row, left to right: Zachary, Pipgras, Collins, Koenig, Heimach, Ruth, Grabowski, Lazzeri, Meusel, Combs. Center row, left to right: Dickey, Durocher, Matthews, O'Leary, Huggins (manager), Fletcher, Johnson, Hoyt, Durst, Gehrig. Front row, left to right: Woods, Gazella, Dugan, Bennett (mascot), Paschal, Thomas, Robertson, Ryan.*

Jackie Breaks the Color Barrier

When Jackie Robinson joined the Brooklyn Dodgers on April 10, 1947, he broke the color barrier in major league baseball. "Robinson arrived at Ebbets Field shortly after 1 o'clock," wrote the *Post*'s Arch Murray that day. "He was besieged by youngsters seeking his autograph. Jackie said he was in good shape, although his stomach was a little upset."

Jackie Robinson was named Rookie of the Year in his first year with the team. He was named the league's Most Valuable Player in 1949 and stayed with the Dodgers through his entire career. Robinson's claim to fame as the man who integrated professional baseball was the first of many achievements that made him a legend. He was a great player who never flinched under the enormous pressure put on him as the first black man on the field, and he led his team to six pennants in ten years.

Three years after joining the Dodgers, Jackie starred in a film about his life, *The Jackie Robinson Story*. He retired in 1956 and was inducted into the Baseball Hall of Fame in 1962.

James Wechsler, *Post* editor in chief from 1949 to 1961,

renowned for his passionate, heart-on-his-sleeve writing, discussed Jackie Robinson's move to the major leagues in the context of the nation's Civil Rights Movement in his autobiography, *Reflections of an Angry Middle-Aged Editor*. Writing in 1960, he stated:

No issue has more cruelly exposed the small political men of our time than the Negro's quest for equality. . . . The guilt it stirs increases the tension of the debate; men are never more vociferous than when they dimly perceive their faithlessness to themselves.

Civil rights has become to the politics of the present what the drive for union organization was to the politics of the 1930's. . . . But the pace of history has quickened. . . . There has been greater improvement in the status of the American Negro in the last fifteen years than in the previous fifty; we are committed as a nation to new advances . . . who could have imagined two decades ago that a man named Jackie Robinson would be only the first of a long line of distinguished ballplayers to win acceptance in the major leagues?

New York Post

NEW YORK, 6, THURSDAY, APRIL 10, 1947

BLUE FINAL

FIVE CENTS

Dodgers Buy Jackie Robinson; 'You Can Win Pennant'---Durocher

ABOVE: *The front-page headline announcing Jackie Robinson's history-making purchase by the Brooklyn Dodgers.* BOTTOM LEFT: *Jackie Robinson.* (Post *archives*)

Amazing Mets

The Mets were formed in 1962 and played their first seasons in the Polo Grounds before moving to Shea Stadium in Queens in 1964. One year after this photo was taken, the Mets pulled off one of the most exciting feats in all of professional sports—coming from the bottom of the league standings they made a stunning reversal and won the National League pennant in three games against the Atlanta Braves. They then defeated the heavily favored Baltimore Orioles to win the 1969 World Series.

BELOW: *Jon Matlack, left, and Tom Seaver opening champagne, after the* Mets' *playoff victory in 1973.* (Post *photo*).

The Shot Heard 'Round the World

At the end of the 1951 season the New York Giants and the Brooklyn Dodgers found themselves tied for first place in the National League. After splitting the first two playoff games the Giants were trailing 4-2. With two Giants on base and one out, Dodger manager Leo Durocher was taking no chances and called ace pitcher Ralph Branca to the mound to face Bobby Thomson.

Thomson proceeded to nail the now famous "shot heard 'round the world" over the left field fence giving the Giants the pennant. A moment later, in the dugout, a *Post* photographer captured not only Branca's disappointment, but the frustration of every Brooklyn Dodger fan that day.

The Giants went on to lose the World Series to the New York Yankees that year, but fortunately 1951 also marked another important milestone for the team as Willie Mays began his incredible career.

Willie Mays, the "Say Hey Kid," was a swift-footed young man from Alabama who gave his fans plenty of ammunition for their arguments after he joined the team in 1951.

His spectacular, over-the-shoulder catch in the 1954 World Series against the Cleveland Indians, in deep center field at the Polo Grounds, solidified his legend. It has been called the greatest catch of all time.

Mays played baseball with an enthusiasm and exuberance seldom seen today. His staggering career stats include 3,283 hits, 660 homers and a .302 lifetime average. The electrifying center fielder was National League Rookie of the Year in 1951 and a two-time MVP. He accumulated 12 Gold Gloves and played in four World Series.

After the Giants fled the city in 1957, he moved with them west to San Francisco, but returned to join the New York Mets in 1972. He played for only one more year, but still managed to charm the city with the ebullience that earned him a place in its hall of heroes as well as baseball's Hall of Fame.

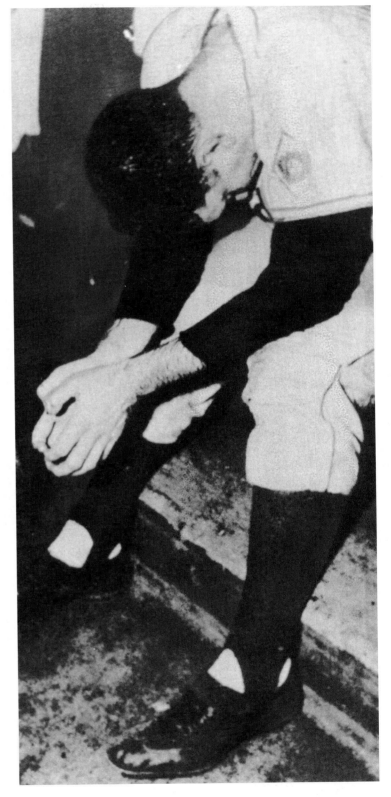

ABOVE: *Willie Mays.* RIGHT: *Dodgers' pitcher Ralph Branca in the dugout after Thomson hit the "shot heard 'round the world."* (Post *photos*)

Yankees: On Top of the World

The New York Yankees won four World Series in five years: 1996, 1998, 1999 and 2000. In the Subway Series of 2000 between the Yankees and Mets, the two home teams matched up for the first time since 1956.

ABOVE (FROM LEFT TO RIGHT):
1996 win over Atlanta Braves.
1998 win over San Diego Padres.
1999 win over Atlanta Braves.
2000 win over the Mets.

BELOW: *Roger Clemens' famous bat-throwing incident during the 2000 subway series. (Post photo)*

Basketball

Swissssh!

No New York team has taken its fans on an emotional roller-coaster ride like the Knicks.

In 1970, they stormed to their first NBA title behind a cast that included Walt "Clyde" Frazier and "The Captain," Willis Reed.

After six games, the Knicks and Lakers were tied 3-3. Game 7 approached and the Knicks looked doomed because Reed was out with an injured right leg.

But moments before tip-off, "The Captain" bounded onto the court to a deafening roar from the Madison Square Garden crowd. Imagine the roar a few minutes later when he hit a jumper. Imagine it a few hours later when the Knicks won their first title.

The team earned its second championship in 1973 and has given its fans plenty to marvel at just about every year since then.

In the eighties, Knicks fans cheered the dynamic scoring of Bernard King, the lottery jackpot that landed center Patrick Ewing, and the feverish coaching of Rick Pitino.

In the nineties, Coach Pat Riley made the Knicks a powerhouse and took three division titles with a team that featured All-Star Ewing, rugged forward Charles Oakley and athletic guard John Starks.

The legend continues today. The team's latest coach, Jeff Van Gundy, has retooled the team with a roster of new players that look certain to keep the Knicks faithful on a thrill ride for many years to come.

INSET: *New York's first basketball team, the Knickerbockers, was founded on June 4, 1946. This ad announces the team's first home game.* ABOVE: *Patrick Ewing slams one in for the New York Knicks.* (Post *photo*)

LEFT: Post *photographer Louis Liotta's famous photo of aerialist Diane Terdick as she slips and falls while performing the Iron Jaw stunt—hanging by her teeth 20 feet in the air without a net—on East 48th Street. She survived but suffered two broken ankles and a fractured spine.*

BELOW LEFT: *Cardinal John O'Connor (1920–2000) at St. Patrick's Cathedral, 1986.*

BELOW: *An aerial view of the Spiderman balloon in the Macy's Thanksgiving Day Parade.* (Post *photo*)

BOTTOM: *Subway riders in the 1950s.* (Post *photo*)

The Post Is Photos

What's a Tabloid without Photos?

In a newspaper like the *New York Post*, photographs are the cement that holds it all together. A dramatic picture can have a powerful impact long after the last sentence of the story has been read, and from the moment the first photographs appeared in the paper, the *Post* has enjoyed a long tradition of hard-edged news and sports images. Photographs have only been a presence for the last third of the paper's life, but in that relatively short time have come to be as synonymous with the paper as its headlines.

In the early days the *Post* had a small staff of photographers. The primary focus back then was politics, celebrities and general slice-of-life photos. From 1933, the daily comings and goings around City Hall warranted a full-time shooter, Tony Calvacca, and it's likely that no mayor in office took a breath while not under the close scrutiny of his lens.

Another early staff shooter was Barney Stein who, when not chasing celebrities arriving on the steamship lines and covering the doings at El Morocco and the Stork Club, doubled as the official photographer for the Brooklyn Dodgers.

Another of the *Post*'s legendary photographers was Louis

Liotta, who shot for the paper from 1946 until his death at 78 in 1996. Louis learned his trade from Weegee, who was also a frequent contributor to the paper, and maintained a flock of carrier pigeons to transport film to and from the *Post*'s offices. Louis specialized in spot news. His most famous photo was of the reaction of two construction workers in a window as a girl falls past them (see page 242). His last great scoop was the exclusive coverage of the shooting of a busload of Hasidic scholars on the Brooklyn Bridge, a story that brought him out of retirement and got him international acclaim. For Louis it was just another day of doing what he did best.

Post photographers have always stopped at nothing to get the shot, even when the subject matter was difficult, gruesome or just plain scandalous. High art? Well, sometimes. Memorable? Always.

The combinations of our headlines and photography have made front pages that are still making waves. The murder of mobster Carmine Galante in 1979 yielded a front page featuring a gruesome close-up photograph of Galante's blood-spattered face, a cigar still in his mouth. The headline: GREED! An instant classic, and no documentary about the Mob has ever been complete without including that front page.

From canoodling celebrities caught on camera to tragedy to sports triumphs to just plain everyday life, *Post* photographers continue to be there. No matter how tough the story or how trying the circumstances, they never lose their humanity. The same photographer can go from shooting a happy sunny-day weather picture to shooting an emotionally draining human tragedy and never lose sight of the fact that their pictures are reaching out to the reader to tell the whole story.

ABOVE: *Newlyweds John F. Kennedy and Jacqueline Bouvier Kennedy in Newport, Rhode Island, September 12, 1953.* LEFT: *Bernhard Goetz, subway-passenger-turned-vigilante who turned on his would-be attackers with a .38.* (Post *photos*)

BELOW: *Ricky Martin greets New York fans.* (Post *photo*)

ABOVE: *Two coiffed Standard Poodles await their time in the limelight at the Westminster Dog Show in Madison Square Garden, February 1999.* (Post *photo by Tamara Beckwith*)

LEFT: *Sailors on deck the USS* John F. Kennedy *as it entered New York Harbor for Fleet Week, May 1998.* (Post *photo by Tamara Beckwith*)

BELOW: *Wynton Marsalis, artistic director of Jazz at Lincoln Center and director of the Lincoln Center Jazz Orchestra, May 1998.* (Post *photo by W.A. Funches, Jr.*)

ABOVE: *Julie Andrews, left, and Liza Minnelli at Sardi's Restaurant on West 44th Street, October 3, 1996, where they announced that Minnelli would be the temporary replacement for Andrews in the Broadway musical* Victor/Victoria. *(Post photo by Francis Specker)*

ABOVE: *Riker's Island (Post photo)*

ABOVE: *The Bowery (Post photo)*

RIGHT: *Brooklyn street scene. (Post photo)*

LEFT: *David N. Dinkins, Mayor of New York from 1989 to 1993. The city's first black mayor, Dinkins served during a period of high crime and racial unrest including the riot in Crown Heights, Brooklyn, a neighborhood inhabited by Lubavitch Hasidim and black immigrants.* (Post photo)

OPPOSITE: *A John Lennon fan lights a candle for the slain rock star outside the Dakota apartment building. Lennon was shot by Mark David Chapman with a .38 revolver in front of the luxury Upper West Side building on December 8, 1980, while he was returning home with his wife, Yoko Ono.* (Post photo)

BELOW: *Vice President George Bush, President Ronald Reagan and Soviet President Mikhail Gorbachev in New York, 1988.* (Post photo)

NEW YORK POST

JOHN
LENNON
SHOT D

Gunned down at
His wife Yok

Beatles

Post Pearls

By ERIC FETTMANN, Associate Editorial Page Editor

The list of those who have spent time working at the *New York Post* reads like a Who's Who of American journalism. Indeed more than 40 Pulitzer Prize winners—including awardees for history, biography, drama and poetry—either began or finished their careers at the *Post*.

The paper itself has won two Pulitzer Prizes, including the second one ever awarded; it went, in 1918, to reporter Harold A. Littledale for an investigation into conditions at the New Jersey state prison. The other *Post* Pulitzer, for international correspondence, was awarded in 1931 to H.R. Knickerbocker for a series of articles on the Soviet economy. *Post* staffers have gone on to win Oscars, Tony and Grammy awards, as well.

The roster includes some of the most famous journalistic names of the past two centuries.

Famous *Post* journalists include Franklin P. Adams, whose famous column, "The Conning Tower," ran in the *Post;* Heywood Broun, Samuel Grafton, Norman Hapgood, Joseph Kahn, Murray Kempton, Ray Kerrison, David Lawrence (founder of *U.S. News and World Report* magazine), Max Lerner, Mike McAlary, Edgar Ansel Mowrer, Paul Scott Mowrer, Rollo Ogden, Westbrook Pegler, Norman Podhoretz, Ernie Pyle, Victor Riesel, Leland K. Stowe, Mark Sullivan, Raymond Gram Swing, Dorothy Thompson, William V. Shannon, Lincoln Steffens (the first great muckraker), Oswald Garrison Villard, Jimmy Wechsler. Like Wechsler, the legendary I.F. Stone served as editor of the paper's editorial page. And veteran journalistic gadfly George Seldes was a special correspondent.

Among the present-day journalists at other publications who honed their skills at the *Post:* Ken Auletta and John Cassidy of *The New Yorker; New York Times* columnists Clyde Haberman, Joyce Purnick and Robert Lipsyte and reporters Jane Perlez, Joyce Wadler, Joseph Berger and Warren Hoge; *Newsday* columnist Jimmy Breslin; *Wall Street Journal* columnist Dorothy Rabinowitz; *Daily News* film critic Jami Bernard and sports columnist Mike Lupica; *Newsweek* columnist Anna Quindlen and *Village Voice* editor Donald Forst.

Two TV news giants saw their bylines in the *Post:* Even as he was broadcasting from London during World War II, Edward R. Murrow wrote articles for the *Post* as a special correspondent. And his CBS colleague, anchor/correspondent Eric Sevareid, wrote a political column for the paper in 1960, until forced to abandon it by the network.

Many other network TV journalists got their start at the *Post:* Robert Bazell of NBC; Myron Kandel, Jonathan Karl, Elsa Klensch and Jill Brooke of CNN; Douglas Kennedy of Fox News Channel. Local TV reporters who worked at the paper include Barry Cunningham of the WB11; Katie Kelly of WNBC/Ch. 4; Jerry Nachman of WCBS/Ch. 2 and both Anthony Prisendorf and Aida Alvarez (later appointed head of the U.S. Small Business Administration) of WNEW/Ch. 5.

Legendary radio talk-show host Barry Gray served two stints at the *Post:* as a political columnist in the '50s and then again as host of a drive-time program emanating from the paper's newsroom in the late '70s. Another celebrity columnist was Orson Welles, who actually considered giving up Hollywood to pursue a full-time journalism career with the *Post*.

The *Post* was a trailblazer when it came to hiring women and minority journalists. Rheta Childe Dorr became the first female war correspondent when the *Post* sent her to cover the Russian revolution in 1917. Jesse White Mario, whose husband served with Garibaldi, filed dispatches from Italy and became one of the heroines of the Risorgimento. Dixie Tighe was a World War II correspondent in the Pacific Theater. Sylvia F. Porter was the nation's first female financial writer and soon became the nation's most famous personal finance columnist. Wilella Waldorf in 1941 became the first female first-string drama critic, and Elizabeth King was the paper's first female correspondent in both Albany and Washington right after World War I.

ABOVE: *Walt Whitman contributed a handful of pieces to the* Post *in the 1860s. (National Archives and Records Administration)*

In 1946, the *Post* hired Ted Poston, the first African-American reporter on a mainstream U.S. newspaper and sent him down South to cover the Civil Rights Movement. Fifteen years earlier, noted African-American writer George Schuyler was made a special correspondent to investigate the African slave trade. Famed short-story writer Langston Hughes and ballplayer Jackie Robinson both wrote political columns for the *Post*—the first blacks to do so at a major paper—as did José Torres, a former light heavyweight boxing champ who became the first Hispanic columnist.

The *Post* pioneered in gossip and celebrity reporting, with columnists like "Saloon Editor" Earl Wilson, Leonard Lyons, Elsa Maxwell, Aileen Mehle ("Suzy"), George Sokolsky, Eugenia Sheppard, Sidney Skolsky, James Brady and Claudia Cohen. Dr. Rose Franzblau wrote one of the earliest psychiatric advice columns.

Famous novelists, screenwriters and playwrights have written for the *Post*: Russel Crouse (*Of Thee I Sing, Life With Father*), Nora Ephron (*Sleepless in Seattle, When Harry Met Sally, Heartburn*), Pete Hamill (*Flesh and Blood*), Laura Z. Hobson (*Gentleman's Agreement*), Sinclair Lewis (*Main Street, Babbitt*), Dudley Nichols (*Stagecoach, Pinky, The Bells of St. Mary's*), Clifford Odets (*Golden Boy, The Country Girl, Sweet Smell of Success*), Tom Topor (*Nuts, The Accused*) and Lewis Grossberger. It includes poets: William Rose Benét, Amy Bonner, William Cullen Bryant, Bret Harte, Walt Whitman and Joseph Rodman Drake. There were famous historians, like Allan Nevins, Joseph P. Lash (*Franklin and Eleanor*), Burton J. Hendrick, George Cary Eggleston and Arthur Schlesinger. And noted short-story writers like James Thurber and Joel Chandler Harris (Uncle Remus).

Plus famed cartoonists like Rollin Kirby, Edmund Duffy and C.D. Bachelor—who won seven Pulitzer Prizes among them—as well as Oscar Cesare, John Pierotti and Paul Rigby, and noted artists like Arthur Szyk and celebrity caricaturist William Auerbach Levy.

ABOVE: *Inside the offices of the* Post *at West Street, opened in 1920.* (Post *125th Anniversary Edition*)

There were celebrated chroniclers of music, both popular and classical: Al Aronowitz, Henry T. Finck, Harriet Johnson, Speight Jenkins, Olga Samaroff. And notable writers on the theater and movies: John Mason Brown, Richard Watt, Frank Rich, Archer Winsten, Jerry Tallmer, Martin Gottfried, Judith Crist, Nina Darnton. And some of the century's most celebrated sportswriters: Jimmy Cannon, Dick Young, Leonard Cohen, Larry Merchant, Fred Lieb, Mike Lupica, Leonard Shecter, Milton Gross and Harry Cross. During the 19th and early 20th centuries, the *Post*—then the *New York Evening Post*—was considered the nation's most important newspaper, with such writers and editors as William Leggett, Carl Schurz, E.L. Godkin, Horace White, Fabian Franklin, Simeon Strunsky and Charles Nordhoff.

There was Joseph Bucklin Bishop, later secretary of the Panama Canal Commission and Teddy Roosevelt's official biographer; Bronson Howard, considered America's first great native playwright; Franklin Clarkin, who covered the Spanish-American War and later helped smuggle Czar Nicholas' ashes out of Russia; Francis Ellington Leupp, later the U.S. commissioner for Indian affairs; John Reuben Thompson, the paper's first literary editor, had been assistant secretary of state for the Confederacy; William Conant Church, whose brother wrote the famous "Yes, Virginia, There Is a Santa Claus" editorial.

At least two future presidents—Martin Van Buren and Woodrow Wilson—contributed articles to the *Post* early in their careers. So did another presidential nominee, future New York Gov. Samuel Tilden. And one president—Franklin Delano Roosevelt—was actually a co-owner of the paper, between 1922 and 1924. FDR's interior secretary, Harold Ickes, wrote a column after leaving government. So did former Mayor Ed Koch and former UN Ambassador Jeane Kirkpatrick.

Some of the country's most famous editors also worked at the *Post*: James Aaronson (*The National Guardian*), Abraham Cahan (*Jewish Daily Forward*), Horace Greeley, David Lawrence (founder of *U.S. News and World Report*) and Henry Raymond (founder of the *New York Times*).

Epilogue

The Post's History Is the Nation's Own

By ERIC FETTMANN, Associate Editorial Page Editor

In the two centuries since its founding on November 16, 1801, the *New York Post* has mirrored New York. And, like the city, it has survived against the odds far longer than anyone expected it to.

Over the years, its political philosophy has turned like a weather vane. It has at varying times been Federalist, Democratic and Republican—switching almost overnight from crusading liberal to staunch conservative. Once it led the way in denouncing sensationalism as "the closest thing to hell on earth"; later, its dramatic headlines became the subject of endless controversy and debate.

It has been written about in books—the main character of Gore Vidal's novels *Burr* and *1876* is a *Post* reporter and the books' pages are filled with real-life characters from the paper's history. A biography of one of its early editors, John Bigelow—Margaret Clapp's *Forgotten First Citizen*—won a 1948 Pulitzer Prize.

What the *Post* has done best is to survive, watching dozens of its bigger-name competitors fall by the wayside. As a result its record of daily publishing—nearly 70,000 issues—is unmatched by any other American newspaper. And it now becomes the first and only paper in American history to celebrate 200 years of continuous daily publishing.

The *New York Post* had distinguished parents: It was started by many founders of the republic, including Alexander Hamilton, father of the U.S. economy; John Jay, the first Chief Justice; Oliver Wolcott, signer of the Declaration of Independence; Rufus King and Gouverneur Morris, signers with Hamilton of the Constitution. Summoned by Hamilton, they met in secret at merchant Archibald Gracie's country home—now known as Gracie Mansion, home of New York City's mayor—in the summer of 1801 to raise $10,000 for a new political organ.

What they had in common was their politics: All were Federalists, and their party had been voted out of office for the first time since the nation's founding; their leading foe, Thomas Jefferson, was in the White House and they wanted a new, prestigious organ to lead the opposition. Although heavily in debt, Hamilton—who had earlier helped two other journalists, including dictionary author Noah Webster, start up newspapers—offered $1,000 of his own money toward the $10,000 needed to launch the new journal. He personally selected as editor 32-year-old William Coleman, a former journalist and onetime law partner of Hamilton's hated rival, Aaron Burr. Michael Burnham, a 25-year-old printer from Hartford, Connecticut, took charge of the business affairs.

The new paper looked far different from today's lively editions. Ads filled three of the four folio pages, including the entire first page. And there was little in the way of actual news—just political comment, some of it biting. Two men and a boy, working out of a ramshackle building at 40 Pine Street (the site now called 1 Chase Plaza) in today's financial district cranked out 600 copies on a small hand-fed press, then hand-delivered them to subscribers, who paid for a full year in advance.

The first *Post* was the paper of the financial elite, written for merchants and businessman, to whose interests the editor openly promised to tend. It certainly wasn't meant for the average worker—its $8 annual subscription price was the equivalent of 10 days' average wage. For the benefit of out-of-town readers, the paper published a semiweekly mail edition, known first as the *New York Herald* and later as the *New York Evening Post For the Country*, which lasted until 1919.

Hamilton's name never appeared on the masthead. But he was its guiding force, spending hours every night with Coleman drafting the next day's editorial matter from his home at 26 Broadway. "As soon as I see him," Coleman once said, "he begins in a deliberate manner to dictate and I to note down in shorthand—when he stops, my article is completed." Political opponents derisively referred to Coleman as "Hamilton's typographer."

The first day's prospectus read in part: "The design of this paper is to diffuse among the people correct information on all interesting subjects; to inculcate just principles in religion, morals and politics and to cultivate a taste for sound literature." It was widely hailed for its clean look and typography, which one paper called "beyond all comparison the most elegant piece of workmanship ever seen."

Coleman fully came into his own after Hamilton was killed by Aaron Burr in the famous 1804 duel. His eye for a well-turned phrase won wide acclaim and earned him the nickname "Field Marshal of the Federalist Press." His flair for a well-earned fight, however, eventually cost him his life. Although a fierce opponent of dueling, he engaged in several—once killing his opponent, then calmly returning to the office to put out the next edition. His tongue was equally sharp; rival editors were denounced as "vile reptiles" and "little monkeys." In 1818, he was beaten by a political opponent and never fully recovered.

But he was the first in a long line of crusading editors—and he

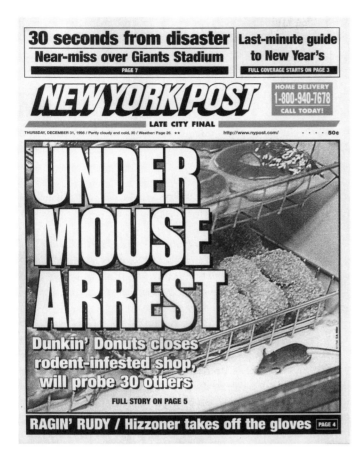

was not above sacrificing needed advertising income in favor of principle. In 1805 he banned all ads for quack medicines; a dozen years later, he threw out all lottery advertising, which then accounted for one-tenth of the paper's income.

Under Coleman, the *Post* opposed the War of 1812 with Britain as "unjust and calamitous." Public sentiment was aroused to such an extent that the editor, who'd received death threats, persuaded Mayor DeWitt Clinton to post a military guard at the paper's offices; armed friends stood watch at Coleman's Hudson Street home.

Although Coleman's primary concern was politics, the paper published several significant news beats. It was the first New York paper to report Robert Fulton's initial steamboat trip and the first American journal to publish the news of the burning of Moscow during the Napoleonic Wars and of Napoleon's defeat at Waterloo.

After Coleman's death in 1829, the *Post* continued as a political organ under its new editors, the celebrated poet William Cullen Bryant and his fiery associate, William Leggett. The latter, who ran the paper when Bryant took a year-long trip to Europe, was the city's leading advocate for abolition and trade unionism. But his vitriolic and scorched-earth style—he believed less in espousing opinions than in denouncing opponents—nearly doomed the paper in Bryant's absence, as readers and advertisers fled. Still, Bryant eulogized him after his premature death, saying that public opinion sometimes needs people to "boldly take it by the beard and tell it

The Wood
Famous Front Pages

Ink-stained tabloid newshounds call it "the wood"—the bold-faced front-page headline that trumpets each day's biggest story.

For years, the *Post*'s wood has been a fundamental part of every New Yorker's day.

One front page—the legendary April 15, 1983, headline HEADLESS BODY IN TOPLESS BAR—is perhaps the most famous tabloid headline ever and even became a movie.

The list of other unforgettable front pages, including those shown above, is almost as long as the paper's history and includes events both grave and sensational—from the headline EVIL COWARDS, exclaiming outrage over the Oklahoma City bombing, to ZORBA THE STUD, announcing the birth of 70-something actor Anthony Quinn's love child.

NEW YORK POST

HOME DELIVERY
1-800-940-7678
CALL TODAY!

LATE CITY FINAL

FRIDAY, MARCH 13, 1998 / Cloudy, 35-40 / Weather: Page 83 ★★   http://www.nypostonline.com/   · · · · 50¢

KISS YOUR ASTEROID GOODBYE!

PAGES 2 & 3

Don't worry, it'll miss Earth by 600,000 miles

---

the things it ought to do." In a final poetic tribute, he wrote of "the words of fire from his pen" that "still move, still shake the hearts of men, amid a cold and coward age."

But in 1835, James Gordon Bennett brought out the *New York Herald*, the first paper to stress news coverage over political opinion. Like most of Bennett's rivals, Bryant tried to ignore the instantly popular paper, attacking its "nauseous practice" of "adopting a light and profligate tone in the daily reporting of crime and depravity." Before long, however, the *Post* too began adding news coverage to its spirited editorials.

Under Bryant, editor for an unrivaled 49 years, the *Post* became the most respected newspaper of its day. Bryant assembled a highly respected staff of reporters and contributors and his pen goaded the city into making necessary improvements—particularly to Central Park, which Bryant first proposed in an 1844 editorial. The *Post* was helped immensely by the addition of John Bigelow as part owner and associate editor; he would go on to become a leading political and diplomatic figure; at his death in 1911, he was hailed as "First Citizen of the Republic."

A fierce abolitionist—he broke with the Democrats in 1848 over slavery—Bryant also helped found the Republican Party and played a key role in pushing the presidential candidacy of Abraham Lincoln, serving as host of the famous 1860 Cooper Union speech that introduced Lincoln to Eastern audiences.

During the Civil War, however, Bryant lost patience with Lincoln, attacking his "incompetence, inaction and overcaution"—even publishing his own military strategy for conquering the South. In 1864, his son-in-law and associate editor, Parke Godwin, was part of a small but influential group that tried to deny Lincoln the Republican nomination; eventually, the paper rejoined the Lincoln camp.

Although the *Post* did not have an extensive battlefield reporting staff like its larger rivals, it enjoyed its share of exclusives. Shortly before the war began, a *Post* reporter stowed away on board a ship sent from Washington to reinforce Fort Sumter and filed a breathtaking report. In 1865, the *Post* obtained Sgt. Boston Corbett's exclusive story of how he had shot Lincoln's assassin, John Wilkes Booth.

But the war also brought embarrassment and scandal to the paper when its publisher, Isaac Henderson, faced criminal charges of war profiteering as a Navy Department agent. He was acquitted, even as Bryant tried unsuccessfully to pressure Lincoln into dropping the charges. Henderson, described as an "adroit rogue," wanted total control of the *Post* and almost got it—by 1877, he owned half the paper, including the building, and his son-in-law was managing editor.

But an investigation after Bryant's death showed Henderson had embezzled $400,000 from the company. When Bryant's family learned Henderson planned to turn his shares over to the notorious speculator Jay Gould, they sold the paper in 1881 to railroad tycoon Henry Villard, who had been a Civil War correspondent for Horace Greeley's *New York Tribune* after being turned down for a *Post* reporter's job in 1857.

Villard named a distinguished triumvirate of editors: Carl Schurz, the former U.S. interior secretary, who instigated the sale and ran the paper for the first two years; E.L. Godkin, founding editor of *The Nation* (which was included in the deal and became the *Post*'s weekly supplement); and Horace White, co-founder of the Western Associated Press. Under Godkin's restrained news coverage (he was almost solely concerned with the editorial page), circulation sank—but the *Post* was still the most influential paper in town because of its choice readership and fierce politicking.

Godkin, it's been written, "won a reputation for uncompromising fidelity to high and austere ideals—and for the bitterest tongue in the country." Theodore Roosevelt in particular hated the paper; "I can never take the *Evening Post* after a hearty meal," he once said.

(Roosevelt wasn't alone: Presidents Thomas Jefferson and Dwight Eisenhower canceled their subscriptions because of the paper's political coverage; Ike even banned the paper from the White House premises. And when President Grover Cleveland, subject of a recent editorial attack, was asked if he still read the paper, he replied: "Yes, I read the waifs"—referring to a small column of jokes. On the other hand, President Calvin Coolidge in 1926 pressed the button that started the *Post*'s presses on the first day in its new building on West Street.)

Under Schurz and Godkin, the *Post* for the first time hired a sports editor: Charles Pike Sawyer, who had ridden with Buffalo Bill against Geronimo. Sawyer, who held the job for 34 years, pioneered in the use of telephones, rocket guns and carrier pigeons to rush the results of sports events back to the paper in time for deadline.

After Villard's death, his son, Oswald Garrison Villard, took over in 1903. Unlike other owners, the younger Villard was less interested in running the paper than in writing for it; he served as both Washington correspondent and editorial writer.

In 1909, the activist Villard wrote the famous "Call for the Lincoln's Birthday Conference" that was the founding document of the NAACP.

But his outspoken pacifism hurt the paper; he was publicly accused of pro-Germanism. The criticism mounted after America entered World War I, and Villard was convinced to sell the paper to banker Thomas Lamont (who, like Henry Villard, was a onetime *Tribune* reporter and whose brother, Hammond, had been the *Post*'s managing editor); Villard retained control of *The Nation*.

Lamont hoped to create an American counterpart to the *Manchester Guardian* or London's *Economist*. But the *Post* was losing money for the first time; its equipment was outmoded and its staff dispirited. Lamont, trying to remain a hands-off owner, appointed as editor Edwin F. Gay, founder of the Harvard Business School and the country's leading economic historian. He and Lamont agreed that the paper should become "liberal, progressive, constructive, not fanatical or smugly self-righteous."

Lamont held on until 1922, when, faced with growing losses, he decided to sell. But buyers weren't flocking to his door; the only offer came from Frank Munsey, the notorious "consolidator" of newspapers, who made clear that a sale to him would mean the end of the *Post*. When Lamont balked, Gay organized a consortium of 34 financial backers, longtime progressives and civil reformers, including Franklin D. Roosevelt, who just two years earlier had been the Democratic nominee for vice president.

FDR took a healthy interest in the paper; indeed, he can fairly be called the paper's savior: Twice in the future, with the *Post* on the verge of folding, he found buyers to rescue the paper from death. Meanwhile, he told Gay of his "real satisfaction that we have saved the good old *Post* from extinction or from being Munseyized." And he kept peppering the editor with suggestions—at one point, complaining that "the editorials are either vapid or wholly reactionary."

To that end, Gay tried unsuccessfully to recruit the celebrated William Allan White to take charge of the editorial page. But he strengthened the paper's Washington and literary coverage; when the next owner decided to fold the paper's weekend literary supplement, the editors resigned and began publishing it themselves as the acclaimed magazine *The Saturday Review*.

Gay's clumsy arrangement—derided by the *New York Times* as "journalism by mass meeting"—ended in 1924, when the paper ran out of cash and was sold to magazine publisher Cyrus Curtis, who popularized the *Saturday Evening Post*. Curtis shifted its politics sharply to the right and stressed financial news. In an unusual and

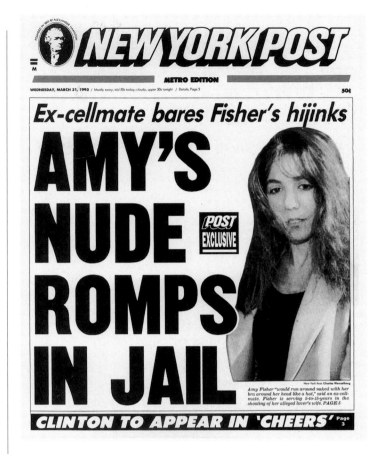

Ex-cellmate bares Fisher's hijinks

AMY'S NUDE ROMPS IN JAIL

POST EXCLUSIVE

Amy Fisher "would run around naked with her bra around her head like a hat," said an ex-cellmate. Fisher is serving 5-to-15-years in the shooting of her alleged lover's wife. PAGE 5

CLINTON TO APPEAR IN 'CHEERS' Page 3

daring move, Curtis in 1933 made the paper a tabloid—but not in the style of other tabloids. Curtis' *Post* was a "conservative" tabloid, similar in layout to a broadsheet newspaper. Analysts debated whether it would work; but the experiment was abandoned after Curtis died suddenly after a few months and his heirs looked to close the paper.

Conventional wisdom said the *Post*'s days were numbered. As usual, however, conventional wisdom was wrong.

FDR, now president, pressured his friend J. David Stern, publisher of the pro–New Deal *Philadelphia Record*, to rescue the paper. Stern dropped the "Evening" from its title and reshaped the *Post* into a lively, liberal organ, specializing in crusading journalism and tabloid instincts. In the reverse of Curtis' experiment—a conservative broadsheet masquerading as a tabloid—Stern's paper featured a tabloid style in broadsheet format.

Within months, circulation actually quadrupled—helped largely by contests and other promotions. But depression-era advertising was scarce and losses mounted to $4,000 a day. The other New York papers offered Stern $250,000 to shut down, but he refused. In 1939, FDR again intervened, persuading his friend, City Councilman George Backer—who prevailed on his wife, banking heiress Dorothy Schiff—to rescue the paper and install him as editor.

Mrs. Schiff later admitted that she thought the idea "ridiculous." And her instinct at first seemed justified: In their first two

Night in jail for deadbeat dad
See Page 3

H'wood honcho gets top Disney post
See Pages 3, 26 & 27

Woman cop nabbed in boyfriend slaying
See Page 14

NEW YORK POST

LATE CITY FINAL

TUESDAY, AUGUST 15, 1995 / Partly sunny today, 90; muggy tonight, 75 / Details, Page 22 ★★ 50¢

REQUIEM FOR A SLUGGER
Mantle laid to rest today

Full coverage: Pages 4, 5, 6, 7, 68 & 69

years, circulation dropped by 150,000 and the paper lost $2 million. A dispirited Backer wanted to "dump the paper in the river," but his wife said she wanted to try to run things. Backer refused, saying he would "go home to my mother." She showed up anyway, and Backer walked out.

She replaced him—as both editor and husband—with Ted Thackrey, who instituted some of the most dramatic changes in the paper's history. In March 1942, the *Post* became a real tabloid, emphasizing local and feature news together with more pictures and columnists. Three years later, she bought the failing *Bronx Home News* and absorbed it into the *Post*, adding a new base of readers. The combination proved popular and the *Post* finally began turning a profit in 1949.

At Thackrey's suggestion, the *Post* in January 1945 started a Paris-based European edition, the *Paris Post*—a tabloid that competed against the more established *International Herald Tribune*. The paper, which carried many familiar *Post* features, lasted for nearly four years until it was forced to shut down because of labor troubles.

But the Thackreys, too, had differences, both business and political. In 1948, he endorsed independent presidential candidate Henry Wallace, whose campaign was dominated by the Communist Party, while she backed Republican Tom Dewey; they battled each other in a series of bitterly competing editorial columns (neither

backed the eventual winner, Harry Truman). Shortly after the election, the pair divorced and Thackrey resigned, starting a short-lived paper, the *New York Compass*.

In a surprise move, Mrs. Schiff named the paper's 33-year-old Washington bureau chief, James Wechsler, editor of both the news and editorial pages. He turned the *Post* into New York's liberal gadfly, building a staff of solid reporters, columnists and feature writers and taking on such political sacred cows as Joe McCarthy, J. Edgar Hoover, Walter Winchell and Robert Moses. In 1952, the *Post* broke the story of vice presidential candidate Richard Nixon's "slush fund"—a story Nixon responded to in his famous "Checkers" speech. A few years later, it played a major role in breaking the TV quiz show scandals.

The 1950s-era *Post* was a profitable paper. But against such direct competition as the *Journal-American* and the *World Telegram & Sun*, its inevitable demise was again widely predicted. In 1961, Mrs. Schiff decided to separate the news and opinion sections; Wechsler remained in charge of the latter and became one of the nation's most important political columnists; Paul Sann was named executive editor and immediately broadened the paper's news and sports coverage.

In 1966, the *Post* unexpectedly found itself alone in the afternoon field after its rivals combined with the *Herald-Tribune* to form the *World Journal Tribune*. Against that combination of newspaper giants, everyone said the *Post* didn't stand a chance. But the *WJT* folded after just 11 months. The *Post*'s circulation soared to 700,000, only to fall back to 489,000 by 1976, when—to everyone's surprise—Mrs. Schiff sold the paper to Rupert Murdoch.

Under Murdoch, the *Post* entered a new, revitalized era. Long features, a *Post* specialty under Wechsler and Sann, gave way to sharp, hard-news stories. The paper's politics gradually turned conservative, while the news side was anything but: In short order, the *Post*'s controversial Page One headlines, written in classic tabloid news formula, were the talk of the town. More important, the *Post*'s initial emphasis on crime coverage had a dramatic and lasting impact on the course of American journalism—and began driving the coverage of its local competitors, as well.

Typical of the *Post*'s journalistic initiative was the work of reporter Charles Lachman during the 1984 U.S. invasion of Grenada. While Washington-based journalists ranted against the Pentagon's decision to set up reporters' pools, Lachman flew to Miami, chartered a boat and arrived on the island 24 hours before any other journalist—filing an exclusive about how the United States had inadvertently bombed a local mental hospital.

The new *Post* was a hit with readers: by 1983, circulation reached 961,000—making the *Post* America's fourth-largest daily newspaper. It also fended off challenges from competitors, most notably the *Daily News*, which lost $20 million with a short-lived afternoon paper.

In the mid-1980s, economic woes saw the rapid disappearance of several major New York department stores. That meant a dropoff in retail advertising, and the *Post*—like every other paper—felt the hit. The *Post* also switched its publication schedule, becoming first an all-day paper with nine editions, later settling into the morning field.

The most turbulent era in the *Post*'s history began in 1988, when the paper was caught by surprise after Sen. Ted Kennedy quietly slipped through Congress a budget-bill rider prohibiting newspaper publishers from buying broadcast outlets in the same city. Murdoch had recently bought Channel 5 as the flagship of his new Fox TV network; suddenly, he found himself forced to sell the *Post*.

The successful bidder was real-estate developer Peter Kalikow, who named as editor Jane Amsterdam, the first woman to edit a major New York newspaper. She was replaced after a year by columnist Jerry Nachman, who brought a sense of New York street smarts to the paper.

Nachman's biggest triumph was his controversial decision to publish the answers to that day's upcoming Regents exams after reporter Timothy McDarrah obtained them from a high-school student via fax. When the state was forced to cancel the exams, the *Post* was denounced by political officials and some rival papers: *Newsday* sniffed that "we can't think of one sound journalistic reason" for publishing the answers. But the *New York Times* came to the *Post*'s defense, saying in an editorial that "what really happened . . . is a mischievous newspaper did its job; it exposed a cheating scandal."

Meanwhile, staff reductions and other forced savings allowed Kalikow to cut back losses severely; so with performance running ahead of projections, Kalikow in 1989 launched a Sunday edition of the *Post*.

It was a mistake; the paper never took off and lost at least $25 million. Moreover, papers across the country were being hurt by a slumping economy—and Kalikow took a double hit as the New York real-estate market collapsed. By August 1991, the paper twice had teetered at the precipice, coming only hours away from folding. Then Kalikow declared personal bankruptcy.

At first, the *Post* wasn't affected—until it became clear that the paper's financial situation was much worse than initially suspected.

In January of 1993, Kalikow was forced to give up control of the *Post*. The three-month roller coaster ride that followed—the likes of which had never been seen in the annals of newspaper history—has been widely reported: the arrivals of Steve Hoffenberg and Abe Hirschfeld, the hiring and firing of Pete Hamill, the wild staff revolt and legal maneuvering in bankruptcy court.

It all ended with the most unexpected development of all: Rupert Murdoch stepping forward to reclaim the paper he had been forced to sell. Flanked by new editor Ken Chandler, Murdoch returned to the *Post* on March 29, 1993, declaring: "It's good to be home."

The ride wasn't without its initial bumps: The FCC granted Murdoch a permanent waiver of its cross-ownership rule, but a walkout by the Newspaper Guild nearly shut the paper down for good. Since then, however, the *Post* has proved that it has many more lives ahead. Circulation has increased in every reporting period since Murdoch's News Corp. reacquired the paper—a feat unmatched by any other newspaper in America.

In recent years, the *Post* has jumped successfully into new technology. Its Web sites, nypost.com and pagesix.com, are resounding successes. The paper is also taking technology to new heights with the opening of its new, state-of-the art color printing plant. For the first time, the *Post* will be able to print full-color editions—up to 64 pages of color per issue, providing a crisp, clean quality.

Indeed, the *Post*'s 21st-century look will be much like what admirers hailed two centuries ago: "Beyond all comparison the most elegant piece of workmanship ever seen." And, by building its plant in the Bronx, the *Post* is sending an important message about its commitment to New York City.

Now the *New York Post* is celebrating its 200th birthday, a milestone in daily publishing of which no other United States newspaper can boast. But in celebrating its past, the paper is looking ahead to its equally promising future.

Against all odds, the *Post* has survived. And now it's moving forward, drawing on its proud record with new, innovative and exciting plans. If the years ahead are as exciting as the ones just passed, it should be a helluva ride.

Bibliography

A Century of Journalism: An Anthology of Outstanding Feature Articles from the New York Post, 3 volumes. New York: *New York Post*, 1943.

Cuozzo, Steven. *It's Alive: How America's Oldest Newspaper Cheated Death and Why It Matters*. New York: Times Books, 1996.

Johnson, Curtiss S. *Politics and a Belly-full: The Journalistic Career of William Cullen Bryant*. New York: Vantage Press, 1962.

Nevins, Allan. *The Evening Post: A Century of Journalism*. New York: Boni and Liveright, 1922.

Press Time. New York: Books Inc., 1936.

Wechsler, James A. *Reflections of an Angry Middle-Aged Editor*. New York: Random House, 1960.